SIN

AND

GRACE

'This excellent discussion is both thorough and accessible, seasoned with pithy analogies and illustrations, and tested over decades of teaching. One of the world's leading Calvin scholars and an authority on the historical debates on justification, Lane has a remarkable depth and breadth of knowledge but uses it judiciously and unobtrusively. Operating clearly within biblical and evangelical parameters he displays independent judgement, cogently presented, but free from anything partisan. For a wide readership beyond the popular level, this is the best single book on sin and grace of which I am aware.'

Robert Letham, Professor of Systematic and Historical Theology, Union School of Theology and Visiting Fellow, Faculty of Religion and Theology, Texts and Traditions, Vrije Universiteit Amsterdam

SIN
AND
GRACE

EVANGELICAL
SOTERIOLOGY
IN HISTORICAL
PERSPECTIVE

GRACE

TONY

LANE

APOLLOS (an imprint of Inter-Varsity Press)
36 Causton Street, London SW1P 4ST, England
Email: ivp@ivpbooks.com
Website: www.ivpbooks.com

First published 2020

British Library Cataloguing-in-Publication Data
A catalogue record for this book is available from the British Library.

ISBN: 978–1–78359–672–0
eBook ISBN: 978–1–78359–673–7

Set in Minion Pro 10.75/13.75pt
Typeset in Great Britain by CRB Associates, Potterhanworth, Lincolnshire

Inter-Varsity Press publishes Christian books that are true to the Bible and that communicate
the gospel, develop discipleship and strengthen the church for its mission in the world.

IVP originated within the Inter-Varsity Fellowship, now the Universities and Colleges Christian
Fellowship, a student movement connecting Christian Unions in universities and colleges
throughout Great Britain, and a member movement of the International Fellowship of
Evangelical Students. Website: www.uccf.org.uk. That historic association is maintained,
and all senior IVP staff and committee members subscribe to the UCCF Basis of Faith.

To Clara, Carys and Jaya

Contents

Contents

Preface

This book is based on a module that I taught to second-year students at London School of Theology from 2007 to 2016. My thanks are due to all of those who took the module and who stimulated its development by their questions. A number of folk are due special thanks.

Ian LaRiviere kindly supplied me with an electronic copy of his lecture notes as he had written them up. These were a starting point for the written text. My former colleague Bob Letham also read and commented helpfully on the whole text. Susanne Wigram read and commented helpfully on chapter 25 and she and Steve Motyer read and commented helpfully on chapter 26.

This volume follows on from my *Exploring Christian Doctrine* (SPCK, 2013), which was taught to the same students in their first year. With the books, as with the lecture courses, there is inevitably some degree of repetition as the same topics are covered again at a higher level. In places the identical material is reproduced, but these form only a small proportion of the whole book.

I have previously written on many of the topics of this book and in places have used and modified this material. Some material has been drawn from the following works:

'Calvin's Doctrine of Assurance Revisited', in David W. Hall (ed.), *Tributes to John Calvin: A Celebration of His Quincentenary* (Phillipsburg: P&R, 2010), 270–313. Taken from *Tributes to John Calvin*, ed. by David Hall, ISBN 978-1-59638-096-7, pp. 270–313, used with permission from P&R Publishing Co., PO Box 817, Phillipsburg, NJ 08865, USA, <www.prpbooks.com>.
'Did the Apostolic Church Baptize Babies? A Seismological Approach', *TBul* 55:1 (2004), 109–130. Reproduced by permission.
'Dual-Practice Baptism View', in D. F. Wright (ed.), *Baptism: Three Views* (Downers Grove: InterVarsity Press, 2009), 139–171. From 'Dual-Practice Baptism View' by Anthony N. S. Lane in *Baptism: Three Views*, ed. David F. Wright. Copyright © 2009 by Anne-Marie Wright. Used by permission of InterVarsity Press, Downers Grove, IL, USA. <www.ivpress.com>

'Irenaeus on the Fall and Original Sin', in R. J. Berry and T. A. Noble (eds),
  Darwin, Creation and the Fall (Nottingham: Apollos, 2009), 130–148.
  Reproduced by permission.
*Justification by Faith in Catholic–Protestant Dialogue: An Evangelical
  Assessment* (London: T&T Clark, 2002). Used by permission of
  Bloomsbury Publishing Plc.
'Justification', in Geoffrey Wainwright and Paul McPartlan (eds), *The Oxford
  Handbook of Ecumenical Studies* (Oxford: Oxford University Press, 2017;
  online edn).
'Lust: The Human Person as Affected by Disordered Desires', *EvQ* 78 (2006),
  21–35. Reproduced by permission.
'What's So Dangerous About Grace?', *Whitefield Briefing* 6:4 (July 2001).
  Reproduced by permission.
'The Wrath of God as an Aspect of the Love of God', in K. Vanhoozer (ed.),
  Nothing Greater, Nothing Better (Grand Rapids: Eerdmans, 2001), 138–167.
  Reproduced by permission.

Quotations from the Bible are taken from the anglicized English Standard
Version. References to Calvin's *Institutes* are by book, chapter and section,
rather than by page numbers, and likewise to the Catechism of the Catholic
Church by paragraph number. This is because, as with the Bible, there are a
number of editions and page numbers help only those with the same edition.

My colleague Matthew Knell has also written on sin and grace.[1] I was
relieved to discover that we are not in competition as his work is a historical
survey with extensive quotations from Christian theologians down the ages.
It would be an excellent companion to the present volume for those wishing
to go deeper into the historical texts. For another way to do this, especially for
those wishing to use this book as a textbook for a taught course, there is at the
end a list of classic texts that can be read in conjunction with particular
chapters.

Finally, this book is dedicated to my three granddaughters, Clara, Carys
and Jaya Woodhams. It is my prayer that they may each, like their parents and
grandparents, come to see themselves as created by God and fallen into sin
and that they might embrace the grace of God and walk on the path to glory.

---

[1] Knell, *Sin, Grace and Free Will* – two volumes so far with a third to follow.

Abbreviations

AD	anno domini
ANF	Ante-Nicene Fathers (Grand Rapids: Eerdmans, 1969–73 reprint of various nineteenth-century editions)
BkConc	Robert Kolb and Timothy J. Wengert (eds), *The Book of Concord: The Confessions of the Evangelical Lutheran Church* (Minneapolis: Fortress, 2000)
c.	circa
can.	canon
CCC	Catechism of the Catholic Church
Comm.	Commentary/Commentaries
CT	*Christianity Today*
d.	died
dist.	distinction
ET	English Translation
EvQ	*Evangelical Quarterly*
ICC	International Critical Commentary
Inst.	John Calvin, *Institutes of the Christian Religion*, ed. John T. McNeill, tr. Ford Lewis Battles, LCC vols 20–21 (London: SCM; Philadelphia: Westminster, 1960)
JTS	*Journal of Theological Studies*
LCC	Library of Christian Classics
LW	Martin Luther, *Luther's Works* (Philadelphia: Fortress; St. Louis: Concordia, 1955–86)
LXX	Septuagint
NET	New English Translation
NPNF	Nicene and Post-Nicene Fathers, First Series (Grand Rapids: Eerdmans, 1956–71 reprint of various nineteenth-century editions)
NPNF[2]	Nicene and Post-Nicene Fathers, Second Series (Grand Rapids: Eerdmans, 1968–73 reprint of various nineteenth-century editions)
NTS	*New Testament Studies*

q.	question
RefConf	James T. Dennison (ed.), *Reformed Confessions of the 16th and 17th Centuries in English Translation*, 4 vols (Grand Rapids: Reformation Heritage, 2008–14)
SBET	*Scottish Bulletin of Evangelical Theology*
SJT	*Scottish Journal of Theology*
SWJC	John Calvin, *Selected Works of John Calvin*, ed. Henry Beveridge (Calvin Translation Society edn) (Grand Rapids: Baker, 1983 reprint of various nineteenth-century editions)
TBul	*Tyndale Bulletin*
Them	*Themelios*
tr.	translator, translated by
WCC	World Council of Churches
ZECNT	Zondervan Exegetical Commentary on the New Testament

Introduction

'I will tell about your righteousness,
and all day long proclaim your salvation,
though I cannot fathom its full extent.'
(Ps. 71:15; NET Bible altered)

Importance of these doctrines

Ever since the Evangelical Revival of the eighteenth century, the doctrines of justification and sanctification have been central to evangelical theology. In the last generation, however, evangelicals have been preoccupied with many other things, such as involvement in politics and wider social issues. This is not necessarily a bad thing and can be seen as the mark of increasing self-confidence, where evangelicals feel able to move beyond the defence of their core beliefs to a more fully rounded biblical theology. But there is an accompanying danger that they neglect their central doctrines and drift away from them. This is what happened in the nineteenth century. In the middle of that century evangelicalism was the dominant force in British church life, but by the end of the century it had largely ceased to be evangelical and had become just a shadow of its former self. Currently, evangelicalism is arguably the strongest element in British church life, but there is no automatic guarantee that it will not again suffer the fate of its nineteenth-century ancestor. Alister McGrath rightly warns that evangelicalism has lost its way before to rationalism and that there is no guarantee that this will not happen again.[1] So it is vital that we continue to focus on these core doctrines.

It is the doctrines of grace and redemption that, as Wilberforce noted, divide evangelical Christianity from moralism:

> My grand objection to the religious system still held by many who declare themselves orthodox Churchmen . . . is, that it tends to render Xtianity so much a system of prohibitions rather than of privilege and hopes, and thus the injunction to rejoice so strongly enforced in the New Testament

---

[1] McGrath, *Evangelicalism and the Future of Christianity*, 188–190.

is practically neglected, and Religion is made to wear a forbidding and gloomy air and not one of peace and hope and joy.[2]

The doctrine of sin may not seem to be joyous, but it is of course the other half of grace and redemption. It is because of human sin that Christ needed to come to save us. Those who have a low view of sin tend to have a correspondingly low view of Christ and grace.

John Barclay, in a Grove Booklet that very helpfully summarizes some of the key ideas of his magisterial *Paul and the Gift*, points out the wide range of meanings of the word 'grace' and lists six different senses in which grace might be 'free'.[3]

- *Grace is superabundant.* Almost all Christians would agree.
- *God is only gracious.* This idea is associated with the heretic Marcion and we shall engage with it in chapters 5 and 6 especially.
- *Grace precedes any human response.* This is known as prevenient grace and we shall engage with it in chapter 8 especially.
- *Grace is incongruous*, given without regard for the merit of the recipient. That theme recurs in this book.
- *Grace is efficacious.* We shall engage with this in chapters 8 and 9 especially.
- *Grace is non-circular, without the expectation of any return.* The necessity of a response of repentance, faith and good works recurs in this book.

Wesleyan Quadrilateral

On what basis will we be discussing these doctrines?

John Wesley, the great eighteenth-century revivalist and founder of Methodism, held that our theology should be based on Scripture, which is to be interpreted with the help of reason and tradition and in the light of our experience. This has come to be known as the 'Wesleyan Quadrilateral'.[4] These four authorities are not equal in authority. Scripture is supreme, and the other three are aids to the correct understanding of Scripture. As the *Westminster Confession of Faith* (1647) put it:

The supreme judge by which all controversies of religion are to be determined, and all decrees of councils, opinions of ancient writers, doctrines

---

[2] Pollock, *Wilberforce*, 46, citing a letter to Lord Carrington of 17 August 1829.
[3] Barclay, *Paul and the Subversive Power of Grace*, 3–5.
[4] See Thorsen, *Wesleyan Quadrilateral*.

of men, and private spirits, are to be examined, and in whose sentence we are to rest, can be no other but the Holy Spirit speaking in the Scripture.[5]

This is the method that has been followed in this book.

Scripture

Scripture is the witness to God's revelation in Christ (John 5:39) and is the test by which to assess all doctrine. But Scripture needs to be interpreted. There are those who think that any issue can be resolved by quoting a passage of Scripture. So, for example, there are those who think that merely citing Genesis 1 proves that creation took place in seven 24-hour periods and accuse those who disagree with them of denying the truth of Scripture. But Genesis 1, like every other passage of Scripture, needs interpretation. Augustine believed in the total truthfulness of Scripture but regarded the days of Genesis 1 as figurative. Also, for many doctrines, different passages can be cited to support different theories. Citing one passage does not settle a dispute. Dietrich Bonhoeffer, in a helpful analogy, compared the exegesis of Scripture to walking on thin ice. If you do not want to fall through the ice it is important not to remain stationary in one place, but to move around.[6] At times we shall see the importance of holding in tension complementary truths, as in chapters 11 and 17, for example. The biblical teaching on a particular topic is not what is said by one or two verses taken in isolation but what is taught by the biblical canon as a whole. So, for example, Proverbs teaches that those who lead a righteous life are rewarded, Job and Ecclesiastes protest that this is not always so, and the New Testament squares the circle with the idea of rewards in the Age to Come.

Tradition

In this book we shall treat Scripture as the test by which to assess all doctrine, but in seeking to interpret Scripture we shall listen to the voices of those who have interpreted it over the ages. We shall not examine issues like election and justification as if no one before us has ever sought to explain them, but will do so in conversation with the great theologians of the past such as Augustine and the Reformers. When we ask whether or not babies were baptized in New Testament times, we shall take into account the evidence of what happened in subsequent generations. We shall also from time to time quote credal statements from the past.

---

[5] Ch. 1:10 (*RefConf* 4:236).
[6] Bonhoeffer, *Christ the Center*, 76. Bonhoeffer used the analogy to make a slightly different point from mine.

Wherefore we do not condemn the holy treatises of the fathers, agreeing with the Scriptures; from whom, notwithstanding, we do modestly dissent, as they are deprehended to set things down merely strange, or altogether contrary to the same. Neither do we think that we do them any wrong in this matter; seeing that they all, with one consent, will not have their writings matched with the canonical Scriptures; but bid us allow of them so far forth as they either agree with them, or disagree, and bid us take those things that agree, and leave those that disagree.[7]

Reason

It is impossible to interpret Scripture without some use of reason. When it comes to a question like the historicity of the fall it is unwise to ignore the contribution of modern science. Psalm 19 refers to what has been called the 'two books of God'. Verses 1–6 state that the heavens declare the glory of God; verses 7–11 state that God's will is revealed by his written Law. The book of nature/creation and the book of Scripture are both from God.[8] Science and theology must relate to one another. Some might object that scientists have often been mistaken and that they disagree with one another. True, but it is not unknown for theologians to err and to disagree with one another! Some would contrast the fallible conclusions of science with the infallible truth of Scripture. A better comparison is between the fallible conclusions of science and the fallible conclusions of theologians seeking to interpret the Word of God.

Experience

Luther and Calvin both recognized the important role that experience plays in the theological task. Luther's theology was forged on the anvil of his personal struggles,[9] and he stated this in a typically graphic way: it is by living, indeed by dying and by being damned that one becomes a theologian – not merely by understanding, reading and speculation.[10]

Calvin's was also a theology of experience. He repeatedly appeals to experience, often using traditional refrains such as 'experience teaches'. When expounding his doctrine of the inner witness of the Spirit, Calvin claims that he speaks 'of nothing other than what each believer experiences within himself'.[11]

---

[7] *Second Helvetic Confession* (1566), ch. 2, written by Heinrich Bullinger (*RefConf* 2:812–813).
[8] For the idea in Isaac Newton, see Janiak, 'Book of Nature, Book of Scripture'.
[9] See Althaus, *Theology of Martin Luther*, 55–63, 173–178.
[10] *Lectures on Psalms*, 5:11.
[11] *Inst.* 1:7:5.

One way that experience functions is as a test of doctrine. For example, some have argued that Christians should never suffer from ill health. Such beliefs may spring up from time to time, but they always fade away in the light of experience. The same can be said for the belief that it is possible to live without sin, which will be covered in chapter 30. We shall refer to experience at times, as for example in the discussion about the possibility of losing one's salvation in chapter 28.[12]

Sola scriptura?

Some might wish to argue against the Wesleyan Quadrilateral on the basis of the Reformation principle of *sola scriptura* (Scripture alone). There are several reasons why this is mistaken. First, the *sola scriptura* slogan did not emerge at the time of the Reformation itself, but came later.[13] It can, however, be seen as encapsulating a key idea of the Reformation. What was that idea? The Reformers certainly did not see the Bible as the sole source or resource in doing theology. They made considerable use of earlier teaching, such as that of Augustine. They did not regard the Bible as the sole authority since they were very ready to draw up new confessions of faith which had authority in their churches. The key point, though, was that all of these resources and authorities were subordinate to the supreme authority of Scripture and were to be tested by it. The Wesleyan Quadrilateral is in line with the Reformers on these points.

---

[12] For more on the role of experience, see Marshall (ed.), *Christian Experience in Theology and Life*.
[13] See Lane, '*Sola Scriptura?*'

Part 1

THE NEED: SIN

1
Creation and fall

Frameworks for theology

The topic of this book is sin and grace, but these cannot be understood properly unless they are placed in a wider context. As we shall see, seeking to understand the whole Christian faith from the perspective of sin and grace can be seriously distorting.

It is important to get the basic structure or framework of Christian doctrine right in order to understand theology correctly. If you build a house the foundations are very important. If you want a square house, circular foundations are not a good start. Likewise, getting the foundations or basic framework of theology right is important. There are a number of different structures that have been used in the past for theology in general, and for the understanding of humanity in particular.

Sin–grace (Lutheran)

At times Lutheranism has operated with a basic sin–grace framework. This has the merit of reminding us that the biblical gospel is about human sin and how God redeems the situation by his grace. It would appear to be a promising approach for a book about 'Sin and Grace', but viewing everything in terms of sin and grace can lead us to forget the fact that the world is God's creation, as we shall see below.

Nature–grace (Thomist)

Catholic theology, especially that influenced by Thomas Aquinas, has sometimes approached theology with the basic framework of nature and grace. Nature is how we are as a result of God's initial creation and grace elevates us beyond that and brings us into a spiritual relationship with God.[1] Again, there is some validity in this distinction, but the danger is that it fails to mention sin.

---

[1] Thomas's basic principle was that grace does not destroy nature, but perfects it (*Summa Theologiae* 1a:1:8; Wawrykow, *A–Z of Thomas Aquinas*, 98–99.

(Thomas himself did not fall into that danger.) Grace does not just elevate us; it also deals with the ravages of sin.

Creation – fall – redemption (Reformed)

The traditional Reformed framework is creation – fall – redemption. This has the merit of incorporating both of the previous two frameworks. It is still not complete, however.

Nature – grace – future glory (Moltmann)

Jürgen Moltmann in one place critiques the Thomist framework of nature–grace, and in particular the tenet that grace does not destroy nature but perfects it. He objects that this model does not give weight to the coming eternal glory, to our ultimate eschatological destiny.[2] This is important, as a key feature of the New Testament view of salvation is the contrast between 'already' and 'not yet'. There is a sense in which we already enjoy it, but another sense in which it is postponed until the end. Moltmann does well to draw attention to the need to incorporate glory, but the ensuing framework still makes no mention of sin.

Creation/nature – fall/sin – redemption/grace – future glory

Synthesizing these frameworks produces a *fourfold framework* for theology:

1 creation and nature
2 fall and sin
3 grace and redemption
4 future glory and our final destiny.

This fourfold framework is not a recent novelty. To give a few examples, the moderate Puritan William Perkins in 1597 wrote a book entitled *A Reformed Catholike*, in which he states that 'Man must be considered in a foure-fold estate, as he was created, as he was corrupted, as he is renewed, as he shalbe glorified.'[3] This became the structure of a major book by the Scottish theologian Thomas Boston in 1720: *Human Nature in Its Fourfold State*. These states are set out in the subtitle: primitive integrity, entire depravity, begun recovery and consummate happiness or misery. But there is a much older precedent, in Peter Lombard's *Sentences*, a work that was the standard

---

[2] Moltmann, *God in Creation*, 7–9.
[3] Perkins, *Reformed Catholike*, 11.

theological textbook for nearly half a millennium. He states that there are 'four states of man: first before sin, second after sin and before grace, third under grace, fourth in glory'.[4]

This fourfold approach can be illustrated by considering the correct attitude first towards creation in general; then towards 'natural' human desires in particular.

Attitudes towards creation

As created

The first point to make is that God created the physical universe so it is inherently good. 'Everything created by God is good, and nothing is to be rejected if it is received with thanksgiving' (1 Tim. 4:4). As C. S. Lewis put it, '[God] likes matter. He invented it.'[5] This needs to be stated in opposition to a number of rival positions. In the first and second centuries, the Platonist and Gnostic view was that there is one supreme God but that the world was created by a lesser deity, the Demiurge, using pre-existent matter. One Gnostic writer maintained that the universe emerged by accident as the result of a belch by a junior deity – not exactly a ringing endorsement of physical matter! The Platonist/Gnostic view of man was that the human soul is a *divine spark*, embodied in flesh that is *grossly inferior*. So they had a very high view of the soul but a low view of the physical creation. The Bible, by contrast, has a lower view of the soul (not divine but created by God) and a higher view of the body (part of God's good creation).

One consequence of a weak view of creation is asceticism, for more on which, see the excursus below. The early Christians were influenced by their intellectual climate, and this sometimes led to extremes of asceticism. So for example (according to Athanasius) Antony (the first monk) ate in private because he was ashamed that he needed to eat.[6] Underlying this shame was the idea that the physical is shameful. Antony did not actually say that because he would have realized that it was contrary to the Christian doctrine of creation. Antony's asceticism was effectively driven by an idea that he did not (and could not) openly acknowledge. Karl Rahner refers to this phenomenon as 'cryptogamic heresy', where our thoughts and behaviour are shaped by

---

[4] Book 3, dist. 16, ch. 2 (Lombard, *Sentences, Book 3*, 67).
[5] *Mere Christianity*, 62.
[6] Athanasius, *Life of Antony* 45 (NPNF[2] 4:208).

subliminal ideas that we never openly formulate, because if we did we would have to acknowledge that they are heretical.[7]

Rahner is referring to something that is very common. To give a simple example, the majority of Christians affirm, with Hebrews 11, that we are pilgrims in this world, heading for an eternal destiny beyond. Yet most of us live for much of the time as if this world was all there is – a doctrine that we could not affirm because we would immediately recognize that it was heretical. That is why the test of works is so important.

Another consequence of a weak view of creation is an extreme other-worldliness. Some especially fervent groups have fallen into this trap, with people feeling that any non-religious activity is 'worldly' and unworthy – because of a sin–grace model that leaves out creation. 'Would you want Jesus to return and find you playing tennis?' This sort of other-worldliness belittles the physical creation. It can appear very 'pious' but reflects Platonist and Gnostic, rather than Christian, beliefs. Marcion was a second-century heretic who believed in two entirely separate Gods: the God of the Old Testament, who created us and condemns us, and the gracious God of the New Testament who saves us.[8] So for Marcion and for the Gnostics, salvation was effectively being saved from the physical universe, but Christ came to save us not from the physical creation, but from sin.

A third consequence of a weak view of creation is the reverse of the first. If the physical creation is despised, one possible reaction is licence, the belief that any behaviour is acceptable because the material world is unimportant. Some of the Gnostic heretics of the second and third centuries followed this line of argument. Paul argued against a precursor of it in 1 Corinthians 6:12–20.

As fallen

There are plenty today who operate with a nature–grace model that side-lines sin. The classic example of this, which is very common, is when people refer to some moral failing and respond that 'God loves you just as you are – that's how he made you.' The fallacy is that it ignores the issue of the fall and sin, that it assumes that we are unfallen creatures just as God originally intended. It may be appropriate to say to someone who is, for example, very short, 'God loves you just as you are, the height you are – that's how he made you.' It is not appropriate to say to someone, 'God loves you just as you are, a paedophile – that's how he made you.' God does love paedophiles, but not 'just as they are'. He loves

---

[7] Rahner, *Theological Investigations*, vol. 5, 497–512. This is not the same as hypocrisy, but is not unrelated to it.

[8] For more on Marcion, see chapter 5.

them, as he loves us all, in that he sent his Son to save them and us from our sin, be that paedophilia or whatever else our own besetting sin may be.

This is the origin of our term 'second nature'. Augustine contrasts the original, first nature with which we are created, with the second, sinful nature that follows from Adam's fall.[9]

As redeemed

Christ came to redeem us and to redeem creation from sin. Christians are those who have been transformed. As part of God's good creation they have fallen into sin, but now they have been saved. Salvation has already begun. But, as every Christian knows from experience, it is not yet complete. New Testament theologians describe this tension by saying that salvation is something that we enjoy 'already but not yet'. Paul's statement 'You have died, and your life is hidden with Christ in God' (Col. 3:3) leads on to the command 'Put to death therefore what is earthly in you: sexual immorality, impurity, passion, evil desire, and covetousness . . . Put on then, as God's chosen ones, holy and beloved, compassion, kindness, humility, meekness, and patience . . .' (3:5–14). We *have died* with Christ, but we also need to *put to death* all that is sinful. We enjoy the new life in Christ 'already, but not yet', a formula popularized by G. E. Ladd.[10] Paul's usual description of Christians is not as those who are 'saved' but as those who are 'being saved' (1 Cor. 1:18; 15:2; 2 Cor. 2:15). John expresses the same contrast in different terms: 'We are God's children now, and what we shall be has not yet appeared; but we know that when he appears we shall be like him' (1 John 3:2). For more on this, see chapter 27.

In glory

When Christ returns, the 'not yet' will be replaced by 'fully'. This is true of us as Christians, and also of the created order. In Romans 8 Paul states that the creation is currently subject to futility, but that it will be set free (8:19–22).

Attitudes towards 'natural' human desires

Having considered attitudes towards creation in general we shall now consider the specific example of attitudes towards 'natural' human desires. The United

---

[9] *City of God* 12:3 (NPNF 2:228). In 15:6 he states that sin is not part of our original nature but a defect of nature (NPNF 2:287).

[10] This formula is often attributed to Ladd, *Gospel of the Kingdom*, where the idea is found (derived from Oscar Cullmann) but not yet the slogan 'already but not yet'. Barrett, *From First Adam to Last*, 105, refers to 'this formula "Already – Not yet"' as 'the fundamental pattern of the Christian life'.

States Declaration of Independence states that 'We hold these truths to be self-evident, that all men are created equal, that they are endowed by their Creator with certain unalienable rights, that among these are Life, Liberty and the pursuit of Happiness.' What are we to make of this? In its eighteenth-century context it might have meant something different, but today it is understood by many as the right to gratify all of our natural desires. Advertising seeks to stimulate such desires in order to create a market for products. How should we assess this? We need to consider our desires as created, as fallen, as redeemed and as in glory.

As created

Contrary to some extreme ascetics, it is wrong to suggest that all desires are wrong. We have desires for food, drink, sleep and sex and without these we would not exist. You might well object that we can exist without sex, which is true of the individual, but none of us would be here unless our parents had indulged. Human desires are not sinful *as created*, although the sin–grace framework might lead one to suppose that. They are, however, now affected by sin.

As fallen

As a result of the fall, our desires have been affected by sin. This means that to a greater or lesser extent they have become inordinate (excessive) and disordered (wrongly directed). The desire for and enjoyment of food is a good gift of God's creation; gluttony is a perversion of this into an inordinate desire and unhealthy eating into a disordered desire. The desire for and enjoyment of sleep is a good gift of God's creation; sloth is a perversion of this into an inordinate desire. The desire for and enjoyment of sex is a good gift of God's creation; sexual immorality is the perversion of this into an inordinate desire and paedophilia into a disordered desire. Without these natural desires we would be in danger of starving, dying of exhaustion or failing to propagate ourselves, but unfortunately in our present sinful state these desires have become inordinate and disordered. The fact that we need to wear clothes in public is testimony not just to the inclement weather, but also to the inordinate nature of our sexual desires. One might say that our desires become inordinate and lustful when we seek ultimate satisfaction outside God. One profession that knows all about human lusts is the advertising industry, which knows how to exploit them to sell products.

Calvin set out clearly how our desires are good as created but spoilt by sin:

We recognise as deriving from the original creation of our nature all the feelings which naturally occur in man, such as, for example, married love, also the love of parents for children, friendship, joy at a happy outcome, sorrow at bereavement, widowhood, and all adversities; fear of hunger, cold, want, danger, disgrace, scandal, and on the other hand the desire for, and seeking after, the necessary resources for life. We do not teach that these feelings developed through sin, but that they were implanted in our nature from its very creation. We do teach that the disorder with which we are all too familiar, that is, the unregulated overflowing of the feelings which causes us to have evil desires and by these desires to become rebels against God, was born of our corruption, and was not inborn in our nature from the beginning . . . Father loves son, husband [loves] wife. It is a pure love and one which even merits praise. But in the present corrupt state of [human] nature this love will not be found in man without some smack of defilement.[11]

One of the purest and most self-giving forms of love is the love of a mother for a child. And yet Calvin says that this is not to be found in fallen humanity 'without some smack of defilement'. At first sight it may seem shocking to say that such love can be sinful, but on further reflection it is not so odd. C. S. Lewis describes a fictional woman called Mrs Fidgett.[12] She 'lived for her family' but in such a way as to bind and oppress them. Her love for them was based on her need to love. This is a caricatured portrait, but points to the reality that even our self-giving love for others can be tainted and, given the all-pervasive effects of sin (for more on which see the next chapter) always is tainted to some extent or other.

As redeemed

Christ redeems our desires, but this is not yet complete. As Christians, our desires begin to be conformed to God's will, but very imperfectly. Augustine famously stated, 'Love, and do what you will.'[13] This is often quoted today; what is less often mentioned is that he used this principle in order to justify the coercion of heretics! 'Love' is so easily used as a justification for our own base desires. For more on this, see chapter 25.

What about the desire for possessions? Is this legitimate? Paul states that we should be content if we have food and clothing (1 Tim. 6:8). Does this mean that it is wrong to seek to better one's lot? Does it mean that a young married couple who live in a rented one-bedroom apartment should be content to

---

[11] Calvin, *Bondage and Liberation of the Will*, 186–187.
[12] Lewis, *Four Loves*, 48–50.
[13] *Homilies on 1 John* 7:8 (LCC 8:316).

remain living there even when they have eleven children? We shall return to this question in chapter 29.

In glory

Our 'natural' desires are good as created, distorted by sin and (partially) set right by grace. In the Age to Come there will be no more sinful desires and our wills will be perfectly aligned with that of God. It will then be true that we can 'Love, and do what we will', although even then this will involve paying attention to what God has commanded.

Excursus: asceticism

Asceticism can be defined as the discipline of leading a life of voluntary austerity. This can involve activities such as fasting, celibacy and the voluntary embrace of poverty. Some have taken asceticism to extremes, such as wearing hair shirts and self-flagellation.

Before Christianity some strands of Greek Philosophy, such as Platonism, exalted the ascetic ideal. (By contrast, the Epicurean philosophy was to 'eat, drink and be merry'.) Underlying this was a failure to acknowledge the goodness of creation, as we have seen. The *soul* was seen as a 'divine spark', but the *physical* universe (including the body) was seen as the product of the 'Demiurge' – not the supreme God but a junior deity. So the physical creation was seen as imperfect and in some ways undesirable. Platonism encouraged people to cultivate the soul, and renounce the passions of the body.

Greek philosophy (in particular a blend of Platonism with other philosophies) was the spiritual context of early Christianity, and was very influential on the early church.[14] What made it especially influential was the fact that there are obvious similarities with the teaching of the New Testament that we should cultivate the soul and the spiritual life, renouncing the sinful passions of the flesh. The key difference lies in the Christian doctrine that the physical universe is the good creation of God.

What about the New Testament? The nearest we get to asceticism in the New Testament is the idea of voluntarily renouncing things for the sake of the coming kingdom. The parables of the hidden treasure and the pearl (Matt. 13:44–45) refer to giving up that which is good for the supreme prize of the kingdom of heaven. The rich young man was likewise challenged to sell all that he had, give it to the poor and follow Jesus (Mark 10:17–22).

---

[14] The Jewish context was also important, as is shown by Finn, *Asceticism in the Graeco-Roman World*.

Again, Jesus refers to those who have 'made themselves eunuchs for the sake of the kingdom of heaven' (Matt. 19:12). The idea behind this is not that possessions or sex are impure or defiling, but that they are good things that should where necessary be put aside for the far greater benefit of the kingdom.

John the Baptist in the desert has been seen as an example of a form of asceticism:

> What did you go out into the wilderness to see? A reed shaken by the wind? What then did you go out to see? A man dressed in soft clothing? Behold, those who wear soft clothing are in kings' houses. What then did you go out to see? A prophet? Yes, I tell you, and more than a prophet. (Matt. 11:7–9)

Jesus went into the desert for forty days after his baptism. On the other hand, he contrasted himself with John:

> For John came neither eating nor drinking, and they say, 'He has a demon.' The Son of Man came eating and drinking, and they say, 'Look at him! A glutton and a drunkard, a friend of tax collectors and sinners!' (Matt. 11:18–19)

What about the church of the early centuries? This was much influenced by the Greek Platonist world-view and asceticism, as we saw in the example of Antony, above. Asceticism was also seen as a training for martyrdom. In the second and third centuries Christians were, from time to time, faced with a simple choice: throw some incense on to a pagan altar or be executed. How would they react when faced with this choice? Some saw asceticism as a form of discipline that reduced one's attachment to this world and prepared one to make the correct decision when faced with the ultimate choice.

With the conversion of the emperor Constantine in 312 the threat of martyrdom receded. Around the same time monasticism came into existence, with Christians gathering into communities to lead an ascetic life together. Some forms of asceticism were extreme, as with 'pillar saints' like Simeon Stylites, who lived for nearly 40 years at the top of a 40-foot-high pillar. He was greatly revered, with even emperors seeking his advice. A far more moderate form of asceticism was found in the sixth-century Rule of Benedict and the monasteries that observed it, where the monks led celibate lives in community, but were not particularly worse off than the peasants around them. Asceticism was strongly admired in the early church and the few people who argued against it were condemned for their views.[15]

In his response to the rich young man who sought eternal life, Jesus tells him that 'If you would be perfect, go, sell what you possess and give to the poor, and you will have treasure in heaven; and come, follow me' (Matt. 19:21). In the Middle Ages this verse was used to develop a theory of a *Double Standard*.[16] There are *precepts*, which are binding on all Christians, such as the Ten Commandments. Then there are *counsels*, which are to be seen as non-obligatory advice for those seeking perfection. These are optional extras. They were also seen as *works of supererogation*, which means going over and above what is required, and thus acquiring merit. These ideas came under heavy fire at the Reformation, as in Article 14 of the Thirty-nine Articles:

Voluntary Works besides, over and above, God's Commandments, which they call Works of Supererogation, cannot be taught without arrogancy and impiety: for by them men do declare, that they do not only render unto God as much as they are bound to do, but that they do more for his sake, than of bounden duty is required: whereas Christ saith plainly When ye have done all that are commanded to you, say, We are unprofitable servants. [Luke 17:10]

A better way of viewing the contrast is to think in terms of different *callings*. John Stott, for example, renounced marriage, an academic career and even the offer of a bishopric, not in order to gain merit or to press on to perfection, but because he sensed a primary calling to a particular pastoral ministry.[17] His huge international ministry would not have been possible if he had been married with a family. Likewise many people who move into Christian ministry do so at great financial cost. They embrace this not in order to gain merit or to press on to perfection, but because it goes with the territory. If they inherited a substantial sum of money they would not feel obliged to give it all away in order to retain the merit of frugal living.

---

[15] E.g. by Jerome in his *Against Vigilantius*.
[16] The earliest trace of this is found in Clement of Alexandria.
[17] See http://howardsnyder.seedbed.com/2013/04/19/john-stotts-celibacy>, accessed 3 May 2013.

2
Sin and bondage

This and the following four chapters are negative in tone, focusing on the disease from which we all suffer. The aim is not to focus on the bad news for its own sake but as a prelude to the good news that follows. The Christian faith is centred on the cure that God has provided to counteract sin. The cure is very drastic, namely God's sending his own Son to die for us, which shows just how serious the disease is. Luther pointed out that without sin there is no need for salvation, and therefore no gospel at all.[1] The bad news sets the scene for the good news.

What is sin?[2]

There is a lot of confusion about the idea of sin in today's culture. I read recently that the law of the land had declared that a certain activity was no longer sinful. That is to confuse sinful with illegal or criminal. Gossiping, for example, is sinful but not illegal. Conversely, in some countries it is illegal to convert to Christianity, but it is certainly not sinful to do so.

Scripture uses many different words to describe sin, involving the following ideas:[3]

- failure or missing the mark
- going astray, trespass, transgression
- rebellion against God, ungodliness
- breaking God's laws, disobedience
- perversity, wickedness, iniquity
- unrighteousness, injustice
- lust, evil desire.

There have been different attempts to identify one root cause that captures the essence of sin:

---

[1] Althaus, *Theology of Martin Luther*, 257–258.
[2] For a study of sin, see Plantinga, *Not the Way It's Supposed to Be*.
[3] Cf. Alexander et al. (eds), *New Dictionary of Biblical Theology*, 781–788.

- Augustine regarded pride as the root of all sin.[4] His analysis has been followed by many, including C. S. Lewis.[5]
- Luther identified unbelief as the root cause of all sin.[6]
- Others have seen the essence of sin as selfishness. This has the merit that the opposite to selfishness is love and the two great commandments are love of God and neighbour.
- Others similarly have seen the root of sin as self-centredness, which leads to pride and selfishness. Luther graphically described sinners as *incurvatus in se*, curved in on themselves.[7] The Lord's Prayer, by contrast, starts with prayer that God's name be hallowed, his will be done and his kingdom come.

There is truth in all of these accounts, but sin is too complex to be traced back to one sole root cause. We must avoid the 'one size fits all' approach that seeks to reduce it to just one thing.

Furthermore, sins of omission are as important as sins of commission. 'Whoever knows the right thing to do and fails to do it, for him it is sin' (Jas 4:17). In Matthew 25:41–46 the lost are condemned for what they did *not* do: 'I was hungry and you gave me no food, I was thirsty and you gave me no drink, I was a stranger and you did not welcome me, naked and you did not clothe me, sick and in prison and you did not visit me.'

Fundamentally, sin is failure to love God with all our heart, soul, mind and strength and failing to love our neighbour as ourselves. This is very different from the modern conception that anything is acceptable so long as it does not harm others.

Whether we sin by doing or by not doing we sin simply because we are sinners. Sin manifests itself most obviously as specific deeds or 'sins', but these are the outward manifestation of a deeper reality. Sin starts as orientation of our lives, as a disposition of the heart, which leads to sinful desires, which lead to sinful thoughts, which lead to sinful deeds (Jas 1:14–15). The sin in our lives may be compared to the ground elder in a garden, which manifests itself all over the place and is extremely hard to eliminate. Tackling its visible manifestation above the surface is no more than a holding operation. Similarly with sin, we need to fight it vigorously and concertedly, but we shall never be able to get rid of it completely in this life.

---

[4] E.g. in *City of God* 12:6 (NPNF 2:229), citing Ecclesiasticus 10:13, which in the Vulgate translation states that the beginning of all sin is pride. Also, *City of God* 14:13 (NPNF 2:273).

[5] *Mere Christianity*, 106–112.

[6] E.g. in his *Preface to Romans* (LW 35:369).

[7] Jenson, *Gravity of Sin*. See Luther's *Lectures on Romans* (LW 25:245, 291–292, 313, 345, 351, 513).

It is wrong to suggest that all sin is equal before God. The Bible contains many distinctions between different types of sin. For example:

- unintentional sin versus defiant sin (Num. 15:27–31);
- sins of ignorance versus deliberate sins (Luke 12:47–48);
- light versus grave sins (John 19:11);
- sins that do not lead to death versus those that do (1 John 5:16–17);
- different sins lead to differing degrees of judgement (Mark 12:40).

In the Sermon on the Mount Jesus compared lust to adultery: 'You have heard that it was said, "You shall not commit adultery." But I say to you that everyone who looks at a woman with lustful intent has already committed adultery with her in his heart' (Matt. 5:27–28). He similarly compared anger to murder (5:21–22). It is important to be clear what Jesus is saying. Lust in the heart is sinful, but clearly to go on to commit the deed is worse. If anyone really believed that to commit murder was no worse than to be angry with someone, you would do best not to meet with them without a bodyguard! There are those who deny this and say that the deed is no worse than the thought. It may be significant that one person I knew who argued for that view subsequently went on to commit the deed of adultery, presumably encouraged by the thought that this was no worse than his previous sin of lust.

So, to call something sinful does not mean putting it on a level with murder. Failure to help someone in need is sin. Having a proud disposition is sin. Not loving God with all our heart, soul, mind and strength is sin. Indeed, in chapters 19 and 30 we shall be asking whether Christians can ever, in this life, be without sin.

The universality of sin

Sin is a disease from which we all suffer. Scripture repeatedly states that all have sinned in one way or another; no one is exempt. In Romans 1:18–3:20 Paul develops an argument for the universality of sin, reaching the conclusion that 'all have sinned and fall short of the glory of God' (3:23). We sin not just from time to time, but consistently throughout our lives. We cannot escape from it and the whole of human nature is affected by sin: our reason (Eph. 4:17), our will (John 8:34), our emotions and our feelings. There is no aspect of human nature that is unaffected. This is the original meaning of the potentially misleading term 'total depravity' (on which see the excursus to chapter 9) – not that there is no goodness left in people, nor that we are as bad as we could possibly be, both of which are manifestly false, but that every part of us is to some extent spoiled and tainted by sin.

Our problem is not that we sin from time to time but that our hearts are sinful. Jesus pointed out that a healthy tree cannot bear bad fruit and a diseased tree cannot bear good fruit (Matt. 7:17–18). Just trying harder is no solution and what we need is no less than a heart transplant: 'I will give you a new heart, and a new spirit I will put within you. And I will remove the heart of stone from your flesh and give you a heart of flesh' (Ezek. 36:26). The drastic nature of the cure indicates the seriousness of the disease. There is a science fiction story in which an invention brings it about that everyone can read everyone else's mind. The result is that no two people can bear to be with one another and the human race faces extinction. More mundanely, how many people could face the world if all of their thoughts from the last 24 hours were publicly broadcast?

Psychology confirms this capacity of the heart, showing that the majority of mental life is subconscious. What we are aware of is only the tip of the iceberg, the 10% that is above the surface. From time to time nasty things rise up into our conscious minds. Sometimes we find ourselves thinking or even saying things that shock us and are inclined to ask, 'Where did that come from?' The things we do spontaneously can serve to reveal to us the reality that lies beneath the surface. As Jesus put it, 'From within, out of the heart of man, come evil thoughts, sexual immorality, theft, murder, adultery, coveting, wickedness, deceit, sensuality, envy, slander, pride, foolishness' (Mark 7:21–22). This shows us what the fallen human heart is really like and I can vouch for its accuracy. The same point is made in a secular psychology book by Robert Simon, entitled *Bad Men Do What Good Men Dream* – and the bad news for women is that he is using 'man' in the inclusive sense of human being, not just males!

We need to hold in tension two different truths taught in Scripture. On the one hand, Scripture teaches that we are all sinners, we have all fallen short of the glory of God (Rom. 3:23). If we forget this truth we can easily become arrogant, like the Pharisee in the parable who thanked God that he was righteous, not like the sinners around him (Luke 18:11–12). On the other hand, Scripture frequently distinguishes between the righteous and sinners, as for example in Psalm 1:1, 5–6.

It is important to maintain both sides of this tension. Without the first point (the universality of sin) the righteous are tempted to look down on 'sinners' and despise them. But without the second point (the contrast between righteous and sinners) we end up with a moral relativism, where there is nothing to choose between a Stalin and a Mother Teresa. As someone once put it, 'We are all of the same mould, but some are mouldier than others!'

Corporate sin

Sin is not solely individual, but is also corporate. Scripture often refers to national sin and the guilt that flows from it: Ezra confesses and associates himself with the sins of the nation (9:6–15). Isaiah in the presence of God identifies himself with the sins of the nation: 'Woe is me! For I am lost; for I am a man of unclean lips, and I dwell in the midst of a people of unclean lips' (6:5).

So also today, the sins of nations can lead to judgement. Sin can be found in the structures of society as well as in individuals. One only has to think of the slave trade, the Holocaust, communism, apartheid or the abortion industry. During the 'troubles' in Northern Ireland there was much violence including murder. As a former paramilitary put it, it was not that Ulster had been hit by a crime wave. People were caught up in rival causes and those who might otherwise have led law-abiding lives indulged in violence. While this was the action of individuals, they were not merely making personal choices but were involved in a system. Reducing all sin to personal individual choices is an error of Western individualism. While there has of late been a relative neglect of the doctrine of sin among evangelicals, one positive change is a greater willingness to take seriously the corporate and social dimension of sin, rather than viewing it in purely individual terms.

The corporate character of sin is seen especially in the doctrine of original sin, the topic for the next chapter. Also, just as there is a corporate dimension to sin, the same is true of sanctification, as we shall see in chapter 27.

The effects of sin

Sin is far reaching in its effects:

Sin deceives and blinds us to the truth

The root of sin lies in the heart, yet we conceal it both from others and from ourselves.

> The heart is deceitful above all things,
> and desperately sick;
> who can understand it?
> (Jer. 17:9)

It is becoming recognized that we use reason not just to ascertain the truth but to justify ourselves, whether excusing our bad deeds or justifying our ethical, political or religious views. When people are confronted with compelling evidence against their political stance, it often has the effect not of changing their views but of bolstering their conviction.[8] We are biased towards that which serves the interests of ourselves as individuals and groups to which we belong.[9]

To commit sin is bad but to approve it as if it is good is worse. Paul concludes his (highly relevant to today) catalogue of the sins of the Gentile world in Romans 1:24–32 with, 'Though they know God's decree that those who practise such things deserve to die, they not only do them but give approval to those who practise them.' Jeremiah refers to those who do not even know how to blush:

> Were they ashamed when they committed abomination?
> No, they were not at all ashamed;
> they did not know how to blush
> (6:15 = 8:12)

This charge can be true of different sins in different societies. In the 1950s a top hotel in Nairobi had a sign saying, 'No dogs or blacks beyond this point.' Younger people today find it hard to believe that that could have happened. It is not that there is no longer any racism today, but it is now almost universally recognized to be wrong. By contrast, today almost any sexual activity is acceptable, in a way that would have disgusted most people in the 1950s. It is not that sexual misdemeanours were unknown at that time (or at any time in human history), but that they were then very widely recognized to be wrong.

Sin brings alienation

In Genesis 3 we see four different ways in which sin alienates us:

- *from God*: 'And they heard the sound of the Lord God walking in the garden in the cool of the day, and the man and his wife hid themselves from the presence of the Lord God among the trees of the garden' (3:8).
- *from one another*: 'The man said, "The woman whom you gave to be with me, she gave me fruit of the tree, and I ate"' (3:12).

---

[8] Cf. Haidt, *Righteous Mind*.
[9] This is spelt out by Cone, *Theology from the Great Tradition*, 313–316.

- *from ourselves*: 'Then the eyes of both were opened, and they knew that they were naked. And they sewed fig leaves together and made themselves loincloths' (3:7), introducing the idea of shame.
- *from creation*: 'Cursed is the ground because of you; in pain you shall eat of it all the days of your life' (3:17–19) – back to the ground elder! Today we see the effects of this disharmony in the issues of pollution and climate change.

Sin leads to bondage to sin

Fallen human nature has a bias to sin and is enslaved to it. We are in bondage (slavery) to sin, until we are set free by Christ. 'Everyone who commits sin is a slave to sin' (John 8:34). 'The mind that is set on the flesh is hostile to God, for it does not submit to God's law; indeed, it cannot. Those who are in the flesh cannot please God' (Rom. 8:7–8).

We cannot avoid sin – it is not something that we can just give up for Lent. This is not to say that one cannot resist particular temptations, just that we are not capable of avoiding sin altogether. After all, even the alcoholic can sometimes decline a drink. The three traditional sources of temptation are the world, the flesh and the devil. All three are named in Ephesians 2:1–3: 'You were dead in the trespasses and sins in which you once walked, following the course of *this world*, following *the prince of the power of the air*, the spirit that is now at work in the sons of disobedience – among whom we all once lived in *the passions of our flesh*, carrying out the desires of the body and the mind.' As the final phrase indicates 'flesh' refers to sinful human nature, whether or not physical. We cannot completely escape from lust, pride and self-centredness, and we fall short of completely loving our neighbours as ourselves.

We are not all tempted by the same sins. As someone once put it, some men have no more desire to sleep with another man's wife than to brush their teeth with his toothbrush! But we are all to some extent enslaved to particular lusts, to inordinate and disordered desires, as we saw in the previous chapter. The classic trio is Money, Sex and Power.[10] Each of these is valid and necessary in its proper place. Many people suffer from some sort of addiction – whether to drugs, alcohol, pornography, chocolate, work, shopping, smart phones and social media . . . Some of these (such as chocolate) are 'respectable' and people can even boast of their addiction; others (such as pornography) are not respectable and people go to pains to hide their addiction. These are the 'besetting sins', referred to in Hebrews 12:1. Sometimes a sin is a deliberate choice; but

---

10 The opposites of these three lusts are the monastic vows of *poverty*, *celibacy* and *obedience*.

some sins seem to have us in their grip so that our ability to resist is very much weakened.

Sin leads to guilt, judgement and punishment

In chapter 5 we shall consider guilt and judgement and in chapter 6 the wrath of God.

Sin leads to death

'The wages of sin is death' (Rom. 6:23), both as a natural outworking and as a punishment imposed by God. Sin leads to physical death, to spiritual death (alienation from God) and to eternal death (final separation from God).

What about free will?

Talk about bondage to sin raises the question of free will. People often boldly proclaim that the Bible teaches free will, but the term never appears in Scripture. Before deciding whether or not we have free will we need to distinguish between various different meanings of the term:[11]

- Most people assume that free will refers to indeterminacy or unpredictability, sometimes called 'libertarian' free will. With this type of free will we can go either way. Personally I like both cheesecake and Black Forest gateau and if offered a choice between these I cannot predict in advance which I would choose – it is unpredictable. If unpredictability is what is meant by free will, God does not have it. We need not worry that tomorrow he might change his mind and become evil.
- There is also the perfect freedom of being unchangeably good. God is free in this sense in that he is perfectly good. Clearly we do not yet enjoy this freedom. To serve God, to be totally committed to the good, is the ultimate freedom. The prayer of St Chrysostom in the Anglican liturgy refers to God, 'whose service is perfect freedom'.
- According to the final meaning of free will, which we can call free choice, there are areas where our behaviour is not unpredictable but we still choose freely. Faced with a choice between a cat or a dog as a pet, I shall inevitably choose a cat. It is a genuinely free choice, but also completely predictable. Likewise whenever curry is served at lunch I invariably go for the non-spice alternative. It is a free choice, but totally predictable.

---

[11] For different secular views on free will and determinism, see Fischer et al., *Four Views on Free Will*.

With these different definitions of free will, we can see what sort of freedom we have in each of the four states described in the previous chapter.

1 As originally created Adam and Eve were able to sin and able not to sin. The outcome could not have been predicted. They had both free choice and indeterminacy.

2 As fallen sinners, by contrast, we cannot avoid sin completely. We are not able not to sin; we have lost indeterminacy, but not free choice. We sin inevitably, but voluntarily; it is of our own free choice, not because of external coercion. Putting it differently, while we can do what we desire (within limits), we cannot control what we desire. As fallen sinners we are in bondage to sin not in the way that hostages may be held prisoner by terrorists against their will, but in the way that addicts are enslaved, but still act of their own choice. Sin controls us from within, not in the way that a puppet's movements are imposed externally. While we can to some extent choose whether or not to commit *particular* sins, we cannot avoid sin completely. We cannot completely give it up; we act according to our nature. Such bondage is not incompatible with responsibility. Someone who jumps into a deep pit is unable to escape – but is responsible for the situation. Someone who starts smoking may be unable to give it up – but is responsible for the situation. This issue will be discussed further in the next chapter.

3 As Christians now, in this present age, we *begin* to be liberated from sin. We are united with Christ 'so that we would no longer be enslaved to sin' (Rom. 6:6). But this is not yet complete. If we do not recognize this inability to be perfect, it will lead to hypocrisy as we cover up our sins to conform to our expectations of achieving high standards and to the image of ourselves that we hold. But is it possible to live without sin for a period of time? We shall consider that question in chapters 19 and 30.

4 In the Age to Come we shall attain the perfect freedom of being un-changeably good. There will be no more sin and no more danger of sin, and we shall not be able to sin. This entails no loss of free choice because we shall no longer *want* to sin. The inability to sin will not be like the inability of the smoker to smoke when deprived of cigarettes.[12]

The condition of the will in the same four states (innocence, sin, grace, glory) is clearly set out in the *Westminster Confession of Faith* (1647):

---

[12] Augustine, *City of God* 22:30 (NPNF 2:510), makes the same point, without mentioning cigarettes.

1 God hath endued the will of man with that natural liberty, that it is neither forced, nor by any absolute necessity of nature determined to good or evil.

2 Man, in his state of innocency, had freedom and power to will and to do that which is good and well-pleasing to God; but yet mutably, so that he might fall from it.

3 Man, by his Fall into a state of sin, hath wholly lost all ability of will to any spiritual good accompanying salvation; so as a natural man, being altogether averse from that good, and dead in sin, is not able, by his own strength, to convert himself, or to prepare himself thereunto.

4 When God converts a sinner, and translates him into the state of grace, He frees him from his natural bondage under sin; and, by His grace alone, enables him freely to will and to do that which is spiritually good; yet so, as that by reason of his remaining corruption, he does not perfectly, or only, will that which is good, but does also will that which is evil.

5 The will of man is made perfectly and immutably free to good alone, in the state of glory only.[13]

Neglect of the doctrine

The doctrine of sin is undoubtedly unpopular. Most people prefer to hear about innate human goodness. But as with any disease, correct diagnosis is necessary if we are to identify the cure. Doctors do their patients no favours by telling them that they are well when they are not. I suffered for a while from a dentist who did just that, with dire consequences. The comforting diagnosis that he offered to me, as to his other patients, was 'Leave well alone, old boy.' Unfortunately we were confronted, when he retired, with a long and expensive list of neglected problems.

Today sin is often excused on genetic, social (bad upbringing) or psychological (dropped on the head as a child) grounds.[14] All three of these factors are real, but not so as to eliminate the element of personal choice, except in the most extreme of examples.[15]

Taking a low view of the seriousness of sin has been characteristic of liberal theology since the nineteenth century. Typically this low view of sin leads to

---

[13] Ch. 9 (*RefConf* 4:246).

[14] The psychiatrist Karl Menninger protested against the elimination of the category of sin and argued for its legitimate place in psychotherapy (*Whatever Became of Sin?*; e.g. p. 46).

[15] For some extreme examples, see Madueme and Reeves (eds), *Adam, the Fall, and Original Sin*, 246–247; <http://news.bbc.co.uk/1/hi/health/2345971.stm>, accessed 5 June 2020.

a low view of the work of Christ (limiting his role to that of example and teacher), which in turn leads on naturally to a low view of the person of Christ (reducing him merely to a good man). Today the marginalization of the doctrine of sin can even be found in much of evangelicalism. Evidence for this can be seen in modern choruses and worship songs, the majority of which emphasize themes like glory and power, with relatively little mention of sin and its cure. As the Danish philosopher/theologian Søren Kierkegaard commented, 'Remove the anguished conscience, and you may as well close the churches and turn them into dance halls.'[16]

In the next chapters we shall consider original sin (3) and its source in the fall (4). We shall also consider how sin leads to guilt, judgement and punishment (5) as well as looking at God's wrath or displeasure against sin (6).

---

[16] Kierkegaard, *Works of Love*, 406.

3
Original sin

Procedure

In the last chapter we considered the nature of sin and our bondage to sin. In this chapter we shall consider the doctrine of original sin and in the next chapter the doctrine of the fall. Some might object that it would be more logical to follow the chronological order and to move from the fall (the origin) to original sin (the outcome) to sin in general (the outworking). This is indeed a more logical approach, and has been the traditional order of proceeding, found both in works of theology and in credal statements, but I would suggest that it is the wrong order (especially today), for three reasons.

1 The primary emphasis of the Bible lies on the universality of sin, which is proclaimed from beginning to end. By contrast, there are few passages that trace this back to the fall and original sin. Genesis 3 and Romans 5 are the main passages that speak of the fall and apart from these there are only a few isolated statements. Even in Romans, Paul first, at some length (1:18 – 3:20), establishes the universality of human sin and only later, in the context of Christ's work, turns to the origin of sin in Adam's fall (5:12–21). In Scripture the fact and universality of sin are the primary concern, while the doctrines of the fall and original sin are relatively secondary and rarely mentioned. To start with the fact of sin before moving on to the fall and original sin is, therefore, to follow the emphasis and approach of Scripture.[1]

2 The reality of sin is clear in everyday life, while the doctrines of the fall and original sin are less evident. Pascal aptly described original sin as a great mystery:

> Nothing jolts us more rudely than this doctrine [of original sin], and yet, but for this mystery, the most incomprehensible of all, we remain

---

[1] This is also argued by Ramm, *Offense to Reason*, 57, citing James Orr.

incomprehensible to ourselves. The knot of our condition was twisted and turned in that abyss, so that it is harder to conceive of man without this mystery than for man to conceive of it himself.[2]

It is a sound principle always to work from that which is plain to that which is obscure, not the other way round. Following this principle, it makes sense to start from the doctrine of sin, which is relatively plain, and to move on to examine the more obscure doctrines of the fall and original sin.

3 The first two reasons apply in any generation, the third relates to the last 150 years in particular. The twentieth century produced ample evidence for the fact of human sin. This was partly because of the evils perpetuated in that century and partly because, unlike previous centuries, so much of it was recorded on film and broadcast on TV. Americans experienced the horrors of the Vietnam War in their own living rooms, while most civilians in the First World War had no idea of what was happening in the trenches. The idea of original sin, that we are all born with a bias towards sin, is much more plausible today than it once was. But since Darwin and the idea that humanity is the product of a process of evolution over millions of years, the concept of a fall has become more problematic.

Original sin[3]

The doctrine of original sin proclaims that sin is not purely an individual matter but that the human race corporately has taken a wrong turn, and is born under sin. That is, babies are born not morally pure or neutral but with an inbuilt bias towards committing sin. There is significant evidence for the basic doctrine in the early church fathers, but it was Augustine (354–430) who set it out clearly and developed it.

Pelagius (c. 350 – c. 425) denied the doctrine.[4] He accepted that Adam's fall led to the universality of death, but he did not accept that children were born with any inbuilt bias towards sin. They are born pure. How come, then, that they grow up to sin? Pelagius held that children learn sin from their environment and by example from other people. He also claimed that some people never sin at all. Pelagius was a monk from Scotland or Ireland (Latin *Scotus*)

---

[2] *Pensées* 131.

[3] For studies of original sin, see Blocher, *Original Sin*; Shuster, *Fall and Sin*; Madueme and Reeves (eds), *Adam, the Fall and Original Sin*. See also Stump and Meister (eds), *Original Sin and the Fall*.

[4] On Pelagius's teaching, see Evans, *Pelagius*, especially 72–73, 82–85, 96–106.

and one of his opponents, Jerome, complained that his theology was muddled because his head was befuddled with too much porridge! Pelagius's teaching is today regarded as heretical by almost all churches.

Augustine encountered Pelagius's teaching in 411 and devoted the rest of his life to refuting it. His own doctrine had mostly been formulated before his encounter with Pelagius, but the controversy forced him to clarify it.[5]

Augustine taught that Adam (with Eve) was created good, but with the potential of sinning by disobedience. He did not need to sin – he was 'able to sin', and also 'able not to sin'. His time in the garden was a time of testing and probation. He had a genuine and unpredictable choice. If he had not sinned, his will would have been fixed permanently in a good state.

As we know, Adam did in fact sin. The consequence was that he (and the whole human race) became subject to concupiscence, or lustful desires. The flesh lusts against the Spirit (Gal. 5:17). This includes sexual desire, but also other lusts such as the lust for money or for power. Basically Augustine's argument is that we have turned from God to seek satisfaction in material things. A look at society today suggests that, despite being 1,600 years old, Augustine's teaching might have a lot to teach us today. The result of the fall is that instead of being 'able not to sin' we are now 'not able not to sin'.

Augustine taught that original sin was transmitted from generation to generation by the sexual lust involved in procreation. This explains the need for the Virgin Birth. Christ came 'begotten and conceived . . . without any indulgence of carnal lust, and therefore bringing with him no original sin'.[6] Augustine did not invent this idea, but inherited it from others before him.[7] Augustine's views on the mechanics of the transmission of original sin are not integral to his doctrine of original sin and the former can be abandoned without prejudicing the latter. Augustine's doctrine of original sin is still held by many today, but I am not aware that his explanation of the *transmission* of original sin has much support.[8] TeSelle comments that 'original sin is not biological for Augustine. It does not affect the genetic makeup of man; rather it is a kind of malfunction in the development of the personality.'[9] Attempts to locate original sin in our DNA are mistaken.

---

[5] On Augustine's teaching, see TeSelle, *Augustine the Theologian*, 258–266, 316–319. His teaching on original sin can be found, among other places, in his *The Merits and Remission of Sins and on the Baptism of Infants*, Book 1 (NPNF 5:15–43), and *City of God*, Book 14 (NPNF 2:262–283).

[6] *Enchiridion* 41 (NPNF 3:251).

[7] Kelly, *Early Christian Doctrines*, 363.

[8] For a discussion of how original sin is transmitted, see Letham, *Systematic Theology*, 381–396.

[9] TeSelle, *Augustine the Theologian*, 318.

Sin as a punishment for sin?[10]

Augustine portrays the imposition of concupiscence as God's punishment for the sin of Adam. At first sight this appears to be an odd procedure. There are four main components to contemporary theories of punishment: retribution, rehabilitation, prevention and deterrence. Augustine clearly sees this punishment as *retributive* and this makes sense so long as one grants that the responsibility for the sin is a corporate human responsibility rather than merely Adam's own private sin. But the imposition of concupiscence far from enabling *rehabilitation* serves to exclude the very possibility, except by the costly intervention of God's grace. Again, far from *preventing* further sin the imposition of concupiscence actually guarantees continued sin. Finally, while the example of Adam's punishment may conceivably have some *deterrent* effect, this is more than cancelled out by the fact that concupiscence makes it impossible not to sin. In short, given that God does not approve of sin, the punishment of Adam's sin by imposing a bondage to sin appears distinctly odd. Yet before we abandon our attempt to make sense of it we should remember the fact that Augustine's account does square rather well with the empirical reality of humanity as it now is and as Scripture describes it and also that if we accept the goodness of God's original creation, the reason for this present state must be traced back to human sin.

At first sight it may seem odd to state that the punishment for sin is more sin. Pelagius thought so and attacked Augustine at this point. The latter responded by showing that this is a scriptural principle, pointing to Romans 1:21–32[11] and to other examples such as the hardening of Pharaoh.[12] The process described in Romans chapter 1 is not without empirical verification in human history, so rather than reject the idea of sin as the punishment for sin we should seek to make sense of it.

There are two ways of interpreting Augustine's claim. Retreating armies routinely sabotage equipment that they have to leave behind. Should we think of the legacy of the fall in these terms? Should we think of Adam and Eve as independent creatures who in themselves had a moral perfection that God deliberately spoiled as a punishment for their sin? That is to misread the Genesis account. There it is precisely a state of moral autonomy, being like God knowing good and evil, that the serpent offers to Eve and Adam (3:5) and that God confirms that they received (3:22).[13] There is another way of interpreting

---

[10] On this, see Lane, 'Lust: Human Person as Affected by Disordered Desires'.
[11] *Nature and Grace* 22:24 (NPNF 5:129).
[12] *Grace and Free Choice* 20:41 (NPNF 5:461).
[13] For more on this see the next chapter.

Augustine's claim. Adam and Eve lived a holy life not by virtue of an inherent perfection but in dependence upon the Spirit of God. By turning away from God, by ceasing to trust him and setting themselves up as their own moral arbiters, they *by definition* ceased to live in dependence upon God. Irenaeus portrays Adam as stating that 'I have by disobedience lost that robe of sanctity which I had from the Spirit'.[14] Again, he remarks that it is those who reject the Spirit's counsel that become enslaved to carnal lusts.[15] If the essence of the fall, and of human sin in general,[16] is to live as autonomous moral agents rather than in dependence upon the Spirit of God, then *by definition* its consequence must be the loss of the moral integration that results from turning away from God.

If this account be accepted, then the consequence of human sin is not to be seen as an arbitrarily imposed penalty, like a judge imposing a fine for drunk driving, but rather as an inevitable outworking of the implications of sin. It would be very odd for a judge to punish drunk driving by forcing the offender to continue to get drunk on a regular basis; it is not odd for the consequence of substance abuse to be addiction to that substance. As Jesus stated, 'everyone who commits sin is a slave to sin' (John 8:34).

One possible way of thinking about how original sin operates on us is to use the analogy of excessive alcohol, which breaks down inhibitions and so reduces emotional control; likewise the effect on us of original sin is that we do not have the same level of control over ourselves that we would otherwise have. This coheres with Augustine's teaching that the effect of concupiscence is that the harmony of body and soul is lost and the soul no longer has full control over the body.[17]

On what grounds did Augustine defend his belief in original sin?

- Primarily *Scripture*: Genesis 3, Romans 5, together with other verses such as Psalm 51:5; Job 14:4; Ephesians 2:3; John 3:3, 6.
- *Tradition*: Augustine did not invent this doctrine and he cited material from earlier church fathers that supported his position, though not with the clarity that he brought to it.

---

[14] *Against Heresies* 3:23:5 (ANF 1:457).

[15] *Against Heresies* 5:8:2 (ANF 1:534).

[16] I assume that Gen. 3 is to be read *both* as an account of the first sin or as the introduction of sin into human history *and* as a paradigmatic account (showing us the nature of human sin in general). See the next chapter.

[17] *The Merits and Remission of Sins* 2:22:36 (NPNF 5:59); *Nature and Grace* 25:28 (NPNF 5:130–131); *City of God* 14:15 (NPNF 2:274–275).

- Augustine argued from the increasingly popular practice of *infant baptism*. If babies are without sin, why do they receive the one baptism for the remission of sins (Nicene Creed)? Today the direction of this theological argument has been reversed: people baptize babies *because* of their original sin.
- Augustine appealed to his *experience* of small children. It should perhaps be pointed out that Pelagius was an unmarried monk, whereas Augustine had experience of parenthood.

Modern rejection of Augustine

The doctrine of original sin has had its ups and downs. In the medieval West Augustine's doctrine was modified in various ways, but these can all be seen as variants of Augustinianism. The Reformers re-emphasized Augustine's teaching, perhaps strengthening it slightly and the Catholic Reformation reacted against them, but we are still talking of debates within Augustinianism. Article 2 of the Lutheran *Augsburg Confession* expresses the view of the Reformers:

> It is taught among us that since the Fall of Adam, all human beings who are born in the natural way are conceived and born in sin. This means that from birth they are full of evil lust and inclination and cannot by nature possess true fear of God and true faith in God. Moreover, this same innate disease and original sin is truly sin and condemns to God's eternal wrath all who are not in turn born anew through baptism and the Holy Spirit.[18]

It was the Enlightenment that seriously challenged the idea of original sin. An 'optimistic' view of human nature, that dispensed with the idea of original sin, emerged in the eighteenth century. So crime was blamed on ignorance, poverty, lack of education, and so on, but not on human nature. Jean-Jacques Rousseau was an early exponent of this and through him it made its mark upon modern educational theory. Marxism had a clear doctrine of a fall but located this in political and economic structures, affirming the inherent goodness of human nature. Once these structures are put right, the evil in society will vanish – as happened in the workers' paradise that followed the Russian revolution.

---

[18] *BkConc* 36, 38 (translation of the German text of the article).

There was no major war in Europe between the exile of Napoleon in 1815 and the outbreak of the First World War in 1914 (though Europeans were busy fighting elsewhere in the world and the French and Prussians had a brief spat) and it was easy to imagine that humanity had progressed to a higher level. But nineteenth-century optimism took a hammering in the twentieth century, with two world wars, and it has been said, with pardonable exaggeration, 'Our grandfathers in their simplicity found it hard, if not impossible, to believe in Original sin; it is not so with us; perhaps among the traditional dogmas this one alone can now be accepted as almost self-evident.'[19] More recently, David Owen, who was Foreign Secretary in the 1970s, and not a particularly religious man, wrote in his autobiography, 'When will we ever learn that evil remains, and that there is such a thing as original sin?'[20]

Nineteenth-century liberal theology had little concept of the inherent sinfulness of fallen human nature. These denials of original sin were, of course, strengthened by the rise of Darwinianism, which offered an alternative explanation for the evil in the world. But after the First World War liberal theology was largely superseded by Neo-Orthodoxy. Theologians such as Barth, Brunner and Niebuhr vigorously restated the Christian doctrine of original sin, which they saw in terms of the paradox between free will and bondage to sin, between personal choice and universal sinfulness. All three of them stressed human sinfulness and were highly critical of naive liberal optimism. There were of course differences between them, but they were agreed about the radical sinfulness of humanity and saw this especially in human pride and attempted independence from God. Reinhold Niebuhr spelt this out most perceptively in terms of its effects on all human civilization and culture. Each civilization sees itself as free from prejudice, while in fact it is dominated by an ideology that in fact furthers the interests of one particular group, whether the nobility, the middle class or the *apparatchiks*. Each civilization sees itself as final but each in turn is brought down because of the corruption in the human heart.[21] This last theme was developed by Herbert Butterfield in his *Christianity and History*. He showed that what happens in history is that successive civilizations try to create a stable society based on selfishness, but that all civilizations thereby contain within themselves the seed of their own destruction, as such a basis will work only for a time.[22] Original sin was brilliantly popularized in the works of D. R. Davies, under whose fiery preaching I sat as a young boy.

---

[19] A. G. Smith writing in 1954, quoted by Walgrave, 'Incarnation and Atonement', 153.
[20] Owen, *Time to Declare*, 361.
[21] E.g. Niebuhr, *Beyond Tragedy*, ch. 2; *Nature and Destiny of Man*, vol. 1, 221–242.
[22] Butterfield, *Christianity and History*, ch. 2.

He wrote that we need to come to terms with the fact that we are sinners, and to stop thinking of ourselves as better than we really are.[23]

Original sin has political implications. Reinhold Niebuhr argued that because of it individuals and cliques cannot be trusted with untrammelled power and so democracy is needed to hold them accountable. Again, because of original sin, the voice of the people is not always the voice of God and so checks and balances are needed. In the USA this takes the form of the Supreme Court, which is supposed to ensure that legislation is in line with the Constitution. This is not the complete solution, however, as the Supreme Court can itself become an unelected and unaccountable elite that imposes on the rest of the country fashionable progressive ideas contrary to the will of the people and the original aims of the Constitution. As Butterfield noted, there is no foolproof system given the corruption of the human heart.

Original sin as paradox

The doctrine of original sin can be stated in terms of a paradox. This can be expressed in various ways:

- Sin is inevitable, a statistical certainty – yet it is our responsibility (for some of us less so than others). It would not be possible to run society on the basis that people are not responsible for their own actions.
- We are enslaved to sin and in bondage to it; yet we choose it freely.
- Sin is universal (everybody sins); yet it is our personal choice.

There is a logical problem with each of these pairs, but they are supported both in Scripture and by experience and it is wrong to deny either side. Both are clearly taught by Scripture. Furthermore, both accord with our human experience. Sin is a statistical certainty. When a baby is born we might ask, 'Is it a boy or a girl?' but we do not ask, 'Will she grow up to be a sinner?' We know the answer. Yet even though it is inevitable that we shall all sin, we are also held responsible for our behaviour. This statistical certainty and our responsibility for sin are both clear in Scripture and both also accord with human experience.

Almost everyone would agree at least that other people fall short of what they should be. At the same time we treat people as responsible for their behaviour. The paradox accords with the complexities of real life. As a graffito once put it, 'Don't adjust your sets, the fault lies with reality.' Of course it is true that

---

[23] E.g. Davies, *Sin of Our Age*; Davies, *Down Peacock's Feathers*.

different people have different opportunities in life, but these do not fully determine our actions; we retain free will. Some academics may write against the reality of human responsibility, but it is unlikely that they will live their private lives according to this theory.

But does it make any sense to talk of a baby being sinful? Undoubtedly there is a *relative* innocence in children. They have as yet committed few personal sins and are not yet hardened in sin, but they also have an inherent tendency to sin and before long this will bear fruit. We have an inbuilt tendency to be sentimental about the very young, but although baby scorpions may look cute, they grow into adult scorpions. Likewise human babies are also baby sinners. Children may have a relative innocence but there is also an original violence. Steven Pinker summarizes this well:

> The most violent age is not adolescence but toddlerhood . . . 'The question . . . we've been trying to answer for the past 30 years is how do children learn to aggress. [But] that's the wrong question. The right question is how do they learn not to aggress.'[24]

The same point is made by William Golding in his classic novel *Lord of the Flies* (1954). 'If infants do no injury, it is for lack of strength, not for lack of will.'[25]

This has implications for child rearing and education. Until the Enlightenment, the goal was to curb evil; since then it has increasingly been to nurture the goodness inherent in human nature. Clearly this is not a simple either-or matter and there is a role for both sides – but whereas earlier generations may have overemphasized the negative side and neglected the positive, there is no doubt that today the pendulum has swung heavily in the other direction. The *Catechism of the Catholic Church* aptly comments that 'ignorance of the fact that man has a wounded nature inclined to evil gives rise to serious errors in the areas of education, politics, social action and morals'.[26]

Original guilt

'Original sin' usually refers to the idea that we are born with a bias towards sin, a doctrine that is very widely held; 'original guilt' refers to the idea that we are born with some measure of guilt, a much more controversial doctrine. A newborn child has not committed any personal sins, but is there a corporate

---

[24] Pinker, *Blank Slate*, 316, quoting R. E. Tremblay.
[25] Augustine, *Confessions* 1:11, as paraphrased in Chadwick, *Augustine*, 69.
[26] CCC §407.

guilt of the human race? Does a newborn child need salvation, and if so, from what? Another way of looking at this is to ask whether Christ died for all, including those who are stillborn or who die in infancy, or did he die only for those who live to an age of moral responsibility?

The key passage for answering this question is Romans 5:12–21. Verse 12 states that 'Just as sin came into the world through one man, and death through sin, so death spread to all people *because / inasmuch as / in whom* [i.e. Adam] all sinned.' The italicized words reflect the Greek words *eph hō*. Death spread to all because all sinned. But how? There are three main options.

1 All die because all have committed personal sins. This was Pelagius's interpretation of the passage. But what about babies who die without having committed any personal sin? Paul was writing at a time when infant mortality was high, and it is unlikely that he would have left such a gaping hole in his argument. Also, verses 13–14 point out that sin is not counted where there is no law, but nonetheless death reigned from Adam to Moses. Why?

2 Because of Adam's sin all have a sinful nature (original sin) and are guilty as a result. This was Calvin's interpretation of the passage. The problem with this is the *justice* of the situation: if we are born with a sinful nature then how are we to be responsible for our sin?

3 All human beings sinned *in Adam*. This was Augustine's interpretation of the passage. 'We were all in that one man, since we all *were* that one man.'[27] Augustine was using the Old Latin translation, which translated the words *eph hō* as 'in whom' meaning 'in Adam'. This is probably an incorrect translation of Romans 5:12.[28] But while it may be a mis*translation* of those two words, it is arguably a correct *interpretation* of the argument of the passage as a whole (5:12–21). One trespass (or the trespass of one) led to all being condemned (5:18).[29]

The idea of a 'corporate' inherited sin because of Adam's disobedience is a real problem for us today, because of the strong individualism of Western culture. This leads us to assume that all responsibility is individual, but it is not. For

---

[27] Augustine, *City of God* 13:14 (NPNF 2:251).
[28] For discussions of the correct translation, see Cranfield, *Epistle to the Romans*, vol. 1, 274–282; Thiselton, *Discovering Romans*, 131–138; Thielman, *Romans*, 282–283.
[29] For a discussion of different views, including Augustine's and Calvin's, see Letham, *Systematic Theology*, 375–380.

example, if the prime minister of the UK declares war, then the whole country is at war. Every culture clashes with Christian beliefs at some point and for modern Western culture individualism is such a point. For more on this see the next chapter.

4
The fall

Did it actually happen?

The idea of a historical fall, of an event in the past that actually happened, is widely questioned today. Even those who believe wholeheartedly in the doctrine of original sin do not all accept the idea of the fall as an event. As noted in the previous chapter, the idea of original sin, that we are all born with a bias towards sin, is much more plausible today than it once was. But since Darwin and the idea that humanity is the product of a process of evolution over millions of years, the concept of a fall has become more problematic.

Our concern here is not with the question of how literally to interpret Genesis 3. (Was there a literal tree and a literal snake?[1]) The more fundamental question is whether or not the chapter refers to an event that actually happened, regardless of whether the account is literal or figurative.

Mirror or window?

Much modern theology views Genesis 3 not as a *window* on the past, but a *mirror* on the present. That is, it is seen not as an account of an actual past event, but as a picture of what we are like now. In the last chapter we saw that many Neo-Orthodox theologians reaffirmed and expounded the doctrine of original sin, but most of them did not see this as being the result of a fall.

Karl Barth affirmed the doctrine of original sin, but did not believe in a historical fall. He spoke of Adam as a real person, but stated that the first man immediately became the first sinner. He saw Genesis 3 as a mirror to show what human nature is like. Adam is not a fate that affects us, but the truth concerning us. 'It is the name of Adam the transgressor which God gives to world-history as a whole.' Genesis 3 teaches that human history is a history of pride and rebellion.[2]

---

[1] For an excellent account of this, see Blocher, *In the Beginning*. For a variety of views, see Halton (ed.), *Genesis: History, Fiction, or Neither?* See also Stump and Meister (eds), *Original Sin and the Fall*.

[2] Barth, *Church Dogmatics* IV/1:507–513.

The view that Genesis 3 is a mirror, not a window, is already found in second-century Judaism: 'Adam is, therefore, not the cause [of judgement], except only for himself, but each of us has become our own Adam' (*2 Baruch* [= *Syriac Apocalypse of Baruch*] 54:19).

What about Genesis 3 itself? It certainly does function as a mirror in that it shows us how temptation works and how we can fall for it. But the chapter is also about the origin of sin, for three reasons.

First, consider the structure of Genesis. In chapters 1 and 2 we have a world that is good and indeed 'very good' (1:31). Yet by Genesis 4 we see brother killing brother. That is bad and very bad. So what has gone wrong? The answer is to be found in Genesis 3. Adam and Eve turned away from God and for this there were consequences. But this is not an answer at all, unless the chapter is about an actual event. It does not matter whether every detail (e.g. the snake) is taken literally. What does matter is that this refers to an actual event where the human race turned against God. So Genesis 3 is not just a mirror but also a window on to something that happened in history. If the chapter is simply saying that this is the sort of people that we are, it offers no answer to the question of how God's 'very good' creation became such a mess.

Secondly, Paul sees Adam's sin as pivotal in Romans 5:12–21 and 1 Corinthians 15:21–22: 'For as by a man came death, by a man has come also the resurrection of the dead. For as in Adam all die, so also in Christ shall all be made alive.' He sees Genesis 3 as not just an account of our present plight but as also giving the reason for our plight, its cause.

Thirdly, why is it that *all* people sin? There are four possible answers.

1 That it is a coincidence, that the billions of people that have lived all just happen to have made the same choice. Statistically this is effectively impossible. It is also not something that people believe. As mentioned previously, sin is a statistical certainty and we do not ask whether a newborn child will grow up to be a sinner.

2 That God created us that way. If so, sin is God's responsibility. We would not need to feel guilty about being sinful, any more than we need to feel guilty about growing hair or not knowing everything. Reinhold Niebuhr, who vigorously expounded a doctrine of original sin, stated that 'Original sin is the inevitable taint upon the spirituality of a finite creature.'[3] Speaking for myself, I do not feel guilty about the fact that I am finite. If original sin is a consequence of finitude, we need not feel responsible for it or guilty about it – any more than we feel guilty

---

[3] Niebuhr, *Beyond Tragedy*, 30.

for not being omnipotent. There is also a worse consequence. In the age to come we shall remain finite, so presumably inevitably tainted with original sin.

3 That sin is the result of evolution, a hangover from our evolutionary past. Here again, this might explain *why* we sin (though that is open to question) but it does not establish any ground for our responsibility. We would be no more responsible for sin than if God had directly created us sinful.

4 That *God made us good but the human race turned away from God to sin* – as portrayed in Genesis 3. This explanation fits the facts of experience (original sin), explains why all people sin and avoids blaming this on God's good creation.

There is an obvious objection to this answer. It establishes *human* responsibility for sin in that it is the consequence not of God's good creation but of the fall. But it does not establish *individual* responsibility in that it was not I who sinned in the beginning. There are a number of points that can be made in response.

In the previous chapter we noted that original sin involves paradox, including that between universal sinfulness and personal choice.

As stated by Pascal,[4] original sin is an 'incomprehensible mystery', though one that helps us to make sense of ourselves.

This does not sit well with our modern individualism. The idea of communal responsibility may feel foreign to our Western mindset, but is not such a problem in other cultures. Modern Western culture regards people as free-standing individuals and regards this as self-evident, but at this point it is opposed to almost every other culture from the past or present. We tend to see ourselves as independent individuals, as if the human race were like a collection of stones on a beach. A better analogy may be to see ourselves like apples on a tree – clearly distinct from one another but inseparably inter-connected. Paul describes Christians as organs in a body (1 Cor. 12:12–27). The Western emphasis upon individual rights and responsibilities has brought many benefits, but has also had negative effects on society. As Westerners we need to move beyond our culture of individualism and regain a sense of the solidarity of the human race. We are a community, not just autonomous individuals. We need to recognize that there is a corporate as well as an individual side to sin and responsibility. There is such a thing as national guilt – as well as national pride. Every culture clashes with the Christian faith at some point and this is a major way in which our culture clashes. We must not make the

---

[4] Pascal, *Pensées* 131.

mistake of absolutizing our own culture and relativizing Christian revelation. What seems absolute truth in one culture often appears to be simple error in another culture.

In 1624 John Donne famously expressed the corporate dimension of human existence:

> No man is an Island, entire of itself; every man is a piece of the Continent, a part of the main; . . . any man's death diminishes me, because I am involved in Mankind; And therefore never send to know for whom the bell tolls; it tolls for thee.[5]

It is not just the doctrine of original sin that requires the idea of corporate solidarity. The belief that Christ died for our sins is hard to understand if sin and guilt are purely individual.

One reason why many today choose to regard Genesis 3 as a mirror, but not a window, is the desire to make peace with the scientific account of human origins. What is this? Life on earth is billions of years old, the genus *Homo* is up to 2.5 million years old, anatomically modern humans (*Homo sapiens*) have been around for some 190,000 years and civilization began about 10,000 years ago. Also, human beings have evolved from the most primitive life forms. Does such an account leave any room for the idea of a fall? It all depends on what sort of fall.

The nature of the fall

Historically there have been two contrasting ways of viewing the fall. Following Augustine, it became traditional to see Adam and Eve as inhabiting a perfect world. There was a tendency to think of them as immortal. At times they were seen as morally and intellectually all but perfect. The result was that Genesis 3 was understood as a fall from a great height. All of this creates intolerable tensions with the modern scientific view. The Garden of Eden becomes like the lost city of Atlantis, the scene of a primitive culture of great value. This view creates problems both with the existence of death before the fall and with the evolutionary account of human origins.

There is, however, an alternative approach. Irenaeus, the second-century opponent of Gnosticism, portrayed Adam and Eve before the fall as morally and intellectually children. They were meant to grow closer to God by a long

---

[5] John Donne, *Meditation* 17.

process, but disobeyed and turned from the path.[6] Whereas the Augustinian model clashes seriously with modern science, the Irenaean model can more easily be harmonized with it. That may be seen as an incentive for adopting the Irenaean model, but the more important question is which model coheres with Scripture. We shall examine in turn the three points mentioned above, together with a fourth.

A perfect world?

The idea of a perfect world conflicts with Tennyson's portrayal of 'nature red in tooth and claw'.[7] That is brought home to us very clearly in the many nature programmes on television. And this conflict is not something recent, beginning with the fall, but is a feature of life on earth from the beginning. But while Genesis portrays the world as very good (1:31), it does not say that it was perfect. Furthermore, there are hints in Genesis 3 itself that evil has entered God's good world. Eve was tempted by the serpent, who was clearly in opposition to God. Human sin was not the first rebellion against the Creator in the universe. The serpent is later identified as Satan, in Revelation 12:9; 20:2. Adam and Eve were expelled from the garden. Are we to understand by this that paradisal conditions were at that time confined to the garden? Genesis 2:8 and 3:23 could be taken to imply that. There are certainly no grounds for dogmatically stating that the whole world was at that stage perfect. It has also been suggested that what changed was not the physical nature of things but our rapport with nature, our ability to control it.[8]

Also, it is not the Bible that tells us that animals were pacifists and vegetarians before the fall. Isaiah 11:6–9 and other passages present a picture of harmony and peace in the animal kingdom, with the wolf and lamb dwelling together, as also the leopard and the goat, the lion and the calf. But this is a vision of the end, not the beginning. Apart from Origen, no Christian theologian of stature has fallen into the mistake of supposing that the end will simply be a restoration of the beginning. A comparison of Genesis 1 – 2 with Revelation 21 – 22 shows that the end far excels the beginning. The ability not to sin will be replaced by the inability to sin.

Confusing the end with the beginning has one serious implication. If the end merely restores the beginning, the whole process of fall and redemption could happen all over again – as Origen conceded. Jesus makes it clear that the New Age will not merely be a restoration of Eden when he declared that there

---

[6] For more on this, see Lane, 'Irenaeus on Fall and Original Sin'.
[7] Tennyson, *In Memoriam A.H.H.* 56.
[8] Lucas, *Can We Believe Genesis Today?*, 146–147.

would be no marriage there (Mark 12:25), while in Eden there was marriage between Adam and Eve.

Were Adam and Eve morally perfect?

Before the fall, Adam and Eve were not yet morally perfect. They were on trial. They had not yet sinned, but nor had they yet learned obedience. Their state was that of being 'able to sin and able not to sin'. There was the possibility of *becoming* perfect and the possibility of *becoming* sinful. The garden was a time of trial or probation, not a time of perfection as at the end. They had not reached the state of being 'not able to sin'. Had they reached it, the fall would have been impossible! It is therefore wrong to think of Adam and Eve as falling from a great moral height. Rather, they were setting out on a path of moral testing and at an early stage they took a wrong turn. They were changeably good, but not unchangeably perfect.[9] 'Very good' (Gen. 1:31), but liable to change.

To say that they were not yet perfect is not to say that they were sinful. We read of Jesus, 'Although he was a son, he *learned* obedience through what he suffered. And being *made* perfect, he became the source of eternal salvation to all who obey him' (Heb. 5:8–9). Being obedient is more than simply not disobeying. A table has never disobeyed – but nor has it ever obeyed. As Jesus grew up he learned to obey, without ever disobeying. Adam and Eve could have done the same, had they not chosen the wrong path.

Were Adam and Eve immortal?

Were human beings immortal before the fall? Genesis 3 and Romans 5 both blame death on the fall. How can this be squared with an evolutionary account of the origins of life? It is important to note what Genesis does and does not say. Death is the penalty of sin, but it is not stated that Adam and Eve were immortal before they sinned. In fact they could not have been, since by definition an immortal being cannot die! Rather they had access to the tree of life and this access was denied to them after their sin. What they had was the *potential* of *future* immortality. They had access to the tree of life from which they were debarred because of their sin (Gen. 3:22). We were created from nothing, and so by definition can return to being nothing. It is only God's sustenance that keeps us alive (Job 34:14–15).

It is clear that this picture does not clash with an evolutionary picture of human origins. Immortality is portrayed by Genesis as something that was held before us, to which we never attained. There is no need to postulate an

---

[9] Farley, *Providence of God*, 236.

immortal state of unfallen humanity. Genesis is at this point compatible with a picture of humanity emerging from a brutish origin.

Is the human race descended from a single pair?

Traditionally Christians have argued that the whole human race is descended from a single pair, Adam and Eve, and the Bible can easily be read this way, but need not be. Contrary to many English translations, the Greek of Acts 17:26 does not say that God made the nations from one *man*. On the other hand, Genesis 4 implies that Cain left his family to confront other people and refers to his building a city. The current scientific evidence supports the idea that the human population was low at certain stages, but not that the human race is descended from a single pair.[10] What about 1 Corinthians 15:22: 'as in Adam all die, so also in Christ shall all be made alive'? Adam's role has often been seen as 'federal headship', which does not necessarily involve our direct physical descent from him. And, clearly, there is no question of physical descent from Christ.[11]

Looking at these points, the Augustinian model of morally perfect and immortal beings in a perfect world clashes both with the modern scientific account *and* with the scriptural account. The Irenaean model of Adam and Eve as morally and intellectually children who were meant to grow closer to God by a long process, but disobeyed and turned from the path, coheres better both with Scripture and with modern science. All that is necessary for the doctrine of the fall is that human beings were created good and at some early point took the wrong turn, away from God. There is no conflict between this and what science claims, although science involves interpretation and is changeable. Indeed it is hard to see how *any* scientific evidence could ever disprove it.

The knowledge of good and evil

The serpent promised Adam and Eve that they would become 'like God, knowing good and evil' (Gen. 3:5). Preachers often portray this as a lie, but it was not, since according to the statement of God himself that is exactly what did happen (v. 22).

What does 'knowing good and evil' mean?[12] It cannot mean omniscience, as some interpreters suggest, since that was manifestly not the outcome of the

---

[10] Collins, *Language of God*, 126, 206–210.

[11] This is a controversial issue. For a number of different views, see Barrett and Caneday (eds), *Four Views on the Historical Adam*; Madueme and Reeves (eds), *Adam, the Fall, and Original Sin*, 3–81.

[12] See Blocher, *In the Beginning*, 126–133, on the meaning of the phrase. See also Westermann, *Genesis 1–11*, 240–248; Hamilton, *Book of Genesis Chapters 1–17*, 163–166.

fall – as students taking exams know all too well. Nor can it mean the *experience* of doing both good and evil, since God does not have that. It must mean moral autonomy and independence, setting oneself up as one's own judge of what is right and wrong. This is precisely what Adam and Eve did. The serpent challenged them to become like God by setting themselves up as their own arbiters of good and evil, in opposition to God. This is the essence of sin – setting oneself up against God. Thus the first sin was a declaration of moral independence, a premature step into adult independence, a wrong turning that took us forward in the wrong direction rather than a fall from a state of perfection already achieved. We are like teenagers who have asserted their independence of their parents and made a mess of their lives, but cannot simply go back to being children again. In the last chapter we examined some of the implications of this.

5
Sin and guilt

Sin and guilt

In both Old and New Testaments we see a pattern. Sin leads to guilt leads to judgement and punishment. There is nothing odd about this. In the secular realm, crime leads to guilt, which leads to judgement and punishment. This process is stated positively in Scripture. Also, Scripture focuses on the cure for this. Atonement leads to forgiveness – which implies the existence of sin and guilt. Worship includes times of confession and absolution – which also imply the existence of sin and guilt. Some have criticized the Penal Substitutionary doctrine of the atonement for focusing on guilt, but any theology that includes the forgiveness of sins implies that there is a need for it, because of sin and guilt.

There is a difference between objective and subjective guilt, between actual guilt and mere feelings of guilt. Some people are actually guilty but have no guilty feelings. I remember when I was first confronted directly with the gospel and saying that I could not think of anything wrong that I had done: an indicator of my blindness rather than my innocence. Others, by contrast, experience obsessive guilt feelings and are unable to accept the fact of forgiveness, even when they have repented, believed and confessed their sin. We see the same contrast when it comes to health. Some people refuse to face up to alarming symptoms and blindly remain confident of good health; others are hypochondriacs, the 'worried well', who are constantly concerned lest they have this or that disease.

When it comes to preaching, I have sat under ministers whom others have accused of 'making me feel guilty'. In fact they were simply presenting clearly the challenges of Christian discipleship. I wonder whether those who complain of being made to feel guilty have fully grasped the gospel. The aim of preaching is not to tell everyone that they are fine as they are and to instil a sense of complacency. Nor is it to make people feel guilty. But we need to be told how far short we fall of fulfilling the two great commandments (love of God and neighbour), told about the forgiveness of sin, and encouraged to press on and grow. We shall return to this in chapter 17, below.

Judgement and punishment

Today judgement and punishment are considered harsh words that many people try to avoid, thinking that surely a God of love would never do anything so nasty as punish anyone. But that is not what we see with the God of the Bible.

God hates sin and brings it into judgement, both now and at the end. In Scripture both judgement and punishment are found repeatedly. In the Old Testament the prophets pronounced judgement on the nations and on the people of God. Both Israel and Judah were sent into exile. There is also repeated reference to the judgement and punishment of individuals. To mention but two examples, David is punished for his sin with Bathsheba (2 Sam. 12:1–14) and Ananias and Sapphira are punished for lying to the Holy Spirit (Acts 5:1–11). The final judgement at the end includes, as the name implies, judgement and leads to punishment for some (e.g. Dan. 12:2; Rev. 20:11–15).

Those who imagine to themselves a God who neither judges nor punishes are not thinking of the God of the Bible, nor of the God of the New Testament on its own. Apart from final judgement at the end, sin is sometimes punished in this life, sometimes not. As Augustine put it:

> For if every sin were now visited with manifest punishment, nothing would seem to be reserved for the final judgment; on the other hand, if no sin received now a plainly divine punishment, it would be concluded that there is no divine providence at all.[1]

As one who has never received a speeding fine I can vouch for the accuracy of the first part of Augustine's comment!

The idea of a 'God' who never judges or punishes goes back to the heretic Marcion in the second century, who was excommunicated in AD 144.[2] He believed in two literal Gods. The creator God of the Old Testament is the Lawgiver and Judge, a wrathful God of justice who is not good. The God and Father of Christ is the good and merciful God of love, who has nothing to do with creation and came to rescue us from both the Creator and the creation. The latter God is revealed in those parts of the New Testament that remained after Marcion had, as Tertullian put it, exercised textual criticism with the knife rather than the pen.[3] Marcion's Bible consisted only of truncated versions

---

[1] Augustine, *City of God* 1:8 (NPNF 2:5).
[2] On Marcion, see Hoffmann, *Marcion: On Restitution of Christianity*. For the classic refutation, see Tertullian, *Against Marcion* (ANF 3:269–474).
[3] Tertullian, *Prescription Against Heretics* 38 (ANF 3:262).

of Luke's Gospel and Paul's letters, edited to remove any affirmation of the God of the Old Testament. As Irenaeus wittily expressed it, Marcion 'circumcised' Luke![4] Tertullian sarcastically described Marcion's view thus:

A better god has been discovered, one who is neither offended nor angry nor inflicts punishment, who has no fire warming up in hell, and no outer darkness wherein there is shuddering and gnashing of teeth: he is merely kind. Of course he forbids you to sin – but only in writing.[5]

No one today believes that there are literally two Gods, but Marcion's approach of setting the New Testament *portrayal* of God against that of the Old Testament is still to be found.

Nineteenth-century liberal theology took up the opposition between love and justice. While it did not affirm the literal existence of two Gods, like Marcion it contrasted the Old Testament portrayal of God as a God of judgement and punishment and the New Testament portrayal of a God of love. The wrath of God was a feature of the Old Testament, not the New. (We shall consider God's wrath more fully in the next chapter.) Such ideas are still found today, in a dilute form, in those who portray a God who never judges or punishes. It is true, of course, that we read that 'God *is* love' (1 John 4:8, 16), but that does not mean that love is all that we have to say about God. The same letter proclaims that 'God *is* light, and in him is no darkness at all' (1 John 1:5). Throughout the Bible we see God as a God of love *and* as a God of holiness and purity. Both themes come out clearly in the Old Testament. The teaching of Jesus proclaims God's love, but it is also true that the majority of the teaching on hell in the New Testament is found in the teaching of Jesus. Paul tells Christians never to avenge themselves – but on the grounds that vengeance is God's and *he* will repay (Rom. 12:19). He then proceeds to spell out how one way that this happens is through the organs of the state (Rom. 13:1–5).

Today many pride themselves that society has become non-judgemental. What they mean is that almost any sexual activity other than paedophilia is now regarded as acceptable. Jonathan Sacks laments the situation that prevails in our society. In our society, he maintains, the word 'judgmental' is used 'to rule out in advance the offering of moral judgement'.[6] A worthy and biblical reticence in passing judgement on individuals has been confused with an

---

[4] Irenaeus, *Against Heresies* 1:27:2; 3:11:7 (ANF 1:352, 428).

[5] Tertullian, *Against Marcion* 1:27, in Evans (ed.), *Tertullian Adversus Marcionem*, vol. 1, 77.

[6] Sacks, *Faith in the Future*, 37–39, referring to sexual issues especially.

unwillingness to make moral judgements, to distinguish between what is morally good and what is evil. Morality becomes a matter of taste and choice. The judgement of God rescues us from just such a moral relativism by showing us that right and wrong are objectively real and pointing us to the moral significance of our deeds. The doctrine of God's displeasure with sin points to the fact that morality is not simply a matter of personal taste and choice.

In other respects, though, we have become increasingly judgemental. Prominent people are being no-platformed for espousing views that do not conform to the latest progressive orthodoxy, and this is happening even in leading universities. The views censored would often have been considered completely uncontroversial a few years back. People have lost their jobs for views expressed in private, sometimes years in the past. Liberal tolerance used to mean the toleration of views with which one does not agree, but for the new fascist liberalism it means conforming to the latest understanding of what is meant by inclusivity.[7]

Sin has effects or consequences:

Can a man carry fire next to his chest
and his clothes not be burned?
(Prov. 6:27)

The trouble is that people often do not want to hear this:

They are a rebellious people,
lying children,
children unwilling to hear
the instruction of the LORD;
who say to the seers, 'Do not see',
and to the prophets, 'Do not prophesy to us what is right;
speak to us smooth things,
prophesy illusions,
leave the way, turn aside from the path,
let us hear no more about the Holy One of Israel.
(Isa. 30:9–11)

---

[7] See on this Carson, *Intolerance of Tolerance*. Tim Farron's 2017 Theos Annual Lecture makes similar points. See <https://www.theosthinktank.co.uk/in-the-news/2037/11/28/what-kind-of-liberal-society-do-we-want-theos-annual-lecture-2017-full-text>, accessed 5 June 2020.

The purpose of punishment

Traditionally punishment has been seen as retribution, maintaining the principles of law and justice in society. In the nineteenth century, Utilitarians presented an alternative view of punishment in terms of reform and deterrence. Imprisonment also performs the function of prevention in that while a burglar (for example) is in prison he cannot be burgling. Some people still reject the idea of punishment as retribution, but it is now widely accepted by criminologists that there is a role for all four elements: retribution, reform, deterrence and prevention.[8]

The idea of *retribution* is clear in Scripture. Today it is out of favour in many circles, but C. S. Lewis's essay 'The Humanitarian View of Punishment' points out that without the idea of retribution, punishment is simply unfair.[9] What makes punishment fair and just is that it is deserved; otherwise it degenerates into social engineering. In the Soviet Union and other Communist states people were sent to 're-education camps' to be 'reformed', as has been happening since 2017 to the Uyghurs in the province of Xinjiang in Communist China. Since this was not a deserved punishment, people could in principle remain there indefinitely (or indeed be executed) if they did not embrace the required ideology. Such treatment rightly strikes us as unjust, because we retain the notion that punishment must be deserved. In the words of Gilbert and Sullivan's *The Mikado*, the aim is to 'let the punishment fit the crime'. Or, as Immanuel Kant put it:

> Judicial punishment can never be used merely as a means to promote some other good for the criminal himself or for civil society, but instead it must in all cases be imposed on him only on the ground that he has committed a crime.[10]

An important component of punishment should be *reform*. The nineteenth century saw the idea that the goal of prison is to reform and rehabilitate. This remains a goal, in theory at least, though in practice prison too often functions as a finishing school for crime. Ezekiel states that an outcome of the Babylonian exile would be to cleanse the Jews from idol worship (Ezek. 37:23). As a simple fact of history this is what happened, since after the return from exile Jews were never again guilty of worshipping physical idols. Again, Hebrews states that God 'disciplines us for our good, that we may share his holiness' (12:10).

---

[8] Cf. Stott and Miller (eds), *Crime and the Responsible Community*, especially 44–50.
[9] Lewis, *Undeceptions*, 287–300.
[10] *Metaphysics of Morals* §49E.I, in Kant, *Metaphysical Elements of Justice*, 138.

More recently, restorative justice is a method of reforming petty criminals by allowing them to face their victims.

Again, *deterrence* has always been one of the purposes of punishment – but not the only purpose. If punishment were solely for deterrence, then one could eliminate parking on yellow lines by hanging offenders from the nearest lamp post. This would prove very effective, but it would be unjust because the punishment would not fit the crime. Again, locking up criminals serves to *prevent* crime, but people should be imprisoned only for crimes that they have actually committed, not merely because they might in future commit other crimes. The concept of retribution is vital in order to prevent the abuse of punishment for purposes of reform, deterrence or prevention.

Deterrence brings in the question of *fear*. People brake before speed cameras because they fear the consequences of getting caught. There are two opposite errors here. One is to suppose that obedience motivated by fear is sufficient. Augustine rightly noted that 'the man who only fears the flames of hell is afraid not of sinning, but of being burned; but the man who hates sin as much as he hates hell is afraid to sin'.[11] It has always been recognized that the mark of true repentance is not fear of consequences but hatred of sin. The opposite error is to suppose that there is no positive role to be played by fear. 'The fear of the LORD is the beginning of wisdom' (Prov. 9:10). Jesus told his disciples to 'fear him who, after he has killed, has authority to cast into hell' (Luke 12:5). We shall consider this question further in chapter 25.

Finally, what about the *lex talionis* principle? This appears in the Mosaic law in a number of contexts:

- In the context of a pregnant woman being hurt in a struggle between two men and having a miscarriage: 'If there is harm, then you shall pay life for life, eye for eye, tooth for tooth, hand for hand, foot for foot, burn for burn, wound for wound, stripe for stripe' (Exod. 21:23–25).
- In the context of personal behaviour: 'If anyone injures his neighbour, as he has done it shall be done to him' (Lev. 24:19).
- In the context of deliberate false witness in court: 'You shall do to him as he had meant to do to his brother. So you shall purge the evil from your midst. And the rest shall hear and fear, and shall never again commit any such evil among you. Your eye shall not pity. It shall be life for life, eye for eye, tooth for tooth, hand for hand, foot for foot' (Deut. 19:19–21).

---

[11] Augustine, *Letter* 145:4 (NPNF 1:496).

The point is not the method of punishment, but the principle of proportionality, which is a fundamental principle of justice. The punishment must fit the crime, not go beyond it. This prevents the escalation into feuding that unbridled retribution could initiate, and was an important step forward when first expressed legally in the Torah, in the context of official courts of law rather than personal revenge.

But what about Jesus' teaching in the Sermon on the Mount?

You have heard that it was said, 'An eye for an eye and a tooth for a tooth.' But I say to you, Do not resist the one who is evil. But if anyone slaps you on the right cheek, turn to him the other also ... And if anyone forces you to go one mile, go with him two miles.'
(Matt. 5:38–41)

Jesus here is talking about taking vengeance as an individual and about how we relate to others. He is not referring to justice administered by the state. We shall consider this further in chapter 25.

6

The wrath of God[1]

Does God get angry with us?

'Where is the God of love in the Old Testament?' people sometimes ask. The same people are also liable to ask, 'How can you believe in a God of love with so much suffering in the world?' What they do not seem to notice was that the Old Testament and empirical reality cohere; it is the sentimental liberal concept of the love of God that is out of step. The sentimental view of the love of God proclaimed almost without respite by many Western churches may appear very attractive, but it is not in the last resort credible.

God's love involves hatred of evil. Romans 12:9: 'Love must be genuine.' The next word comes as a shock. In most Bible translations it is 'Hate.' 'Hate what is evil.' For most Western Christians 'hate' is the last word that would be associated with love. But a love that does not contain hatred of evil is not the love of which the Bible speaks. It is not that we need to balance God's wrath with his love, as rival attributes, but that *God's love itself implies his wrath, his displeasure against sin. Without his wrath God is simply not loving in the sense that the Bible portrays his love.*

The neglect of the wrath of God

Today there is a widespread silence regarding God's wrath. But it was not always thus. The most notorious sermon on the topic is probably Jonathan Edwards's *Sinners in the Hands of an Angry God*, preached to great effect at Enfield in New England in 1741. In this sermon Edwards is unrestrained in the language he uses to describe God's wrath:

> The bow of God's wrath is bent, and the arrow made ready on the string, and justice bends the arrow at your heart, and strains the bow, and it is nothing but the mere pleasure of God, and that of an angry God, without

---

[1] For a fuller version of this chapter, see Lane, 'Wrath of God'.

any promise or obligation at all, that keeps the arrow one moment from being made drunk with your blood . . . The God that holds you over the pit of hell, much as one holds a spider or some loathsome insect over the fire, abhors you and is dreadfully provoked. His wrath towards you burns like a fire; he looks upon you as worthy of nothing else, but to be cast into the fire; he is of purer eyes than to bear to have you in his sight; you are ten thousand times more abominable in his eyes than the most hateful venomous serpent is in ours. You have offended him infinitely more than ever a stubborn rebel did of his prince. And yet it is nothing but his hand that holds you from falling into the fire every moment.

O sinner! consider the fearful danger you are in. It is a great furnace of wrath, a wide and bottomless pit full of the fire of wrath, that you are held over in the hand of that God, whose wrath is provoked and incensed as much against you, as against many of the damned in hell. You hang by a slender thread, with the flames of divine wrath flashing about it, and ready every moment to singe it and burn it asunder . . . Consider this, you that are here present, that yet remain in an unregenerate state. That God will execute the fierceness of his anger implies that he will inflict wrath without any pity. When God beholds the ineffable extremity of your case, and sees your torment to be so vastly disproportionated to your strength, and sees how your poor soul is crushed and sinks down, as it were, into an infinite gloom; he will have no compassion upon you, he will not forbear the executions of his wrath, or in the least lighten his hand; there shall be no moderation or mercy, nor will God then at all stay his rough wind; he will have no regard to your welfare, nor be at all careful lest you should suffer too much in any other sense, than only that you shall not suffer beyond what strict justice requires. Nothing shall be withheld because it is so hard for you to bear. Ezekiel 8:18, 'Therefore will I also deal in fury; mine eye shall not spare, neither will I have pity; and though they cry in mine ears with a loud voice, yet will I not hear them.'[2]

Today one would have to travel far to hear a sermon remotely like Edwards's. The problem with today's theology and preaching is not that the wrath of God is exaggerated but rather that it is muted or even suppressed. Most people today feel that, if God exists, it is his purpose to make us happy. He is there to serve *our* agenda, not we to serve *his*. The unspoken attitude is not 'What do we owe him?' but 'What does he owe us and why isn't he doing a better job

---

2 Sermon 7 in Edwards, *Select Works*, vol. 2, 183–199, with the punctuation modernized in places.

of delivering it?' To slightly modify Question 1 of the *Westminster Shorter Catechism*, 'What is God's chief end in life? It is to make us happy.' If there is a God, then he most definitely ought to respect human rights – human rights as *we* define them. God's love is understood in sentimental terms, God being a heavenly Grandfather, whose role is to indulge us, rather than our Father, whose role includes discipline. Many people's concept of God is comparable to Santa Claus. Such a view of God leads to a benign scepticism and apathy. A proclamation of God that includes his displeasure against evil is likely to attract hostility rather than apathy, but in some people it will engender a conviction of sin.

There are four different ways in which the wrath of God is neglected by Christians today.

The first way is simple denial of the wrath of God. This is often found today, even in some evangelical churches, as such denial fits in well with our secular culture. They dismiss it as a crude idea found in the Old Testament which has no place in Christian theology. Liberal theology takes this approach.

The second way, more sophisticated than philosophical denial, is the theological approach of Marcion, described in the previous chapter. He differentiated between the wrathful God of justice revealed in the Old Testament and the merciful God of love revealed in the New Testament. While no one today believes that there are literally two Gods, Marcion's approach of setting the New Testament *portrayal* of God against that of the Old Testament is still to be found.

The third way in which God's wrath is muted is that found in the majority of Western evangelical churches today. The wrath of God is not denied and is indeed given formal recognition. But in practice it is neglected. In preaching and teaching it is ignored, largely or totally.

> Those who still believe in the wrath of God . . . say little about it . . . The fact is that the subject of divine wrath has become taboo in modern society, and Christians by and large have accepted the taboo and conditioned themselves never to raise the matter.[3]

There is a fourth and more subtle way in which the wrath of God is undermined. C. H. Dodd offered a reinterpretation of the concept. Talk of God's anger is too anthropomorphic. There is no place for the wrath of God in the teaching of Jesus. 'Paul never uses the verb, "to be angry", with God as subject.'

---

[3] Packer, *Knowing God*, 164.

While the original meaning of 'the wrath of God' was the passion of anger, by the time of Paul it has come to refer to an impersonal process of cause and effect, the inevitable result of sin. In Paul the wrath of God describes not 'the attitude of God to man', but 'an inevitable process of cause and effect in a moral universe'. We live in a universe where there are moral consequences that have been set up by God in creation – for example, getting drunk at night leads to a hangover the next morning. 'In the long run we cannot think with full consistency of God in terms of the highest human ideals of personality and yet attribute to Him the irrational passion of anger.'[4]

How should Dodd's approach be assessed? There are some positive points to acknowledge. First, it must be recognized that talk of God's wrath is anthropomorphic (or, to be pedantic, anthropopathic). While God is rightly described in human terms, we must recognize that these terms are true by analogy rather than univocally. Almost every writer on this topic emphasizes the dangers of understanding God's wrath in terms of human anger. Our human anger is so often flawed by selfishness or loss of control. But of course, this is not true only of the wrath of God. Talk of God's love is also anthropomorphic and we must not fall into the error of equating the divine love with human love in all its imperfection and distortion. To concede that talk of God's wrath is anthropomorphic is not, of course, to deny that there is a reality to which it corresponds. What that reality is is precisely the point at dispute.

Secondly, the wrath of God should not be understood in a crudely literal fashion. The divine wrath is very different from human wrath. It should certainly not be understood as an irrational rage or passion, to use Dodd's words. As Stott puts it, God's wrath against sin

> does not mean . . . that he is likely to fly off the handle at the most trivial provocation, still less that he loses his temper for no apparent reason at all. For there is nothing capricious or arbitrary about the holy God. Nor is he ever irascible, malicious, spiteful or vindictive. His anger is neither mysterious nor irrational. It is never unpredictable but always predictable, because it is provoked by evil and by evil alone.[5]

The wrath of God is his settled displeasure against sin.

Thirdly, it can be conceded that, relative to the Old Testament, there is in the New Testament a tendency to depersonalize the wrath of God. MacGregor

---

[4] Dodd, *Romans*, 47–50.
[5] Stott, *Cross of Christ*, 173.

softens and qualifies Dodd's position in such a way as to bring out the validity of his case. 'God's "wrath" in the N.T., and particularly in Paul's letters is conceived of in terms less completely personal than is his love.'[6] This casts doubt on the wisdom of Edwards's sermon. Edwards heightens the affective character of God's wrath by bringing together in concentrated form the strongest elements of the Old Testament teaching, while the New Testament writers seem to move in the opposite direction. The New Testament speaks of God's wrath almost entirely in terms of its effects rather than God's disposition.

Finally, it should be recognized that wrath is not fundamental to God in the same way that love is. Isaiah describes God as rising up in wrathful judgement

> to do his deed – strange is his deed!
> and to work his work – alien is his work!
> (Isa. 28:21)

Loving parents will feel similarly about the exercise of discipline – they prefer rewarding their children to punishing them. Although discipline is a part of love it is not a *pleasant* part, but saddens parents. God *is* love, yet one could not say that God *is* wrath. In other words, love is a fundamental and eternal attribute of God, while wrath is no more than an outworking of God's character in response to sin. Wrath is not an attribute of God in the way that his love or holiness is. His wrath is his response to something outside himself. It is also true that before creation God had no occasion to exercise his mercy. But this does not put wrath and mercy on the same footing. The Old Testament repeatedly affirms God's reluctance to exercise his wrath and his delight in showing mercy. The Bible often states that God is slow to anger, and that he grieves over sin. Jonah states that the Lord is 'a gracious God and merciful, slow to anger and abounding in steadfast love, and relenting from disaster' (4:2). So his wrath is the displeasure of one who mourns over sin.

There is much that is true in Dodd's thesis. God's wrath is an anthropomorphism not to be taken in a crudely literal fashion. It is not to be put on the same level as the love of God and the New Testament tends to speak of it in less personal terms than the Old Testament does. But having gladly conceded these points we must point to the serious deficiency in the Dodd thesis: the reduction of the wrath of God to an impersonal process of cause and effect, to

---

[6] MacGregor, 'Wrath', 103, cf. 104–105.

the inevitable consequences of sin in a moral universe. Of course, God's wrath does indeed work in this world primarily in the way Dodd describes. God's wrath normally operates through means. The problem lies not with what Dodd affirms but with what he denies.

The seriousness of this issue can be seen by a simple example. Dodd denies that God's wrath involves feelings or emotions and that God has a personal feeling like 'displeasure'. It must follow, therefore, that God views the sexual molestation and murder of a little child without any feeling of displeasure or indignation. Is this really the New Testament picture of God's wrath?

Dodd's position is not immune from the charge of Deism. God's judgement on sin is not to be thought of as the moral equivalent of the law of gravity. The aim in talking about impersonal wrath appears to be to dissociate God from wrath and punishment, to portray wrath as a mere by-product of sin, not actually willed by God. Such a position smacks of Deism.

Similarly, Dodd in particular is not exempt from the charge of neo-Marcionism. He argues that in the New Testament 'anger as an attitude of God to men disappears, and His love and mercy become all-embracing'.[7] Wrath and punishment are the impersonal by-product of the moral order and God is dissociated from them. This approach is avowedly contrary to the teaching of the Old Testament and is based upon a particular interpretation of Paul and is supported by a truncated (as we shall argue) appeal to the teaching of Jesus. The similarities with Marcion are striking.

The biblical evidence

What of the biblical evidence? First, the Old Testament. Morris lists over twenty different words used for the wrath of God a total of more than 580 times.[8] This wrath is God's displeasure and his venting of it, the opposite of his good pleasure.

What of the New Testament? Dodd claims that the wrath of God 'does not appear in the teaching of Jesus, unless we press certain features of the parables in an illegitimate manner'.[9] Dodd appears to look solely at the use of the *word* wrath, a procedure criticized by James Barr in his *The Semantics of Biblical Language*. It is true that Jesus in the Synoptics uses the word 'wrath' only once, but there are many passages where he clearly expresses the divine hostility to all that is evil, though without using the actual term 'wrath'. In John, Jesus

---

[7] Dodd, *Romans*, 50.
[8] Morris, *Apostolic Preaching of the Cross*, 149–150.
[9] Dodd, *Romans*, 50.

does affirm the wrath of God: 'Whoever does not obey the Son shall not see life, but the wrath of God remains on him' (3:36).

What of Paul? The impersonal character of his talk about God's wrath should be acknowledged, but not exaggerated. While much of Paul's talk about God's wrath is *relatively* impersonal, the evidence of his writings as a whole is that he did not wish to eliminate the concept of wrath as a disposition on the part of God. Paul presents God's personal judgement in 2 Thessalonians 1:6–9; there is no question of its being an impersonal cause and effect.

Hebrews refers to God's wrath on the sin of the Israelites during the wilderness period:

> I was provoked with that generation,
> and said, 'They always go astray in their heart;
> they have not known my ways.'
> As I swore in my wrath,
> 'They shall not enter my rest.'
> (3:10–11)

We also see God's judgement on sin elsewhere in the New Testament, such as the account of Ananias and Sapphira (Acts 5:1–11), the judgement on Herod (Acts 12:23) and on 'Jezebel' (Rev. 2:22).

The case that God's wrath is *purely* an impersonal process of cause and effect, the inevitable consequence of sin in a moral universe can be maintained only with considerable difficulty. It necessitates rejection of the clear teaching of the Old Testament, dubious interpretation of some passages of the teaching of Jesus and Paul and the rejection of other New Testament passages. This neo-Marcionite procedure (rejection of the Old Testament teaching and selective use of Jesus and Paul) yields no more than a silence about the affective side of God's wrath. No passage in either Testament is alleged that *denies* the personal nature of God's wrath. The case rests simply on an argument from the (alleged and highly contestable) silence of Jesus and Paul.

With what or whom is God angry? In both Testaments we see that God hates sin and is angry and displeased with evildoers. What about the saying that God hates the sin and loves the sinner? This is certainly true of the gospel, where God seeks the salvation of the lost. It is not true, however, if it is taken to mean that God is indifferent to whether or not sinners repent and turn from their sins.

God's wrath is to be understood neither as purely impersonal nor in crudely anthropomorphic terms. So to what *does* 'the wrath of God' refer? Drawing on a range of authors, we can say that it is God's personal, vigorous opposition both to evil and to evil people. This is a steady, unrelenting antagonism that arises from God's very nature, his holiness. It is his indignation at sin. It is God's revulsion to evil and all that opposes him, his displeasure at it and the venting of that displeasure. It is his passionate resistance to every will that is set against him.

The wrath of God and the love of God

What is the relation between the wrath of God and the love of God? In the popular imagination they are simply opposed to one another. Yet, as has often been observed, the opposite of love is not wrath but indifference. God's wrath should be seen as an aspect of his love, as a consequence of his love. God's wrath both expresses his love and can be contrasted with it – though it may be happier to contrast wrath with *mercy*, seeing both as expressions of God's love.

First we should note that there is no true love without wrath. Paul's injunction that love be sincere is followed by the command to hate what is evil (Rom. 12:9). A husband who did not respond to his wife's infidelity with a jealous anger would thereby demonstrate his lack of care for her. The loving husband would also grieve over his wife's infidelity, as does God over his people's infidelity. Which parents love their children more: those who do not care how they behave or those who seek to instil moral character into them? Loving parents take care to discipline their children (Heb. 12:5–8).

Failure to hate evil implies a deficiency in love. 'Absolute love implies absolute purity and absolute holiness: an intense burning light . . . Unless God detests sin and evil with great loathing, He cannot be a God of Love.'[10] A 'God' who did not detest evil would not be worthy of our worship.

The fallacy of those who deny the wrath of God lies in the attempt to reduce God *purely* to love. John Henry Newman, in one of his famous University Sermons, preached against the Socinian dogma that 'the rule of Divine government is one of benevolence, and nothing but benevolence', the error being the neglect of justice.[11] P. T. Forsyth opposed the same error with his talk of 'the holy love of God'. Our starting point should be 'the supreme holiness of God's love, rather than its pity, sympathy, or affection', this being 'the watershed between the Gospel and the theological liberalism which makes religion no more than the crown of humanity'. 'If we spoke less about God's

---

[10] Watson, *My God Is Real*, 39.
[11] Sermon 6 'On Justice, as a Principle of Divine Governance', in Newman, *Fifteen Sermons Preached before University of Oxford*, 99–119, quotation at 104.

love and more about His holiness, more about His judgment, we should say much more when we did speak of His love.'[12]

There may be some value in considering the disciplining of a child as an analogy. Suppose a child wilfully and maliciously hurts another child. In what way is the disciplining of that child an expression of love? It expresses the parent's love for righteousness and detestation of cruelty. It expresses love for the victim in the form of concern for what has been done. It expresses love for the perpetrator in that it is intended as discipline. Finally, it expresses love for society in the disciplining of the child. Those who let undisciplined children loose on society show not love but lack of concern for their children and even greater lack of concern for their future victims in the rest of society.

The social implications apply also to God's wrath, which must not be understood in purely individual terms. A ruler would not be showing love for his people if he were to allow an enemy to run roughshod over them. Lactantius also emphasizes that the wrath of God is needed to maintain good order in society, which is incumbent upon God if he is loving.[13] Paul, of course, teaches that God's wrath functions in part through the organs of law and order (Rom. 13:4–5). The claim that God's wrath is an expression of love is wider than the claim that it expresses love for its victim. It is also an expression of God's love for other human beings. There may be situations, such as with God's wrath against the impenitent in the final judgement, where wrath expresses love without expressing love for its object.[14]

The love of God and the wrath of God are not ultimately in contradiction, but there is a tension between them. This does not prevent us from exploring the correlation between God's wrath and his love, but it does warn us against imagining that we have completed the task.

---

[12] Forsyth, *Cruciality of the Cross*, 6, 73.

[13] Lactantius, *A Treatise on the Anger of God* 17–18, 21, 23 (ANF 7:273–280).

[14] Augustine (*City of God* 21:24 (NPNF 2:470)) and Thomas Aquinas (*Summa Theologiae* 1a:21:4) mention the idea that even there God's justice is tempered with mercy in that the lost are punished more mildly than they deserve.

Part 2
BECOMING A CHRISTIAN

7
The need for grace

Are we capable, through free choice, of keeping God's law?

'Keeping God's law' in this question does not mean merely avoiding murder or theft but positively loving God with all our heart, soul, strength and mind and loving our neighbour as ourselves.

There are those who hold that 'ought implies can', that if something is required of us, that proves that it is possible for us. Ironically, this principle was proclaimed by someone whose name was Kant[1] – the philosopher Immanuel Kant (pronounced the same as 'can't')! 'Ought implies can' summarizes his teaching on this matter, but his philosophy is complex and convoluted and he never expressed it in such simple terms. Kant was not original here as the principle goes back to the heretic Pelagius in the fifth century.

To answer this question properly we have to consider it in relation to the four states of human nature, as set out in chapter 1 – as created, fallen, redeemed and in glory.

As created

When it comes to human nature as created, Pelagius and Kant are right. Refraining to eat of the tree of the knowledge of good and evil was not unduly difficult, and certainly not impossible. God commanded nothing that was beyond the ability of Adam and Eve. He commands nothing of us that is beyond the capacity of human nature *as created*. He does not command us to do things like stay awake for a week or grow a third arm.

---

[1] Kant, *Critique of Practical Reason*, 147–151. The German original appeared in 1788.

As fallen

Pelagius,[2] who denied the doctrine of original sin (chapter 3) taught that Adam's sin introduced death, but that it did not introduce any bias to sin. Babies are born pure, without any inclination to sin. So why do we sin? Pelagius maintained that we learn to sin by the example of others, and that it then becomes a habit. He also held that even before Christ it was possible to live without sin, and indeed that some people actually had. In particular Joseph is one person in the Old Testament who is never criticized for sin. He acknowledged that habit can lead to 'a certain necessity of sinning', but also believed that if we make the effort we can overcome sin.

Pelagius identified three stages in any good deed: the ability, the will and the deed itself. So consider the process that leads to the good deed of turning off the television and studying this book. The ability to do this comes to us from creation and is a gift of God. In other words, whatever God commands is possible for us. The will to do it comes from ourselves, from our free will, which is a gift of creation. Likewise, the deed follows from our choice and comes from ourselves. So Pelagius's basic message is that God has already, in creation, given us all that we need to obey him and it is simply up to us to get on with it.

However, both the Bible and Christian tradition referred to God's grace. How did Pelagius understand that? He identified grace with three things. First, there are the gifts given to us by God in creation, especially free will. Secondly, God has graciously told us how to behave in the commands of the Law, which are his instructions for living. Finally, should anyone despite this actually sin, God graciously offers the forgiveness of sin.

Pelagius was able to speak of grace, in this threefold sense, but there is one important sense in which he did not believe in it. The New Testament occasionally, and later tradition more consistently, uses the word 'grace' to refer to the inner working of the Holy Spirit. Paul refers to 'those who through grace had believed' (Acts 18:27). Pelagius's theology had no room for this inner help of the Holy Spirit. So he strongly objected to a prayer of Augustine in his *Confessions*: 'Give what you command and command what you will.'[3] In other words, Augustine is asking God both to tell him what he should do and to give him the will to do it. Pelagius thought that this second part was just an excuse for laziness and disobedience. God has *already*, in creation, given us

---

[2] On Pelagius's teaching, see Evans, *Pelagius*, especially 90–121.
[3] Augustine, *Confessions* 10:29:40 (NPNF 1:153).

all the ability that we need. We should simply get on with it. Augustine and other critics accused Pelagius of denying the reality of grace. Some recent scholars[4] have responded by pointing out that Pelagius did believe and talk about grace – as described above. That is true, but in the sense that Augustine and the Christian predominantly understood the term (the inner working of the Holy Spirit), Pelagius did not believe in it.

Pelagianism has been called the national heresy of the English (especially of 'public-school religion'), though Pelagius himself was either Scottish or Irish. Just about all churches regard Pelagianism as heresy, in theory at least, though many have in practice lapsed into it from time to time.[5]

Pelagius at least acknowledged the force of habit, but one of his more extreme disciples, Caelestius, came out with what must count as one of the most naive statements in history: 'it is the easiest thing in the world to change our will by an act of will'.[6] A more realistic assessment of the power of free will is found in the quip regularly attributed to Mark Twain: 'It's easy to give up smoking. I've done it many times!'[7] My own experience of trying to give up sugar in coffee is similar.

Augustine encountered Pelagius's views in AD 411, and spent the remaining 20 years of his life combating them.[8] He wrote many works against Pelagius and his disciples and one of the best and most famous is his *The Spirit and the Letter*. The title of the book is taken from 2 Corinthians 3:6 ('The letter kills, but the Spirit gives life'), and Augustine interprets it by means of an exposition of Romans, especially chapter 7. *The Spirit and the Letter* was, after the Bible, the greatest literary influence on Luther and the Reformation. There are four points to note from this work.

The letter kills. This refers (both in 2 Corinthians 3:6 and in Augustine's work) to the written law, which comes to us as a command or demand from outside us. As Paul argues in Romans 7:7–12, this command does not produce obedience. When we hear the command to love God with all our heart or not to covet, we are unable to obey. The best that the law can produce is an *external* obedience, through fear of consequences, but true obedience comes from the

---

[4] Mentioned by Evans, *Pelagius*, 109–113.

[5] For a blog drawing out the parallels between Pelagius and the contemporary psychologist Jordan Peterson, see <https://unherd.com/2018/05/jordan-peterson-shares-pelagius/?=refinnar>, accessed 5 June 2020.

[6] Brown, *Augustine of Hippo*, 373, citing Augustine, *Man's Perfection in Righteousness* 6:12.

[7] There are many minor variants of this but it is uncertain whether any of them actually go back to Mark Twain.

[8] For Augustine on sin and grace, see Brown, *Augustine of Hippo*, 146–157, 340–407; TeSelle, *Augustine the Theologian*, 156–165, 258–266, 278–294, 310–338. For his writings against Pelagius, see Lehmann, 'Anti-Pelagian Writings'.

heart arising from a love of righteousness. For this we need the help of the Holy Spirit as unaided free will cannot produce it.

Augustine was very good at producing 'one-liners', or sound bites, that summarized his argument concisely. Here he states that 'The law makes sin to be known rather than shunned.'[9] This follows from Paul's statement that through the law comes not obedience from the heart but the knowledge of sin (Rom. 3:20).[10] Pelagius held that the law gives us knowledge of human ability (because 'ought implies can'); Augustine follows Paul in stating that the law gives us the knowledge of sin, thus showing us our need.

The Spirit gives life. If we are to obey God's law we need grace; that is, the inner working of the Holy Spirit. The Holy Spirit gives us love for God, which then enables us to keep the law. Augustine made frequent use of a number of key texts and regularly cited Romans 5:5: 'God's love has been poured into our hearts through the Holy Spirit who has been given to us.'[11] When we have love we can then truly obey God from the heart. For Augustine, 'the Spirit gives life' is exemplified in his prayer to God to 'give what you command'.

External versus internal law. Fundamental to the book is the contrast between the external and internal laws, the letter and the Spirit. The external law makes demands and threatens retribution. This is true whether it is the Old Testament law, natural law, the law of the land, or whatever. By contrast, the internal law written on our hearts by the Holy Spirit (Jer. 31:33; 2 Cor. 3:3) gives us the love that enables us to obey God and his law.

Order of Salvation. The law is a tutor to lead us to grace (Gal. 3:24),[12] through which we go on to fulfil the law. 'The law was given that grace might be sought, grace was given that the law might be fulfilled.'[13] This process is summed up in a catena that sets out an 'order of salvation', which begins with law and ends with law:

> By the law comes the knowledge of sin; by faith comes the obtaining of grace against sin; by grace comes the healing of the soul from sin's sickness; by the healing of the soul comes freedom of choice [i.e. liberation

---

[9] §8 (LCC 8:200).

[10] §14 (LCC 8:204).

[11] Commentators today mostly interpret this to mean that the Holy Spirit gives us an awareness of God's love for us, rather than giving us love for God. If that is true, it does not prove Augustine wrong as there are other passages that refer to God's giving us love, such as the statement that love is the fruit of the Spirit (Gal. 5:22).

[12] This is another verse that is mostly interpreted differently today, but Augustine's point is implied by Rom. 7:7–12.

[13] §34 (LCC 8:220).

from sin]; by freedom of choice comes the love of righteousness; by the love of righteousness comes the working of the law.[14]

The *Reformers* followed Augustine here. They spoke of three uses or functions of the (moral) law: to convict us of sin; to restrain the ungodly (especially through the law of the land); to guide the godly as to how to live.[15] The first use of the law is to convict us of sin, show us our moral inability and to point us to Christ and the gospel. This was closely modelled on what Augustine understands by 'the letter kills'.

Augustine's position has scriptural warrant. According to Paul, 'Those who are in the flesh cannot please God' (Rom. 8:8). Jesus taught that 'apart from me you can do nothing' (John 15:5). But does this mean that unbelievers can do no good? From the human point of view, many unbelievers live good lives and keep the external law. Indeed, there are unbelievers whose lives put many believers to shame. How should we understand that? We shall return to this issue in chapters 19 and 27.

So is fallen human nature capable, through free choice, of keeping God's law? No.

As redeemed

As redeemed, Christians are new creatures. 'If anyone is in Christ, he is a new creation. The old has passed away; behold, the new has come' (2 Cor. 5:17). So we now begin to have true love for God and neighbour, and thus *begin* to fulfil God's law. But do we have full and perfect obedience?

Pelagius believed that we can live lives of perfect obedience – even without God's grace (the inner help of the Holy Spirit). After his conversion *Augustine* initially believed that *with the help of the Holy Spirit* it was possible to achieve perfection, and hoped to achieve this before too long. But after a few years' experience, and after studying Paul's letters, he arrived at a different view. This found expression in his *Confessions* (397–401), in which he portrayed Christians as *not yet* cured of sin but *being* cured. He came to see the church more as a hospital for those being cured, than a club for those already fully cured. In *The Spirit and the Letter* he admitted a theoretical possibility of living sinlessly,[16] probably because he did not want to alienate those who believed that but wanted to unite them behind his drive against Pelagius. At the end of

---

[14] §52 (LCC 8:236).

[15] Calvin, *Inst.* 2:7:6–13. Luther clearly affirmed the first two functions (Althaus, *Theology of Martin Luther*, 253–256), but was ambivalent about the third (270–273). For the second and third uses, see chapter 25.

[16] §3 (LCC 8:196–97).

the book, however, he notes that 'In the righteousness that is to be made perfect much progress in this life has been made by that man who knows by his progress how far he is from the perfection of righteousness.'[17] Noah is called perfect in Genesis 6:9 (some translations) and Augustine comments that he was perfect not in the sense that we shall be in the age to come but only so far as perfection is possible in this earthly pilgrimage.[18]

As his position became more secure Augustine withdrew this concession and at the Council of Carthage in AD 418 the idea of sinlessness in this life was condemned. The council cited scriptural passages like 1 John 1:8 ('If we say we have no sin, we deceive ourselves, and the truth is not in us'), the prayer for forgiveness in the Lord's Prayer and James 3:2 ('for we all stumble in many ways'). It also rejects the idea that we should say such things not because they are true but out of humility. Humility is not pretending to be worse than we are but soberly facing the truth about ourselves,[19] for more on which see chapter 26.

Is redeemed human nature capable of keeping God's law in this life? We shall pursue the question of perfection more fully in chapter 30, but for the moment we can conclude that with the help of the Holy Spirit we can *begin* to obey God's law in this life,[20] but that we shall not reach perfection or escape sin until the Age to Come.

In glory

We shall attain perfection when we are in glory in the Age to Come. Adam and Eve were able to sin and able not to sin; fallen human beings are not able not to sin; in glory we shall not be able to sin. That is not because we shall lose free will (in the sense described in chapter 2), but because we shall no longer have any desire to sin. It is not that we shall want to sin but be unable (like the addict deprived of drugs), but that we shall be perfectly good and will desire only to please God.

Will redeemed human nature be capable of keeping God's law in glory? Indeed it will.

---

[17] §64 (LCC 8:248).

[18] City of God 15:26 (NPNF 2:306).

[19] Neuner and Dupois (eds), *Christian Faith in the Doctrinal Documents of the Catholic Church*, 544–546.

[20] What about Old Testament believers prior to Pentecost? This is a complex issue, but suffice it to say that one must avoid the opposite errors of either supposing that they were no better than pagans or thinking that the coming of Christ made no difference.

8
Prevenient and efficacious grace

Can we take the initiative in turning to God for grace?

In the previous chapter we saw that it is impossible for fallen human beings to keep God's law by their own free will, without the grace of God, that is without the inner working of the Holy Spirit. That raises a further question. If we need the Holy Spirit in order to obey God, can we take the initiative in turning to God and asking for this grace? We shall first look at the teaching of Augustine, then at the Semi-Pelagian alternative that he opposed. Finally we shall look at the teaching of Scripture.

Augustine

As we saw in the previous chapter, the thrust of Augustine's argument in his *Spirit and the Letter*, one of his first works against Pelagius, is that the law leads us to the knowledge of sin, which leads us to seek God's grace. This concerns the issue of the message we preach, what it is that we call upon people to do. This is not 'You have the ability already so get on with it', but 'You do not have the ability so turn to God and seek his grace or the help of the Holy Spirit.'

This leads to a further question, the topic of this chapter. When we preach that message, does God simply confront the hearers externally, with the preached word, or does the Holy Spirit also work within them internally to draw them to faith? This question affects our understanding of how God works in the process of conversion; it does *not* affect the message that is preached. Augustine devotes the first fifty-two sections of his *Spirit and the Letter* to the question of the message to be preached, in opposition to Pelagius, and then turns tentatively to the other question only in the closing sections (§§53–60) of his book. There was a good reason for this. Augustine's prime aim at that point was to ensure the rejection of Pelagianism. To this end he did not want to alienate potential supporters who might disagree with him over the other question, how God works in us. Politically, he needed to maintain a united front against Pelagius.

A biblical passage that moved Augustine to see that God makes the first move was 1 Corinthians 4:7: 'What do you have that you did not receive? If then you received it, why do you boast as if you did not receive it?' If we took the first move to God, then the answer to Paul's first question would be 'faith'; faith would be something that we have but did not receive. Augustine developed this argument more fully in his *Letter* 217, to Vitalis, written in AD 426 or 427.[1] When we pray to God for the conversion of unbelievers, is this a pious pretence or do we actually expect God to work within them to draw them to himself? Likewise if we give thanks for the conversion of a friend, is this a pious pretence or do we believe that God was actually at work within them? Augustine appealed to Scripture to support this argument. In his letter to the Philippians Paul states that 'It is God who works in you, both to will and to work for his good pleasure' (2:13). Augustine also often cited Proverbs 8:35, from the Septuagint version: 'The will is prepared by the Lord.'

So Augustine argues that it is God who makes the first move, that it is the Holy Spirit who works within us to lead us to faith. This work of the Spirit is called prevenient grace, the word being derived from the Latin *praevenire*, meaning 'to come before'.

As John Newton's hymn 'Amazing Grace' puts it:

'Twas Grace that taught my heart to fear
And Grace, my fears relieved.
How precious did that grace appear
The hour I first believed.

Semi-Pelagianism

While Augustine denied that we can take the first move, there were others in the early church who held either that we must or that we can ourselves take the initiative. These people believed that God approaches us externally, through preaching for example, and that we can then of our free will turn to God. At that point we receive God's grace, the inner working of the Holy Spirit, to enable us to obey and serve God. This was the approach of a number at the time, especially in the Eastern church, and indeed it was the view of Augustine himself for the first ten years or so after his conversion in 386. More on that shortly.

This view is now known as 'Semi-Pelagianism', but it did not acquire that name until the seventeenth century and the name is misleading, for several reasons. First, this view predates Pelagius since many held to it before the time

---

[1] Augustine, *Letters*, vol. 5, 75–96.

of Pelagius. Secondly, the name gives the impression that it is partly tainted with Pelagianism, whereas on the key issue, our need for the grace of the Holy Spirit, this view is at one with Augustine.[2]

To give an analogy, consider the situation of shipwrecked sailors at sea. Pelagius held that they have the capacity to swim to shore on their own and should just get on with it. The others all agree that there is no chance of getting to shore without being picked up by a lifeboat, but disagree as to whether we can swim to the boat ourselves or whether we have the option of declining when we are hauled into the boat. These are significant questions, but as nothing compared to the issue of whether or not we can swim to the shore by ourselves.

At the end of his life Augustine was confronted with Semi-Pelagianism in the teaching of a group of monks based in Marseilles in the south of Gaul (France), especially John Cassian. These were not Pelagians. They completely agreed with Augustine that we cannot love and serve God without the help of the Holy Spirit. But they also believed in the ability of fallen humanity to turn to God and seek his grace. They cited in support Matthew 7:7, 'Ask, and it will be given to you; seek, and you will find; knock, and it will be opened to you.' They admitted that sometimes God may take the initiative (as with Paul), but also that we have the capacity to make the first move and that many do so.[3]

Augustine responded to them in a major work entitled *The Predestination of the Saints*. There he treats them not as heretics (such as Pelagius) but as erring brethren. There was a century-long controversy over this issue in the south of France and this was finally resolved at the Second Council of Orange in AD 529. This council produced twenty-five 'canons', setting out and condemning contrary views. Canon 4 states:

If anyone maintains that God awaits our will to be cleansed from sin, but does not confess that even our will to be cleansed comes to us through the infusion and working of the Holy Spirit, he resists the Holy Spirit himself who says through Solomon, 'The will is prepared by the Lord' [Prov. 8:35 LXX] and the salutary words of the Apostle, 'It is God who works in you both to will and to accomplish.' [Phil. 2:13][4]

---

[2] In some Reformed circles there is the unfortunate practice of unfairly branding as Pelagian views that are deemed to be insufficiently Augustinian, but that are far removed from Pelagius.

[3] These points are all found in Cassian, *Conferences* 13 (Third Conference of Abbot Chaeremon) (NPNF² 11:422–435). See also Chadwick, *John Cassian*, 110–136.

[4] Leith (ed.), *Creeds of the Churches*, 38.

Orange declared Semi-Pelagianism to be heretical for the Western church. (Eastern Orthodoxy has not taken a clear stand against it.) However, from the tenth century the canons of the council were forgotten as they were not included in the standard compilations of council teaching. They were re-discovered in 1538, when they were included in a published collection of material from councils.[5] The Reformers appealed to them against the Semi-Pelagianism then being taught by some within the Roman Catholic Church.[6]

In the late Middle Ages (fourteenth and fifteenth centuries) a more extreme form of Semi-Pelagianism had emerged, taught by Gabriel Biel (d. 1495) among others.[7] This declared not just that we can make the first move by turning to God and asking for grace, but that we need to *merit* God's grace. God gives his grace to those who do their very best (*facere quod in se est*), to those who turn from sin and love God above all else. This is what was required of people *before* they receive God's grace. If it is possible to do all of this without grace, one wonders why we need grace at all.

Martin Luther was taught by the disciples of Gabriel Biel. It caused him spiritual problems as he was not convinced that he was doing enough to be worthy of God's grace. He saw God as one who condemned him and as a consequence hated God. More on this in chapter 16.

Scripture

Scripture supports the idea that it is God who makes the first move, not us. In addition to the passages cited above, Jesus twice affirms in John that we cannot come to him unless drawn by the Father (6:44, 65). Rather than our taking the initiative, it is the Holy Spirit who convicts us of our sin and need (John 16:8). Why is this necessary? Because without his intervention we are blind (2 Cor. 4:3–6) and indeed spiritually dead (Eph. 2:1–2), as we saw in chapter 2.

Does prevenient grace make conversion possible (for all), or inevitable (for some)?

If we are unable to turn to God without his making the first move, does he give this prevenient grace to all, leaving us to decide whether to respond or not, or is this grace given to some only in such a way that our response is guaranteed? This is the point at which Calvinists and Arminians diverge. We shall examine each view in turn, focusing especially on Augustine and Arminius.

---

[5] Crabbe, *Concilia Omnia* 1:339B–341A.
[6] Desiderius Erasmus and Albert Pighius were both guilty of this.
[7] On Biel's theology, see Oberman, *Harvest of Medieval Theology*, 120–184.

Augustinianism/Calvinism

What is today often known as 'Calvinism' was taught in the fourth century by *Augustine*. He did not always hold that view. When he was first converted in AD 386 he believed that he had made this move without the help of the Holy Spirit. He also believed that perfection would come very soon. At this point he had a low view of sin and a high view of the capacity of human free will. All of that changed between AD 394 and 396, in what has been called his 'second conversion'.[8] Three factors caused this change. First, his own experience did not support his earlier optimistic views of the capacity of human free will. Secondly, he was working on an exposition of Romans and was challenged by the teaching of Paul. Thirdly, Augustine responded to questions on Romans 7 and 9 posed by Simplician, who had been one of the human agents instrumental in his conversion at Milan in 386. In his response he was struck by 1 Corinthians 4:7 (as noted above) and also by the teaching of Romans 9. It is in the second part of his response, on Romans 9, that Augustine arrived (in 396) at his mature teaching on predestination, which he would put forward in response to Pelagius in the closing decades of his life. As he himself put it, 'In trying to solve this question I made strenuous efforts on behalf of the preservation of the free choice of the human will, but the grace of God defeated me.'[9] He then wrote his *Confessions* (397–400), in which he reinterprets the events of his life in the light of his new insights into grace and election.

So what was Augustine's mature view? He believed that conversion comes about through God's 'operating grace'; that is, God's working on us. (This is to be contrasted with 'cooperating grace', on which see chapter 28, below.) This operating grace is, as we have seen, prevenient – that is, God makes the first move. It is also efficacious – it does not merely make our conversion possible but effects it, brings it about. This grace infallibly achieves its goal – which is our conversion, that we repent, believe and respond gladly and willingly to the gospel. God works in such a way that we shall respond; we cannot resist him because we do not *want* to; we are fully won over. God changes the will without forcing or violating it; he wins it over. At the end of his life Augustine wrote a work entitled *Grace and Free Choice* (426/27).[10] God operates on us preveniently in such a way that we *freely* and willingly respond and repent.[11]

---

[8] TeSelle, *Augustine the Theologian*, 156–165; 176–182.

[9] *Retractations* 2:1, as cited by Chadwick, *Augustine*, 117.

[10] NPNF 5:436–465, where the title is translated *Grace and Free Will*. This is unfortunate as Augustine distinguished between 'will' (*voluntas*) and 'choice' (*arbitrium*).

[11] For a range of views on the relationship between God's sovereignty and human freedom, see Basinger and Basinger (eds), *Predestination and Free Will: Four Views*.

Effectual grace is known by other names. Some Calvinists use the term 'effectual calling':

> *Question*: What is effectual calling?
> *Answer*: Effectual calling is the work of God's Spirit, whereby, convincing us of our sin and misery, enlightening our minds in the knowledge of Christ, and renewing our wills, he doth persuade and enable us to embrace Jesus Christ, freely offered to us in the gospel.[12]

Others have sometimes used the term 'irresistible grace' (a term used neither by Augustine nor Calvin), but this is unhelpfully ambiguous. The statement 'I couldn't resist him' might appear in an account of falling in love – or in an account of rape. If God's grace is irresistible it is only in the first of these senses.

Augustine appealed extensively to Scripture for this teaching. He cites Matthew 13:11 and John 10:26–29, which state that the secrets of the kingdom of heaven are given only to some, and Christ gives eternal life to his sheep, who are given to him by the Father. He refers to passages from Acts, like the statement that the Lord opened Lydia's heart (16:14). Finally, he makes heavy use of Ephesians 2:8 (salvation by grace as a gift of God) and Philippians 2:13 (God works in us 'both to will and to work for his good pleasure').

In the Middle Ages many (though not all) theologians took the Augustinian position. In the sixteenth century all the Reformers took this position, although Luther's colleague Melanchthon later changed his mind and moved to the Arminian view.

Semi-Augustinianism/Arminianism

While Augustine and Calvinists believe that prevenient grace is efficacious for the elect, Arminians believe that prevenient grace is merely 'sufficient'. It works in people in such a way as to leave to them the ultimate choice as to whether or not to accept it. It is sufficient to enable us to turn to God, should we so choose. In other words, prevenient grace makes it *possible*, but *not inevitable*, that we respond to God's call. To pursue the lifeboat analogy, we are offered a helping hand into the boat, but we have the option whether to accept or reject this helping hand. Classic Arminianism is *not* Semi-Pelagianism since Arminius agreed with Augustine that we cannot make the first move towards God. It is more accurate to call Arminianism Semi-Augustinianism, because it

---

[12] *Westminster Shorter Catechism* (1647), q. 31 (*RefConf* 4:357).

shares with Augustinianism the belief that we can do no spiritual good without God's prevenient grace.[13]

Jakob Hermandszoon, more commonly known by his Latin name Arminius, was a Dutch pastor and theologian who grew up in the Reformed tradition. He studied for a time in Geneva, under Theodore Beza, Calvin's successor. But at the beginning of the seventeenth century he reacted against the Calvinist tradition and became an Arminian. His teaching provoked a controversy, but he died soon after in 1609.[14] The following year a group of Arminian pastors wrote a *Remonstrance* that contained five articles. Article 4 states that we need God to make the first move, but that when he does so it is not irresistible:

> This grace is the beginning, the increase, and completion of every good thing; to be sure even that the regenerate person himself is not even able to think, will, or accomplish good, nor resist any temptation to evil apart from or preceding that prevenient, moving, accompanying, and cooperating grace, so that all good works and actions which are able to be conceived must be ascribed to the grace of God in Christ. As for the rest, what pertains to the manner of operation of this grace – that it is not irresistible, since indeed it is written about many that they 'resisted the Holy Spirit,' Acts 7[:51] and several other places.[15]

In response to this the *Synod of Dort* (or Dordrecht) met in the south of Holland (1618–19) and condemned Arminianism, re-endorsing the Augustinian position.[16]

Arminians point to passages of Scripture that speak of people resisting the Spirit (Acts 7:51), grieving the Spirit (Eph. 4:30) or quenching the Spirit (1 Thess. 5:19). For Arminians these prove that grace is not efficacious, that it does not always infallibly achieve its goal. The Holy Spirit seeks to 'rein us in' but leaves us the choice of accepting or rejecting his prompting. In response Calvinists would concede that there are times when God's grace is resisted, but also claim that God works efficaciously to ensure that the elect will eventually respond to him and be saved.

---

[13] Olson, *Arminian Theology*, 137–178, who also acknowledges the existence of Semi-Pelagianism at the popular level (16–18).

[14] McGonigle, *Sufficient Grace*, 19–34. Bangs, *Arminius*, 140–141, n. 141, questions whether Arminius had ever been a Calvinist. Contrary to popular misunderstanding, it is not necessary to come from Armenia to be an Arminian.

[15] *RefConf* 4:43. Arminianism is correctly seen as one strand of Reformed theology.

[16] Canons of Dort, Third and Fourth Heads (*RefConf* 4:135–143). For the early years of Arminianism, see Harrison, *Beginnings of Arminianism*.

John Wesley was an Arminian and is considered the father of evangelical Arminianism. He was emphatic on the need for God to make the first move and was no Semi-Pelagian. But he also held that *all* people, without exception, receive prevenient grace. This comes especially through the medium of conscience and people are then saved or not according to their response to this grace. Even those who never hear the gospel receive God's prevenient grace through their conscience, and are judged according to their response to this inner grace. So every human being, whether or not they hear the gospel, has the opportunity to be saved. Given this belief it may seem strange that Wesley continued to ride on horseback round the country preaching the gospel until the age of 87. Why this passion for evangelism, if all receive an opportunity anyway? Wesley believed that when people hear the gospel they have *more* opportunity to respond. Also, when people do hear the gospel, faith is required for them to be saved.[17]

The essence of Arminianism is to believe that prevenient grace makes conversion possible, but not inevitable, that it leaves us with the final choice. Not all Arminians believe that all without exception receive prevenient grace, but such a belief coheres fully with the Arminian concern to leave the final decision to human free choice. If some are lost through never having an opportunity, that is effectively a form of negative predestination.

It is worth noting that this question cannot be settled by analysing our own experience, let alone other people's, since both Calvinists and Arminians agree that God makes the first move and that conversion occurs when *we* respond. For example, C. S. Lewis described his own conversion in Calvinist-sounding terms, but his own theology was rather different.[18] Conversely someone might have had no conscious sensation of God's grace at work in them before their conversion and yet for theological reasons reach a Calvinist position. Augustine began by ascribing his conversion to his own free will but eventually ascribed it to God's grace and wrote his *Confessions* to express this conviction.

Classical Arminianism is clear that we can make no move towards God without his prevenient grace; some calling themselves Arminians today would hold to a Semi-Pelagian position, claiming that we can turn to God without any prior move on his part.

In the next chapter we shall consider the question of election and predestination, which is essentially the same question that we have just been considering, but viewed from a different angle.

---

[17] Williams, *John Wesley's Theology Today*, 39–46; McGonigle, *Sufficient Grace*, 318–330.
[18] Lewis, *Surprised by Joy*, 182–183; Lewis (ed.), *Letters of C. S. Lewis*, 251–252 (Letter of 8 August 1953); Lewis, *Undeceptions*, 152–153.

9
Election and predestination

Do we choose God or does he choose us?

Introduction

Scripture clearly teaches that we are called upon to choose God, as for example in Deuteronomy 30:19, where the people of Israel are called to choose between life and death, blessing and curse. Yet Scripture also teaches, for example, that God 'chose us in [Christ] before the foundation of the world, that we should be holy and blameless before him' (Eph. 1:4). The question therefore is, which causes the other, which is ultimate? There are two main answers to this question, often called Calvinism and Arminianism. These names are somewhat misleading in that both views go back to the early church, over a thousand years before the time of either Calvin or Arminius.

The issue here is the same as in the previous chapter, but viewed from a different angle. Does God give sufficient grace to 'all' (as with Arminius and Wesley), which means that the ultimate choice lies with us? Or does God give efficacious grace to some only whom he has chosen (as with Calvin), which means that the ultimate choice is God's?

Both views were found at the time of the eighteenth-century Evangelical Revival. The Wesleys and others were Arminians; George Whitefield and others were Calvinists. This caused Wesley and Whitefield to go their separate ways, but the division was not acrimonious. John Wesley preached at Whitefield's funeral, at the latter's request. The Calvinists mostly stayed within the Church of England; the Arminians mostly became Methodists. Since then evangelic-alism has always embraced both Calvinists and Arminians, though the relative proportions have varied from time to time. In the 1960s there was a strong revival of Calvinism in the UK, though today it would not be so popular. In the last ten years there has been a revival of Calvinism in the USA.[1]

---

[1] For companion volumes setting out each side, see Peterson and Williams, *Why I Am Not an Arminian* and Walls and Dongell, *Why I Am Not a Calvinist*. See also Brand (ed.), *Perspectives on Election: Five Views*.

It would be wrong to suggest that all evangelicals are either Calvinists or Arminians. While there are significant numbers who openly subscribe to one or another of these views, there are also significant numbers who do not come down on either side, either regarding this as a secondary issue or claiming to hold a middle position. Charles Simeon (1759–1836) commented that Calvinists and Arminians alike wish that Paul had phrased himself differently in places and that the truth lies not at one extreme or the other but at both extremes.[2] There are churches where Calvinism or Arminianism is very explicitly taught from the pulpit. There are other churches where neither is explicitly taught and where one can attend for years without hearing a clear answer to the question posed at the head of this section.

The Calvinist view is perceived by many as offending against the principles of modern Western culture, a culture that favours a democratic inclusive egalitarianism and stresses the rights of the individual. Arminianism sits more happily with these principles. This in itself does not prove it right or wrong, but it is worth noting why ideas become more or less popular at different times. Anthony Kenny, a Roman Catholic theologian who left the Roman Church, described his theological training in Rome. He recalls how disgusted many of his American fellow students were to discover how inegalitarian was Roman Catholic teaching on grace, as taught at the Council of Trent (1545–63).[3] We must not allow our cultural prejudices to decide the issue for us, but should examine the teaching of Scripture and see how we can hold the various strands together.

Augustine (354–430)[4]

Augustine held that because all have sinned no one *deserves* salvation, but God freely elects or chooses some for salvation. On what basis? It is not because of any prior merit, nor for any previous deeds. Nor is it because of any foreseen merit, God knowing in advance that we shall believe or that we shall do good works. Putting it differently, election is not God's 'backing a winner'. Election is not based on *anything* in us, past, present or future. Despite this, Augustine denied that God's choice is arbitrary – like the selection of the winner of a lottery. God has a reason, but his reasons are not known to us.

Some object that the doctrine of election is unfair in that God does not give the same opportunity to everyone. It should be remembered that as sinners we

---

[2] Moule, *Charles Simeon*, 77–81. Olson, *Arminian Theology*, 61–77, argues that while they share considerable common ground, there is no coherent hybrid of Calvinism and Arminianism.
[3] Kenny, *A Path from Rome*, 78.
[4] See TeSelle, *Augustine the Theologian*, 319–332.

are in the same situation as the elderly lady who objected to an artist's portrayal of her. 'You haven't done me justice,' she complained. 'Madam, what you need is not justice but mercy,' was the response!

The elect, those whom God has chosen, are predestined for eternal life, predestined to be saved. This does not mean that they will be saved regardless of whether they believe or not, but rather that God saves them by bringing them to faith – as Paul describes in 1 Thessalonians 1:4–5. Again, it is not that God would reject the non-elect if they believed but rather that no one comes to faith except through God's grace. Election does not mean that there is no need for evangelism or for pastoral care, for it is *through* such means that God saves his elect. Augustine argued this in a book called *Rebuke and Grace*.[5] Predestination is God's decision to save someone through the gospel and their response to it, not to save them regardless of how they live.

What about those who are not elect, who are 'reprobate'? These are simply allowed to continue in the path of sin and to be lost at the end. In other words, while election leads to God's active intervention in the form of prevenient and subsequent grace, reprobation consists primarily in God's passive non-intervention, in God's leaving the reprobate to their own devices. Augustine held that those dying unbaptized in infancy or dying in unbelief as adults will all be lost. He saw no way of salvation for those not encountering the gospel.

What about the fall? Did God predestine it? According to Augustine, God foresaw the fall and decided to permit it, but did not ordain it. So election is his selective rescue operation in the light of a foreseen fall.

Why does Augustine believe this? He appealed in part to experience. Two infants are born and then die. One dies before receiving baptism – and therefore is lost, according to Augustine. The other dies after receiving baptism – and so is saved. This has nothing to do with any difference in merit between the two infants. Again, some adults die without hearing the gospel and having the opportunity to repent and believe. This has nothing to do with any merit or demerit on their part. More significant, though, for Augustine is the teaching of Scripture. Some of these passages will be found below.

Finally, Augustine held that not all of those who have received prevenient efficacious grace, not all converted Christians who have repented, believed and been baptized, will be saved. Some but not all of them are elect and will be given the gift of perseverance to the end. Others, who are not elect, are not given that gift and will fall away and be lost. More on this in chapter 28, below.

---

5 NPNF 5:471–491.

Augustine was hugely influential upon the Middle Ages. The Second Council of Orange in AD 529 emphatically affirmed his doctrine of prevenient grace, but referred this to baptism especially. All who have been baptized have the ability and responsibility to achieve salvation, with the aid and cooperation of Christ. It also forcefully rejected the idea of predestination to evil.[6] During the Middle Ages many leading theologians held to an Augustinian position regarding predestination. Others held rather to a Semi-Augustinian (later known as Arminian) position. Thomas Aquinas, the most influential of the medieval scholastic theologians, held to a Semi-Pelagian position in his early years, based on his reading of the early Augustine, but when he read Augustine's anti-Pelagian writings he moved to a fully Augustinian position.[7]

John Calvin (1509–64)

Calvin, like all of the magisterial Reformers (apart from Melanchthon),[8] followed Augustine on election. As with Augustine, he appealed to experience. People do not all have equal opportunity to hear the gospel; people have different upbringings; not all live where the gospel is preached; some die in infancy. But, as with Augustine, his primary emphasis is on the teaching of Scripture. He devoted four chapters of his *Institutes* to election and predestination, and one of these is devoted to 'Confirmation of This Doctrine from Scriptural Testimonies'.[9] He appeals especially to Paul (passages such as Rom. 9 and Eph. 1) and to the teaching of Jesus in John. Some of these passages will be found below.

Where Calvin differs from Augustine, and also from a number of his fellow Reformers, is on the issue of reprobation. Augustine argued that God permitted the fall. He then works for the salvation of the elect, passively allowing the reprobate to go their own way. Calvin, by contrast, argued that God positively willed and ordained the fall. He refers to this as God's awesome or dreadful decree (*decretum horribile* in the Latin).[10] God also positively predestines the reprobate to damnation, rather than (as Augustine held) merely permitting them to go that way. So God is the ultimate cause of the fall and of reprobation, but that does not mean that he brings them about in the same way that he created the universe or raised Jesus from the dead. God is the *ultimate* cause, but there are *immediate* causes. So God ordained the fall but Adam had the free will to sin or not sin and fell entirely of his own

---

[6] Leith (ed.), *Creeds of the Churches*, 44.
[7] Wawrykow, *A–Z of Thomas Aquinas*, 67–68.
[8] Magisterial Reformers, seeking reform of the state churches in cooperation with the magistrates/rulers, as opposed to radicals such as Anabaptists wishing to plant new churches.
[9] *Inst.* 3:21–24, of which 3:22 is devoted to scriptural testimonies.
[10] *Inst.* 3:23:7–8.

will.[11] His sin was his own fault.[12] Again, those who are lost are condemned for their own sinful nature.[13]

Why should Calvin have held this view? In a real sense he was 'predestined' to this position by his doctrine of providence. Calvin held to a very strong doctrine of providence, believing that *all* that happens is positively ordained by God and not merely permitted.[14] Indeed, 'Not only heaven and earth and the inanimate creatures, but also the plans and intentions of men, are so governed by his providence that they are borne by it straight to their appointed end.'[15] If that is so, it clearly follows that the fall and reprobation must have been positively ordained by God.

But *why* should God ordain this? Calvin took a very principled stand against speculation beyond what is revealed – not just on this doctrine but across the board. He believed that this was the teaching of Scripture and accepted that. He also argued that the fact that God wills it proves it to be right. This is a dangerous argument. It could mean that if God wills something it must be right because God would never will anything that was wrong. Or it could mean that if God wills something that *of itself* makes it right. So, for example, it could mean that if God chose to condemn someone innocent, that would be right simply because God chose it. If that is so, the statement that God is good would become a mere tautology.

Calvin did not invent any of this. Zwingli and Luther both had a slightly stronger doctrine of predestination than Calvin's. The idea that God predestined the fall and reprobation goes further back to the late Middle Ages. It was held by Thomas Bradwardine, who was Archbishop of Canterbury for forty days in 1349, before dying of the Black Death.

Most of the Reformers did not follow Luther, Zwingli and Calvin in holding that God predestined the fall and reprobation. Nor have the majority of those who have called themselves Calvinists. It is important to distinguish between what Calvin himself taught and what is taught by 'Calvinists'. As we have seen, Calvin held that God predestined the fall. On that issue the majority of those who call themselves Calvinists have sided rather with Augustine. On the other hand, many Calvinists today (not all, and probably not even most) teach a doctrine of limited or definite atonement, denying that Christ died for all. Calvin did not teach this.[16] Those holding this view often

---

[11] *Inst.* 1:15:8.
[12] *Inst.* 3:23:8.
[13] *Inst.* 3:23:3.
[14] *Inst.* 1:16–18.
[15] *Inst.* 1:16:8.
[16] This is a controversial claim, contested by some of those who themselves hold to limited atonement.

subscribe to the mnemonic TULIP, on which see the excursus at the end of this chapter.

Infralapsarianism and Supralapsarianism

Theodore Beza (1519–1605), who was Calvin's successor in Geneva, introduced speculation about the *order* of God's decrees.[17] This is a question not of chronological order, since all agreed that God transcends time, but of *logical* order. Two different models emerged, which are known as infralapsarianism and supralapsarianism. These correspond broadly to the positions of Augustine and Calvin, though neither of them entered into such speculation about the order of decrees.

According to infralapsarianism, God decided first to create humanity and to allow Adam to sin. The result was that Adam did sin, so God then decided to predestine some for salvation and to allow the rest to go their own way to damnation. Thus predestination comes after (*infra*) the fall (*lapsus*).

According to supralapsarianism God decides first of all that some people should be blessed and others lost. To that end he creates humanity and decrees that the fall will take place. That being so, he predestines some to salvation and others to damnation. Thus predestination comes further back (*supra*) than the fall.

William Perkins (1558–1602), an Elizabethan Puritan theologian, wrote a book called *A Golden Chain* (1591) in which he produced a famous chart that illustrates the order of God's eternal decrees and their execution in time.[18] This presents a clearly supralapsarian approach, with the decree of reprobation preceding creation and fall.

One does not hear much about supralapsarianism today, but its importance lies in the role it played in the development of Arminianism.

Arminius (1560–1609)

The view that ultimately it is our choice was widely held before Augustine and remains the view of the Eastern Orthodox Church. It was held by many in the Middle Ages. Luther's colleague Melanchthon broke ranks with the other Reformers on this issue, as did Arminius in the seventeenth century.

As we saw in the previous chapter, Arminius was a Dutch pastor and theologian who studied under Beza in Geneva, before returning to the Netherlands as a pastor. A controversy arose there between supralapsarianism and infralapsarianism. As a student of Beza's, Arminius was invited to defend

---

[17] See Berkouwer, *Divine Election*, 254–277; Beeke, 'Theodore Beza's Supralapsarian Predestination'.

[18] Breward (ed.), *The Work of William Perkins*, 169–259 (parts omitted), with the chart inserted at p. 169.

supralapsarianism, but as he thought more about it he came not only to reject supralapsarianism but also the whole Augustinian doctrine of predestination. And so he became a Semi-Augustinian, an Arminian.[19]

Arminius held that there were two forms of election. First, God chooses to save *whoever* will repent, believe and persevere to the end – this is like a blank cheque, where the name is still to be added. Secondly, he also understood election to refer to God's choice of specific individuals based on God's foreknowledge of what they will freely choose. God chose Paul because he foresaw his faith.[20]

Arminius also, like infralapsarians and supralapsarians, set out God's decrees in their logical order:[21]

1 God appoints Christ as Saviour.
2 He determines to save all who repent, believe and persevere to the end.
3 He determines to give people grace *sufficient* to enable them to repent and believe.
4 He elects specific people for salvation, based on his foreknowledge that they will (aided by prevenient and subsequent grace) repent, believe and persevere.[22]

The fundamental issue for Arminians is the fact that God loves everyone and desires that *all* should be saved,[23] on which, see the passages quoted below. There is also a strong emphasis on the role of human free will in salvation. (On the question of free will, see chapter 2.) Finally, there is also an emphasis on the fact that God 'shows no partiality' (Acts 10:34).

In 1610, the year after Arminius died, a group of Arminian pastors produced a *Remonstrance*, containing five articles. The first of these concerned predestination:

> God, by an eternal and unchangeable decree in his Son, Christ Jesus, before laying the foundation of the world, determined, out of the human race fallen in sin, to save those in Christ, on account of Christ, and through Christ, who through the grace of the Holy Spirit, would believe on his

---

[19] See chapter 8, n. 14.
[20] McGonigle, *Sufficient Grace*, 26–34.
[21] Speculation about God's decrees was the fashion of the time, not confined to extreme Calvinists.
[22] Arminius, 'Declaration of Sentiments', in *Works of James Arminius*, 1:653–654. This was preceded by his critiques of supralapsarianism (1:614–645) and infralapsarianism (1:646–653), and is followed by his defence of his own position (1:654–656). Cf. Bangs, *Arminius*, 350–355
[23] Olson, *Arminian Theology*, 97–114, argues that the heart of Arminian theology is God's love and character, rather than an emphasis upon free will.

same Son, and who would persevere in that very faith and obedience of faith, through the same grace without ceasing to the end; but on the other hand, to leave the obstinate and unbelieving under sin and wrath, and condemn them as alienated from Christ, according to the word of the gospel ... (John 3:36). To which other expressions of Scripture correspond.[24]

In response to Arminianism, the Reformed Church summoned the Synod of Dort/Dordrecht, in the province of South Holland (1618–19), which produced a number of 'canons'.[25] Article 7 of the First Head portrays Reprobation as God simply leaving people to the fruit of their own sin:

Election is the unchangeable purpose of God, whereby, before the foundation of the world, He has out of mere grace, according to the sovereign good pleasure of His own will, chosen from the whole human race, which had fallen through their own fault from their primitive state of rectitude into sin and destruction, a certain number of persons to redemption in Christ, whom He from eternity appointed the Mediator and Head of the elect and the foundation of salvation.[26]

The teaching of the Synod is infralapsarian, although supralapsarianism is not actually condemned.

Karl Barth

Finally, mention should be made of Karl Barth who offered a radical re-interpretation of the Reformation (i.e. Augustinian/Calvinist) doctrine of predestination – or at least claimed to have done so.[27] He accused that doctrine of tearing God and Christ asunder, in the sense that Christ brings the gospel but behind this lies the hidden decree of election.[28] Christ is reduced, he claims, to the role of executing God's hidden decree. Against this, Barth insists that election is not something that lies behind the gospel but that it is in fact the gospel itself. He based this on his principle that God is known only in Christ.

How so? Barth proposed a doctrine of double predestination, but not in the sense that some are elect and others reprobate. Barth's doctrine can be summed

---

[24] *RefConf* 4:42.
[25] On election and reprobation, see Canons of Dort, First Head (*RefConf* 4:121–130).
[26] *RefConf* 4:122.
[27] Barth, *Church Dogmatics* II/2, §§32–35.
[28] Barth, *Church Dogmatics* II/2:60–76.

up in three (not five!) points. First, Christ is himself the electing God. It is not that the Father selects some (but not others) independently of Christ, but that Christ himself is the electing God. Secondly, there is only one person who is reprobate, that is predestined to damnation, and that is Christ himself. On the cross he bore God's rejection and the wrath that is due to us. He has borne it for all, so no one else is reprobate. Thirdly, Christ is also the elect one, and all others are elect 'in him' (Eph. 1:4). For Barth the gospel message is not that we shall be accepted by God if we repent and believe, but that we are already accepted and just need to recognize that fact. In a famous sermon to the inmates in Basel prison, he tells them that 'the door of our prison *is* open, even though, strangely enough, we prefer to remain within'.[29] For more on this issue, see chapter 25.

What should we make of this? First, does the New Testament present faith as waking up to a reality that is already true or as laying hold of something that is freely on offer? Barth's message is attractive in many ways, but is it biblical? He has been accused of undermining the seriousness of the decision that we are all called upon to make. Secondly, Barth's message appears to point clearly to universalism, the doctrine that all will eventually be saved. It is reported, though, that Barth stated of universalism, 'I do not teach it, but I also do not not teach it.'[30]

There is another way to view Barth's teaching here. If he is unable to affirm universalism, it would appear that when he claims that all are elect he is referring to something different from election as it was understood by Augustine, Calvin or Arminius. His teaching that Christ is the only reprobate one because he bears God's wrath upon the cross suggests that he is talking not about the question of who will or will not be saved at the end (which is what election has traditionally been about) but about the work of Christ in dying for our sins on the cross. His message is that by giving his Son to die for us God has made a choice for us and in that sense all are elect, but without that implying necessarily that all will actually be saved. It can be argued that he has subtly reinterpreted the traditional language of election and reprobation, using it to refer to God's salvific intentions at the cross, rather than God's plan for who will/will not be saved. His election of all in Christ is more about his desire that all will be saved than his determination that this *will* take place.

---

[29] Barth, *Deliverance to the Captives*, 35–42, quotation at 40. See also Barth, *Church Dogmatics* II/2:313–325. Cf. Hunsinger, *How to Read Karl Barth*, 128–135, especially 130–131.

[30] Jüngel, *Karl Barth*, 44–45. See also Barth, *Church Dogmatics* II/2:417–419. Cf. Bettis, 'Is Karl Barth a Universalist?'; Colwell, 'Contemporaneity of the Divine Decision'; Crisp, 'On Barth's Denial of Universalism'.

Scripture

Calvinists stress the efficacy of God's saving purposes and point to many passages of Scripture that speak of election and predestination. Paul refers to God's choosing us in Christ before the foundation of the world and predestining us for adoption (Eph. 1:4–5). The Thessalonians had repented because God had chosen them as the first fruits to be saved (2 Thess. 2:13). In Romans 9 he argues on the basis of Exodus 33:19 that 'it depends not on human will or exertion, but on God, who has mercy,' so God 'has mercy on whomever he wills, and he hardens whomever he wills' (9:16, 18). There is a remnant of Israel, chosen by grace and not works (11:5–6).

Also cited are passages from the Gospels, such as John 15:16 where Jesus tells the apostles that they did not choose him, but he chose them and appointed them. Also passages from Acts, like the statement that 'as many as were appointed to eternal life believed' (Acts 13:48). The belief in election arises not from philosophical speculation but from a concern to be faithful to the teaching of Scripture in passages like this.

Arminians, by contrast, stress God's love for *all* and point to passages of Scripture that refer to God's desire that none should perish. In Ezekiel God states that he takes no pleasure in the death of anyone but desires that they should turn from their way and live (18:23, 32). Paul tells us that God 'desires all people to be saved and to come to the knowledge of the truth' (1 Tim. 2:4). Peter likewise states that God does not wish that any should perish but that all should reach repentance (2 Peter 3:9). It is in line with this universal desire that Jesus laments over Jerusalem and states his desire to have 'gathered your children together as a hen gathers her brood under her wings, and you would not!' (Matt. 23:37).

Romans 8:29 states that those whom God foreknew he predestined to be conformed to the image of Christ. Arminians see that as proof that God predestines those whose future repentance and faith he foresees. Calvinists point to Amos 3:2, where God knows the people of Israel in the sense of choosing them and see Romans 8:29 as stating that God predestines those whom he has chosen.

The will of God

How should these two bodies of texts be held together? Medieval theology, drawing on Augustine, distinguished between different senses of the 'will of God' and the Reformers drew upon this tradition.[31] The fundamental difference

---

[31] For a very helpful account of this, see Foord, 'God Wills All People to Be Saved', 179–203.

is between God's will in the sense of what he commands or prohibits and God's will in the sense of what he purposes, whether by ordaining it or permitting it. Clearly these two wills are not identical. God commanded Abraham to sacrifice Isaac, but this was clearly not his purpose, as he intervened to stop Abraham from going ahead (Gen. 22). The actions of Pilate, Herod and the Jews in killing Jesus were clearly contrary to God's law, yet they were also according to his purpose (Acts 2:23; 4:27–28). Augustine, most of the medievals and the Reformers saw the 'Arminian passages' as referring not to God's will in the sense of his sovereign purpose (since all are not saved) but in various other ways, such as pointing to our obligation to preach to all, or as being conditional upon our repentance and faith.

Excursus: TULIP (The 'Five Points of Calvinism')

The mnemonic TULIP refers to what are often somewhat inaccurately called the Five Points of Calvinism. These five points do *not* go back to Calvin himself. Nor are they, as is sometimes claimed, the five 'heads' or points taught by the Synod of Dort (1618–19). In fact TULIP appears to have been coined in the twentieth century.[32]

T = Total Depravity. The whole of human nature, including the mind and will, is corrupted and sinful, which means that we cannot perform works which are truly good in God's sight and cannot make the first move towards God. Arminius and traditional Arminians (such as Wesley) also teach this. It does not mean that sinners are as evil as they could be or are unable to do good deeds such as acts of kindness. It has been suggested that a more helpful term might be 'total spiritual incapacity'.[33] For more on this see chapters 7 and 19.

U = Unconditional Election. God's election of who will be saved (predestination) is not based on any foreseen merit in us, whether faith, works or future potential. This was taught by Augustine and was rejected by Arminius, who held that God elects those whom he foresees will repent, believe and persevere.

L = Limited Atonement. The purpose of Christ's death was to save the elect only – sometimes called 'particular redemption' or 'definite atonement'.[34] This

---

[32] See Stewart, 'Points of Calvinism'; *Ten Myths About Calvinism*, 75–96.
[33] Raith, *After Merit*, 92–96.
[34] On this topic, see Naselli and Snoeberger (eds), *Perspectives on Extent of Atonement*.

doctrine was not taught by Calvin but was developed after him.[35] Historically the majority of those who have called themselves Calvinists have not accepted this point. It must not be equated with the oft-repeated statement of Peter Lombard that Christ's death is sufficient for all but efficient for the elect alone,[36] which is relatively uncontroversial. Almost all Christians would accept that the death of Christ is of sufficient value (and more) to save all human beings.[37] That it is efficient for the elect alone is simply to say that only the elect are actually saved, which is a tautology (true by definition). The advocates of limited atonement often ask whether the death of Christ makes our salvation certain or merely possible. The answer is that our salvation is made certain, not merely possible, by the combined work of Father, Son and Holy Spirit.

I = Irresistible Grace. When God sovereignly acts to convert someone, that individual certainly will be converted. Augustine and Calvin both taught this, though neither called grace 'irresistible', which is not the happiest of terms. (For more on this, see chapter 8.) It is sometimes called 'efficacious grace' or 'effectual calling'. It is not that grace is never resisted (Acts 7:51) but that God sovereignly brings about the conversion of the elect and in that situation his grace is effective, not merely sufficient (the Arminian view of prevenient grace).

P = Perseverance of the Saints. Also called the 'preservation of the saints' or 'eternal security'. Those whom God has drawn to himself he keeps faithful to the end. Truly converted Christians will not fall away and be lost. Those who do fall away either never had true faith to begin with or will return. This is not to be confused with the idea that converted Christians will all be saved regardless of whether they persevere to the end. For more on this topic, see chapter 28.

---

[35] Many books have been written on Calvin's view. For an excellent recent study see Hartog, *Calvin on Christ's Death.*

[36] Book 3, dist. 20, ch. 5 (Lombard, *Sentences, Book 3*, 86).

[37] So Canons of Dort, Second Head, Article 3, states that Christ's sacrifice 'is of infinite worth and value, abundantly sufficient to expiate the sins of the whole world' (*RefConf* 4:130).

10
Christian initiation

How does one become a Christian?

What must we do to be saved? What is Christian initiation? In Acts there are fourteen passages that describe how people became Christians.[1] Looking at these, a clear pattern emerges.

Fourfold initiation

In these fourteen passages we see four things repeatedly occur (see Table 1 on page 94):

- repentance (mentioned 9 times – twice being indirect mentions)
- faith in Jesus (mentioned 12 times – once in a variant reading)
- baptism (mentioned 10 times)
- receiving the Spirit (mentioned 7 times).

Looking at the book of Acts as a whole it is clear that becoming a Christian involves all four: repentance, faith, baptism and receiving the Spirit. Although not every account describes all four steps, we see a clear pattern. Luke did not regard any of these as optional extras for some only. There are three reasons for affirming this.

1 Explicitly mentioning all four every time would be tedious and Luke is too good a writer for that. Also, on one occasion (Peter preaching in the temple) the events were interrupted and so the process may not have not have been completed all at once (4:1–4).

---

[1] In addition to these fourteen accounts, there are others that *briefly* speak of people becoming Christians, usually mentioning just faith.

Table 1 The four spiritual doors

	Acts	Repentance	Faith	Baptism	Receiving Spirit
1	2:37–41, 44 (Peter's Pentecost sermon)	✓	✓	✓	✓
2	3:17–20; 4:3–4 (Peter and John in the temple)	✓	✓	Interrupted (4:1–3)	
3	8:12–24 (Conversion of the Samaritans)	✓	✓	✓	✓
4	8:36–38 (Conversion of the Ethiopian eunuch)	–	(v. 37)	✓	–
5	9:17–18 (Conversion of Saul/Paul)	–	–	✓	✓
6	10:34–35, 43–48 (Conversion of Cornelius)	(v. 22)	✓	✓	✓
7	11:15–18 (Peter's report of the conversion of Cornelius)	✓	✓	✓	✓
8	15:7–9 (Peter's further report of the conversion of Cornelius)	–	✓	–	✓
9	16:14–15 (Conversion of Lydia)	–	✓	✓	–
10	16:30–34 (Conversion of Philippian jailer)	–	✓	✓	–
11	17:30–34 (Paul's preaching at Athens)	✓	✓	–	–
12	19:1–7 ('Disciples' at Ephesus)	✓	✓	✓	✓
13	20:20–21 (Paul's account of his ministry at Ephesus)	✓	✓	–	–
14	22:10, 14–16 (Paul's account of his conversion)	(v. 10)	–	✓	–
Totals		7 + 2	11 + 1	10	7

2 Furthermore, the accounts are compressed, as can be seen by the fact that when the same event is described on different occasions different points are mentioned. So Peter's account of the conversion of Cornelius in 15:7–9 mentions only faith and the Holy Spirit, but the original account of this mentions all four items (10:34–35, 43–48) as does Peter's further account in 11:15–18. The original account of Paul's conversion mentions only baptism and the Spirit (9:17–18), while the later account in 22:10, 14–16 mentions only baptism, with repentance implied. Acts 9:11 states that Paul is praying, which suggests that Luke thinks of him as having repented and believed.

3 When the Samaritans are converted they do not receive the Spirit, and this has to be rectified (8:14–17). Likewise, in the same event, Simon is deemed not to be genuinely converted because of his lack of repentance (8:22). Paul encounters some 'disciples' at Ephesus who had not even heard of the Spirit and this needed to be rectified (19:1–7). These examples all show that Luke did not see any of these four items as optional.

James Dunn refers to 'the *three* most important elements in conversion-initiation', but that is because he treats faith and repentance as one, 'being the opposite sides of the same coin'.[2] David Pawson in a more popular book, *The Normal Christian Birth*, sets out these four elements, which he calls the 'four spiritual doors', an obvious allusion to the famous 'Four Spiritual Laws'.[3] He points out that repentance and faith, which he brackets together under the heading of 'conversion', refer to what we do; baptism and receiving the Spirit, which he brackets together under the heading of 'regeneration', refer to what God does. All four also correspond to what have been identified as the four components of conversion: changes in belief, belonging and behaviour, in the context of an experience of God.[4] Gordon Smith identifies 'seven elements of a good conversion'.[5] These are our four, except that he divides faith into intellectual belief and emotional or affective trust, and repentance into (negative) remorse and rejection of sin and (positive) volitional commitment and allegiance. He also adds the corporate component – incorporation into the Christian community, citing Acts 2:38–42. The last point can be seen as an effect of baptism, as we shall see in chapter 12. We shall consider conversion further in the next chapter.

---

[2] Dunn, *Baptism in the Holy Spirit*, 91 (my emphasis).
[3] Pawson, *Normal Christian Birth*. The title is intentionally an echo of Watchman Nee's *The Normal Christian Life*.
[4] Kreider, *Change of Conversion and Origin of Christendom*, xv.
[5] Smith, *Beginning Well*, 138–153.

How does this compare with evangelism today? I have made a study of this, looking at evangelistic books both in the 1960s and in the current century, at the booklets given to enquirers in those two periods, and also at online resources available today.[6] The need for repentance and faith is clearly taught – though in much evangelism this is reduced to an unbiblical phrase such as 'invite Jesus into your heart'. The Holy Spirit is usually mentioned, but most do not portray receiving the Spirit as an aspect of Christian initiation. There is a danger of producing converts who, like the disciples at Ephesus, can say 'we have not even heard that there is a Holy Spirit' (Acts 19:2). Baptism is the missing dimension, playing no part in the process of becoming a Christian as set out by these writers, though some of them refer to the need for baptism at other points in their account. It cannot be said that any of the works reviewed *in practice* allow any role for baptism in Christian initiation. Most evangelism today offers something less than the full fourfold New Testament initiation and as a result we are in danger of producing stunted and defective births. Evangelical tradition has prevailed over the pattern set out in Scripture.

Repentance

Repentance is more than just acknowledging that one is a sinner, and it is more than just being sorry or regretful. The Greek word *metanoia* means a change of mind and heart, a turning from sin to God. It involves repentance for specific sins as well as a general state of sinfulness. The Old Testament prophets taught this, as did John the Baptist, who issued specific instructions to tax collectors and soldiers (Luke 3:12–14). Where necessary, repentance involves making restitution, and Zacchaeus was willing to restore fourfold what he had fraudulently acquired (Luke 19:8). At times this can be very costly. A couple who became Christians confessed to the Inland Revenue that they had previously failed to declare income and it cost them their house. As the *Westminster Confession of Faith* puts it, 'Men ought not to content themselves with a general repentance, but it is every man's duty to endeavour to repent of his particular sins, particularly' (15:5).[7]

Repentance also involves accepting the lordship of Christ over the whole of our life. There are no no-go areas, contrary to the approach of one king in the Dark Ages. He decided to become a Christian and arranged for his whole army to be baptized by marching through a river – but with their sword arms raised because he did not wish their baptism to affect that area of their lives.[8]

---

[6] Lane, 'Becoming a Christian'.

[7] *RefConf* 4:251.

[8] For a similar story, involving King Clovis of the Franks, see Kreider, *Change of Conversion*, 87–88.

There is tension here that needs to be maintained. Thomas à Kempis notes the phenomenon of those who confess sins and yet the next day commit the same sins again, those who resolve to guard against sins and yet succumb again within the hour.[9] In his play *Androcles and the Lion*, Bernard Shaw makes fun of an early Christian called Spintho, who wants to be martyred as a sure route to heaven, but not because he actually hates sin. His nerve fails him and he renounces his faith:

> I'll repent afterwards. I fully mean to die in the arena: I'll die a martyr and go to heaven; but not this time, not now, not until my nerves are better. Besides, I'm too young: I want to have just one more good time.[10]

How are we to respond to this? There are two opposite dangers to avoid. On the one hand we must warn against a hypocritical confession and repentance that involves no real intention to change; on the other hand we must not exclude those who are genuinely struggling against a besetting sin, a habit, an addiction. What differentiates the two groups is a genuine hatred of sin. The test of whether love is sincere is whether we hate what is evil (Rom. 12:9), which Spintho did not. It can be hard enough to read our own hearts here and we should not presume to judge others. We shall consider this further in the next chapter.

Faith

In Acts we see that people believe both in the Lord Jesus and in the gospel. For example, John wrote his Gospel 'so that you may believe that Jesus is the Christ, the Son of God, and that by believing you may have life in his name' (20:31). In other words, the object of faith in the New Testament is Christ, Christ as presented in the gospel – who he is and what he has done.

Saving faith is not just accepting facts in our head.

Faith needs to *move from the head to the heart* in the form of trust. There is a well-known story about the tightrope walker Charles Blondin, who many times crossed the Niagara Gorge. On one occasion he asked a spectator if he believed that Blondin could safely carry him across in a wheelbarrow. The man said that he did believe – but declined to put it to the test. That was probably a wise decision, since Blondin was a fallible man, though a better illustration would be deciding to trust Blondin in order to escape a fierce lion.[11] Either

---

[9] Kempis, *Imitation of Christ* 1:22 (p. 39).
[10] Shaw, *Complete Plays*, 695.
[11] For the historical event underlying this story, involving the Prince of Wales in 1860, see Wilson, *Everybody's Heard of Blondin*, 62–64.

way, Christian faith is about being prepared to put it to the test, about getting into the wheelbarrow. Faith does involve believing certain things in our minds (against an anti-intellectualism) but it is more than mere head knowledge.

It also needs to *move from the heart to the lips*; faith must be confessed openly. This takes place initially in baptism. Paul's account of confession of faith in Romans 10:9–10 probably refers to baptism.

Faith must also *move from words to actions*, as James repeatedly affirms: 'So also faith by itself, if it does not have works, is dead' (2:17); 'As the body apart from the spirit is dead, so also faith apart from works is dead' (2:26). The Reformers taught that we are justified by faith alone, and not by works, as we shall see in chapter 18, but they agreed that it is not possible to be saved *without* works. Justification is not *by* works, but nor is it *without* works.

Baptism

Baptism is mentioned in ten of our fourteen passages. It is not mentioned in the Acts 3 incident, because Peter's address was interrupted before he could conclude it. It is not mentioned in Peter's report of Cornelius's conversion (15:7–9), but we know from chapters 10 and 11 that Cornelius was baptized. It is also missing from the account of Paul's preaching in Athens (17:30–34) and in his address to the Ephesian elders (20:20–21). It would be fair to say that in the New Testament all Christians were baptized. Baptism is an integral part of the initiation process described in Acts, being mentioned in ten of the fourteen passages. Ephesians 4:4–6 lists baptism as something that unites all Christians – Paul could assume that all of his readers had been baptized. After the day of Pentecost (Acts 2) there is not a single example of an unbaptized Christian in the New Testament.

According to the New Testament, one becomes a Christian at least in part by baptism, as will be seen in chapter 12. This is something that many find it hard to accept, for two main reasons. First, there has been a polarization between Protestants, who teach that we become Christians by faith, and Catholics, who teach that we become Christians by baptism. The New Testament knows no such dichotomy. Secondly, the legacy of Christendom means that in Europe in particular we are faced with hordes of baptized unbelievers, people who were baptized as babies but in many cases have had no other exposure to the Christian faith. Needless to say, that was not an issue for the New Testament writers. When they wrote of faith they meant the faith that expressed itself in baptism (as in Acts) and when they wrote of baptism they meant the baptism that was an expression of faith. Faith and baptism are the proverbial two sides of the coin. We shall consider the relation between them further in chapter 12.

The story of Naaman the Syrian, who came to Elisha to be healed of leprosy (2 Kings 5:10–14), illustrates the relation between faith and baptism. Naaman had to believe the word of Elisha, but he wasn't actually healed until he submitted to washing himself in the river Jordan, as commanded. It was only then that 'his flesh was restored like the flesh of a little child, and he was clean' (v. 14). This story was seen as a picture of baptism in the early church, for example by Irenaeus.[12] The intimate link between conversion and baptism can be compared to the way in which some evangelists invite those responding to their message to come forward – in fact such a practice has been seen as a surrogate baptism, an attempt to fill the void that comes from ignoring baptism. It is helpful to have an outward visible response to the gospel, not as a substitute for an inner invisible response but as confirmation of it.

What is the origin of the rite of baptism? Christian baptism follows on from the baptism of John the Baptist, but where did he get the idea? We cannot be certain, but there are two possible antecedents. The Qumran community practised baptism for ritual purity and John the Baptist did baptize in the desert (Mark 1:4), in the geographical proximity of Qumran. Like John, the Qumran community also practised asceticism and looked for the coming of the Messiah. Another possible antecedent is proselyte baptism, given to those who convert to Judaism.

We shall consider baptism at greater length in chapters 12 to 15.

The timing of baptism

In Acts we see that baptism was immediate. It always took place on the same day as conversion, with one exception. The Philippian jailer was baptized the same hour of the *night* (16:33)! Paul did not suggest that they should get some sleep and have the baptism in the morning. It was so much part of the initiation process that it happened on the spot. It was not an optional extra. The apostles did not ask their converts, 'Will that be with or without baptism, sir?' It was not delayed until the new convert requested it, nor until their genuineness was proved. It was clearly part of the gospel message according to Acts. Baptism is part of the so-called Great Commission, which commands baptism but makes no mention of faith (Matt. 28:19–20).

During the second century we see the beginning of a shift from the immediate baptism of Acts to the idea of a period of preparation and instruction before baptism. In the *Apostolic Tradition*, traditionally attributed to Hippolytus at Rome, this time of preparation had been extended to three years,

---

12 Irenaeus, *Fragment* 34 (ANF 1:574).

though with the proviso that those who do well should be judged by their character and conduct, rather than the length of time spent in catechesis.[13] By the fourth century baptism was normally practised on Easter Sunday, preceded by 40 days of fasting and an all-night vigil.[14] The aim of the preparation was to ensure high moral standards in the baptismal candidates, and in this the early church was remarkably successful, at least until the influx of converts following the conversion of Constantine. But there was the danger of turning baptism into a reward that needed to be earned rather than a free gift of God's grace. The 40 days were clearly modelled on Jesus' forty days of fasting in the wilderness, but with the significant change that while his period of fasting *followed* his baptism, it now preceded baptism. The New Testament pattern clearly proclaims the priority of grace over law. The grace of baptism is given freely at conversion. Discipleship is something that follows. By the third century baptism was delayed not just in order to allow time for instruction but also to test the lives of the candidates. The situation emerged where the candidates had to provide witnesses to prove that they were worthy of baptism. Law now precedes grace. Baptism is now seen as a reward for good behaviour. One has to put one's life right before being accepted by Christ rather than coming to him to have one's life put right. Rather than receiving the Spirit in order to live a holy life one is required to live a holy life in order to receive the Spirit.[15]

But is it not wise to allow for a period of instruction? Is it not rash to baptize before one can test the genuineness of the conversion? Those churches which take time before baptizing still have the problem of those who later lapse. Of course instruction is important, but why must this precede baptism? It is noteworthy that with the postponement of baptism its place is often taken by some other ritual. To give one example, many evangelists would pray a prayer of commitment with those wishing to become Christians. Should this prayer be delayed for three years to allow further instruction? Should it be delayed until the uprightness of the convert's moral life can be verified? If it is possible to pray a prayer of commitment together at the point of commitment, what is the problem with doing it the New Testament way and using baptism instead? It may not be practicable today to practise baptism at the actual point of conversion, but if the delay could be reduced to a few days or even a few weeks, that would make a big difference. Someone baptized, for example, one week

---

[13] Attridge (ed.), *Apostolic Tradition: A Commentary*, 96–98 (ch. 17). For catechesis in the third century, see Kreider, *Change of Conversion*, 21–32.

[14] For catechesis in the fourth century, see Kreider, *Change of Conversion*, 43–53.

[15] For Augustine's defence of the change, see Kreider, *Change of Conversion*, 60.

after conversion would a year later look back on the process as effectively a single drawn out event.

Receiving the Spirit

Receiving the Spirit is mentioned in just seven of our fourteen passages, but that does not mean that it was an optional extra. It was expected to happen and when it did not, steps were taken to rectify the situation. This happens twice in Acts. When Philip evangelized Samaria the converts were baptized, but did not receive the Spirit. Peter and John came down from Jerusalem and laid hands on them, and they then received the Spirit (8:14–17). This can be seen as an extended initiation process, which takes place over a few days. Paul at Ephesus met some 'disciples' of John the Baptist who had never heard of the Holy Spirit and had received only John's baptism. One wonders whether they had even heard of Jesus. Paul preached to them and they were then baptized in the name of the Lord Jesus and received the Spirit after Paul laid hands on them (19:1–7).

In Acts receiving the Spirit is expected to come at the time of baptism/ conversion, not as a second blessing but as part of Christian initiation.[16] Indeed Paul states, 'Anyone who does not have the Spirit of Christ does not belong to him' (Rom. 8:9).

The Spirit came upon Jesus at his baptism and in line with that we see people receiving the Spirit in Acts when they believe and are baptized. Sometimes this happens after baptism, as at Pentecost (2:38), and sometimes beforehand, as with Cornelius (10:44; 11:15). In Acts, as well as this initial reception of the Spirit, which is what is meant by baptism in the Spirit, there are times when people are filled with the Spirit specifically for a particular task. This is not a one-off experience but happens more than once to the same person. The apostles and others are twice said to be all filled with the Spirit (2:4; 4:31). The same is said of Peter another time (4:8) and later of Paul (13:9) as well as other disciples (13:52). For more on the ideas of a 'second blessing' and of being filled with the Spirit, see the excursus to chapter 27.

Does receiving the Spirit always lead to some spectacular event, such as praying in tongues or prophesying? David Pawson maintains that it always does.[17] Certainly this often happened in Acts, but there is no theological reason why it should always happen. Indeed, to the contrary, Paul rejects the idea that all should have any particular gift: 'Are all apostles? Are all prophets? Are all teachers? Do all work miracles? Do all possess gifts of healing? Do all

---

[16] On this, see Turner, *Holy Spirit and Spiritual Gifts*; *Baptism in the Holy Spirit*.
[17] Pawson, *Normal Christian Birth*, 71–77.

speak with tongues? Do all interpret?' (1 Cor. 12:29–30). Also, if no one can receive the Spirit without such a manifestation then the devastating conclusion follows that the overwhelming majority of Christians throughout history never received the Spirit – and so were not even Christians according to Romans 8:9! This would include many leading evangelists and missionaries. We need rather more evidence to unchurch such a multitude than the fact that such manifestations took place in *some* of the incidents recorded by Luke.

Three times in Acts there is reference to the laying on of hands to receive the Spirit. We have already mentioned the episodes of the Samaritan converts (8:17) and the Ephesian 'disciples' (19:6). In addition, Ananias laid hands on Paul so that he could regain his sight and be filled with the Spirit (9:17). There is not enough evidence to be dogmatic, but it is likely that this was the regular practice as part of Christian baptism, despite Luke's mentioning it only occasionally. Support for this can be found in Hebrews 6:1–2, where the author mentions as foundational repentance, faith, baptisms (plural) and the laying on of hands. In this context the last of these most likely means the laying on of hands to receive the Spirit. Certainly this was part of the regular practice by the second century.

There is a lot of sense in making the laying on of hands to receive the Spirit part of the ceremony of baptism, especially where it is a new convert that is being baptized. Otherwise there is always the danger that no one remembers to mention the Holy Spirit and then the new convert will be able to say, like the disciples at Ephesus, 'we have not even heard that there is a Holy Spirit' (Acts 19:2). One of the functions of ritual and ceremonies is precisely to ensure that what is important does not get forgotten, rather than just 'trusting to luck' that it will happen. When I leave home in the morning I have a routine procedure to ensure that I am not leaving anything behind.

In the second century the ceremony of baptism included the laying on of hands and anointing with oil. By the fourth century this was seen as a rite separate from baptism – confirmation. In the Eastern Orthodox Church infants normally receive confirmation at the same time as baptism. In the Roman Catholic Church confirmation normally comes later and is accompanied by a reaffirmation of baptismal vows. The reason for the different timing was that in the Roman Catholic Church confirmation must be done by a bishop, and bishops are not normally available at the point of infant baptism. In the Eastern Orthodox Church, by contrast, confirmation is performed by ordinary priests, using oil that has been consecrated by a bishop.[18]

---

[18] See Kelly, *Early Christian Doctrines*, 207–211, 432–436.

In popular understanding confirmation is the occasion for a young person to 'confirm' their faith and their baptismal vows for themselves. This is no doubt a worthwhile function, but it is not what confirmation traditionally meant, which is that *God* confirms or strengthens the candidate with the Holy Spirit. The Confirmation service of the Church of England's sixteenth-century Book of Common Prayer refers to the candidates ratifying and confirming the baptismal vows made on their behalf, upon which the bishop prays that they may be strengthened with the Holy Spirit and defended with God's grace. In today's *Common Worship*, by contrast, the bishop lays hands on the candidate and prays that God would confirm them with his Holy Spirit.

11

Conversion

What is conversion?[1]

This is not as simple a question as may at first sight seem. There are a range of different issues to be considered. First, what is the relation between conversion and repentance? There are two Greek words: *metanoeō*, which is translated 'repent', and *epistrephō*, which is translated 'turn' or 'convert'. The Bible is composed of a number of 'occasional' writings: works addressed to specific occasions or situations. As a consequence, words are sometimes used differently by different authors, or by the same author in different works, or even by the same author in the same work, or even by the same author in the same sentence. In Romans Paul uses the word 'law' in many different ways and in 3:21 states that God's righteousness is manifested apart from law (written sets of commands) although the Law (the five books of the Pentateuch) and Prophets bear witness to it. When it comes to writing theology, however, it is rightly expected that words will be used with clearly defined meanings.

So how will we use the words 'convert' and 'repent'? *Metanoia* bears the meaning of 'change of mind' and *epistrephō* bears the meaning of 'change of direction'. We shall, therefore, follow common usage and by 'conversion' refer to the whole process of turning and becoming a Christian, and by 'repentance' refer specifically to the change of mind regarding sin, this together with faith being part of the process of conversion. In Acts they are twice used together. 'Repent therefore, and turn again' (3:19). 'The Gentiles . . . should repent and turn to God' (26:20).

So conversion embraces what we *do* in becoming Christians: believe, repent, change direction. Regeneration embraces what we *receive* in becoming Christians: baptism, the Holy Spirit. Some mistakenly call baptism a work, something we do, but it is something we receive. Regeneration also refers to the change God brings about when we become Christians and are made new creatures (2 Cor. 5:17).

---

[1] On the topic of this chapter, see Smith, *Beginning Well*.

Fourfold initiation and presenting issues

As we saw in the previous chapter, repentance, faith, baptism and receiving the Spirit are the components of full Christian initiation. But the way in which conversion manifests itself in situations varies according to the historical and cultural situation and according to individual circumstances, which will determine what is the 'presenting issue' involved.[2]

For the *apostle Paul* the key issue was the recognition of Jesus as the Jewish Messiah.

Justin Martyr was a pagan Greek who was converted to Christ in the early second century. For him conversion came as the culmination of a search for the true philosophy. He describes the way in which he tried various philosophies, culminating in a meeting with an old man who pointed him to Christ and to the Old Testament Scriptures. His account ends by stating how he had now at last found the true philosophy:

> A flame was kindled in my soul; a love of the prophets and of the friends of Christ possessed me; and whilst revolving his words in my mind, I found this philosophy alone to be safe and profitable. Thus, and for this reason, I am a philosopher.[3]

Cyprian was an upper-class pagan Roman who was converted in the middle of the third century. For him conversion came as the culmination of a search for moral renewal, as he describes in a letter to a friend:

> I was myself so entangled and constrained by the very many errors of my former life that I could not believe it possible for me to escape from them, so much was I subservient to the faults which clung to me. And in despair of improvement I cherished these evils of mine as if they had been my dearest possessions. But when the stain of my earlier life had been washed away by the help of the water of birth, and light from above had poured down upon my heart, now cleansed and purified, when I had drunk the Spirit from heaven, and the second birth had restored me so as to make me a new man, then straightway in a marvellous manner doubts began to be resolved, closed doors to open, dark places to grow light.[4]

---

[2] For many such examples, see Kerr and Mulder (eds), *Famous Conversions*.

[3] *Dialogue* 8 (ANF 1:198). In his *Second Apology* 12 (ANF 1:192) Justin also mentions the effect on him of seeing Christian martyrs face death fearlessly.

[4] Letter 1:4 to Donatus 4 (Bettenson, *Early Christian Fathers*, 272 – punctuation changed).

Augustine was raised as a Christian but strayed from the faith and for a while joined the Manichaean heresy. His conversion involved both a search for the truth and the quest for moral purity, as he describes in his *Confessions*.

For *Luther* the issue was the search for a gracious God, for more on which see chapter 18:

> [Re Rom. 1:17: God's righteousness is revealed in the gospel] I began to understand that the righteousness of God is that by which the righteous lives by a gift of God, namely by faith ... The righteousness of God is revealed by the gospel, namely, the passive righteousness with which the merciful God justifies us by faith.[5]

For *Calvin* the issue was the quest for true religion:

> Since I was too obstinately devoted to the superstitions of popery to be easily extricated from so profound an abyss of mire, God by a sudden conversion subdued and brought my mind to a teachable frame, which was more hardened in such matters than might have been expected from one at my early period of life.[6]

John Wesley's conversion concerned his quest for assurance of salvation, after his disturbing experience as a missionary in North America:

> I felt my heart strangely warmed. I felt I did trust in Christ, Christ alone, for salvation: And an assurance was given me, that he had taken away *my* sins, even *mine*, and saved *me* from the law of sin and death.[7]

It should be noted, though, that while this experience was a turning point in Wesley's life, it is not about his coming to faith but about his coming to full assurance of faith. For more on this see chapters 20 and 27.

For *C. S. Lewis* a key point was the acceptance of the existence of God,[8] a point that was not in question for the other named figures.

The main issue in someone's experience of conversion depends on where they are coming from.

---

[5] Preface to the 1545 edition of his Latin writings (*LW* 34:337).
[6] Calvin, *Commentary on the Book of Psalms*, vol. 1, xl (preface).
[7] *Journal of John Wesley*, 35 (24 May 1738) (his italics).
[8] Lewis, *Surprised by Joy*, 170–183. Cf. McGrath, *C. S. Lewis*, 135–146.

For a *Jew* the issue may be believing that Jesus is the Messiah. The purpose of John's Gospel is to bring people to believe that 'Jesus is the Christ, the Son of God' (20:31).

For a *Muslim* it is of less interest that Jesus is the Jewish Messiah and the key issue will be something else, like recognizing Jesus as the Son of God.

For an *atheist* the main issue may be acknowledging God's existence.

For a *nominal Christian* it may be seen as moving beyond a merely formal religion into a personal relationship with God through Christ.

So the 'presenting issue' in the human biography of conversion may vary according to historical situation, culture and individual history, but the biblical pattern of fourfold initiation stands as a theological norm or criterion by which to test the genuineness of conversion. The atheist who comes to believe in God, but refuses to embark upon a life of discipleship, may have undergone some sort of conversion, but not Christian initiation.

Is conversion necessarily instantaneous?

The conversions described in Acts are all instantaneous, with the converts being able to name the day and hour of their conversion. Evangelicals have traditionally emphasized the need for conversion and many would echo the words of Charles Wesley's hymn 'And can it be':

> Long my imprisoned spirit lay,
> fast bound in sin and nature's night;
> thine eye diffused a quickening ray;
> I woke, the dungeon flamed with light;
> my chains fell off, my heart was free,
> I rose, went forth, and followed thee.

Theologically conversion is a single event and the New Testament has no concept of a 'half-Christian'. But in practice the process of conversion can be drawn out. In tropical regions it is usually very clear when the sun rises; in regions nearer the poles a sunrise can take longer and it can be hard to say exactly when it happens. The important thing is that the sun has risen, not that we can time it precisely. Similarly, when crossing some borders one knows exactly when one changes country; with other borders there may be a long period when it is not clear which country one is in, even though at every point one is actually in one country or the other. The traditional evangelical emphasis on conversion has sometimes pushed people into emphasizing a single event where the reality has been more one of a process.

The picture is also complicated by the fact that we have identified four distinct components of full Christian initiation. In Acts these normally come all together, but even there this is not always the case. The Samaritans did not receive the Spirit at the time they were baptized (8:14–17). Paul preached to some at Ephesus who were already 'disciples' – but of John the Baptist (19:1–7). Theologically the four components are a unity, and initiation is a single event with four aspects, not four separate events or four stages. Salvation is not parcelled out between the four components, as if we get one benefit from faith, another from repentance and another from baptism. Nor is it like passing three successive years of study in order to gain a degree. But while the four steps should be seen as a single event ideally or theoretically, in practice they are often drawn out over a period of time. When this happens, we should think of one extended event rather than four separate events, of a *fourfold* initiation. Real life is usually more messy than our neat theories. What is of prime importance is neither the *timespan* nor even the *order* of the four components, but the fact that all four actually take place.[9]

With adult converts converting to Christ from *outside* the Christian community, the four components sometimes do occur close together in time, even if rarely all on the same day. But for those raised in a Christian home the process of initiation is often spread over years. It is rare, but not unknown, for those brought up in a Christian home to undergo a sudden or instantaneous conversion. And where such people speak of becoming a Christian on a specific date it is often that this was the occasion of just one significant step in a much longer process. For the great majority of those becoming Christians out of a Christian upbringing this is a gradual process of growing into faith, often with one or more crisis events on the way. In many years' experience of hearing testimonies from prospective students I noticed it was very common for there to be two crisis events, one in their early teens and one in their later teens. Some spoke in terms of conversion followed by recommitment, others in terms of an initial challenge followed by a later conversion. Perhaps in the majority of cases these were just staging posts on a long journey. Again, there are others who cannot remember any time when they did not know God.

---

[9] Smith, *Beginning Well*, 144–156, argues similarly.

Is conversion a single event or a lifelong process?

Most evangelicals think of conversion or regeneration as a single event. By contrast, Calvin and other Reformers viewed regeneration and repentance as a lifelong process – the process that evangelicals call 'sanctification'. So who is right? We need not think of the two views as mutually exclusive. They should be seen as two sides of the truth. Conversion is an event or a crisis (whether sudden or otherwise) that leads on to a lifelong process. The word 'marriage' has the same dual meaning. Wedding invitations often refer to the 'marriage' of the two people, meaning by that the service at which they enter into marriage. The word also refers to the permanent state that people enter at their weddings. Similarly the words 'conversion' or 'regeneration' can be used to refer either to initiation or to the lifelong process. The important point is not how one uses the words but making it clear how one is using them. In this book I use them to refer to the initial change, unless the context makes clear otherwise.

Does conversion involve total commitment?

How radical or total is conversion? Does conversion involve immediate total commitment, or is it just the first step towards this? The answer is both. Conversion implies a 180-degree turn, not just a 120-degree turn – but does this total commitment come at the beginning of the Christian life, or is it the goal? Putting it differently, should we think of this total commitment as promise, or as delivery? Repentance involves total commitment *in principle*, but at conversion this is still only theoretical. A long time ago I belonged to a Young People's Fellowship and we sang songs pledging our total commitment to Christ. Now we can look back at half a century of varying degrees of delivery. The same is true of marriage. At the wedding various all-embracing vows are made of fidelity and commitment. What lies ahead is a lifetime of seeking to live up to those vows. Likewise, the Christian life is a lifetime of seeking to put into practice the commitment promised at the beginning.

As we saw in chapter 1, a key feature of the New Testament view of salvation is the contrast between 'already' and 'not yet'. There is a sense in which we already enjoy it, but another sense in which it is postponed until the end. Likewise, there is a sense in which becoming a Christian means 'already' being totally committed, another sense in which that will 'not yet' be fully achieved in this life. Augustine notes that there is truth both in 1 John 3:9, which states that no one born of God sins, and in 1 John 1:8, which states that we deceive ourselves if we say that we have no sin.[10]

The same issue arises with preaching about sanctification. Should this involve calling people to total commitment or is it calling them to take one more step on a journey? *Both* are necessary. If all we do is call people to total commitment, we shall be in danger of teaching an unrealistic perfectionism. This will lead either to *discouragement*, as people are all too aware of how far they fall short, or to *hypocrisy*, as people claim to have reached a level of commitment they have not yet attained. On the other hand if all we do is call people to take one more step on the journey, we shall be in danger of leading people to complacency and of accepting a merely nominal Christianity. Augustine before his conversion famously prayed, 'Lord, make me chaste, but not yet!'[11] I have a hundred-year plan for my sanctification in which the next thirty years involve some very small steps in the right direction.

There is a tension here.

On the one hand one cannot be a Christian without following Christ; we cannot have Christ as Saviour without having him as Lord. There is no forgiveness of sins without repentance. At a wedding the bridegroom does not promise his bride Sundays to Fridays but reserve Saturdays for his mistress.

Yet on the other hand we are not required to sort our lives out before God accepts us. We do not come to Christ because we have been sorted out; we come in order to be sorted out. We are all a work-in-progress. If you bring in a builder to sort out the dry rot this means being committed to the task. You do not ask him to do every room but to leave the rot in the kitchen.

Does conversion require giving up drug taking – or giving up slave trading? When it comes to today's situation it is hard to see how a slave trader could be a Christian. Yet in the eighteenth century John Newton, the author of the hymn 'Amazing grace', continued as a slave trader for some time *after* his conversion. At that time slave trading was not perceived to be as evil as widely as it is today.[12] There is no universal culture-free answer to the question of what we need to give up when becoming Christians. It will vary according to different social contexts and the awareness within the church itself of what is right and wrong. It will also vary according to people's experience before conversion. It is unrealistic to expect that someone coming out of an addiction will never again lapse into it. The Christian life usually involves ups and downs, with temporary backslidings.

---

[10] *The Correction of the Donatists* 9:40 (NPNF 4:647).

[11] *Confessions* 8:7:17 (NPNF 1:124).

[12] Pollock, *Amazing Grace: John Newton's Story*, 94–128, especially 120.

One way of thinking about conversion is as a *paradigm shift* – a shift of understanding and allegiance that takes time to work out in practical terms. There is an initial commitment, which then takes time to work through to become a reality. I had a similar experience in the realm of political commitment. Having for many years held to one persuasion, in 1986 I watched a series of short programmes on the television that changed my underlying perspective, that involved a paradigm shift. I knew that there would be implications, but at that point was unclear what they would be. After a period of reflection (during which I managed in one year to be a member of three different parties without actually changing my views!) I ended just over two years later in the party of which I am now a member. The change took place in principle in 1986; the working out of its implications took two years.

Conversion and the struggle against sin

Conversion leads to a real change – a new heart, love for God and the desire to serve him. Sin no longer *reigns* over us, but *remains* in us.[13] Sin moves from being a citizen to being an illegal alien. We still have sinful desires and lusts that lead us into sin. So the Christian life is a daily struggle against sin.

Conversion is the *beginning*, not the *end*, of the serious struggle against sin. As Augustine put it, it is better to be in conflict with vice rather than enjoy peaceful bondage to it.[14] Sometimes with the exhilaration of initial conversion (during the honeymoon period) people are misled into thinking that sin has gone, as John Wesley noted.[15] The Christian life is a slow and steady progress towards a goal, with no quick fixes and no short cuts. There is no perfection in this life – on which see chapter 30, below. In his *Institutes*, Calvin offers a realistic picture of expectations. This is a marathon, not a sprint, as Calvin described.[16]

It is right, therefore, that we should be aware of our sinfulness and grieve for it. But Calvin urges the need for moderation. If we focus exclusively or excessively on our sinfulness, there is a danger of falling into despair or lethargy. Sorrow for sin must be combined with rejoicing in God's grace and blessings.[17] This is an important pastoral point and I have known someone who fell into the danger described by Calvin. Today, however, that would be

---

[13] *Inst.* 3:3:11.
[14] *City of God* 21:15 (NPNF 2:465).
[15] Sermon 43:5–6 ('The Scripture Way of Salvation'), quoted at the end of chapter 30.
[16] *Inst.* 3:6:5, quoted at the end of chapter 30.
[17] *Inst.* 3:3:15.

rare and we need to be urged not to focus exclusively on God's grace and blessings but to remember also to grieve for our sins. We shall revisit the need for this balance in chapter 17 and again when we consider self-esteem in chapter 26.

Does faith or repentance come first?

Calvin argued strongly that repentance comes after faith and forgiveness of sins.[18] Why? First because, as we have seen, he defined repentance as a *lifelong* process. Secondly, he argued that obedience from the heart flows from knowing that one's sins are forgiven, which in turn comes through faith. In other words, the message of the gospel is not 'put your life right and God will forgive you' but 'come to God and he will put your life right'. Luther's early problems came precisely because he had been taught that he needed to do his very best, turn from sin and love God above all else *before* God would give him his grace. A similar situation emerged in early seventeenth-century Puritanism in England where some taught that you cannot come to Christ until you have been through a process of conviction of sin and grieving for it. This caused John Bunyan huge problems, as he described in his autobiography *Grace Abounding to the Chief of Sinners*. Rather than ask whether we are fit to come to Christ we should come to him to be made fit. This is an important point – theologically, pastorally and evangelistically. It is well expressed in Charlotte Elliott's famous hymn 'Just as I am':

> Just as I am, and waiting not
> To rid my soul of one dark blot;
> To Thee whose blood can cleanse each spot,
> O Lamb of God, I come, I come!

While this is true, it is not, however, the whole truth. First, there is no forgiveness of sin without repentance. In Luke 24:47 Jesus commands that 'repentance and forgiveness of sins should be proclaimed in his name to all nations' – a verse Calvin often quoted. Calvin's point was not that faith can exist *without* repentance, but that faith leads to repentance. He was totally against the idea, taught by some today, that it is possible to have faith and the forgiveness of sins *without* repentance and discipleship. For more on this, see chapters 16 and 18.

---

[18] *Inst.* 3:3:1–4.

Where repentance and faith are put together in the New Testament it is in that order – Mark 1:15; Acts 20:21; Hebrews 6:1. There is an important sense in which turning to Christ, coming to faith, is itself a form of repentance or 'change of mind', because it implies a desire for change. In his 1554 Commentary on Acts 20:21 Calvin clarifies the twofold relation between faith and repentance. 'The beginning of repentance is a preparation for faith.' This 'beginning' he goes on to explain as 'the dissatisfaction with ourselves, which drives us, when we have been moved by a serious fear of the wrath of God, to seek for a remedy'.[19] In his 1539 *Reply to Sadolet* he says that pastors should first point people to the tribunal of God to discover their sin and guilt and then show them the mercy of God made known in Christ.[20]

We shall return to this issue in chapter 25.

---

[19] Calvin,*Acts of the Apostles* 14–28, 176–177.
[20] *SWJC* 1:41–42; Calvin, *Theological Treatises*, 234–235.

12
Efficacy of baptism

What does baptism do?[1]

For many the answer is very simple: 'Nothing whatsoever!' Baptism is just a sign, just a way in which we profess our faith. It is true that we confess our faith in baptism, but it is mistaken to see this as all that baptism does. There are seven things that baptism involves, according to the New Testament.

Confession of faith

Baptism was an occasion for the confession of faith. Ananias tells Paul to call on the name of Jesus as he is baptized (Acts 22:16). Romans 10:9–10 mentions confessing 'with your mouth that Jesus is Lord'. This does not explicitly mention baptism but it was at baptism that such faith and outward confession took place and these verses are widely and rightly seen as referring to baptism. This confession took place because faith is a condition of baptism. Philip tells the Ethiopian eunuch that he can be baptized if he believes with all his heart (Acts 8:36–38).[2]

There is a significant difference between the confession of faith that took place then and the way in which it commonly occurs today. In Acts the converts' confession concerned who Jesus was – that he is Lord, Christ, Son of God. Today the confession of faith is so often not about who Christ is but an account of the conversion of the one being baptized. In line with our narcissistic culture it is all about us, and in some instances Jesus may not even be mentioned. For more on this, see chapter 26.

What is never found in the New Testament is the idea of baptism as testimony *to unbelievers* – indeed there is no recorded example of an unbeliever being present at a baptism. So, for example, the Philippian jailer and his family were baptized at night (Acts 16:33) and there was no thought of waiting till morning and inviting the neighbours to witness it. Today in many churches

---

[1] For the answer to this question, see Beasley-Murray, *Baptism in the New Testament*, ch. 5, and for a more popular version, *Baptism Today and Tomorrow*, chs 2–3.
[2] Verse 37 is a variant reading but at the very least expresses an early Christian viewpoint.

baptism is seen as a way of testifying to one's faith before unbelieving friends and family. There is nothing wrong with this and it can be a powerful form of witness. What is wrong is to pretend that this is the meaning or purpose of baptism in the New Testament, since it is neither.

Salvation

Baptism is linked with salvation. Peter bluntly states, 'Baptism . . . now saves you . . . through the resurrection of Jesus Christ' (1 Peter 3:21). The longer ending of Mark contains the statement 'Whoever believes and is baptized will be saved' (16:16).[3] Paul states that 'if you confess with your mouth that Jesus is Lord and believe in your heart that God raised him from the dead, you will be saved. For with the heart one believes and is justified, and with the mouth one confesses and is saved' (Rom. 10:9–10). As already noted, this probably refers to baptism.

Union with Christ (in his death, burial and resurrection)

Paul states that 'as many of you as were baptized into Christ have put on Christ' (Gal. 3:27). Being baptized into Christ means being baptized into his death, and being buried with him by baptism so that, as he was raised from the dead, we might walk in newness of life (Rom. 6:3–4). Elsewhere he puts this more strongly, stating that in baptism we are not just buried with Christ but also raised with him, through faith (Col. 2:11–12).

Forgiveness of sin and washing

John's baptism was a baptism of repentance for the forgiveness of sins (Mark 1:4). Peter likewise, on the day of Pentecost, called upon his hearers to 'repent and be baptized . . . for the forgiveness of your sins' (Acts 2:38). And Ananias called upon Paul to 'rise and be baptized and wash away your sins, calling on his name' (Acts 22:16).

Paul in turn told the Corinthians that they were washed, sanctified and justified 'in the name of the Lord Jesus Christ and by the Spirit of our God' (1 Cor. 6:11). He also stated that Christ cleansed the church 'by the washing of water with the word' (Eph. 5:26). God 'saved us, not because of works done by us in righteousness, but according to his own mercy, by the washing of regeneration and renewal of the Holy Spirit' (Titus 3:5). Hebrews likewise refers to 'our hearts sprinkled clean from an evil conscience and our bodies washed with pure water' (10:22). These references to washing probably all refer to baptism.

---

[3] The longer ending of Mark may not be part of the original Gospel, but at the very least expresses an early Christian viewpoint. See Black (ed.), *Perspectives on Ending of Mark*.

Regeneration or new birth

The idea of regeneration or new birth is not often mentioned in the New Testament, which is why it has been given different meanings. Jesus told Nicodemus that one cannot see the kingdom of God unless one is born again (John 3:3). He goes on to say that one cannot enter the kingdom of God 'unless one is born of water and the Spirit' (3:5). Given that Christian initiation in Acts involved baptism in water and receiving the Spirit, it is hard to deny that water here refers to baptism. This is how the early church understood it from the second century and how the great majority of commentators today understand it. Paul likewise states that we are saved 'by the washing of regeneration and renewal of the Holy Spirit' (Titus 3:5).

Earlier in John we read that it is those who believe in Jesus who become children of God, being 'born, not of blood nor of the will of the flesh nor of the will of man, but of God' (1:12–13). Elsewhere the New Testament talks of regeneration as happening through the word of truth (Jas 1:18), through Christ's resurrection (1 Peter 1:3) and through the word of God (1 Peter 1:23).

Receiving the Holy Spirit

Peter, at the conclusion of his Pentecost sermon, tells his hearers that if they repent and are baptized they will receive not just forgiveness of sins but also 'the gift of the Holy Spirit' (Acts 2:38). The Ephesian 'disciples' encountered by Paul received Christian baptism and, after Paul laid hands on them, 'the Holy Spirit came on them' (Acts 19:5–6). There is a parallel here with the way in which the Spirit descended upon Jesus after his baptism (Mark 1:9–10). On the other hand receiving the Spirit sometimes preceded baptism, as with Cornelius and his family (Acts 10:44; 11:15).

Entry into the church

Baptism is not just a private matter between God and the individual, but involves the community and implies entry into the community. It is performed by someone else on behalf of the church. Almost all denominations understand baptism to bring a person into the universal church. On the day of Pentecost those who were baptized were 'added' to the church (Acts 2:41). 'In one Spirit we were all baptized into one body' (1 Cor. 12:13). In almost all churches, while anyone may attend, one cannot belong to the local church without having been baptized. In other words, baptism does make a difference, so we should be careful to whom it is given. Baptism without real faith does not bring salvation, but it does bring entry into the visible church. This can be compared to the way in which matriculation makes one a member of a university, or to the bestowal of nationality.

Some object to giving baptism any role in salvation on the grounds that it is a 'work', but this is wide of the mark. Baptism is not something we do but something done to us, something we receive. It speaks not of our performance but of our coming with empty hands to receive God's grace.

The relationship between faith and baptism

Today we have a polarization between the belief that salvation is by baptism (Roman Catholics) and the belief that it is by faith (evangelicals).[4] The New Testament takes no sides here, because conversion and baptism are always held together, so we must resist the false dichotomy. The New Testament teaching on baptism, expounded above, makes no sense while we think of faith and baptism as separate, as alternative ways to salvation. From that starting point we are forced to choose between salvation by faith or salvation by baptism – it must be one or the other. In the New Testament, however, faith was expressed in baptism and baptism was the outward expression of faith. This is what we see in Acts. From this perspective it does make sense to talk of salvation by faith and baptism, as in Mark 16:16. That is why Paul can talk both about salvation through faith and about salvation through baptism. For New Testament Christians, baptism was the decisive turning point. This is still true today for converts from Islam and Judaism, who often when asked for the date of their conversion will point to their baptism. It is when one of their number is baptized that Jews and Muslims regard them as having become Christians, not when they merely talk about believing in Jesus. At that point Orthodox Jews hold a funeral service for them, with an empty coffin. Muslims are liable to do the same – with a full coffin. Many modern Western Christians find it hard to conceive of baptism this way, but they are the ones who have departed from the New Testament.

For New Testament Christians, who were baptized at the point of coming to faith, it was natural to see these as two sides of the one coin. So Paul could switch from referring to one to the other. 'In Christ Jesus you are all sons of God, through faith. For as many of you as were baptized into Christ have put on Christ' (Gal. 3:26–27). He tells the Colossians that they were buried with Christ in baptism and raised with him through faith (2:12). That is very confusing if we think of faith and baptism as two separate events, but not if

---

[4] Baillie, *Baptism and Conversion*, 13–15, states the issue with great clarity, and after reviewing different approaches sets out his 'Attempted Conclusion' (41–48).

we think of baptism at the point of conversion, as in Acts. Likewise, in Romans Paul expounds justification by faith in chapters 3–5, then turns to baptism in chapter 6. This is not a change of topic. The faith described in chapters 3–5 is a faith that expressed itself in baptism; the baptism described in chapter 6 is the baptism that came at the point of conversion. Paul could glide naturally from faith to baptism because the two went together and are not separate.

Today, we need to recover the New Testament concept of the unity of faith and baptism. We can do this in three stages:

1 We need to *think* of faith and baptism as a unity, not as two separate things.
2 We need to *teach* this, whether from the pulpit or when talking to a non-Christian friend. Baptism is part of the gospel message: 'Go therefore and make disciples of all nations, baptizing them in the name of the Father and of the Son and of the Holy Spirit' (Matt. 28:19). In Acts, as we have seen, baptism is part of Christian initiation. It is something to be discussed with those interested in becoming Christians, not something to be deferred to a later date.
3 We should seek to *practise* this unity, to recover the largely extinct practice of converts' baptism. We shall not be able to do this in all cases in the modern West, for a variety of reasons.

A high number of Christians today were brought up in a Christian home and the majority of these grow into faith gradually rather than in one crisis event, making it hard for their baptism to coincide with their conversion. Unless, of course, one took great care to insulate one's children from any contact with the Christian faith and then, when they reached a suitable age, filled the bath with water in anticipation, sat them down and preached to them with the hope that they would repent, believe, be baptized and receive the Spirit all at once!

In addition, many of those raised in a Christian home would already have been baptized as babies.

Apart from those raised in a committed Christian home, many millions of people in Britain (and other European countries) have been baptized or 'christened' but have had little or no other contact with the church.

Given all of these factors, there is no way that all baptisms today will be converts' baptisms, as in Acts. But if as many as 10% of baptisms were like those in Acts, we would then be better able to understand the New Testament approach to baptism because, even if we ourselves had not experienced it, we would know many Christians who have and it would no longer just be something we read about in a book.

There is another reason why converts' baptism is rare today. Many churches feel the need to delay the baptism of new converts in order to check the genuineness of their conversion. Experience shows that such a delay is no guarantee that the baptized convert will continue walking in the faith. For more on this, see chapter 10.

Two stories

The New Testament talks about being a Christian in two different ways. The first story tells how we become Christians by faith, repentance and receiving the Spirit. These are all inward and none of them is visible to others. The second story is about the outward manifestation. Faith leads to confession of faith. Repentance leads to the fruit of repentance in a changed life and good works. The reception of the Spirit leads to outward manifestations as fruit of the Spirit and as gifts of the Spirit. So there are two different stories to tell. The first concerns the inward reality; the second concerns its outward manifestation.

There are two opposite errors to be avoided. The first is to assume that the two stories are identical – that everyone who professes faith has true faith, that everyone who professes repentance has genuinely repented. The New Testament warns against this error. Simon Magus believed Philip's preaching and was baptized (Acts 8:13). Yet shortly after Peter told him, 'You have neither part nor lot in this matter, for your heart is not right before God' (8:21). Jesus refers to those performing charismatic miracles whom he *never* knew (Matt. 7:21–23). There is the recognition elsewhere that not all who profess to be Christians are genuine.

> They went out from us, but they were not of us; for if they had been of us, they would have continued with us. But they went out, that it might become plain that they all are not of us. (1 John 2:19)

As Paul put it, 'The Lord knows those who are his' (2 Tim. 2:19), implying that the rest of us do not always know.

Augustine in the fourth century developed the concept of the 'invisible church'. He distinguished between the 'visible church', the mixed body we see, and the 'invisible church', the body of true Christians. The visible church consists of those who profess to be Christians – those who are baptized and in good standing. Among these are both genuine Christians and nominal Christians,

119

those without true faith or true love. The invisible church is invisible only in the sense that its boundaries are known to God alone. There was no suggestion that one might belong to the invisible church *instead of* the visible church. The idea, rather, was that the boundaries of the true church are invisible to us, but known to God who reads people's hearts. No membership list is infallible because we cannot see people's hearts, only their outward actions. As Archbishop James Ussher put it, while we judge the heart by the actions, God judges the actions by the heart.[5]

It is wrong to assume that the two stories always coincide, that everyone who professes faith is genuine. It is equally wrong to treat the two stories as if they were unconnected, as if all that mattered is the inward story. It is inward faith that is crucial, but genuine faith will always lead to outward manifestation, in words and actions, as set out in chapter 10. Inward repentance is crucial, but genuine repentance always leads to 'fruit in keeping with repentance' (Matt. 3:8). Belonging to the invisible church is crucial, but that is not a substitute for belonging to the visible church. Some Christians try to be more 'spiritual' than the New Testament. Outward observances without the inner attitude of the heart are condemned throughout the Bible. But the opposite extreme, inner change not expressed outwardly and physically, is not commended. We are physical as well as spiritual beings and the gospel addresses us at the physical as well as the spiritual level.

Baptism belongs to the outward story. Being baptized is of itself no guarantee that one has the inward reality. We must not fall into the error of assuming that all who have been baptized are certainly saved. But the outward is also important and no one who declines baptism has the right to claim to be a genuine Christian.

Delayed baptism

The New Testament ascribes an efficacy to baptism, as we have seen. It is one thing to make such statements about baptism that comes at the time of conversion, but what significance does baptism have if it comes much later. Augustine was converted in August 386 but was not baptized until Easter 387. In his *Confessions* he more than once says that in the intervening period he was 'awaiting regeneration', although he was already converted. This is perhaps to fall into the error of parcelling out the benefits of salvation between the four different components of initiation.

---

[5] Cited by Snoddy, *Quicunque Vult*, 160.

Another way of viewing his status at that stage is to pick up on Paul's comment about Abraham's status between Genesis 15, when he was accounted righteous for his faith (15:6) and Genesis 17, when he was circumcised (17:24). 'He received the sign of circumcision as a seal of the righteousness that he had by faith while he was still uncircumcised' (Rom. 4:11). So also, delayed baptism can be seen as a seal upon the benefits received earlier by faith.[6]

Can the benefit of baptism be lost if someone later denies their faith? First, receiving baptism is no guarantee of receiving the benefits of baptism – baptism without faith is not effective. Secondly, there is the vexed question of whether those who fall away were or were not true Christians in the first place, an issue discussed in chapter 28.

What is necessary for salvation?

Are all the four elements of initiation (repentance, faith, baptism, receiving the Spirit) equally necessary for salvation? There are examples in Scripture of those who were saved without one or other of these, most notoriously the thief on the cross. Jesus promised him, 'today you will be with me in Paradise' (Luke 23:42–43). This man was presumably not baptized – though a colleague of mine was taught as a youngster that Jesus did in fact baptize him, by spitting at him! Also, to be pedantic, the pattern of fourfold initiation begins with the day of Pentecost, which was yet to come. But there certainly are believers who die before they are able to receive baptism. Secondly, Old Testament believers did not actually believe in *Jesus*. Thirdly, if it is possible for those who die in infancy to be saved, then they are saved without repenting or believing. So do we conclude that it is not necessary to be baptized, or to believe, or to repent, in order to be saved? No. There is a fundamental difference between those who are *unable* to do these things and those who *refuse* to, between cannot and will not.[7]

It is important to distinguish between the norm and exceptions. Lawyers have a well-known saying: 'Hard cases make bad law.' Laws should be made for normal situations and then allowances made for the exceptions. For example, Sikhs cannot wear motorcycle helmets because of their turbans. The response to this is not to make helmets optional for all but to make special provision for Sikhs. Again, some countries require a yellow-fever vaccination of visitors, but people who are allergic to eggs cannot have this vaccination.

---

[6] I am indebted to George Beasley-Murray for this thought, in a private conversation.

[7] In Num. 9:6–13 there is a distinction between those *prevented* from keeping the Passover by uncleanness or travel and those who negligently fail to keep it.

The response is not to dispense with the requirement, but to allow those with this allergy to enter the country at their own risk.

Likewise our practice here should be based on the New Testament norm, which is fourfold initiation, not on the exceptions or problem cases. We can leave the problem cases for God to handle! We must start with the norm, and then go on to consider any exceptions. The norm is fourfold initiation by repentance, faith, baptism and receiving the Spirit. That is the only model we have the right to offer in telling the gospel. But if someone is prevented from one or other of these, that is a different matter; that is in the hands of God. It is wrong to suppose that a child who dies before it can repent and believe is not saved. Ultimately salvation is by Christ, not by any of the four components of Christian initiation.

Significantly in Mark 16:16 it is 'whoever believes and is baptized' that is saved, while condemnation is for those who do not believe, with no mention of failure to be baptized. Salvation comes through faith and baptism, but it is those who do not believe, not those who are not baptized, who are said to be condemned. Faith is more crucial than baptism. John 3:5 links entering God's kingdom with being born of water and the Spirit, but verse 8 goes on to talk of the sovereignty of the Spirit in a way that does not encourage us to restrict his working: 'The wind blows where it wishes, and you hear its sound, but you do not know where it comes from or where it goes. So it is with everyone who is born of the Spirit.' We cannot limit the working of the Spirit:

> We can set no limits to the power of Christ: he is leading men to salvation in his own way. Yet this does not at all entitle us to hold baptism in contempt. It is not that Christ is bound to baptism as a means of grace, but we in our faith are.[8]

> God has bound salvation to the sacrament of Baptism, but he himself is not bound by his sacraments.[9]

Receiving the Spirit is *the* criterion of whether or not one is a genuine Christian, rather than observable repentance, faith or baptism. Paul states, 'Anyone who does not have the Spirit of Christ does not belong to him' (Rom. 8:9). John the Baptist was filled with the Holy Spirit from his mother's womb (Luke 1:15), so even though babies dying in their mother's womb or in infancy cannot believe and have faith that does not mean they cannot be born again of the Spirit.

---

[8] *Baptist–Reformed Conversation: Report 1977* in Meyer and Vischer (eds), *Growth in Agreement*, 141.
[9] CCC §1257.

Is baptism necessary? Necessary for what? It is necessary in that the church has no right not to practise it and to require it of converts. It is necessary in that it is not optional for those becoming Christians. It is not necessary in that believers who fail to be baptized for some legitimate reason (such as premature death) do not miss salvation.

13
Origins of infant baptism

When did infant baptism begin?[1]

When did infant baptism, the baptism of those too young to speak for themselves, begin? This question has traditionally been answered by considering all of the evidence available from New Testament times, which is notoriously ambiguous. The evidence before the end of the second century is also so meagre and ambiguous that it is widely accepted that a firm verdict is not possible. It may be helpful, therefore, in seeking to answer the question, to work backwards using a 'seismological' approach. Seismologists in New York can observe and measure earthquakes that take place in Los Angeles, without leaving their own laboratories. How do they do this? They can tell what has happened in California by its effects two to three thousand miles away. In a similar manner I would suggest that we can deduce what was the situation in apostolic times by its effects two to three hundred years later. We shall start from a time in church history where it *is* clear what happened and work back from that point to New Testament times. The evidence becomes clearer as the centuries go by, so we shall begin with the third century, move on to the fourth and fifth, then go back to the second century and end with the first century, in line with the principle of working from what is plain to what is obscure.

Third century

From the third century we have five major sources of information: the so-called *Apostolic Tradition*, Tertullian, Cyprian, Origen and inscriptions on Christian tombstones. It is important to distinguish different types of evidence.[2] There are sermons and other writings that contain exhortations either to baptize or not to baptize babies. These testify to the views of the authors and show what views were considered acceptable, but do not in themselves prove that anyone actually followed the advice given. Then there is evidence as to when specific

---

[1] This chapter is based on Lane, 'Did the Apostolic Church Baptise Babies?'
[2] I am indebted to David Wright for this and other points.

individuals were baptized, either through literary biographical information or from inscriptions. In between these two types are church orders and other works regulating practice. These do not give hard statistical information but are clearly a far more reliable indicator as to what actually happened than are exhortatory sermons.

The first of our witnesses, the *Apostolic Tradition* traditionally attributed to Hippolytus at Rome, is a composite work derived from different sources from the second to fourth centuries, the earliest core of the work dating, maybe, from the mid-second century.[3] The earliest material can be seen as evidence of what was happening at the beginning of the third century at the very latest. Chapters 16–23 describe the ceremony of baptism. This is still clearly geared to new converts and the only mention of infants comes in three sentences. After the statement that candidates are to be baptized naked, it is stated that the first to be baptized should be the little children. These should speak for themselves if they can, otherwise one of their family should speak for them.[4] These chapters in general, and the instructions about small children in particular, are found in the earliest core of the document.[5]

What is being described is a ceremony designed for adults in which small children are included – both those who could answer for themselves and infants who were too young. It should occasion no surprise that children are here (and elsewhere) fitted into an essentially adult ceremony since, as we saw in chapter 10, the practice of baptism described in Acts is *converts'* baptism. *Whatever* happened to Christian children at whatever age, it would involve adapting that process to include them. One cannot say how long children had been included by the time of the *Apostolic Tradition*, except that this is unlikely to have been a recent innovation. The practice that is described, and which presumably reflects the reality of what was then happening, included the baptism of little children both at an age when they can speak and at an earlier stage when they cannot. This is an account of a regular baptismal service and so *does not refer to the emergency baptism of dying babies*. While one cannot deduce that all Christians were having their infants baptized, the document is clear evidence that some infants (too young to answer for themselves) were being baptized.

At the turn of the third century *Tertullian*, at Carthage in North Africa, wrote a work entitled *Baptism*. Here he urges that baptism should be delayed, especially for little children:

---

[3] Attridge (ed.), *Apostolic Tradition*, 1–6, 13–15.

[4] Attridge (ed.), *Apostolic Tradition*, 112–113 (ch. 21:4).

[5] Attridge (ed.), *Apostolic Tradition*, 15, 124.

It is preferable to delay baptism, according to the circumstances, disposition and even age, of each individual. Delay is especially preferable, however, in the case of little children ... It is true that our Lord says, 'Forbid them not to come to me.' So let them come – when they are growing up, when they are learning, when they are taught what they are coming to. Let them be made Christians when they have become competent to know Christ. Why should innocency hasten to the remission of sins? ... For no less reason the unmarried should also be delayed since in them the ground of temptation is prepared.[6]

Tertullian opposes the baptism of children, including those too young to speak for themselves (i.e. infants) and so needing sponsors. The fact that he counsels delay also means that the practice that he is opposing is the 'regular' baptism of infants, not the emergency baptism of dying infants. A superficial reading might portray him as a proto-Baptist fighting the emerging practice of infant baptism, but the situation is somewhat different. In the first place, one argument that Tertullian does not use against child baptism is that it is a recent innovation. In the ancient world novelty and innovation were regarded as something bad, not desirable and Tertullian, in particular, elsewhere argued at length that truth is ancient and goes back to the apostles while heresy is recent. He would hardly have neglected to use that argument here if he could. Tertullian was converted to the Christian faith by the mid-190s. At that time he would have known people who had been Christians for some time. If infant baptism had been unknown at the beginning of the African church or in the middle of the second century (whichever is later) Tertullian would have known it. And would have mentioned it.

Tertullian urges against hurrying children to baptism while they are in the age of innocence and need not hasten to the forgiveness of sins. What motivates Tertullian here is the fear of post-baptismal sin. Baptism, it was believed, washes away all previous sin. But what of sins committed after baptism? Finding forgiveness for these was not so straightforward. Given that fact, it was prudent to time one's baptism so as to derive the maximum benefit. So, later in the same passage, Tertullian urges the unmarried and widows to delay baptism until they are married, and thus safely out of temptation's way. Tertullian here is urging delay, but is seeking a change of *established* practice and does so because of his beliefs about post-baptismal sin. Baptism was like a trump card – it is important to play it at the right time. Tertullian believed that baptizing children was inexpedient; he did not claim that it was

---

[6] *Baptism* 18 (Evans (ed.), *Tertullian's Homily on Baptism*, 36–41, commentary on 101–106).

illegitimate, irregular or invalid. In short, Tertullian had no objection *in principle* to infant baptism. This was a question of strategy rather than principle. Tertullian bears witness to the fact that little children were being baptized for reasons other than emergency baptism. His own exhortation that baptism be delayed is not itself proof that his advice was followed, but such proof is found elsewhere.

A generation after Tertullian *Cyprian*, bishop of Carthage and an admirer of Tertullian, also wrote about baptism. His *Letter* 64 to Fidus, written in the early 250s, discusses the question of infant baptism in the light of controversy and reports the conclusions of a council of African bishops held at Carthage. The issues have changed since the time of Tertullian. Now the only point in question is whether or not to delay baptism until the child is eight days old, following the Old Testament pattern with circumcision. Various arguments were invoked in the debate, the most imaginative being that babies' feet are too repugnant at birth to receive the kiss of peace![7] As Cyprian reports, the council resolved that newborn babies should not be hindered from being baptized. It does not follow that all African Christians had their babies baptized, but the fact that there was a serious controversy between baptism at birth and baptism on the eighth day means that a significant number of Christians must have been having their babies baptized.

Origen was a contemporary of Cyprian who lived in Alexandria. Like Cyprian, he justifies infant baptism by an appeal to the doctrine of original sin. New-born babies are not pure and innocent. Origen claims that infant baptism is a tradition from the apostles.[8] Origen did not, of course, have any privileged access to apostolic times, but was born into a Christian family in about AD 185, so his belief would require that infant baptism was an established practice at least by the last quarter of the second century. We cannot be certain whether Origen was himself baptized as a baby, but there can be no serious doubt as to whether infant baptism was at that time being practised. Origen in his youth would have known people who had been Christians for sixty or seventy years. If *none* of these had been baptized as babies it is most unlikely that he would have claimed that the practice was apostolic. Indeed it could be argued that this shows that infant baptism was practised by the early years of the second century.

Too many discussions of this topic play down the significance of tradition. I once heard a lady on the radio tell how her grandmother had described to

---

[7] *Epistle* 64:2–5 (ANF 5:353–354 [numbered 58]).

[8] *Commentary on Romans* 5:9 on 6:5–7.

her seeing Napoleon go into exile in 1815. That event was over two hundred years ago, yet I have heard a second-hand account of it. Theology can of course change subtly over the years, but a simple fact like whether or not babies were baptized can easily be remembered. Polycarp knew from his own experience whether or not babies were baptized in the late apostolic age and it is unlikely that he and others took this information to the grave with them. This does not preclude changes taking place, but it does mean that informed Christians at the end of the second century were not as ignorant of early practice as is usually assumed. Of course, they often had no reason to divulge this information or indeed good reason not to. But had Tertullian, for example, had any reason to suppose that the practice of infant baptism was introduced after the time of the apostles, he had every motive to say so. Origen's claim that infant baptism is from the apostles indicates that he knows of no time when babies were not being baptized. This is not to claim that *all* babies were being baptized at any point, but rather that there was no time accessible to these writers when the practice was unknown. If that is so, the baptism of babies must go back at the very least to the middle of the second century, if not to the beginning of the century.

Given the geographical diversity of Hippolytus (Rome),[9] Tertullian (Carthage) and Origen (Alexandria), their evidence would seem to demonstrate fairly conclusively that by the last quarter of the second century infant baptism was well established across the Roman Empire, in the sense that at least some Christians were having their babies baptized. It would also suggest that the practice was very likely known in the early years of the second century. The *Apostolic Tradition*, Tertullian and Cyprian (and probably Origen too) all describe the 'regular' baptism of infants, rather than the emergency baptism of dying infants.

Another piece of evidence from the third century is found in the *inscriptions on Christian tombstones*.[10] Most of these are undated but many are from the third century and there is no evidence that any of them are earlier. These clearly testify to two points. First, that many babies and children were baptized. Secondly, that many were baptized not at birth but at a later stage when they were in danger of death. None say that a child was baptized as a baby and died at a later age. Emergency baptism was clearly common in the third century, because of the fear that those dying unbaptized in infancy would be lost. It is

---

[9] If the *Apostolic Tradition* be seen as a composite work, it might then reflect the practice of more than one region.

[10] Ferguson, 'Inscriptions and Origin of Infant Baptism'. The text of many inscriptions is given (40–44). A shorter version is found in his magisterial *Baptism in the Early Church*, 372–377.

also noteworthy that emergency baptism was not just for children. There are adults, aged 34 and 51 for example, who were baptized shortly before death. The evidence from the inscriptions reinforces the picture that we have already seen. Infant baptism is practised, but not universally. Why were some not baptized as babies? There is no evidence, here or elsewhere, for any objection in principle to infant baptism. There is evidence elsewhere (as in Tertullian) for the fear of post-baptismal sin and the consequent postponement of baptism. This motive would equally explain the evidence of the inscriptions for the emergency baptism of mature adults as well as children. The inscriptions are valuable evidence in that (like biographical evidence) they tell us what actually happened. They clearly prove that emergency baptism happened for those of every age. They do not prove either that emergency baptism was the only form of baptism or that infants were baptized only in the case of emergency.

Tertullian and the *Apostolic Tradition* give us the first indisputable reference to infant baptism. Baptists sometimes make much of the fact that there is no indisputable evidence for infant baptism before the third century, but this ignores an important point. Tertullian and the *Apostolic Tradition* also give us the first indisputable reference to the baptism at *any* age of someone from a Christian home. The silence before the third century is not just a silence about infant baptism; it is a silence about the church's policy and practice regarding the baptism at any age of those raised as Christians. Regarding this silence, Jeremias aptly notes, 'how seldom in the OT the circumcision of male infants is expressly mentioned'.[11]

Tertullian indicates that although infant baptism may have been practised it was not the only form of initiation being proposed. In the third and fourth centuries many Christian families followed the course he recommended, not having their children baptized. Tertullian's argument for the prudential delay of baptism until the worst onslaughts of temptation were past struck a chord and was followed in the fourth century by emperors and leading Christians. But neither in Tertullian nor in any other figure from that time do we find any objection in principle to infant baptism nor any denial of the claim that it was an apostolic practice.

Fourth and fifth centuries

What of the fourth and fifth centuries? A number of facts are undisputed. Some babies were baptized and not only at the point of death. No one objected in principle to infant baptism. But that does not mean that all Christians practised it.

---

[11] Jeremias, *Infant Baptism in First Four Centuries*, 23.

The fourth-century fathers urged adults not to delay baptism, whether in order to postpone Christian commitment or for fear of post-baptismal sin. But none of them proposed infant baptism as the *only* correct policy. *Gregory Nazianzen's* advice to Christian parents in his fortieth *Oration* is often quoted. Earlier in the oration he appears simply to commend the baptism of babies: 'Have you an infant child? Do not let sin get any opportunity, but let him be sanctified from his childhood; from his very tenderest age let him be consecrated by the Spirit.' But later, and at greater length, he offers a different recommendation. He recommends the immediate baptism of any babies in danger of death. For the rest his advice is to wait until they are about three, 'when they may be able to listen and to answer something about the sacrament; that, even though they do not perfectly understand it, yet at any rate they may know the outlines'. This is the age when they begin to be responsible for their behaviour and their reason is matured![12]

Three general points can be noted from the fourth century. *First*, there was a frank acceptance of a variety of policy. This clearly goes back to the third century, as is shown by the evidence of the inscriptions. Is there any reason for supposing that this variety does not go back further still? It is significant that we have no record in the third or fourth century of anyone objecting in principle to anyone else's policy, nor of anyone's policy being branded as a novelty. This fact strongly supports the theory that the diversity goes back a long way – perhaps even into the apostolic age.

Secondly, many fourth-century Christians did not have their babies baptized. Why not? The biggest motivation for delaying baptism, for which there is clear direct evidence, was the fear of post-baptismal sin. There is no shortage of evidence from the fourth century of *adults* delaying baptism through fear of post-baptismal sin.[13] Apart from Tertullian there is less evidence for this motivation for the non-baptism of children, but it would be extraordinary for it to have caused adults to delay baptism without also motivating delay in the baptism of children. Tertullian argued that it was prudent to wait till youngsters had been through the years of teenage rebellion, sown their wild oats and were ready to settle down. This would be a good time to be baptized, thus effectively availing themselves of a once-only offer of amnesty, and to knuckle under to the rigours of the Christian life and church discipline.

Thirdly, it is clear that the fourth-century Christians had no objection *in principle* to infant baptism. They did, however, see the merits of coming to baptism at the point when its one-off benefits could be used to greatest effect.

---

[12] Gregory Nazianzen, *Oration* 40:17, 28 (NPNF[2] 7:365, 370). I can confirm that when I was baptized at the age of 3 I did not 'perfectly understand it'.

[13] E.g. Chrysostom, *Homily 1 on Acts*, from the very end of the century (NPNF 11:1–10).

It was in the fifth century West that infant baptism increasingly became the norm, especially through the influence of Augustine in the context of the Pelagian controversy. Various factors were at work, including an increasing emphasis on the doctrines of original sin and prevenient grace and the fear that babies dying unbaptized would go to hell. It is then that infant baptism was for the first time expected of *all* children born to Christians.

When was the first objection *in principle* to infant baptism? The defence of an alternative to infant baptism goes back at least to Tertullian. But neither Tertullian nor anyone else in the early church objected in principle to infant baptism. They may have urged prudential considerations for the delay of baptism (not only for infants), but they did not suggest that the practice was unapostolic, illegitimate or invalid. Tertullian was not the sort of polemicist to pull punches like that had they had any plausibility. Augustine cited the practice of infant baptism as evidence for original sin, yet the Pelagians never questioned the validity of the practice. For such an objection in principle we have to wait until some small medieval sects[14] and the sixteenth-century Anabaptists. If the practice was in fact unapostolic it is surprising to say the least that none of those who had hesitations about it in the second to fourth centuries saw fit to draw attention to that fact. Had infant baptism been universally practised in these centuries its opponents today could plausibly argue that its unapostolic origins were for this reason suppressed. But in fact it was far from universally practised and there would have been no such motivation for concealing any suspicions that it was not an apostolic practice.

Second century

What about the second-century church? The direct evidence is much less clear. There are two accounts of baptism. The *Didache*, or so-called *Teaching of the Twelve Apostles*, is probably from around the turn of the century, possibly even from the first century. It contains a few rules about how to conduct baptism but makes no mention of children.[15] *Justin Martyr*, writing from Rome in the middle of the century, gives a fuller description of a baptismal service, also without mentioning children.[16] This proves nothing, as the Jewish tractate *Gerim* gives regulations for proselyte baptism that are designed for adults only, yet elsewhere indicates that children were baptized.[17]

---

14 Robinson, *Baptist Principles*, 51, 58–64, gives examples.
15 *Didache* 7.
16 Justin Martyr, *I Apology* 61 (ANF 1:183).
17 Jeremias, *Origins of Infant Baptism*, 39.

The most significant testimony from the second century comes from *Irenaeus*, who grew up in Asia Minor but was writing from Lyons in the early 180s. In the context of teaching that Christ sanctified every stage of life, he makes the following statement: 'For [Christ] came to save all through means of himself – all, I say, who through him are born again to God – infants, small children, youngsters, youths and old folk.'[18] Given his usage elsewhere, 'born again to God' must refer to baptism. Since infants are distinguished from small children and youngsters, the reference must be to those too young to speak. It is hard to see what Irenaeus can mean if infant baptism is not in mind.

The only substantial evidence for infant baptism from the second century is Irenaeus's statement, although there is the possibility that the instructions in the *Apostolic Tradition* go back to the middle of that century. But, as has been argued above, the evidence *for* the second century is not limited to evidence *from* the second century. Given the fact of tradition, one can draw conclusions from the statements of Tertullian and Origen in the third century about what was happening in the previous century. Finally, we cannot assume that there was one uniform policy. There may have been variations by region and according to individual choice.

First century

If the second-century evidence is weak, for the first we are reduced to hints. Most explicit are the household or family baptisms of Acts 16:15, 33 and 1 Corinthians 1:16. It seems clear that this was the baptism not just of several individuals but of a family unit. Did this include babies? It is hard to be certain. It is unlikely, but not impossible, that none of these families included babies. Other household passages can be taken as pointing the other way. Acts 18:8 refers to a whole family believing. Cornelius is told that it is through a message that his household will be saved (Acts 11:14) and it is implied that it is those who heard the message who received the Spirit and who then were baptized (10:44–48). Some will say that just as these passages must exclude babies, so also the reference to family baptisms cannot include infants. Others have suggested that the concept of the family as a unit means that babies could be referred to as believers. There are third-century epitaphs on the tombs of babies which refer to them as believing on the grounds that they were baptized.[19] The most natural reading of the references to household baptism, especially in the context of the Old Testament background, is that children were included. But this falls short of definite proof.

---

[18] *Against Heresies* 2:22:4 (ANF 1:391 [modified]).
[19] Ferguson, 'Inscriptions', 40.

Jewish proselyte baptism was given to the whole family, including the youngest children. But it was not given to children subsequently born into the family. It has been suggested, on the basis of 1 Corinthians 7:14, that this might mean that babies were baptized when a family converted but that future children were not baptized at all.[20] To suggest that such were never baptized is an interesting theoretical interpretation of that verse, but does not square with history. Paul addressed his readers on the assumption that they were all baptized, while the suggested policy would mean that at Rome, for example, there would by that stage have been young adult Christians who had not been and would never be baptized. There is no evidence in the sources that any group of people were ever exempted from the need to be baptized and such a policy would make nonsense of the New Testament theology of baptism. But the possibility that while existing children were baptized with their parents (as with proselyte baptism) subsequent children were baptized not then but at a later stage should not be discounted. If this were so we would have a variety of practices already in New Testament times and this would account for the non-dogmatic approach taken in the following three centuries.

Mark 10:13–16 has long been cited as a proof of infant baptism. Jesus urges the disciples to let the children come to him. They are not to be hindered, a term that already in the New Testament (Matt. 3:14; Acts 8:36; 10:47; 11:17) refers to obstacles to receiving baptism, and he lays hands upon them. Tertullian refers this to infant baptism, but it is unlikely to have that reference in Mark.

Did the apostolic church baptize babies?

So far we have looked for direct evidence for or against infant baptism. It is widely recognized that the surviving direct evidence does not enable a clear answer to be given until the last quarter of the second century. But our seismological approach provides an alternative way to answer the question. In the third and fourth centuries, the earliest period for which we have clear evidence, there was variety in practice. Christian children were baptized at every conceivable age. How can this variety be accounted for? There are three reasonable scenarios for the earliest apostolic church: either they did not baptize Christian babies or they did or there was already variety at this stage.

Which of these three scenarios is the most plausible, given the evidence? Consider the first scenario: that infants were not baptized. How is the later variety to be explained? Perhaps it began with emergency baptism of sick

---

[20] This passage is discussed by Wright, *Infant Baptism in Historical Perspective*, 13–17.

children and this led on to more regular infant baptism.[21] There is evidence from the inscriptions for the emergency baptism of small children, but the provision in the *Apostolic Tradition* is not for such. Also, there is no hint anywhere in the surviving Christian literature from the first five centuries that anyone objected *in principle* to infant baptism, that anyone considered it improper, irregular or invalid. If it was a post-apostolic innovation, this silence is remarkable. Tertullian sought to discourage infant baptism, but failed to use what would have been his most powerful argument – the claim that it was unapostolic.

Also, there is no single piece of evidence from the first two centuries of a child being brought up as a Christian and baptized at a later age. If the problem with infant baptism is *inconclusive* evidence that it happened in the first 150 years of the church, the problem with the alternative theory is *total lack* of evidence. It is true that the New Testament evidence for the baptism of infants is inconclusive, but at least there are passages which may plausibly be interpreted as implying that infants were baptized – such as Acts 16:33. By contrast there is no New Testament evidence at all for the later baptism of Christian children. There is no record of such a baptism and no hint in the epistles that such children should be seeking baptism.

Consider now the second scenario: that the earliest church did in fact baptize babies. While there is no unequivocal proof that this did happen, there is what can quite plausibly be seen as evidence of it. Whole households were baptized and these incidents can at least plausibly be seen as examples of infant baptism. It is also noteworthy that in the New Testament epistles the instruction given to the churches includes instruction to children (Eph. 6:1–4; Col. 3:20). These children are not encouraged or instructed to be baptized, nor are their parents instructed to work to that end. Instead the children are addressed as Christians, which fits best with the theory that they are baptized. But if the earliest practice was the baptism of infants, how is it that in later centuries not all Christian babies were baptized? Tertullian urges just such a change, on the ground of his fear of post-baptismal sin. If babies were baptized in the earliest church there is no difficulty in accounting for the later variation in practice. Those who delayed the baptism of their babies, not because of any objection in principle to infant baptism but for prudential reasons because of the fear of post-baptismal sin, would of course wish to have those children baptized should they fall ill and be in danger of death. Thus this theory also fully explains the existence of emergency baptism of children. But against it is the

---

[21] As is argued by Ferguson, 'Inscriptions', 44–46; *Baptism in the Early Church*, 377–379.

fact that Tertullian and others who urged delay in baptism were never accused of departing from the New Testament or from apostolic tradition.

The final scenario, variety of practice in the apostolic church is the most likely,[22] based on the later evidence and using our seismological approach. After all, the earliest *unequivocal* evidence for the initiation of Christian children comes from a time (early third century) when we know that there was variety of practice. What could have caused the variety? There are a number of options. We have already proposed the difference between babies born before and after their parents' baptism. Another option would be different policies for Jews, who circumcised their children, and Gentiles who did not. It is also possible that variety was introduced as the church spread into different places. The evidence from the New Testament that babies were baptized is impressive, though not conclusive. The evidence that *all* Christian babies were baptized is of course much weaker. While the New Testament offers no positive evidence for such a variety of practice, the later existence of a variety that is widespread, enduring and unchallenged leads us as seismologists to enquire about its origins and to ask whether it might not go back to the apostolic church. Such a hypothesis would explain the fact that we have no evidence for any objection in principle against either the baptism or the non-baptism of babies. This hypothesis is also supported by the fact that as far back as we have unequivocal evidence of how Christian children were initiated (early third century) we find variety. There is no evidence against the existence of such variety in the first and second centuries.

So what conclusion do we reach as twenty-first-century seismologists, drawing on the reports of witnesses from closer to the epicentre of the earthquake? The meagre evidence from the first two centuries is consistent with the practice of infant baptism but does not demand it. The evidence from the third and fourth centuries unambiguously reveals a diversity in practice where the initiation of Christian children is concerned. There is a total lack of evidence in the first four centuries of any objection *in principle* to either the baptism or the non-baptism of babies. Given this evidence, what is most likely to have occurred in the apostolic church? That the practice of infant baptism was unknown seems to me to be the least likely hypothesis. That it was practised seems very likely. That it was *universally* practised is much less likely given the freedom that later Christians felt not to baptize their children.

---

[22] Jeremias, *Infant Baptism in First Four Centuries*, 43–44, also postulates such variation.

14

Theologies of baptism and infant baptism

The early church

How did the early Christians understand the significance of baptism? From the very beginning baptism was seen as *effective* – that is, actually doing something. Giving someone baptism, like bestowing nationality on them,[1] makes a real difference, so it must be given with care. In particular, it was seen as bestowing regeneration and the forgiveness of *past* sins. Baptism was seen as necessary for salvation because 'unless one is born of water and the Spirit, he cannot enter the kingdom of God' (John 3:5). In his *First Apology*, Justin Martyr states that those who repent, believe and choose to be born again receive the forgiveness of *previous* sins. He states that through baptism they are born again, citing John 3:5.[2] Irenaeus, writing towards the end of the second century, states that through baptism we are made clean and are spiritually born again, also citing John 3:5. He draws an explicit parallel with the case of Naaman.[3] These statements are made with reference to converts' baptism. Because baptism was seen as obtaining forgiveness for past sins only, post-baptismal sins were a problem, leading many in due course to delay baptism until late in life so as to maximize its effect.

In the fourth century, after the conversion of the emperor Constantine, there was a flood of 'converts', as it suddenly became politically expedient to be a Christian. The problem then arose that people were signing up as catechumens preparing for baptism, but forever putting off being baptized and thus becoming subject to church discipline. They were trying to get the best of both worlds, claiming the name of Christian while remaining free of church discipline. They were urged not to delay their baptism, as if they died without being baptized they would not be saved. At this stage the norm remains the baptism of converts, although the process could be drawn out for years.

---

[1] I am grateful to Gerald Bray for this analogy.
[2] Justin Martyr, *I Apology* 61 (ANF 1:183).
[3] *Fragment* 34 (ANF 1:574).

What about infant baptism? Until the fourth century children fit into the existing pattern of converts' baptism, whether by being baptized or by being enrolled as catechumens. By the fifth century, with the conversion of the Roman Empire, adult baptism was becoming rarer and infant baptism becoming the norm. The significance of the efficacy of baptism changes as instant converts' baptism becomes delayed converts' baptism and eventually infant baptism. This shift encouraged a more mechanical view of the effects of baptism, now separated from conversion. This is illustrated by a story told by Augustine. In his Manichee years a friend became seriously ill and his concerned Christian parents had him baptized while he was unconscious. When he came round Augustine joked with him about this, but having been baptized he now rebuked Augustine. Augustine and his friend shared the assumption that baptism made a difference, even if one is unconscious at the time.[4]

Infants were seen to be born again in baptism. For many evangelicals this would seem to imply that baptized infants are guaranteed final salvation, but that is not how it would have been seen. Regeneration was seen more like the sowing of a seed, which needs to germinate and mature to bear fruit, the planting of a new life, which may or may not grow to salvation. Baptism did not cover post-baptismal sins.

Roman Catholicism

The traditional Roman Catholic view is set out at the Council of Trent,[5] and broadly follows the position of the early church as set out above. Baptism is valid if it is administered in the name of the Father, the Son and the Holy Spirit with the intention of doing what the church does.[6] Also baptism is necessary for salvation and is not an optional extra,[7] like the sun roof on a car, though the *desire* for baptism can suffice.[8] Those who are martyred before receiving baptism are deemed to have been baptized in their own blood. This baptism had the merit of excluding post-baptismal sin and any fear of lapse!

In Roman Catholicism there is an emphasis on salvation by baptism and the sacraments, and in the Middle Ages the church came to be seen like a pharmacy 'dispensing' salvation through the sacraments. The Jesuit missionaries who went to India and China in the sixteenth century had a simple

---

[4] Augustine, *Confessions* 4:4:8 (NPNF 1:70).
[5] *Decree Concerning the Sacraments* (1547) (Tanner (ed.), *Decrees of the Ecumenical Councils*, 2:684–686).
[6] Canon 4 concerning baptism.
[7] Canon 5 concerning baptism.
[8] *Decree on Justification*, ch. 4.

technique for conversion: they rang a hand bell so that people would gather round, then baptized them to turn them into Christians!

The traditional Roman Catholic view has been modified in recent years. It remains true that baptism is the way of entry into the church, but the Second Vatican Council (1962–65) recognized that sincere non-Christians, even atheists, can be saved.[9] This comes from a further extension of the principle of the baptism of desire and also the recognition that such folk can belong to the church by an implicit desire, even if they have no explicit knowledge of Christ or even God.

The Second Vatican Council also revealed a shift in the Roman Catholic view of salvation and the sacraments:

> [The sacraments] not only presuppose faith; they also nourish it, strengthen it and express it, both through words and through objects. This is why they are called sacraments of faith. It is true that they confer grace; but, while they are being celebrated, they are also very powerful in opening people up to receive this same grace fruitfully.[10]

These days there is a less mechanical view of the sacraments and less of a tendency to rely upon the sacraments alone.

Luther and Lutheranism

Luther held that baptism 'brings about forgiveness of sins, redeems from death and the devil, and gives eternal salvation to all who believe it, as the words and promise of God declare'. Through it we are born again to eternal life. Baptism is not just a sign but is an effective sign that accomplishes what it signifies. This is not because of the water, but because of the Word of God spoken at the time and because of faith.[11] But Luther differs from the Catholic view. Catholic teaching is that baptism is a one-off event that leads to instant regeneration and the forgiveness of past sins, which leads to issues with post-baptismal sins. For Luther, however, regeneration is a lifelong process that has a beginning but then continues to the end of this life. Luther accordingly saw baptism as acting and being effective throughout the whole of life, not just at one moment.

---

[9] *Lumen Gentium* 16; *Ad Gentes* 7; *Gaudium et Spes* 22 (Tanner (ed.), *Decrees of the Ecumenical Councils*, 2:861, 1017, 1082).

[10] *Sacrosanctum Concilium* 59 (Tanner (ed.), *Decrees of the Ecumenical Councils*, 2:832).

[11] Small Catechism (*BkConc* 359).

Luther vigorously defended infant baptism against the attacks of the Anabaptists. He conceded that it is not taught explicitly in Scripture but argued that it is compatible with Scripture. He appealed to the 'universal tradition' of the church. He also pointed out that if infant baptism is invalid, then for the majority of Christian history, when almost exclusively infants were baptized, there has been no baptism and therefore no church. Luther also defended infant baptism by an appeal to Mark 10:13–16.

But what about the doctrine of justification by faith? How did Luther manage to reconcile with it his doctrine of the regeneration of infants? His views on this topic changed over time. Until 1521 he appealed to the faith of the sponsors, those who bring the child to baptism, but he came to see that justification by the faith of another is not adequate. From 1522 Luther began to teach that infants could believe. It was not that infants were baptized because they believed but rather that infants believed because they were baptized. From the late 1520s Luther shifted his ground again. He continued to insist that it was possible for infants to believe, but held also that it was all right to baptize infants even if they did not believe until later. But their baptism would have no value unless they later believed and would have no value if they ceased to believe.[12]

Reformed views

Zwingli

There are a variety of Reformed views. Ulrich Zwingli (1484–1531) was the pioneer of Reformed theology. His view of baptism was very simple.[13] The sacraments in general, and baptism in particular, are simply signs, not effective means of grace. They are simply signs, but meaningful signs that testify to the work of Christ. They are powerful visual aids that assist and strengthen our faith. Zwingli went back to the original, pre-Christian meaning of the Latin word *sacramentum*. The sacraments are our oath or pledge of allegiance to Christ and thus the way in which we testify to the church that we are Christians. Zwingli opposed the idea that mere outward symbols can be spiritually effective. Their effect is simply their psychological effect as signs.

There are two sides to this stance. On the one side there is a healthy reaction against medieval superstition, against a reliance upon outward rites with an

---

[12] Large Catechism (*BkConc* 462–467).
[13] See Stephens, *Theology of Huldrych Zwingli*, 180–217.

inadequate concern for the inward attitude of the heart. This concern Zwingli shared with all of the Reformers. But Zwingli took this a step further. With him there is also a divorce between the physical and the spiritual, a divorce that owes more to Platonist Greek philosophy than to the Bible. Zwingli seems to be more 'spiritual' than the Bible, in whose pages God clearly works through physical things.

Given Zwingli's view of baptism one cannot help asking what is the point of infant baptism. If baptism is a personal testimony of our Christian faith and pledge of allegiance to Christ, what sense does it make to baptize babies? This question occurred to a number of Zwingli's colleagues at Zurich. One major strand of the sixteenth-century Anabaptist movement was composed of those at Zurich who in the early 1520s took Zwingli's teaching in a more radical direction – to its logical conclusion, as they saw it.[14] Zwingli himself 'wobbled' on the question of infant baptism for a while, but drew back from the brink and defended it, being prepared to put his former colleagues to death over the issue. Ultimately the choice was between a state church to which all belong and a gathered church of voluntary disciples. Zwingli's commitment to the principle of a state church was strong enough to override any hesitations that might have arisen from his definition of a sacrament.

Calvin

Today many Protestants take for granted a Zwinglian view of the sacraments in general and of baptism in particular, but it was very much a minority view in Reformation times. The 1560 *Scots Confession of Faith*, written by John Knox and others, states that 'we utterly damn the vanity of those that affirm sacraments to be nothing else but naked and bare signs'.[15]

On the issue of baptism Calvin stood somewhere between Luther and Zwingli. His view of the sacraments was 'higher' than Zwingli's.[16] The sacrament in general, and baptism in particular, is a 'visible Word', God's word or promise set forth in visible form, just as preaching is God's word in an audible form. There is a strict parallel between the two. When the gospel is preached we hear forgiveness of sins offered, which becomes ours when we receive it with faith; likewise in baptism the washing with water signifies the offer of forgiveness of sins, which becomes ours when we receive it with faith. As with Luther, this faith can come later, so infant baptism is acceptable. A sacrament is an outward sign by which God seals on our consciences the

---

[14] See Pearse, *Great Restoration*, 44–55.
[15] Scots Confession Article 21 (*RefConf* 2:201).
[16] *Inst.* 4:14.

promises of his goodwill and we respond by confessing our faith. It is primarily God's act, though our response is also important.

Unlike most in the sixteenth century, Calvin recognizes that believers' baptism is the norm and in his *Institutes* treats this first, before devoting a chapter to the defence of infant baptism.[17] Baptism is a sign of initiation, *signifying* forgiveness of sins and regeneration; but it is not a *mere* (empty) sign. In baptism God offers us the reality that it signifies, which we have to receive by faith. Baptism is a sign of initiation by which we are received into the church, engrafted into Christ and reckoned as God's children.[18] It signifies the forgiveness of sins, union with Christ, death, burial and resurrection with him and regeneration.[19] For its efficacy, we need to look beyond the outward sign. The one who gives the sacrament is not the human minister but God himself and he gives us not just the outward sign but also the reality signified. While baptism is more than an empty sign (against Zwingli), it is not to be seen as magical (against Rome). It has no power of its own to separate from Christ and the Gospel.[20] It has no value apart from faith and benefits only those who receive it with faith, but this faith need not come at the moment of baptism and may come later, as with infants. Like Luther, Calvin sees baptism as pointing to a lifelong cleansing from sin, not simply to a once-for-all cleansing from past sins only.[21]

Covenant Theology

From Zwingli on the main (though not only) justification for infant baptism within the Reformed tradition has been Covenant Theology.[22] There is a close-knit argument with five main points:

1 God made a Covenant of Grace with Abraham, based on faith not works (e.g. Gen. 12:1–7; cf. Gal. 3:6). Circumcision was later added as the sign of this covenant (Gen. 17:1–14). Children were included in this covenant and males received circumcision.

2 The New Covenant in Christ (promised in Jer. 31:31–34) is essentially the same Covenant of Grace promised to Abraham. The classic New Testament passage where this is found is Galatians 3:15–29, where we

---

[17] *Inst.* 4:15, 16.
[18] *Inst.* 4:15:1.
[19] *Inst.* 4:15:2–6.
[20] *Inst.* 4:15:2.
[21] *Inst.* 4:15:3.
[22] Marcel, *Biblical Doctrine of Infant Baptism*, is a classic statement of the argument; Jewett, *Infant Baptism and Covenant of Grace*, opposes it.

read that Christ is the seed promised in Genesis 12:7 (3:16). So there is only *one* covenant of grace throughout Old and New Testaments.

3 There are differences in administration between the Old and New Covenants. They come in different dispensations and have different sacraments.

4 Baptism replaces circumcision as the sign and seal of the covenant, as the sacrament of initiation (Col. 2:11–12). Circumcision and baptism have the same function and meaning.

5 There is one sole Covenant of Grace and baptism replaces circumcision as the sacrament of initiation. It follows that the children of believers are also in the New Covenant (Acts 2:39)[23] and are therefore to be baptized.

This is a close-knit argument and also one that depends upon every stage. If any one link snaps, the chain as a whole fails. In fact a number of the links are rather weak.

Regarding the third point, there are indeed 'differences in administration' and these are not insubstantial. The material promise of land is changed to a purely spiritual inheritance, at least for this life. The covenant with the elect nation has become a covenant with the elect from every nation. Circumcision is like a passport – with the differences that it cannot be lost and need not be renewed every ten years, but is more embarrassing to produce when required! These are major differences and not without significance for the point at issue.

Regarding the fourth point, is it true that baptism replaces circumcision? This is not stated as such in Colossians 2:11–12, nor anywhere else in the New Testament. If Paul had thought so, Galatians would have been a lot shorter. All he had to say against the Judaizers (who were trying to persuade Gentile believers that they needed to be circumcised) was 'What is the point of Gentiles being circumcised? By baptism they have already received the sacrament of initiation into the one Covenant of Grace. Circumcision is also the sacrament of initiation into that same covenant, so what is the point in giving to Gentiles what they have already received?' If it was true that baptism had simply replaced circumcision that would be a knockdown argument against the Judaizers – but Paul never hints at it, never affirms the identity between circumcision and baptism. Again, Jews who were converted received baptism. But if baptism, like circumcision, is the sacrament of initiation into the one Covenant of Grace, why baptize circumcised Jews? And why did Paul

---

[23] Acts 2:39 does not end with 'your children' but goes on to include 'all who are far off'.

circumcise Timothy (Acts 16:3)? Jewish believers were never told not to circumcise their children.

Of course there are parallels and similarities between circumcision and baptism. At least in some sense it is true that baptism has replaced circumcision in that one becomes a Christian today by baptism just as one once (and still) becomes a Jew by circumcision. But this does not mean that there is a simple identity or that one has simply replaced the other. The Covenant Theology argument relies for its force upon such a substantial identity.

In the Reformed tradition the idea of covenant is often seen as a controlling theological principle. Although this was arguably so in the Old Testament, the idea of covenant does not have the same controlling position in the New Testament. Finally, it is noteworthy that baptism in the New Testament is never explicitly linked with the idea of covenant. Ironically it is the Lord's Supper, not baptism, that is so linked (1 Cor. 11:25). The idea of covenant is not central to the New Testament in the way that it is central to Covenant Theology or, indeed, to the Old Testament. Covenant Theology seeks to defend infant baptism by putting it into an overarching scheme that is foreign to the New Testament approach to baptism.

But suppose for the moment there is only one Covenant of Grace, that baptism does simply replace circumcision, that baptism is the sacrament of initiation into the New Covenant. There still remain important differences in administration that effect the question of who receives baptism. Women are baptized whereas they were not circumcised. The people of God in the Old Testament were an elect nation and one normally enters a nation at birth. There is no nation on earth that treats its children as stateless until they reach mature years and then invites them to choose whether or not to join. The people of God in the New Testament, however, form not an elect nation but the elect from all nations. Given these differences and the differences in administration, it is far from inevitable that children will be baptized because they were circumcised. So because of these differences we cannot just assume that babies must be baptized because (male) babies in Old Testament days were circumcised.

There is, however, some value in the Covenant Theology argument. It could be argued that for the early Jewish converts, faced with the question of what to do with their children, the 'default setting' would have been to baptize them. In other words, they would have assumed that it was right to baptize them unless there was some strong reason to the contrary.[24] It is also true that at

---

[24] Letham, *Systematic Theology*, 721, comments that if infants were denied baptism, 'Pentecost would have been the greatest occasion of mass excommunication in history'!

least some of the arguments used by Baptist polemicists against infant baptism would, if true, equally invalidate infant circumcision. For example, if it is in principle meaningless to perform a ritual ceremony on an unaware infant, then it is meaningless to circumcise unaware infants and so the command to circumcise infants must also have been mistaken. But since the Old Testament clearly commanded the circumcision of infants, the argument must be faulty.[25]

Baptist views

The Baptist approach was pioneered by the sixteenth-century Anabaptists and in the following century was taken over by the Baptists. 'Baptist' in the present context is not used in a narrow denominational sense but to describe those who baptize only those who profess faith for themselves. As well as Baptists in the denominational sense this includes Pentecostals, Brethren and many others.[26]

A representative example of the Baptist approach is found in the 1632 Mennonite *Dordrecht Confession*. Article 7 runs as follows:

> We confess that all penitent believers, who through faith, the new birth and renewal of the Holy Spirit have become united with God . . . must on such Scriptural confession of their faith, and renewal of life, according to the command and doctrine of Christ . . . be baptised with water . . . to the burying of their sins and thus to be become incorporated into the communion of the saints.[27]

It is clear from this statement that of the four elements of Christian initiation, it is three only that effect salvation and that the fourth (baptism) follows on later as a testimony to what has already happened.

Most Baptists follow this Zwinglian approach to the sacraments, seeing them as merely symbolic. Baptism follows repentance, faith, union with Christ, and so on, as a symbol of what has *already* happened. This was expressed in an unfortunate manner by the Baptist theologian A. H. Strong, who described baptism as a symbol of an already existing union, like a wedding service![28] This analogy might have more appeal in an age where many couples cohabit before getting married, but that is hardly what Strong had in mind. The point about a wedding, whether in a church or in a registry office, is that two

---

[25] Calvin makes this point in *Inst.* 4:16:20.
[26] Barth and Moltmann, two hugely significant theologians from the twentieth-century European Reformed churches, both opposed the practice of infant baptism.
[27] Leith (ed.), *Creeds of the Churches*, 298.
[28] Strong, *Systematic Theology*, 946.

individuals enter as single people and emerge as a married couple. On any reckoning a wedding is not just a symbol of an already existing union but itself creates a new form of union. We shall shortly see a happier use of this analogy by another Baptist theologian.

The traditional Baptist approach also views baptism as our response to what God has done in our lives, as our confession of faith. Another traditional emphasis (found in the *Dordrecht Confession*, for instance) is upon baptism as an act of obedience. While in theory any Christian might choose to describe baptism as an act of obedience, in fact it is exclusively those with a Zwinglian view of the sacraments who choose to emphasize this. Since baptism does not actually *do* anything some reason must be given for observing it; hence the emphasis on obedience. There does not seem to be much point in doing it, but we shall do it anyway because it has been commanded! Another implication of the belief that baptism effects and conveys nothing is that there is no point in baptizing infants.

Alongside the majority view there is also a minority Baptist view that rejects the Zwinglian position.[29] George Beasley-Murray argues that the New Testament portrays baptism as being effective.[30] If this is so, what does it mean for the efficacy (or otherwise) of delayed post-conversion baptism? This question needs to be answered by all who wish to see baptism as more than just symbolic. One recent Baptist theologian who wrestles with this is Stanley Grenz. He presents baptism as a response to the Gospel, as a public confession of faith, an oath of fidelity (like Zwingli returning to the original meaning of *sacramentum*). Baptism is like the public vows made at a wedding and the Holy Spirit uses it to strengthen our commitment to Christ.[31] More generally, the sacraments are channels of the Holy Spirit at work in our lives. They are ways of acting out our faith symbolically and the Holy Spirit uses them to facilitate our participation in the realities signified.[32] Grenz is clearly feeling his way towards a position that goes beyond the 'mere symbolism' of the traditional Baptist Zwinglianism.[33]

Baptism, eucharist and ministry

Perhaps the most significant document ever produced by the World Council of Churches (WCC) is *Baptism, Eucharist and Ministry* (*BEM*). This was produced

---

[29] For a history of this minority position, see Fowler, *More than a Symbol*.
[30] Beasley-Murray, *Baptism in the New Testament*, ch. 5.
[31] Grenz, *Theology for Community of God*, 684–685.
[32] Grenz, *Theology for Community of God*, 672–673.
[33] In personal conversation he confirmed the accuracy of this description.

at Lima, Peru, in 1982, under the auspices of the Faith and Order Commission of the WCC. It was the culmination of over fifty years of discussions – not that the same participants were involved throughout the fifty years! A very wide range of churches took part. These included not just the member churches of the WCC (such as the Eastern Orthodox Churches, the Anglican Church, Lutherans, Reformed, Baptists, Pentecostals, Salvation Army), but also the Roman Catholic Church and evangelical churches not belonging to the WCC. The document states where there is perceived common ground and also points to areas of difference.

Infant baptism is the most obvious bone of contention. Baptism on personal profession of faith is, they claim, the most widely attested pattern in the New Testament and it is uncertain whether infant baptism was also practised at that time (§11).[34] The document discerns two rival patterns used today: infant dedication leading to baptism with faith at a later age versus infant baptism leading to a later personal response (§§11–12). Both of these require a similar and responsible attitude towards Christian nurture (Comm. §12). Mutual recognition is encouraged (§15). Some churches actually practise both patterns, regarding them as 'equivalent alternatives'.

> In some churches which unite both infant-baptist and believer-baptist traditions, it has been possible to regard as equivalent alternatives for entry into the church both a pattern whereby baptism in infancy is followed by later profession of faith and a pattern whereby believer baptism follows upon a presentation and blessing in infancy. (Comm. §12)

Baptists are urged to express more visibly the fact that children are placed under the protection of God's care. Paedobaptists, by contrast, are urged to guard against 'apparently indiscriminate baptism' and also to take more seriously their responsibility to nurture baptized children to a mature commitment to Christ (§16).

BEM also rejects anything 'which might be interpreted as rebaptism' (§13). This condemnation has two targets: Roman Catholic 'conditional baptism' and Baptist 'rebaptism'. Many Baptists are unhappy with *BEM* at this point and feel that the Baptist delegates at Lima had conceded too much.

At the beginning *BEM* invites the churches to study it and to respond officially (p. x). An important response came from the World Evangelical Fellowship (WEF).[35] This engages well with *BEM* at a number of points, but itself has a serious weakness. *BEM* appealed to 'the faith of the Church through

---

[34] This statement is too sceptical about infant baptism for some people, too generous for others!
[35] Schrotenboer (ed.), *Evangelical Response to* Baptism, Eucharist and Ministry.

the ages' as an authority (p. x). The WEF criticizes this and insists that Scripture should be normative. This would be fine if they had themselves followed that policy. But in fact they repeatedly reject statements in *BEM* on the grounds that 'most evangelicals' disagree. This is simply to replace 'the faith of the Church through the ages' by 'the view of most evangelicals today'. For example, *BEM* speaks of baptism effecting things. The WEF objects to this not on the grounds that it is unscriptural (it is not!) but that 'few evangelicals' can accept it. It seems that Scripture is authoritative only where it can claim a majority evangelical vote to confirm it. The document in effect rejects *BEM* on the grounds not that it is unscriptural but that it contradicts evangelical tradition. This is a legitimate point for such a document to make, but not while at the same time criticizing *BEM* for its appeal to 'the faith of the Church through the ages'. As David Wright put it eloquently, 'We balk at the indicatives of *Baptism, Eucharist and Ministry* when it is the indicatives of the New Testament that truly bother us.'[36]

Dual practice

Discussions of infant baptism are often polarized. Should children be baptized as babies or at some later stage when they have a personal faith? This is to present two stark alternatives, while there is in fact far more common ground between the two sides than is often recognized. In some churches there is some sort of dedication ceremony after the birth of the child, followed by many years of Christian nurture within the church, concluding (if all goes well) with the grown-up child making a personal public confession of faith in baptism. In other churches the newborn baby is baptized, followed by many years of Christian nurture within the church, concluding (if all goes well) with the grown-up child making a personal public confession of faith in an adult ceremony that may or may not be called confirmation. For those raised in a Christian home, both infant baptism and adult baptism are not isolated events but simply one stage in a lengthy process. To lose this perspective makes any resolution of the issue much harder and effectively impossible. For example, attempts to defend infant baptism as itself complete initiation (rather than the beginning of a process of initiation) are misguided.

As regards the timing of baptism these two strategies are diametrically opposed; apart from that they are remarkably similar. That is why Baptists and

---

[36] Wright, *Infant Baptism in Historical Perspective*, 369. The indicatives he is referring to are statements like 'as many of you as were baptized into Christ have put on Christ' (Gal. 3:27).

Paedobaptists are able to cooperate happily in so many areas without serious tension. In Britain teams work with children at the 'Spring Harvest' Christian family week events without anyone knowing (or caring) whether or not the children attending have been baptized. Those who offer to help in this work are not asked whether they are Baptist or Paedobaptist. Why not? Is this a heroic determination to cooperate despite serious differences? Or is it because the question both seems and is all but totally irrelevant to what is taking place? The programme of Christian nurture, that which takes place between the first and second 'rite', is not significantly different for baptized and unbaptized children. That is why those who publish Bible reading notes for children do not provide separate sets for those who have or have not been baptized.[37]

It is reasonable to regard both of the strategies outlined above as different, but legitimate, adaptations of the converts' baptism of Acts to the changed situation of the nurture of children in a Christian home.[38] Both demand a programme of Christian nurture that, in the last resort, is more important than any of the ceremonies. But how feasible is it to expect churches to treat the two strategies as 'equivalent alternatives'? Many will regard this as hopelessly idealistic,[39] but that is not so. In the first place, wherever we have clear evidence in the early centuries we see children of Christian families were being baptized at every conceivable age. Indeed there is no evidence from the early church that the situation was ever different nor that anyone ever denied the legitimacy of such variety. Also, the dual practice approach has not been unknown in recent centuries. In seventeenth-century England a group of Baptist churches began to accept either practice and the church at Bedford, now named after Bunyan, has maintained this approach down to the present day.[40]

Many if not most Paedobaptist churches today accept the fact that not all Christian parents wish to have their children baptized and make provision for alternative ceremonies such as dedication. The Anglican church today takes this approach and even Roman Catholics have toyed with it.[41] But while Paedobaptists have never denied the validity of believers' baptism, many Baptists regard infant baptism as no baptism at all, or at best highly irregular.

---

[37] On the other hand, the happy cooperation may be because both sides have such a low view of baptism. I am grateful to Bob Letham for pointing this out.

[38] As I argue in Wright (ed.), *Baptism: Three Views*, 139–171.

[39] As does Grudem, *Systematic Theology*, 982–983.

[40] Pearse, *Great Restoration*, 212–213.

[41] E.g. Béguerie and Duchesneau, *How to Understand the Sacraments*, 121–122, citing the pattern of the early centuries, although they are over-optimistic in claiming that 'the church has always known this diversity of positions'. CCC §1250 rejects the idea.

This makes it harder for Baptists to come to terms with the dual practice approach. Accepting the legitimacy of infant baptism is an issue for modern Baptists in a way that it was not for those in the early church who chose not to baptize their babies.

15

Issues behind infant baptism

The majority of discussions concerning the validity of infant baptism focus heavily or exclusively on the question of whether or not the New Testament teaches it, for which see chapter 13. This is obviously a crucial issue, as is the wider question of whether or not it is consistent with the New Testament theology of baptism. But there are also other important theological issues that bear on the question.[1]

Efficacy

How does God work? Are spiritual benefits received *purely* inwardly, spiritually or are they *also* linked to physical things and physical actions – as with the healing of Naaman? This is a fundamental question that affects one's approach not just to infant baptism but also to many other issues. Are the sacraments purely symbolic or are they effective signs through which God works? The former view makes life much simpler. There are no problems with coordinating the efficacy of faith and the sacrament, no questions about the status of someone who has the one but not the other, no dilemmas about situations where the two are separated by a substantial time gap. But is this view biblical? As we saw in chapter 12, the New Testament does not appear to treat baptism as purely symbolic.

So how does God's action through the sacraments relate to the need for faith? There is no problem where the two come at the same time, as with the converts' baptisms of Acts. But what about situations where coming to faith and receiving baptism are substantially separated in time, as with those baptized either in infancy or some years after coming to faith? This question has to be answered by all who would ascribe some efficacy to baptism. Lutherans and Calvinists see baptism as a means of grace, but not effective without faith. The timing issue is resolved by saying that baptism is effective *throughout*

---

[1] There is a vast body of literature on the rights and wrongs of infant baptism. For two books that set out different views in dialogue with one another, see Armstrong (ed.), *Understanding Four Views on Baptism*; Wright (ed.), *Baptism: Three Views*. This chapter draws in part on my material from Wright (ed.), *Baptism: Three Views*, 163–171.

the life of the believer, not just at the moment when it is given. This resolves the question of timing and escapes the Catholic problem of post-baptismal sin, but is this how the New Testament portrays baptism? Does the New Testament support the idea that baptism is efficacious at the moment of reception or throughout life?

The question of timing is also answered by seeing infant baptism both as a pointer to and as an example of prevenient grace. We turn to God because he has already, by his Holy Spirit, been at work in our lives drawing us to Christ. Infant baptism can be seen as part of this process in the lives of those receiving Christian nurture. Baptists who believe firmly in prevenient grace would, however, question whether this is the significance of *baptism* in the New Testament. In the case of those baptized some time after conversion, baptism can be understood as God's seal upon our faith,[2] ratifying and strengthening it.

Some would argue that the question of infant baptism is tied to that of efficacy. They would argue that if baptism achieves nothing, there is no point in baptizing infants, while if it does achieve something it is wrong to deny baptism to infants. There is some truth in this in that the majority of those believing in the efficacy of baptism would support infant baptism and the majority of Baptists would see infant baptism as wrong because baptism is essentially a declaration of what has *already* happened. But it should be noted that Zwinglian paedobaptists believe in infant baptism while denying that it actually achieves anything. Also this discussion assumes that the issue is the efficacy or otherwise of baptism as an isolated event, while if one thinks in terms of the whole process of initiation, that question is partly defused.

Whose work?

Zwinglians (which includes most Baptists) see baptism as something we do. It is our confession of faith and our act of commitment. The other traditions see baptism primarily as God's act, as a gift we receive. It is a means of grace, God's promise, his seal upon our faith. But this is not, contrary to the way in which it is sometimes portrayed, a complete contrast. Zwinglians see baptism as our act – but in response to what God has already done for and in us. Others see baptism as God's act – but also insist that we need to make a personal response of faith. There is a difference regarding the significance of baptism, but it is wrong to suggest that Zwinglians have a Pelagian view that excludes God's work in our lives. It is just that Zwinglians do not see *baptism* as part of that work.

---

[2] As is said of circumcision in Rom. 4:11.

Status of Christian children

Are the children of Christians to be viewed as Christians or as pagans? Sometimes the question is posed in this stark way.[3] But the truth of the matter is not so simple. In practice Christians do not treat their children as pagans. They take their children to church. They teach them to pray – and teach them to pray specifically Christian prayers. If a 9-year-old comes back from school uttering blasphemous expletives he is told that is not acceptable in this household. Again, in practice evangelical Christians do not treat their little children as full-fledged Christians. However high their view of infant baptism (even if, like Luther, they believe in baptismal regeneration) they recognize that the child will need to come to a personal commitment as it grows up. As society becomes more secular, as Christendom becomes more and more a thing of the past, as purely nominal Christianity becomes rarer, this truth is recognized increasingly by Christians across the spectrum. Catholic Christians may once have emphasized that children become Christians at baptism; today they increasingly acknowledge the need for this to become 'interiorized' as a personal decision if the child is going to grow up to be a practising Christian.[4] What was once very much an evangelical distinctive (the need for conversion) is becoming much more widely acknowledged.

There are two sides to the picture. Just as we talk of Jewish, Muslim and Hindu children, so we can also talk of Christian children – that is, those being nurtured in a Christian home. But in the modern secular world parents who presume upon this and imagine their children as being already 'home and dry' are liable to have a rude awakening.

Church membership

Is church membership for adults only, or are baptized people of *all* ages full members of the church? Paedobaptists tend towards the latter view. On this issue the rubber hits the road with respect to taking communion; is it right for, say, a 5-year-old to take communion? Those holding to adult believers' baptism will usually think it right for children to wait until they have made a personal commitment to Christ.

The issue of the status of children poses itself in an acute way for Baptists. What is the status of unbaptized, believing children? The New Testament knows

---

[3] This is a question Colin Buchanan liked to pose in debates on infant baptism.
[4] E.g. Béguerie and Duchesneau, *How to Understand the Sacraments*, 121.

nothing of unbaptized Christians. At what age should children be baptized? This is a dilemma for Baptists. If they emphasize *believers* baptism, why not baptize believing children of 3, 5 or 7 years old, as do the Southern Baptists in the USA? But since children of that age will believe whatever their parents tell them, this policy is no more effective than infant baptism in excluding nominal Christianity or in requiring a truly personal adult faith. If, on the other hand, they emphasize *adult* believers baptism, as do virtually all British Baptists, they have the problem of believers who are denied baptism for up to ten years. This causes no problems for those Baptists who have reduced baptism to a declarative adult public testimony, but is more of a problem for those who take seriously the full New Testament theology of baptism, as set out in chapter 12.

Individual versus corporate

It is significant that the Baptist view emerged and grew in popularity at the same time as the rise of modern Western individualism. The Baptist model is of the baptism of independent autonomous individuals. How should this be assessed? Is the Baptist view a skilful contextualization of the gospel into modern Western society in a culture where people *do* mostly operate as individuals? Or is it an accommodation of the gospel that betrays it to modern Western individualistic culture? The trouble is that one person's contextualization can be another person's accommodation! It would in fact be possible consistently to argue that the early church did baptize infants, that universal infant baptism was a legitimate policy during the period of Christendom when children were reared in a Christian environment, but that in the climate of today's postmodern and individualistic culture the best policy is not to baptize infants.[5]

Baptists will of course protest that it is the gospel, not modern individualism, that urges the individual to put loyalty to God and Christ above loyalty to the family (e.g. Matt. 10:35–37; 12:46–50). This is true, but similar demands are found in the Old Testament, when infants were circumcised, and it remains true that the understanding of these passages to exclude infant baptism came with the rise of individualism.

Paedobaptists lay greater stress on the corporate side of salvation. They would point to the way in which God, in the Old Testament, deals not just with individuals but with families, as with Noah and, supremely, Abraham. Old Testament faith and religion were a family and community matter, not just an

---

[5] Bradshaw, 'Profession of Faith in Early Christian Baptism', ties the issue of whether or not to baptize infants to the question of what decisions it is deemed in a particular culture that parents may appropriately make on behalf of their children.

individual matter. They would see the household baptisms of Acts as being the baptism of a family unit, not just of a collection of individuals all of whom happened to believe. Infant baptism has also, historically, been linked with the doctrine of original sin – either doctrine offering support to the other as the need arose! The doctrine of original sin implies that sin is not purely individual, that there is such a thing as the corporate sin of the human race. Babies are not born totally innocent. This used to provide a compelling motivation for infant baptism when it was feared that infants dying unbaptized would be lost. Indeed, Baptists have argued that infant baptism arose because of a misguided fear of infant damnation. Today, however, the majority of Christians would not accept that dying unbaptized excluded babies from salvation.[6]

Relation between Old and New Testaments

There is a famous tract that reads on the outside, 'What the Bible teaches about infant baptism.' When it is opened the inside pages turn out to be empty![7] It is a clever ploy, but the tract is based upon a particular assumption – that the answer to this question is to be sought in the New Testament alone. Others would want to place some emphasis on the teaching of the Old Testament and, especially, on the fact that infants were circumcised.[8] The question of the relation between the testaments is important and determines people's attitudes on a variety of issues, such as the significance of the Sabbath law, pacifism, the possibility of a state church, and so on. Usually it functions as an *unacknowledged* presupposition, meaning that people are unable to agree because they are arguing from different premises.

In fact all Christians would agree that there is both an element of continuity between the testaments (at the very least, they are both about the same God) and an element of discontinuity (Christians no longer offer animal sacrifices, for example). Where Christians differ is how much weight to put on continuity or discontinuity. Mennonites, for example, stress the discontinuity, emphasizing the newness of the New Covenant. They are pacifists, do not baptize babies, and so on. The Reformed, by contrast, lay more stress on the continuity, baptizing babies and not generally being pacifists. On the issue of baptism,

---

[6] The *Catechism of the Catholic Church* states of children dying without baptism, 'the Church can only entrust them to the mercy of God, as she does in her funeral rites for them', expressing hope that there is a way of salvation for them (§1261).

[7] I have not myself seen such a tract, but a number of people have told me that they have seen them.

[8] Some would also want to point to New Testament passages like the household baptisms.

those emphasizing the continuity between the testaments will stress the one covenant of grace, while those emphasizing the discontinuity will stress the novelty of the *New* Covenant.

Silences of Scripture

The front page of the tract could instead have read, more prosaically, 'What the New Testament teaches about the initiation of children brought up in a Christian home.' There is no explicit answer to this question in the New Testament, though there is material (such as the family baptisms) that can be interpreted as supporting one side or the other. Opponents of infant baptism will correctly point out that there are no documents before the third century that explicitly refer to infant baptism. But it is equally true that there are no documents before the third century that propose the non-baptism of Christian babies. The silence is not just a silence about infant baptism; it is a silence about the church's policy towards Christian babies.

What do we make of this silence in the New Testament? It could so easily have been resolved. All that was needed was the addition of a brief phrase to Acts 16:33. After 'he and all his family were baptized' Luke could have added, 'babies, children and adults', or 'all who were old enough to answer for themselves', or 'all who had reached adulthood', or some other such clause. But it is not there. Why not? Should we regard the silences of Scripture as being as much inspired as the positive statements? Are the silences there in order to leave the church liberty to vary its practice to suit different circumstances?[9] Do they sanction the variety of practices we see in the fourth-century church for instance?

Historical evidence or burden of proof

It is clear that there is no explicit evidence about infant baptism until, at the earliest, the last quarter of the second century. How does one interpret this? Upon which side lies the burden of proof? One line of argument would be that, given the Jewish background infant baptism was all but inevitable. The early Jewish converts were used to infant circumcision and to the Proselyte baptism of infants. They also held to a strongly corporate belief in the solidarity of the family and came from an Old Testament belief that God worked not so much through individuals as through families. Given this background, it is argued,

---

[9] The suggestion is that God might have intended it for this reason, not that this was Luke's motive.

it would have taken an explicit command to prevent the early disciples from baptizing their infants.

Against this must be set the clear evidence that in the third and fourth centuries not all Christian children were baptized. Tombstones which indicate that little children were baptized as death approached equally bear witness to the fact these children had not been baptized as babies. Why not? Given the cultural situation, with the emphasis on family solidarity, is it more likely that infant baptism would be introduced where it did not previously exist (e.g. via emergency baptism of dying infants) or that it would be dropped where it did already exist? On the other hand, it is significant that Tertullian, when he opposed the baptism of children, made no accusation that the practice was a recent innovation. Had he had the slightest suspicion that it was, he would hardly have failed to employ that argument! The opposition to infant baptism and the policy of delaying baptism were based not on the belief that infant baptism was invalid or unapostolic but rather on the belief that it was imprudent because of the difficulty of post-baptismal sin.

Many Baptists would interpret the silence of the New Testament differently. They would argue that the New Testament view of baptism demands a response of faith at the moment of baptism. In Acts, repentance, faith, baptism and receiving the Spirit do not always happen in the same order, but faith does always precede baptism.

The role of diversity

There are some practical issues where the individual must make a choice, but the church can benefit from diversity. An individual cannot at the same time be both married and single. But it is important for the church both that the majority of Christians marry and form Christian families and that a minority remain celibate, like Jesus and Paul, and bear witness to the transcendent values of the kingdom. Again, no individual can both fight and be a pacifist, yet both witness to important aspects of truth. A church composed solely of pacifists would be dangerously out of touch with society; yet a church all of whose members were prepared to fight would have lost an important strand of biblical truth. A related issue is the value of the study of theology both in the public arena, in secular universities and in the confessional setting of the seminary. Each has its complementary strengths and weaknesses and there would be a loss to the church if either ceased to exist. In short, there are practical areas where no one policy can bear witness to the fullness of truth, where different Christians may have contradictory callings and yet together bear witness to the full range of God's truth.

So also with this subject. Any one Christian baby is either baptized or is not, but it is valuable for the church that both policies are followed. Paedobaptists bear witness against the individualism of the postmodern age and point to God's prevenient grace, his dealings with families. Baptists, by contrast, bear witness against the scourge of nominal Christianity and remind us that in the strict sense God has no grandchildren. Believers' baptism warns against the dangers of a second-hand faith, whereas infant baptism can lead those raised in Christian homes to become nominal Christians imagining that they are already Christians without making a personal response of faith.

Each policy leads to anomalies. Infant baptism means the baptism of some who will grow up to be unbelievers. This has become especially scandalous because of the practice of indiscriminate infant baptism, with the result that in Europe tens of millions are baptized but have hardly ever set foot in a church. The problem is far less acute if infant baptism is restricted to those who are going to receive a Christian upbringing, yet even with such there is no guarantee they will in due course come to a living personal faith. But this problem is not confined to Paedobaptists. There is unfortunately no shortage of people who have been baptized as believers but have subsequently abandoned their faith. Also, on the Baptist model there is the anomaly of children who have a living faith but are unbaptized, a situation foreign to the New Testament concept of converts' baptism. The situation is less acute for those who genuinely hold to *believers'* baptism (being ready to baptize four-year-old believers, for example) than for those who believe only in *adult* believers' baptism (being unwilling to baptize believers under twelve years old, or whatever other age has been decreed).

Part 3

BEING PUT RIGHT WITH GOD: JUSTIFICATION

16
Two models of justification

Introduction

In English we have two different families of words, relating to justice and right-eousness. The one family, derived from the Latin and French, includes words like 'just', 'justice', 'justify', 'justification'. The other family, derived from the German, includes words like 'righteous' and 'righteousness', but has no word equivalent to 'justify'. In modern English there are nuances of differences in the meaning given to each family of words, but in the Greek, and also in Latin, there is only one family of words, not two. So English complicates the issue by forcing one to opt for one or other of the two families, where no such requirement or option existed in the original languages. Catholic writers generally use only the 'justice' family of words, which has the advantage that it is clear that 'just', 'justice' and 'justify' all have the same root. My own view is that given the nuances of the words 'just' and 'justice' today it is best to use the words 'righteous' and 'righteousness', while also referring to 'justify' and 'justification'. The important point is to remember that in the original languages there is just the one family of words.

Catholic model of justification

In the early church, from the second to the fourth centuries, there was little interest in the doctrine of justification. It then came into prominence with the controversy between Augustine and Pelagius, most especially in the former's *The Spirit and the Letter*, on which see chapter 7, above. This was one of Augustine's best works, and after the Bible was the most influential book during the Reformation. It is all about how we can be justified.

Definition of justification

What did Augustine mean by 'justify'? He understood it to mean 'make right-eous' in the sense of changing someone from being unrighteous to righteous.

This is what Protestants today would call 'regeneration', being 'born again', being 'sanctified'. Augustine did not invent this understanding, but inherited it from the previous Latin-speaking tradition of the Western church. In *The Spirit and the Letter* Augustine makes it clear how he normally understands the word. He is seeking to explain Romans 2:13: 'the doers of the law . . . will be justified'.

> The word 'justified' is equivalent to 'made righteous' – made righteous by him who justifies the ungodly [Rom. 4:5], so that he who was ungodly becomes righteous ... Alternatively, we must suppose that 'shall be justified' here [Rom. 2:13] means 'shall be held just,' 'shall be accounted just'; as in the case of the lawyer in Luke [10:29] of whom we read, 'and he, willing to justify himself . . . ,' that is, with a view to being held or accounted just.[1]

In this passage Augustine (at the end) toys with the idea that to be justified may mean 'to be accounted/considered just/righteous', but the passage as a whole makes it clear that this is not how he normally uses the word.

Process of salvation

Augustine's understanding of justification is made clear by the argument of the book as a whole, which is about the way in which the Holy Spirit changes and renews us so that we can now obey God from the heart. This can be seen clearly in his order of salvation, quoted in chapter 7, which is not about God's putting us right with himself through the work of Christ on the cross, but about God's changing us within by the work of the Holy Spirit:

> By the law comes the knowledge of sin; by faith comes the obtaining of grace against sin; by grace comes the healing of the soul from sin's sickness; by the healing of the soul comes freedom of choice; by freedom of choice comes the love of righteousness; by the love of righteousness comes the working of the law.[2]

Shortly after, Augustine speaks of Abraham's being counted as righteous, but does not use the word 'justification' to describe that.[3] It is possible to read *The Spirit and the Letter* superficially with the assumption that Augustine is using the word 'justify' in the Pauline/Protestant sense, but that is to misread him.

---

[1] §45 (LCC 8:229).
[2] §52 (LCC 8:236).
[3] §54.

Augustine and Protestant theology both teach justification by faith. For Protestant theology, claiming to follow Paul, this means by faith being put right with God, being accepted by God. For Augustine, following earlier tradition, it means by faith receiving the Holy Spirit, who then changes and renews us, dealing with our sinful wills. Of course, salvation includes both of these things. The point at issue is not whether one of them happens to the exclusion of the other, but which of them is meant by the *word* 'justification'.

When writing about justification there are two verses Augustine repeatedly cites: 'God's love has been poured into our hearts through the Holy Spirit who has been given to us' (Rom. 5:5), which Augustine understands to refer to the Spirit's giving us the love that enables us to obey from the heart, and 'For in Christ Jesus neither circumcision nor uncircumcision counts for anything, but only faith working through love' (Gal. 5:6), which Augustine understands according to the order of salvation just quoted.

Middle Ages (500–1500)[4]

Medieval Western theology broadly followed Augustine's doctrine of justification, setting it in the context of the sacraments. As we saw in chapters 13 and 14, baptism was held to wash away all sin, but the forgiveness of sin after baptism was not so simple. The sacrament of penance was developed to deal with post-baptismal sin. This involved confession to a priest and also the offering to God of some satisfaction for sins.

There were many debates around these topics in the Middle Ages, covering issues such as the different types of grace, the role of human free will and the role for human merit.

Protestant model of justification

The Reformation brought with it a new model of justification, but this did not happen all at once. There is a myth that Luther suddenly grasped the doctrine of justification by faith and that this then led to the break with Rome. That is not how it happened. The controversy began with the issue of Indulgences. Luther wrote his *95 Theses* in 1517, which was the spark that ignited the Reformation, but the theses are all about Indulgences, and contain no mention of the doctrine of justification. At that time Luther still believed in the authority of the pope and the reality of purgatory.[5]

---

[4] For medieval developments, see McGrath, *Iustitia Dei*, 55–207.
[5] For Luther's development to 1519, see McGrath, *Luther's Theology of the Cross*; for developments between 1517 and 1521, see Atkinson, *Trial of Luther*.

It was in the 1520s, after Luther's excommunication and his stand at the Diet of Worms in 1521, that the Protestant doctrine of justification began to be developed, arising especially from renewed interest in the letters of Paul. During the 1520s Luther's own understanding developed. A crucial role was also played by Philipp Melanchthon, his right-hand man at Wittenberg. When it comes to the formal statement of the Protestant doctrine of justification, Melanchthon's role was at least as important as Luther's.[6]

In the 1520s Protestantism began to divide into two groups. Lutheranism was based in Wittenberg and spread through much of Germany, and beyond into Scandinavia especially and into parts of Eastern Europe. At the same time as Luther was introducing the Reformation into Germany, with huge publicity, a quieter Reformation was taking place in Switzerland, starting with Ulrich Zwingli in Zurich and Johann Oecolampadius in Basel. Zwingli's Reformation was mostly independent of Luther's – but not as completely as he claimed. From the beginning there were differences in approach and these soon gave birth to a controversy over the issue of Christ's presence in the Lord's Supper. Reformed Protestantism (as the Swiss model came to be known) spread to France, to the British Isles, to the Netherlands and to parts of Germany and Eastern Europe.

Lutheran and Reformed differed on a number of points, especially the Lord's Supper. When it comes to justification there are nuances of difference, but a much greater common agreement and one can meaningfully speak of the development of a *Protestant* doctrine of justification, rather than separate Lutheran and Reformed doctrines. As significant as differences between Lutheran and Reformed on this topic are the differences *within* Lutheranism. In what follows we shall concentrate on the commonalities while occasionally pointing out differences.

Alister McGrath identifies three distinctive features of the classic Protestant doctrine between 1530 and 1730,[7] and we shall follow these below. The date 1530 is significant – it took time for these points to develop.

Definition of justification

Justification is defined as acquittal, as the not guilty verdict in a law court. This is a legal or 'forensic' definition of justification. It does not imply that our relationship to God can be reduced to legal, forensic terms alone. The New Testament also uses other models such as 'reconciliation' and 'adoption' as God's children

---

[6] For the early Melanchthon, see McGrath, *Iustitia Dei*, 238–241.
[7] McGrath, *Iustitia Dei*, 212–213.

(another legal term). So justification is not the totality of salvation, but is an important part of it. In particular, justification deals with our guilt. To be justified means to be declared, reckoned, accounted righteous by God. It means that God accepts us as if we had never sinned. Justification means that God looks upon us 'just-as-if' we had never sinned. In Pidgin English 'God justifies him' becomes 'God he say him all right'. Christ's righteousness is reckoned or 'imputed' to us. The forensic definition of justification is based upon Paul's use of the term. It can also be seen elsewhere in the New Testament. When Luke states that the lawyer desired to 'justify himself' (10:29) he was not seeking to *become* righteous, but to be seen to be righteous, to be accounted righteous.

Calvin offers this definition in his *Institutes*: 'We explain justification simply as the acceptance with which God receives us into his favour as righteous men. And we say that it consists in [negatively] the remission of sins and [positively] the imputation of Christ's righteousness.'[8] Calvin was consistent in this definition, but things were not so clear in the early years of the Reformation. Luther throughout his life sometimes defined justification as Calvin did, and at other times used it to include the idea of inner renewal. Melanchthon regularly defined justification like Calvin, but also sometimes states that in the New Testament it can 'also' mean being made righteous or being regenerated, since Scripture also uses the term this way.[9] Martin Bucer in his 1536 Romans commentary takes 'justification' to refer both to the remission of sins and the imparting of righteousness by the Spirit,[10] but later sometimes follows the same definition as Calvin.

Justification versus sanctification

One of the distinctive features of the Protestant doctrine is the distinction between justification and sanctification. Justification, as just defined, refers to our standing before God; sanctification refers to God's work in renewing and transforming us into the image of Christ. This distinction can be stated in many different ways. Justification is about God's accepting me; sanctification is about God's changing me. Justification is legal; sanctification is moral. Justification is about my relationship with God; sanctification is about my condition. Justification is about my status or standing; sanctification is about my state. Justification is about how God looks on me; sanctification is what God does in me. Justification is about Christ's dying for me on the cross; sanctification is about Christ's

---

[8] *Inst.* 3:11:2.
[9] *Apology of the Augsburg Confession* (*BkConc* 132). For the changes in Melanchthon's view on this topic, see Wengert, *Law and Gospel*, 179–185.
[10] Wright (ed.), *Common Places of Martin Bucer*, 163–164.

living in me by the Holy Spirit. Justification (like pregnancy) is binary – you either are or you are not; sanctification is progressive and we should become increasingly sanctified. For more on the definition of sanctification, see chapter 27.

The essence of the Protestant doctrine is that justification and sanctification can be distinguished, but not separated. We cannot have one without the other because they both flow from our union with Christ. It is in Christ that we are accepted by God: '*in him* we have redemption through his blood, the forgiveness of our trespasses, according to the riches of his grace' (Eph. 1:7); and it is in Christ that we are made new: 'if anyone is *in Christ*, he is a new creation. The old has passed away; behold, the new has come' (2 Cor. 5:17). We have neither justification nor sanctification independently of or outside Christ. That is why justification is not a 'legal fiction'.

Calvin, like others at the time, illustrates this with the example of the heat and light of the sun.[11] The sun provides us with both heat and light. These are distinct in that we are warmed by the heat, not by the light, and we see by the light, not by the heat. They are also inseparable in that the sun never gives us one without the other. Justification and sanctification can also be compared to the two legs of a pair of trousers, which cannot be separated, unlike a pair of socks, which in my experience can all too easily become separated. When you open the washing machine, finding one leg of a pair of trousers is a guarantee of finding the other; finding one sock provides no such guarantee. The two legs are inseparable because they both emerge from the top of the trousers, just as justification and sanctification flow from Christ.

Whereas the distinction between justification and sanctification is foundational for the Protestant doctrine, Catholic theology has not generally accepted the distinction. Catholic theologians at the time of the Reformation and later repeatedly accused Protestants of teaching that it was possible to be justified while remaining an unchanged sinner – a gross misrepresentation. Here is one example from a distinguished Catholic philosopher of the last century:

> For the first time, with the Reformation, there appeared this conception of a grace that saves a man without changing him, of a justice that redeems corrupted nature without restoring it, of a Christ who pardons the sinner for self-inflicted wounds but does not heal them.[12]

Protestants have in turn often been guilty of caricaturing the Catholic doctrine as justification by works. For what Catholics actually teach, see chapters 21 to 24.

---

[11] *Inst.* 3:11:6.
[12] Gilson, *Spirit of Medieval Philosophy*, 421.

Justification by Christ

The Reformers held that we are acceptable *to* God and accepted *by* God not because of anything in ourselves, but because of what Christ has done for us on the cross. We are right with God because Christ's righteousness is imputed to us,[13] not because of any inherent or imparted righteousness within us. We are justified by Christ alone, through faith alone. Justification comes through faith not because faith is meritorious, not because faith in itself achieves or earns something. The role of faith is simply to receive God's free offer in Christ. The Reformers compared faith to the empty, open hands with which we receive Christ. This is receiving a free gift, not meriting, earning or deserving something. However, the only faith that justifies is faith working through love (Gal. 5:6). Although we are not justified *by* works, we are not justified *without* works.

Comparison of the models

The difference

The Catholic and Protestant models have a certain amount in common. Both hold that we are all in need of salvation because of original sin, as well as our actual sins. Both hold that God justifies us because of Christ and that faith is a crucial part of this process. Both hold that the justified sinner is accepted by God as righteous and also that the justified sinner is renewed and transformed by the Holy Spirit. But there are some crucial differences. For Catholic theology, as defined at the Council of Trent (see chapter 22), justified sinners are accepted by God because of what they have *become*. It is imparted righteousness, the righteousness of Christ within by the Holy Spirit, that makes us acceptable to God. For Protestant theology, by contrast, we are accepted by God because of what Christ has done for us. It is imputed righteousness, Christ's righteousness reckoned to our account that makes us acceptable to God. Related to this, the Reformers all insisted that while we are regenerated by the Holy Spirit and begin to obey the law, our inner righteousness and the works to which it gives birth alike remain imperfect and insufficient to make us acceptable to God. That idea was excluded from Trent's *Decree on Justification*.

---

[13] In the earlier years of the Reformation Bucer, for example, was clearer that righteousness is imputed to us than that it is *Christ's* righteousness that is imputed (Lane, *Regensburg Article 5 on Justification*, 101–102, 124). Some evangelical scholars today deny this last point. For varying views on this, see Husbands and Treier (eds), *Justification: What's at Stake*.

One can say that the difference between the two comes down to being accepted because of imparted versus imputed righteousness. That makes it sound as if the issue is a minor difference between two technical terms. In fact these are ordinary words from everyday language, not purely theological terms. To impart something is to bestow it, to transfer it to someone. Teachers impart knowledge to their pupils. To impute something is different. If I impute a bad motive to someone I am not *giving* them a bad motive but ascribing or attributing a bad motive to them. So, for example, a teacher imparts knowledge to a pupil, who eventually is reckoned to be worthy of an A level.

Are the differences between the two views minor or major?

As noted above, they have a lot in common. And yet the differences are important. They affect the question of the basis for our acceptance by God.

Can the two views be reconciled?

For this question see chapters 21 to 24 where we examine the Roman Catholic Council of Trent and ecumenical dialogues in the sixteenth century and today.

In chapters 18 to 20 the Reformation doctrine is expounded, primarily from the lucid exposition of Calvin in chapters 11–19 of Book 3 of his *Institutes*, with reference as appropriate to the teaching of other Reformers.[14]

---

[14] For a fuller account of Calvin's teaching, see Lane, *Justification by Faith*, 21–43. For different views of justification, see Beilby and Eddy (eds), *Justification: Five Views*.

17

Justification in the New Testament

Paul on justification[1]

Justification by faith alone is taught most clearly by Paul, especially, though not exclusively, in Romans and Galatians. Justification is by faith, not works. In Romans 1:18 – 3:20 Paul talks about human sin, concluding in 3:20 that 'by the works of the law no human being will be justified in his sight, since through the law comes knowledge of sin'. The rest of chapter 3 speaks of the righteousness of God that comes by faith, apart from the law, by grace. 'For we hold that one is justified by faith apart from works of the law' (3:28).

In Romans 4:1 – 5:11 Paul talks about the righteousness received by Abraham. 'Abraham believed God, and it was counted to him as righteousness' (4:3). Abraham was 'reckoned righteous by faith' before he was circumcised and before the law had been given. So Gentiles can become believers and be justified without being circumcised, as was Abraham. 'To the one who does not work but trusts him who justifies the ungodly, his faith is counted as righteousness' (4:5). This justification of the ungodly would have been shocking to Jews, as it runs counter to Proverbs 17:15, which states:

> He who justifies the wicked and he who condemns the righteous
> are both alike an abomination to the LORD.

But this is possible because of the work of Christ, 'whom God put forward as a propitiation by his blood, to be received by faith . . . so that he might be just and the justifier of the one who has faith in Jesus' (3:25–26).

In Romans 10:1–13 Paul contrasts the righteousness of works of the law and the righteousness of God, through faith: 'Being ignorant of the righteousness that comes from God, and seeking to establish their own, they did not submit to God's righteousness' (10:3).

---

[1] There is a vast literature on Paul's doctrine of justification. For an introduction, see Seifrid, *Christ, Our Righteousness*, which builds on an earlier weighty academic tome.

Justification by faith is also the theme of Galatians, especially 2:15 – 3:25: 'a person is not justified by works of the law but through faith in Jesus Christ' (2:16). In Philippians 3:4–11 Paul contrasts his Jewish heritage with his desire to 'gain Christ and be found in him, not having a righteousness of my own that comes from the law, but that which comes through faith in Christ, the righteousness from God that depends on faith' (3:8–9).

Justification is important, but it is wrong simply to equate it with the gospel, as some do. Outside these three letters Paul rarely mentions justification. It is an important part of the gospel message, but not the sum total of it.

Luke on justification

The most down-to-earth account of justification by faith is in Jesus' parable of the Pharisee and the tax collector (Luke 18:9–14), which in today's terms might be a parable of the church leader and the bailiff. The former trusts in his own works – although he did acknowledge that it was due to God's grace that he was better than the tax collector, thanking God for it; he did not ascribe it to his own efforts alone. The tax collector simply casts himself on God's mercy, recognizing the inadequacy of his own works. Jesus tells us that it was the tax collector who was justified, not the Pharisee. He was justified because he recognized his sinfulness and cast himself on God's mercy.[2]

Related to this, when people encounter God in the Old Testament they become aware not of their merit and fitness to stand before God but of their own sinfulness. Isaiah's reaction, for example, was, 'Woe is me! For I am lost; for I am a man of unclean lips, and I dwell in the midst of a people of unclean lips; for my eyes have seen the King, the LORD of hosts!' (6:5). When Job encounters God his reaction is to say:

> I despise myself,
> and repent in dust and ashes.
> (42:6)

James versus Paul?

Paul teaches that we are justified by faith apart from works, but James declares that we are justified by works and not by faith alone (Jas 2:24). Clearly there is a verbal contradiction between them, but we need to look at the meaning of the

---

[2] For a Catholic perspective on this parable, see Johnson, *Gospel of Luke*, 273–274.

words. Theology is not like maths and words do not have one meaning only. The Bible contains almost no 'technical language' – that came later as theology became an academic discipline, for which precise definitions became important. The issue of James versus Paul has been much studied over the centuries and many different theologians have sought to show that there is no ultimate contradiction.[3]

In order to resolve this we can compare Romans 4:2–5 with James 2:21–24, parallel passages both of which focus on the example of Abraham, the apparent contradictions being in italic type (see Table 2).

Table 2 Parallel passages that compare Romans 4:2–5 with James 2:21–24

Romans 4:2–5	James 2:21–24
2 If, in fact, *Abraham was justified by works*, he had something to boast about – but not before God. 3 What does the Scripture say? 'Abraham believed God, and it was reckoned to him as righteousness.' [Gen. 15:6] 4 Now when a man works, his wages are not credited to him as a gift, but as an obligation. 5 However, to the man who does not work but trusts God who justifies the wicked, *his faith is credited as righteousness* [Gen. 15:6].	21 Was not our ancestor *Abraham justified by works* when he offered his son Isaac on the altar? [Gen. 22] 22 You see that his faith and his actions were working together, and his faith was made complete by what he did. 23 And the scripture was fulfilled that says, 'Abraham believed God, and it was reckoned to him as righteousness,' [Gen. 15:6] and he was called God's friend. 24 You see that a person is *justified by works and not by faith alone*.

It will be noted that both writers refer to Genesis 15:6, where 'Abraham believed God, and it was reckoned to him as righteousness.' James also refers to Genesis 22, where Abraham offers Isaac on the altar. The apparent contradictions are between 4:2 and 2:21, and between 4:5 and 2:24. But these are verbal contradictions only, as Paul and James are using the same words with different meanings.

For Paul to be 'justified' means to be 'reckoned righteous by God', as in Genesis 15:6 (Rom. 4:2–3). James likewise teaches that we are reckoned righteous by faith, and also cites Genesis 15:6 in support (2:23) – but this is not what James means by 'justification'. For Paul, justification refers to what happened to Abraham in Genesis 15; for James it refers to what happened to him in Genesis 22, when he was willing to sacrifice Isaac (2:21). They use the word justify with different meanings, but are agreed that it is by faith that Abraham (and we) are reckoned righteous.

---

[3] E.g. Calvin, *Inst.* 3:17:11–12 and Comm. Jas 2:20–21. For a modern discussion, see Bauckham, *James*, 113–135.

Also, Paul and James both use the word 'faith' differently. For Paul faith refers to a living trust in Christ which leads to good works – the 'faith working through love' of Galatians 5:6. James is concerned about a dead faith without works (2:14–17), that is in the head alone and which even the demons have (2:19). 'Faith apart from works is dead' (2:26). Neither Paul nor James thought that *such* a 'faith' could save. When it comes to *that* sort of faith, Paul would have agreed with James that we are not justified by faith alone. If I have 'all faith', but no love, 'I am nothing' (1 Cor. 13:2). The Catholic tradition has generally adopted James's understanding of faith as giving intellectual assent to certain doctrines, while Protestants generally understand it in the Pauline sense of a living trust in Christ.

So they were using the same words but with different meanings; they do not say the same as each other, but their teachings are not in contradiction to each other but should rather be seen as complementary. Catholic theology has often seen Romans 4 as referring to the initial justification of the ungodly and James 2 as referring to the continuing justification of the godly, as can be seen in the Council of Trent (chapter 22).

Judgement according to works

How will we be tested at the last judgement? Many Christians would say that it is on the basis of faith. In fact the New Testament consistently teaches that it is according to *works* that we shall be judged.[4]

This is expressed repeatedly in the Gospels, including a number of times in Matthew. Saying 'Lord, Lord' does not guarantee entry into the kingdom of heaven, unless we also do the will of the Father in heaven (7:21–23). The Son of Man will 'repay each person according to what he has done' (16:27). Those who have 'left houses or brothers or sisters or father or mother or children or lands, for my name's sake' will inherit eternal life (19:29). The parable of the sheep and the goats (25:31–46) is very clear, the judgement being according to how we have treated 'one of the least of these my brothers' (25:40). John's Gospel lays great emphasis on faith, and 'whoever hears my word and believes him who sent me has eternal life' (5:24), but this is immediately followed by a statement of judgement according to works. 'An hour is coming when all who are in the tombs will hear his voice and come out, those who have done good

---

[4] For a variety of views on this, see Stanley (ed.), *Four Views on Role of Works at Final Judgment*. Michael Bird in Beilby and Eddy (eds), *Justification: Five Views*, 154, helpfully points out that in the New Testament (especially Paul) we are justified *through* and *by* faith, but judgement is *according to* works. Christ, received through faith, is the basis for our justification; works are the test or evidence of it.

to the resurrection of life, and those who have done evil to the resurrection of judgement' (5:28–29).

Paul is the great teacher of justification by faith, but he also is clear about judgement according to works. '[God] will render to each one according to his works: to those who by patience in well-doing seek for glory and honour and immortality, he will give eternal life; but for those who are self-seeking and do not obey the truth, but obey unrighteousness, there will be wrath and fury' (Rom. 2:6–8). 'We must all appear before the judgement seat of Christ, so that each one may receive what is due for what he has done in the body, whether good or evil' (2 Cor. 5:10). There are other relevant passages, such as Galatians 6:7–9 and Colossians 3:23–25.

Finally, Revelation describes the last judgement, in which the dead are judged 'according to what they had done' (20:11–13).

So, according to the New Testament we are justified by faith, but the final judgement is according to works. These passages are about the judgement of all people, believers and unbelievers; they are concerned with eternal destiny, not just reward. People sometimes see a contradiction here, but that is not so. It all comes down to the fundamental distinction between cause and symptom. The cause of our acceptance by God is justification by faith; the symptom or evidence of this is good works. The way we live shows what we really believe. The cause of chickenpox is a virus; the symptom, the evidence that we have it, is spots. People do not catch chickenpox by painting spots on themselves, but nor is it possible to have the disease without the symptom, the spots, appearing in due course.

Calvin observes that often in Scripture the mark of true religion is stated in terms of how we treat one another. He comments that it is not that love of neighbour is more important than love of God, but it is easy to pretend to love God and the test of its genuineness is how we treat one another.[5] There was a time when I would have said that I liked porridge. It was only after I lived somewhere that served porridge for breakfast and went some weeks without ever opting for it that I realised that I did not really like porridge. My actions were the proof of my real beliefs.

All the Reformers agreed that there is no salvation without good works; justification by faith alone does not mean that one can be saved without good works. Justification is only one part of salvation. Good works are necessary for salvation – not that they *cause* it, but there is no salvation without them. But what about someone who is converted on their deathbed and has no opportunity

---

[5] *Inst.* 2:8:52; similarly, 1 John 4:20–21.

for good works? The thief on the cross is the classic example, but even he had the opportunity to bear witness to Christ (Luke 23:40–43). It *is* possible to have chickenpox without displaying spots – if one dies before they have time to appear.

Tension to hold[6]

In the New Testament we see a tension. In the parable of the Pharisee and the tax collector (Luke 18:9–14) the Pharisee thanked God for all his good works and that he was better than others. The tax collector by contrast beat his breast and said, 'God, be merciful to me, a sinner.' It was the tax collector, not the Pharisee, who was accepted by God. The only grounds on which we can approach God is the grace of God. But that is only half of the story. A few chapters earlier in the same Gospel (Luke 14:25–33) Jesus speaks uncompromisingly of the demands of discipleship and warns that 'any one of you who does not renounce all that he has cannot be my disciple' (14:33). The promise of acceptance to the worst sinner does not rule out the demand for total commitment from all believers.

The same tension is found in Paul. He teaches justification by faith alone, that we are accepted by God not on the grounds of our good works or merits but solely on the basis of Christ's death for us on the cross (e.g. Rom. 3:21–28). But alongside this comforting message of grace, the same Paul also warns the Corinthian Christians that those indulging in a variety of activities, such as adultery, theft or drunkenness, will not inherit the kingdom of God. 'And such', he says, '*were* some of you' – before they came to Christ (1 Cor. 6:9–11). The good news of free acceptance does not rule out the need for obedience. Likewise 1 John 1:9 teaches that 'If we confess our sins, he is faithful and just to forgive us our sins and to cleanse us from all unrighteousness.' A few verses previously, though, we read, 'If we say we have fellowship with him while we walk in darkness, we lie and do not practise the truth' (1:6).

Being faithful to this tension is a challenge for Christian theology, not just for theologians. The tension is something that needs to be lived out by *all* Christians in their day-to-day discipleship. There are two opposite dangers that threaten us and that we need to avoid. One danger is antinomianism, which says that it does not matter how we live.[7] The other danger is legalism, which says that we need to earn God's acceptance by our works.

---

[6] For more on this, see Lane, 'What's so Dangerous About Grace?'
[7] The term 'antinomianism' is also sometimes used to refer to the view that Christians can rely on the Spirit to guide them and do not need the written law.

We need to live in tension between these two. Tension is not the same as balance. When I stand upright I am balanced; if two people are pulling my arms in opposite directions I am in tension, being pulled in two opposite directions. Living the New Testament in tension means feeling both the pressure towards antinomianism and the pressure towards legalism. Martyn Lloyd-Jones once argued, on the basis of Romans 6:1, that a preacher who is never misunderstood to be teaching antinomianism is probably not preaching justification by faith alone.[8] By the same token, a preacher who is never misunderstood to be teaching legalism is probably not preaching the radical demands of discipleship.

A similar point was made by Dietrich Bonhoeffer, the German theologian who joined the resistance against Hitler and was hanged by the Nazis in the closing days of the war. In his *Cost of Discipleship* he talks of the distinction between cheap and costly grace. Cheap grace breaks our tension by offering forgiveness without repentance, grace without discipleship. Cheap grace proclaims the forgiveness of sins without the resolve to forsake sin. Cheap grace interprets 'grace alone' to mean that we can remain as we are without changing. Costly grace, however, calls us to follow Christ. It is costly because it cost God the life of his Son and because it costs us our life.

> The only man who has the right to say that he is justified by grace alone is the man who has left all to follow Christ . . . Those who try to use this grace as a dispensation from following Christ are simply deceiving themselves.[9]

It is important to maintain this tension in the overall thrust of a preaching ministry. One of my students once told me that at church he expects to hear the basic message 'You're all right. God has accepted you in Christ.' That is certainly an important part of the gospel and in a Western world that is obsessed with the need for self-esteem it is the only message heard in many churches. But there is an equal need for another message: 'You're not all right. Your life falls short of what is expected of a Christian. Don't just relax and enjoy justification but repent and get on with discipleship.' Indeed without this second message the first ceases to be the biblical doctrine of justification by faith and becomes instead a secular message of self-esteem, for more on which see chapter 26. As Luther pointed out, if we take away the law we lose the gospel

---

[8] Lloyd-Jones, *Romans: Exposition of Chapter 6*, 8–10.
[9] Bonhoeffer, *Cost of Discipleship*, 35–47.

as well.[10] We *are* all right in that God has accepted us freely in Christ, but we are *not* all right in that our lives still fall very short of God's goal for us and he will not let up on us until he has reached that goal.

The same tension also works itself out in the doctrine of the church. On the one hand the church is the community of forgiveness. Moral achievement is not a precondition for entry. The church is the school for forgiven sinners, the hospital for those who are being healed from sin. When the church becomes a moralistic club for the respectable it has lost touch with its calling. Yet, at the same time, the church is meant to witness not just to human impotence but to renewal by God's grace. We are rightly scandalized by those episodes of church history where the church has exemplified the basest of moral behaviour. The church has to maintain the difficult balance of welcoming sinners without sanctioning and approving their continuation in sin. To the woman taken in adultery Jesus said, 'Neither do I condemn you; go, and from now on sin no more' (John 8:11). He does not condemn, but nor does he condone. We are not meant to take away the message that adultery is all right. We can come to God just as we are, but are not supposed to stay that way.

It is vital to maintain this tension between the good news of free grace and the call to discipleship not as an optional extra for the zealous but as part of the basic package. Henry Drummond is reported to have said that the entrance fee for the Christian faith is nothing, but the annual subscription is everything. When we are in Christ we receive the free gift of justification but we also need to press on with the arduous task of sanctification. At different times one or other side of this tension has been lost. At times the church has lapsed into preaching cheap grace, as Bonhoeffer put it, and Christians have been shamefully indistinct from the ungodly. At other times the stress has been on the moral demands of Christian faith and the radical message of forgiveness has faded into the background, leaving only a graceless morality. The New Testament gospel offers us forgiveness and encouragement, but does not allow us to think that we are fine as we are.

New perspectives on Paul[11]

So far we have been considering the traditional Protestant understanding of justification, but since the 1970s this has been challenged by what is called 'new perspectives' on Paul. This started with E. P. Sanders, who challenged the older

---

[10] Althaus, *Theology of Martin Luther*, 257–258.
[11] For more on this, see Thompson, *New Perspective on Paul*; Beilby and Eddy (eds), *Justification: Five Views*, 53–82, 176–218.

view that Judaism was a religion of justification by works, against which Paul argued for justification by faith.[12] Sanders claimed that Judaism was based on 'covenantal nomism' – we enter the covenant by *grace*, and stay in it by *obedience*. Sanders's view of first-century AD Judaism has been widely accepted, although it is also recognized that Judaism was not monochrome and there were some who taught a legalistic justification by works of the law.[13]

Following Sanders's work a number of New Testament scholars have proposed a new interpretation of Paul. J. D. G. Dunn agrees with Sanders's views and coined the phrase 'New Perspective' on Paul. He argues that the 'works of the law' that cannot justify us according to Paul relate to specific Jewish 'social boundary markers', such as circumcision and the food laws. So Paul's message of justification by faith is primarily about breaking down barriers between Jews and Gentiles.[14] Tom Wright has a similar, but not identical, approach. He also claims that Paul's doctrine is not primarily about how we find peace with God, but rather about what defines the people of God. Justification by faith is the declaration that those who believe in Jesus are members of the true covenant family; it is about *who* belongs to the people of God, rather than *how* to join.[15] While the views of these two scholars have much in common they are not identical, which is why we should speak of 'New Perspectives', in the plural.

It is too early to start revising the traditional doctrine of justification, for several reasons. First, these new perspectives have by no means won universal acceptance among New Testament scholars and there remains considerable opposition to them. The jury is still out. Secondly, Tom Wright himself has said on a number of occasions that if his view of Paul is correct it would not mean that the Reformation doctrine of justification is mistaken. Rather we should see that doctrine not as itself Paul's doctrine of justification but as an implication of Paul's doctrine. So even if Wright is right it does not mean that the Reformers were wrong. Dunn has also stated that his new perspective supplements rather than supplants the old perspective.[16]

---

[12] Sanders, *Paul and Palestinian Judaism.*

[13] Carson et al. (eds), *Justification and Variegated Nomism.*

[14] For a recent statement of Dunn's view, see his contribution in Beilby and Eddy (eds), *Justification: Five Views*, 176–201.

[15] For a recent statement of Wright's view, see Wright, *Paul and His Recent Interpreters*, 64–131.

[16] In Beilby and Eddy (eds), *Justification: Five Views*, 176–177.

18
Ground of justification

Union with Christ

All of the Reformers were keen to stress that justification cannot be separated from sanctification, that it is not possible to enjoy the forgiveness of sins without a changed life. But *why* should this be so? The answer lies in our union with Christ. This is true for all the Reformers, but is especially clear in Calvin.[1]

Union with Christ is central to Calvin's doctrine of salvation, as can clearly be seen from the structure of his *Institutes* (see Figure 1). Having in Book 2 expounded his doctrine of the person of Christ and what he has achieved for us, in Book 3 he turns to 'The Way in which we Receive the Grace of Christ' (the title of the Book). There he starts by affirming that unless we are united with Christ, 'all that he has suffered and done for the salvation of the human race remains useless and of no value for us'.[2] Until we are united with Christ what he has achieved for us helps us no more than an electricity mains supply that passes our house but is not connected to it. It is the Holy Spirit who unites us with Christ, by faith, and this brings us two major

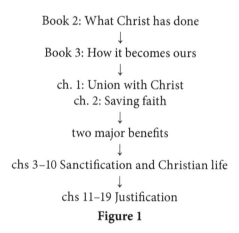

Book 2: What Christ has done
↓
Book 3: How it becomes ours
↓
ch. 1: Union with Christ
ch. 2: Saving faith
↓
two major benefits
↓
chs 3–10 Sanctification and Christian life
↓
chs 11–19 Justification

Figure 1

---

[1] For an excellent study of union with Christ, see Letham, *Union with Christ*.

[2] *Inst.* 3:1:1. Note, 'the human race', not 'the elect'.

benefits – justification and sanctification.[3] These are the theme of most of the remainder of Book 3.

In order to make it abundantly clear that we cannot have justification without sanctification, Calvin first devotes eight chapters to the latter (3:3–10), before turning to the former (3:11–19) – so that it may better appear 'how man is justified by faith alone, and simple pardon; nevertheless actual holiness of life, so to speak, is not separated from free imputation of righteousness'.[4] Justification and sanctification are inseparable, because they both flow from union with Christ:

> As Christ cannot be torn into parts, so these two which we perceive in him together and conjointly are inseparable – namely, righteousness and sanctification. Whomever, therefore, God receives into grace, on them he at the same time bestows the Spirit of adoption, by whose power he remakes them to his own image.[5]

Calvin also refers to the 'double grace' received by partaking of Christ: reconciliation and sanctification.[6]

So faith unites us with Christ and it is 'in him' that we are justified and have new life. Justification is not a benefit Christ confers upon us, which we then possess independently of him. We are justified only by virtue of being in Christ. For Calvin justification and sanctification both follow inevitably from union with Christ. He frequently cites 1 Corinthians 1:30: that Christ is given to us for both righteousness and sanctification. 'Therefore Christ justifies no one whom he does not at the same time sanctify.'[7] It should be noted that Calvin, unlike some of his interpreters, does not speak of justification as the cause of sanctification nor of the latter as the fruit or consequence of the former. Both are the fruit and consequence of union with Christ.

Because of this, justification and sanctification are inseparable. Some people speak of accepting Christ as Saviour when we become Christians and then at some later stage accepting him as Lord. None of the Reformers would have allowed this distinction. There is only one Christ, who is both Lord and Saviour. 2 Peter repeatedly refers to him as 'Lord and Saviour' in that order (1:11; 2:20; 3:2). Of course, the process of sanctification should involve *increased*

---

[3] *Inst.* 3:3:1.
[4] *Inst.* 3:3:1.
[5] *Inst.* 3:11:6.
[6] *Inst.* 3:11:1.
[7] *Inst.* 3:16:1.

recognition of the lordship of Christ and submission to it, but conversion is not possible without the acceptance of it in principle.[8] It was to make this point that Calvin discussed sanctification and the Christian life *before* justification. At the same time, justification is a definitive event, while sanctification is progressive,[9] so in that sense our continuing sanctification is founded on our completed justification.

By making union with Christ central to his doctrine of salvation[10] and deriving justification from it, Calvin was in line with Paul, for whom the theme of being 'in Christ' is much more central than the theme of justification. References to being 'in Christ' come throughout his letters, while justification is found only in Romans, Galatians, briefly in Philippians and a few other passages.[11]

Righteousness of God

A key phrase in the Reformation debates over justification is 'the righteousness of God'. It played a crucial role in Luther's conversion. At the end of his life he describes how he had struggled with Romans 1:17, which states that the righteousness of God is revealed in the gospel. Luther understood this to refer to God as the righteous judge. Since God had already given the law to condemn us, why did he need to condemn us in the gospel as well? Then his eyes were opened:

> I began to understand that the righteousness of God is that by which the righteous lives by a gift of God, namely by faith . . . The righteousness of God is revealed by the gospel, namely, the passive righteousness with which the merciful God justifies us by faith.[12]

Luther went on to say that when he understood this, he felt as if he had been born again and had entered Paradise.

Luther says that he later discovered the same idea in Augustine's *Spirit and the Letter*, which refers to 'the righteousness of God, not that by which God is righteous, but that wherewith he clothes man, when he justifies the ungodly [Rom. 4:5]'.[13] In fact the idea that Romans 1:17 refers to the righteousness by

---

[8] For more on this, see chapters 10 and 11, above, and see on the tension in the New Testament in chapter 17.

[9] For the idea of 'definitive sanctification', see chapter 27.

[10] To say that it is central to his doctrine of salvation is not to make the mistake of calling it the central dogma from which all of his theology is derived.

[11] Being 'in Christ' has a range of meanings in Paul. So the freedom to marry 'only in the Lord' (1 Cor. 7:39) probably means marrying a fellow Christian.

[12] Preface to the 1545 edition of his Latin writings (*LW* 34:337). For the date and significance of this, see McGrath, *Luther's Theology of the Cross*.

[13] §15 (LCC 8:205).

which God justifies us is part of the Catholic tradition from the time of Augustine and is found (after Luther's death) in the Council of Trent's *Decree on Justification*: 'The sole formal cause [of justification] is the righteousness of God – not that by which he himself is righteous, but that by which he makes us righteous.'[14] Luther's discovery was a highly significant event for him personally, but not for the history of theology. So does this mean that there is no difference between the Roman Catholic and Protestant views? Not necessarily. There is the shared understanding that we are justified by God's righteousness, but what sort of righteousness?

The *Roman Catholic view* is that we are accepted by God because of *imparted* righteousness – which could also be called 'implanted', 'inherent' or 'infused'. In other words, we are accepted because we have been born again or regenerated, because the Holy Spirit has changed us to make us acceptable (sanctification).

The *Protestant view* is that we are accepted because of *imputed* righteousness – righteousness 'ascribed' or 'reckoned' to our account. While we are regenerated and are becoming sanctified, this process is not yet complete and so in ourselves we remain sinful and inherently unacceptable, but we are accepted through what Christ has done for us and his righteousness is reckoned to our account.

Faith

Sola fide

Justification is received by 'faith alone', *sola fide* – the Reformation slogan.[15] This is not because our faith has value in itself, but rather because faith unites us with *Christ*, in whom we are justified. Justification is by faith alone not because of what faith merits or *achieves* but because of what it *receives*. Faith has been described as the empty hands by which we receive Christ. Faith appropriates justification not as a worker earns wages but as one accepts a free gift. 'The power of justifying, which faith possesses, does not lie in any worth of works. Our justification rests on God's mercy alone and Christ's merit, and faith, when it lays hold of justification, is said to justify.'[16]

Faith is like an empty vessel, which is then filled. It is not that faith itself is powerful; the power lies in the Christ who is received into our lives by faith. This is quite different from the message proclaimed by Norman Vincent Peale

---

[14] Ch. 7, my own translation based on earlier ones.
[15] For a well-balanced account of this, see Schreiner, *Faith Alone*. See also the excursus below.
[16] *Inst.* 3:18:8.

in his very influential 1952 work *The Power of Positive Thinking*. He taught that faith itself is something active, powerful and positive, by which we can accomplish anything. For him it did not particularly matter what was the object of faith; the key point was the positive thinking. This is completely different from the Protestant doctrine of justification by faith alone, for which the power lies not in the faith itself but in the Christ received by faith. As Richard Hooker put it in 1586, 'God doth justify the believing man, yet not for the worthiness of his belief, but for his [Christ's] worthiness which is believed.'[17]

But why is justification by faith rather than by love, say? It is not because faith is superior to love because it is not: 'faith, hope, and love abide, these three; but the greatest of these is love' (1 Cor. 13:13). This does not imply that we are *justified* by love. 'It is as if someone argued that a king is more capable of making a shoe than a shoemaker is because he is infinitely more eminent.'[18]

The 1563 *Heidelberg Catechism* gives the following answer to the question 'Why do you say that you are righteous by faith only?'

> Not that I am acceptable to God on account of the worthiness of my faith, but because only the satisfaction, righteousness, and holiness of Christ is my righteousness before God; and I can receive the same and make it my own in no other way than by faith only.[19]

Why is this doctrine so important? Melanchthon, in his *Apology [i.e. Defence] of the Augsburg Confession* repeatedly states that those whose consciences are terrified on account of their sins should find rest and comfort in the mercy of God and the promises of the gospel.[20]

The Reformation stress on faith alone was not intended to affirm that faith is to be found on its own but rather to stress that it is only in Christ that we are acceptable. Justification is by faith alone, *sola fide*, but this faith does not stand alone, is not *nuda fides*, a naked faith. As Calvin put it:

> It is therefore faith alone which justifies, and yet the faith which justifies is not alone: just as it is the heat alone of the sun which warms the earth, and yet in the sun it is not alone, because it is constantly conjoined with light.[21]

---

[17] Hooker, Sermon 2:33 in *Works*, 3:538.

[18] *Inst.* 3:18:8.

[19] Question 61 (*RefConf* 2:783).

[20] E.g. *BkConc* 129, 149, 155, 168.

[21] *Acts of the Council of Trent*, can. 11 (*SWJC* 3:152). For further use of the sun analogy, see *Inst.* 3:11:6. The Lutheran *Formula of Concord* likewise states that 'it is faith alone that lays hold of the blessing, apart from works, and yet it is never, ever alone' (*BkConc* 569). Later the same point is made by means of a quotation from Luther that refers to the heat and light of a fire (*BkConc* 576).

We are justified by faith alone, but not without repentance or baptism. There can be no faith without hope nor vice versa.[22] We are justified not by faith without the Holy Spirit, but by faith that receives the Holy Spirit. We are not justified by a faith devoid of love. Saving faith is not to be confused with a dead faith that does not give birth to works of love.[23] 'No other faith justifies but faith working through love [Gal. 5:6].'[24] While works are most certainly not the ground of justification, where there is true faith works will follow. Justification is not *by* works, but nor is it *without* works. All the Reformers agreed that works are necessary for salvation in the sense that there is no salvation without them. 'We dream neither of a faith devoid of good works nor of a justification that stands without them. This alone is of importance: having admitted that faith and good works must cleave together, we still lodge justification in faith, not in works.'[25] Love and good works are a necessary condition in that one cannot be justified without them – just as spots are a necessary condition of having chickenpox. This does not prejudice justification by faith alone in that love no more causes justification than having spots causes chickenpox. The gospel is unconditional in that anyone can come to Christ; it is not unconditional in the sense that we can continue to live how we like. To quote the bumper sticker, it may be true that 'Christians aren't perfect' but it is not true that they are 'just forgiven'. As Paul wrote to the Corinthians:

> Do you not know that the unrighteous will not inherit the kingdom of God? Do not be deceived: neither the sexually immoral, nor idolaters, nor adulterers, nor men who practise homosexuality, nor thieves, nor the greedy, nor drunkards, nor revilers, nor swindlers will inherit the kingdom of God. And such *were* some of you. But you were washed, you were sanctified, you were justified in the name of the Lord Jesus Christ and by the Spirit of our God.
> (1 Cor. 6:9–11)

Luther famously in his translation of Romans 3:28 added the word 'alone', stating that justification is by faith *alone*, apart from works of the law.[26] The Greek contains no word for 'alone', and Luther was criticized for adding it, but he was following the example already set by some late medieval German translations. Interestingly, in the 1530s and 1540s, in the many debates between

---

22 *Inst.* 3:2:42–43.
23 *Inst.* 3:2:41.
24 *Inst.* 3:11:20.
25 *Inst.* 3:16:1.
26 'So halten wir nun dafür, daß der Mensch gerecht werde ohne des Gesetzes Werke, allein durch den Glauben.'

Protestant and Catholic theologians, a number of Catholic theologians agreed that there was an acceptable sense in which we can talk of justification by faith alone, but feared that if this were taught to the 'common herd', people would think that there was no longer any need for repentance and good works.[27]

That fear was also shared by the Reformers. In 1527 Melanchthon, in collaboration with Luther, drew up some brief *Articles* in Latin for use with a visitation of the churches in Electoral Saxony, which was revised the next year and again in 1538.[28] This states forcefully that there is no forgiveness of sins without repentance and to preach the former without the latter leads people astray. They will think that they are already forgiven and lapse into a false sense of security without the fear of God. Preachers are to proclaim the Ten Commandments and to warn people of the judgement that follows from disobeying them. They are to be taught that there is no saving faith without repentance, contrition and the fear of God. There is again a warning against those who think that it suffices to have faith without the fear of God and contrition. Such arrogance and carnal security is *worse than all of the earlier errors under the papacy.*[29]

Luther made a similar point in his *Third Antinomian Disputation* of 1538. Here he argues that at the beginning of the Reformation the gospel was preached to those burdened with sin, those with anxious consciences. Now the situation was different, with people having become secure and evil. He opposed those who 'want to preach sermons for a time of the contrite in a time of the secure'. Those who are secure, lazy and licentious need a different message from those who are afflicted and contrite.[30]

Because of the potential confusion between faith alone and a naked faith that stands alone, some have suggested that it would cause less misunderstanding to say that justification is 'only by faith'. This makes clear the distinctive role of faith without the unfortunate implication that such faith can stand alone. The fact that justification is *by* faith alone does not mean one can be justified *with* faith alone.

Saving faith

Book 3, Chapter 2 of Calvin's *Institutes* is a long and important chapter on the definition and properties of faith. Here he points to a number of inadequate

---

[27] For details, see Lane, *Regensburg Article 5 on Justification*, 236–242.

[28] Bornkamm, *Luther in Mid-Career*, 485–500.

[29] For the specific point being made in this paragraph, see Bornkamm, *Luther in Mid-Career*, 490, 492, 494–495.

[30] McCue, 'Luther and Problem of Popular Preaching', 37–38. For Luther's robust theology of progressive renewal in holiness, see Anderas, *Renovatio: Martin Luther's Augustinian Theology*.

definitions of faith. Saving faith is not merely giving mental assent to the existence of God, to creeds, to doctrine or to the account of Christ found in the Gospels. In fact it is not sufficient to believe that the Bible is an infallible oracle without a change of heart.[31] True faith cannot exist without love and sanctification.

But what about Simon Magus, who in Acts 8:13 is said to believe? What about James's comments about those who believe that God is one (2:19–20)? Calvin accepts that Scripture's use of the word varies, but is himself reluctant to use it of anything less than full saving faith. In line with the other Reformers he admits that there also exists the dead faith referred to by James (2:17, 26), the counterfeit faith described by Paul (1 Tim. 1:5),[32] and the temporary faith mentioned by Jesus (Luke 8:13). He argues that there are people who for a time experience 'almost the same feeling as the elect, so that even in their own judgement they do not in any way differ from the elect', although they do not experience the same degree of assurance. Such people are called hypocrites or play actors because they pretend to have what they do not have, whether consciously or otherwise.[33]

As well as opposing wrong views of faith, Calvin gives what he calls a 'right definition': 'A firm and certain knowledge of God's benevolence towards us, founded upon the truth of the freely given promise in Christ, both revealed to our minds and sealed upon our hearts through the Holy Spirit.'[34]

There are a number of points to note:

- Faith involves knowledge in the mind. It is not just an experience.
- This knowledge is based upon God's promise in Christ, the gospel, the good news.
- It does not stop in the mind but also penetrates to the heart. It is not just an intellectual exercise and is useless if it remains at the level of head knowledge only. It needs also to take root in the heart, the centre of our wills and emotions. At the same time it is not a contentless emotional experience but reaches the heart through the mind.
- It is the Holy Spirit who both reveals it to our minds and seals it on our hearts.
- What does the knowledge involve? It is knowledge of God's goodness and favour to us. It is not the knowledge that God is favourable to some people, but that he is favourable to *me*. For more on this see chapter 20.

---

[31] *Inst.* 3:2:9.
[32] Where English translations refer to a sincere or unfeigned faith the Latin Vulgate has the two words *non ficta* – 'not feigned or counterfeit'.
[33] *Inst.* 3:2:10–12.
[34] *Inst.* 3:2:7.

As well as setting out his own definition of faith, Calvin opposes a number of Roman Catholic ideas. One of these is the idea of implicit faith, that faith is accepting that whatever the church teaches is true, without actually knowing what it teaches. It is in opposition to this idea that Calvin stresses that faith is knowledge, not just signing a blank cheque. He admits, though, that in this life our faith always remains imperfect and mingled with unbelief. But the object of faith is the promise of the gospel as set out in Scripture, not the teaching of the church. Another Catholic idea that Calvin rejects is the distinction between 'formed' and 'unformed faith'. This Aristotelian distinction sees faith as giving assent with the mind, which is not effective until it receives its 'form' from love. This distinction under-lies the claim made by a number at this time that we are actually justified by love rather than by faith. Calvin's definition of faith, however, is of a full saving faith, not the bare intellectual belief described by James, for example.

The ground of justification

The Reformation doctrine excludes a number of wrong ideas about why we are accepted by God.

The basis for acceptance is not the merit of our good works. Paul concludes his account of human sin with the observation that 'by works of the law no human being will be justified in [God's] sight' (Rom. 3:20). The Pharisee thought that he would be accepted on the basis of his works and prayed thus: 'God, I thank you that I am not like other men, extortioners, unjust, adulterers, or even like this tax collector. I fast twice a week; I give tithes of all that I get.' Yet it was not he but the tax collector who 'went down to his house justified' (Luke 18:9–14).

The basis for acceptance is not that 'God loves me just the way I am because he made me that way', as we often hear. That is to forget about the fact of sin. It is one thing to say, 'God loves me just the way I am, 5 feet tall, because he made me that way.' It is quite another thing to say, 'God loves me just the way I am, a burglar, because he made me that way.'

The basis for acceptance is not that I have now become acceptable because of my regeneration and sanctification. The psalmist prayed:

Enter not into judgement with your servant,
for no one living is righteous before you.
(Ps. 143:2)

As Christians we *are* changed, but not such that we can stand before God on the basis of our own righteousness. For more on this, see chapter 19.

The true basis for acceptance is the work of Christ on the cross, whereby Christ took our sin upon himself and made his righteousness ours: 'For our sake he made him to be sin who knew no sin, so that in him we might become the righteousness of God' (2 Cor. 5:21). This becomes effective for us when by faith we are united to Christ.

Excursus: the five 'solas'

The teaching of the Reformation is sometimes summarized in five 'solas'. Some of these go back to the Reformation but others are more recent. They all have value, but are also all capable of being misunderstood unless they are held in tension with other truths.

Faith alone (*sola fide*)

We start with justification by faith alone, which was already a key Reformation slogan by the 1520s. As we have seen, it needs to be balanced by the truth quoted from Calvin above, that while it is faith alone that justifies, the faith that justifies is never alone.

Grace alone (*sola gratia*)

Salvation is by grace alone, but this also needs a balancing truth. Paul expresses the two sides in Philippians 2:12–13:

> Therefore, my beloved, as you have always obeyed, so now, not only as in my presence but much more in my absence, work out your own salvation with fear and trembling, for it is God who works in you, both to will and to work for his good pleasure.

It is God who is at work in us, who is effecting our salvation. However, the lesson to be drawn from that is not 'lie back and let God waft you to heaven' but 'work out your own salvation with fear and trembling'.

Christ alone (*solus Christus*)

The Reformers stressed the completeness of the work of Christ. Jesus Christ is the one way to God (John 14:6). One of the great affirmations of the Reformation was the privilege of the believer to have direct access to God through Christ. We do not need the mediation of the Virgin Mary or the saints but can approach God directly ourselves (1 Tim. 2:5). But at times this emphasis on Christ has led to a neglect of the work of the Spirit.

Scripture alone (*sola scriptura*)

As we saw in the introduction, *sola scriptura* did not become a slogan until after the Reformation. It teaches the important point that all must be tested by Scripture, but must not be misused to imply that all we need is the Bible.

To God alone be glory (*soli Deo gloria*)

This has been added to the list of 'solas' much more recently. It is less of a Protestant distinctive as the motto of the Jesuit order is *Ad maiorem Dei gloriam* – 'To the greater glory of God'. Even this slogan can be misused. In the sixteenth century the different Protestant groups all at times executed those whom they considered heretics. They thought they were doing this for the glory of God, though we today may wish to disagree.[35]

Finally, there are two other 'solas' that have been seen as describing where too many churches stand today.

Feelings alone

The satirical Babylonbee website contains a spoof news item headed 'Progressive Evangelical Leaders Meet to Affirm Doctrine of "Sola Feels"', the essence of the doctrine being that 'one's feelings are the supreme authority in all matters of theology and practice' and 'the infallibility of feelings'.[36] Like all good satire, this contains more than a germ of truth. Feelings rule supreme in many quarters today. Where we once used to sing about God and Christ, many modern worship songs are all about ourselves and our feelings. There is an old story of three people walking on a wall: Faith, Facts and Feelings. While Faith followed Facts and Feeling followed Faith, all was well, but when Faith turned round to look at Feelings both fell off.

Culture alone

Christians have to live in the world and so face the question of how to relate to their surrounding culture. Over the ages the church has adopted different

---

[35] The burning of Servetus at Geneva is one such example but, contrary to the way in which it is portrayed today, not something that marks Calvin or Geneva out but an example of what was happening almost everywhere at the time.

[36] See <https://babylonbee.com/news/progressive-evangelical-leaders-meet-affirm-doctrine-sola-feels>, accessed 20 November 2019.

approaches to the relation between Christian faith and culture,[37] and one of these is 'the Christ of Culture', also called 'Culture Christianity', where Christians simply absorb the values of the surrounding culture without any serious critique. This approach seems to be enjoying something of a revival with many Christians following culture on matters ranging from sexuality to narcissism. For more on the last of these, see chapter 26.

---

[37] A classic study of five different approaches is found in Niebuhr, *Christ and Culture*. Others have offered alternative approaches, such as Scriven, *Transformation of Culture*, and Carson, *Christ and Culture Revisited*. I have commented on these in 'Presenting the Challenge: Christ and Culture'.

19

Value of good works

Can we be justified by works?

In one sense the answer must be yes. James states that Abraham was justified by works and that the same is true for us (2:21–25). We need to phrase the question more carefully: In *what sense* can we be justified by works? Can we be acceptable to God by the merit of our works *outside* Christ?

The standard of judgement

Outside Paul, the classic passage for justification by faith is the parable of the Pharisee and the tax collector (Luke 18:9–14). Calvin argues the Pharisee trusted in the merit of his works only because he was judging them by the wrong standard. He had no idea of the actual standard required by God.

> First, therefore, this fact should occur to us: that our discourse is concerned with the justice not of a human court but of a heavenly tribunal, lest we measure by our own small measure the integrity of works needed to satisfy the divine judgment . . . [God's justice] is held of precious little value if it is not recognized as *God's* justice and so perfect that nothing can be admitted except what is in every part whole and complete and undefiled by any corruption.[1]

When we see God's holiness, his justice, his law, his standards, his requirements, our response can only be that of the tax collector, to cast ourselves on God's mercy alone with trembling and humility. This involves a real humility, not just a feigned, polite modesty. It is nothing less than a sober appraisal of the reality of the situation. Consider the two great commandments. Which one of us loves God with *all* of our heart, mind, soul and strength. Or our neighbour *as* ourselves? If we are going to stand before God on the basis of our own righteousness, then we need to be perfect. I could not respect a God who

---

[1] *Inst.* 3:12:1.

required any less than this. This is not just bad news (showing us our short-comings) but also good news. God will not rest until he has made us like that. Luther pointed out that God's commandments can be read as gospel, that the command 'You shall . . .' can be read as the promise that one day, when God has finished with you, 'You shall indeed . . .'

Calvin explains at the beginning of his *Institutes* that the knowledge of God and the knowledge of ourselves are intimately related to one another. It is only as we come to an awareness of God's majesty and holiness that we begin to appreciate our sinful state. This is what we see in both Old and New Testaments when people are confronted with God.[2] Once we recognize God's holiness and purity we can only respond with the tax collector, 'God, be merciful to me, a sinner!'

We need to assess our good works before God in the light of his holiness and purity. This Calvin does for four different groups of people.

Human virtue

The *first* group are unbelievers.[3] Calvin is aware (from classical antiquity especially) that unbelievers can perform heroic works of moral virtue and he sees these as gifts of God. But since unbelievers' hearts are opposed to God they defile these gifts. Relative to one another, some people are indeed virtuous, but God looks behind the deeds to the motivation of the heart. The 'good works' of such people, thus evaluated, are not genuinely virtuous. Calvin lays stress on their lack of faith. Augustine reached a similar conclusion, but placed greater emphasis on the lack of love.

As I argued in chapter 7, Augustine and Calvin are basically right about this. But that poses a problem. We all know non-Christians whose lives and deeds put many Christians to shame. There are those who give their lives in war to save a comrade, or who risk their lives to help people during a terrorist attack. Less spectacularly, there are those who give their lives sacrificially as long-term carers, sometimes for people they do not particularly like. While I am finally reviewing this text, health workers are risking (and sometimes losing) their lives to treat the victims of the coronavirus. We should not pretend that such virtue does not exist, but should honour it. Nor should we pretend that there is no difference between such people and those who live selfish or evil lives. For more on this see chapter 27. But our present question is, do they meet God's standard? The first and great commandment is to love God with all our heart, and those who do not do so fall short. Without this all of

---

[2] *Inst.* 1:1:1–3.
[3] *Inst.* 3:14:1–6.

our works are flawed. Augustine and most of the Reformers stopped there, but Thomas Aquinas made a distinction between natural and supernatural virtue. Non-Christians are capable of 'natural virtue', but not of the 'supernatural virtue' that flows from love of God.

Calvin considers the *second* and *third* groups together.[4] Nominal Christians are those who are baptized and receive communion, but whose lives deny the faith they profess. Hypocrites are those who conceal their wickedness from others, and indeed from themselves. They appear to others to be regenerate, and even themselves think that they are, when in fact they are not. (For more on this, see chapter 18.) As with unbelievers, their hearts have not been cleansed, so their works remain impure.

There are two different positions on the works of the unregenerate, whether they belong to the first, second or third group. The hard position is that *everything* done by such a person falls short of God's standards and requirements. The soft position is that they *sometimes* fall short, even if on other occasions they may succeed in reaching God's standards. I would side with Augustine and Calvin in taking the hard position, in saying that none of their works pass muster. Some people may be very virtuous compared with other people, but they are not virtuous when measured by God's standards. We are measuring shades of grey, whether fifty or otherwise. To be fully virtuous, works need to be motivated by love for God. But for the purposes of the doctrine of justification by faith, the soft position suffices. Even if people may on occasions act virtuously, we all on many other occasions do not. If you are on trial for fraud it is no defence to say you have never murdered anyone. We all need God's mercy and forgiveness.

The *fourth* group are those who are born again of the Spirit and seek after holiness.[5] Conversion leads to a change of heart, and to love for God and neighbour; this in turn leads to good works. We seek from the heart to obey God. But are these works *perfect* in the eyes of God? The best works of the godly may indeed be motivated by love of God and neighbour, but in this life elements of sinful motivation always remain as well.

The disciples of Christ love him with sincere and earnest affection of heart, and according to the measure of their love keep his commandments. But how small is this compared with that strict perfection in which there is no deficiency?[6]

---

[4] *Inst.* 3:14:7–8.
[5] *Inst.* 3:14:9–11.
[6] *Acts of the Council of Trent*, ch. 11 (*SWJC* 3:132).

It is not that their works are not good but that they are less than 100% good. Judged by the standard of God's holiness and purity they fall short: they are less than perfect. 'There never existed any work of a godly man which, if examined by God's stern judgment, would not deserve condemnation.'[7] In sum, therefore, for Calvin 'we have not a single work going forth from the saints that if it be judged in itself deserves not shame as its just reward'.[8] For more on the possibility of perfection in this life, see chapter 30.

Again, there are two positions on this. The hard position holds that even our *best* works fall short: we *do* love God, but not with all our heart, soul, mind and strength, and we *do* love our neighbours but generally not so much as we love ourselves. So we are not totally pure, but are still tainted by sin. The soft position holds that *some* of the time we may reach the standard of loving God and neighbour, but not all of the time. Sometimes we fall short, and at other times we are all right. The Reformers held to the hard position and were criticized for this by some of their Catholic opponents, though the hard position is not without some support from earlier Catholic tradition.[9]

Some may wish that God would lower his standards, that he would demand less than total holiness. That is a superficially attractive prospect, but I would question whether such a God would be worthy of our worship. Also, as Luther stated, the good news is that God will not rest with us until he has brought us into line with his high standards.

Are our good works acceptable to God?

Double justification

If this were all that we had to say it would be negatively depressing and demotivating. What is the point of seeking to live a godly life if everything we do will be counted as falling short? Why seek to serve God if one's best works will be flung back in one's face as tainted and inadequate? As believers, however, we relate to God not as a strict Judge through the law but as our gracious Father through Christ. This leads to the doctrine of 'double justification', to give it its modern name,[10] a doctrine taught by most if not all of the Reformers.

---

[7] *Inst.* 3:14:11. Even if we hold that *some* of our works are indeed 'wholly pure and perfect', these works are nevertheless tainted by our sins (*Inst.* 3:14:10–11). Cf. Jas 2:10–11.

[8] *Inst.* 3:14:9.

[9] On Thomas Aquinas and John Duns Scotus, see Raith, *After Merit*, 53, n. 74.

[10] That term is also used to describe the pairing of the initial justification of the ungodly and a subsequent justification of the godly, as set out at the Council of Trent for example. See chapter 22.

If we approach God as a just and holy Judge, seeking to be justified by works outside Christ on the basis of law, we are all condemned and furthermore none of our works pass muster. Given this negative attitude towards works, it may come as a surprise to some to learn that for Calvin and other Reformers God both accepts and rewards the good works of the justified believer.[11] In fact this is not so surprising when one sees what are his concerns. Justification by works is excluded 'not that no good works may be done, or that what is done may be denied to be good, but that we may not rely upon them, glory in them, or ascribe salvation to them'.[12] Works are of no value to those who seek justification from them outside Christ. But for the justified believer the situation is different.

When we approach God in faith we are accepted as righteous, in Christ. But it is not only *we* who are accepted. God also accepts our good works in Christ, overlooking whatever defects and impurities may remain in them.

> Therefore, as we ourselves, when we have been engrafted in Christ, are righteous in God's sight because our iniquities are covered by Christ's sinlessness, so our works are righteous and are thus regarded because whatever fault is otherwise in them is buried in Christ's purity, and is not charged to our account.

Thus, 'by faith alone not only we ourselves but our works as well are justified'.[13] The same was taught by the *Westminster Confession of Faith* in the following century:

> The persons of believers being accepted through Christ, their good works also are accepted in him; not as though they were in this life wholly unblameable and unreproveable in God's sight; but that he, looking upon them in his Son, is pleased to accept and reward that which is sincere, although accompanied with many weaknesses and imperfections.[14]

How does this work? This is not God's arbitrarily calling evil works good. It is not that the works of Christians are indistinguishable from those of non-Christians, God's deciding to accept the former but not the latter. These are genuinely good

---

[11] This is spelt out in *Inst.* 3:15:3–4; 3:17:3–10.

[12] *Inst.* 3:17:1.

[13] *Inst.* 3:17:10.

[14] Ch. 16:6 (*RefConf* 4:252). Article 12 of the Thirty-nine Articles likewise states that 'Good Works, which . . . follow after Justification, cannot put away our sins, and endure the severity of God's Judgement; yet they are pleasing and acceptable to God in Christ.'

works in that they are done in faith from a genuine love for God and neighbour. The reason why such works do not justify in their own right is not because they are totally bad but because they are less than totally pure, because being tainted they fall short of the standards of God's holiness. In Christ, God accepts these works by overlooking their blemishes and accepting what is genuinely good in them. 'Everything imperfect in them is covered by Christ's perfection, every blemish or spot is cleansed away by his purity.'[15] God looks with favour both on the godly and on their good works because he embraces them 'in Christ rather than in themselves'.[16] This is not a matter of his calling vice virtue – as if one were to mug an old lady and God were to declare that a righteous deed. Instead it is a matter of his accepting works that are genuinely good, overlooking their defects – as if one were to help the old lady over the road partly out of compassion for her and partly to impress someone else. This doctrine served a number of different purposes.

First, it had a pastoral aim. It is an important and much needed counterbalance to Calvin's teaching about the sinfulness of even our best works. That may be true in the context of our seeking to be justified by God, but leaves the believer with little incentive. What is the point of striving for good works if even one's best efforts are going to be weighed and found wanting? But once we are accepted in Christ the situation is different. Calvin contrasts those who approach God on the basis of law and merit, who cannot please him without perfect obedience, with those who are his adopted children in Christ, whose feeble works he approves with fatherly generosity.[17] 'We . . . remarkably cheer and comfort the hearts of believers by our teaching, when we tell them that they please God in their works and are without doubt acceptable to him.'[18] It is worth pressing on because God is easily pleased and looks with favour upon our feeble efforts. As George MacDonald put it, 'God is easy to please, but hard to satisfy.'[19] That distinction captures the essence of the doctrine of double justification.

Calvin illustrates this from the manner in which loving parents relate to their children. They will encourage and be delighted by the smallest evidence of progress, but they also long for their children to progress to full maturity. Both halves of this statement are important. When a child comes back from school with their first feeble attempt at writing ('Dear Baddy I luv you'), the

---

[15] *Inst.* 3:17:8.
[16] *Inst.* 3:17:5.
[17] *Inst.* 3:19:4–5.
[18] *Inst.* 3:15:7.
[19] As cited by Lewis, *Mere Christianity*, 168–169.

parents are delighted and do not immediately point out all its imperfections. It will be treasured as a great step forward. But if the child's spelling has not improved ten years on, then they will be concerned. God likewise is pleased with and rewards the least progress, but he will not rest until he has brought us to perfection, until he has transformed us into the image of Christ.

Underlying this is a sound pastoral and psychological principle. We need encouragement, and receiving nothing but criticism can be highly demotivating. Some children suffer from such an environment at home and I heard a woman recall such an experience on the radio. She returned home from school to report to her mother that she had gained 98% in a maths test. 'And what happened to the other 2%, dear?' was the only encouragement she received. Some, inaccurately, perceive God to be like this. Encouragement is very important, but if all we give is encouragement people can soon become proud and complacent. We need to be told of the need to improve as well as to be encouraged for the progress we have made. Encouragement alone can lead to complacency and a lazy unrealism about ourselves.

Secondly, the doctrine also had an exegetical and apologetic aim. The Reformers were forced to account for the many biblical passages where the writer appeals to his own righteousness or that speak of God's rewarding good works. How could these be squared with other biblical teaching against human merit? Double justification was a tool to account for the whole range of biblical data. Calvin states that the aim of the doctrine is that 'Scripture may, without quibbling, be duly brought into agreement with itself.'[20] It enabled Calvin to acknowledge that our works do indeed have value before God and that he looks upon them with favour and rewards them – all because of his kindness to us in Christ. The doctrine of double justification is a way of handling a tension found in Scripture and of doing so by contrasting our standing before God as a strict Judge and God as our loving Father. The doctrine of double justification, like the doctrine of the Trinity, is an attempt to make sense of what is clearly found in the New Testament. It was also an apologetic response to Roman Catholic polemical appeals to biblical teaching about rewards.

Should we hope for reward?

In 1647 Thomas Hooker, the founder and Puritan pastor of Hartford, Connecticut, was on his deathbed. A friend told him that 'he was going to heaven to receive the reward for his extensive labors'. 'No,' he replied, 'I am going to receive mercy.'[21]

---

[20] *Inst.* 3:17:8.
[21] Beeke, 'Reading the Best in Puritan Literature', 138.

Calvin would have agreed with Hooker's affirmation of mercy, but not with his denial of reward. As a skilled exegete Calvin was aware of the New Testament teaching on reward. Our works are all tainted by sin and even were they not we would be no more than unprofitable servants (Luke 17:10). Judged strictly, all our works and all our righteousness fall short.

> Enter not into judgement with your servant,
> for no one living is righteous before you.
> (Ps. 143:2)

Yet our good works, which are the fruit of God's grace, are also 'our' works and are acceptable to God (double justification) and even bring a reward, in this life and the next.[22]

But is hoping for reward not an unworthy motive? Should we not serve God freely, out of love and gratitude, rather than desire for reward? This is undoubtedly true as regards our primary motive. Someone who gave *merely* as an investment programme with an eye to future reward would not be acting virtuously. 'If it is only a matter of men looking for reward when they serve God, and hiring or selling their labor to him, it is of little profit. God wills to be freely worshiped, freely loved.'[23] Cynical calculation for reward is not the right spirit. But to stop there is to be more 'spiritual' than Jesus and the apostles, especially Jesus who taught so much about reward.[24] 'He who is justified will not forget that a reward is laid up for him, but be incited by it as the best stimulus to well-doing. And yet he will not look to this alone.'[25] We need to distinguish between our primary motivation and what may serve as an encouragement. Many parents use bribes to induce their children to do things like learn the piano, but the child will not get far if the bribe is the *only* motive. I found the promise of reward a powerful motive in persuading my children to work hard for key exams – but it worked only because they also desired to do well.

The nature of the reward

What is the reward held out to us? There is a difference between 'extrinsic' and 'intrinsic' rewards. A child may be offered a bribe for learning the piano (an extrinsic reward) but the real (intrinsic) reward is being able to play the piano.

---

[22] *Inst.* 3:15:3.
[23] *Inst.* 3:16:2.
[24] Especially (but not exclusively) in Matt. 5:3–12, 46; 6:1–4, 6, 20; 10:41–42; 16:27; 19:29; 25:14–30. At the end of his life Paul looks forward to the reward that awaits him: 'Henceforth there is laid up for me the crown of righteousness, which the Lord, the righteous judge, will award to me on that Day' (2 Tim. 4:8).
[25] *Acts of the Council of Trent*, can. 31 (*SWJC* 3:162).

The ultimate reward for being generous is becoming a generous person. As adults we are better able to appreciate intrinsic rewards, which is not to say there is no place for extrinsic rewards. A colleague used to motivate himself to mark exam scripts by rewards of chocolate, a practice I have happily adopted.

Do all Christians receive the same reward? There are some who argue that they do, basing this on the parable of the vineyard workers (Matt. 20:1–16). Those who work only one hour receive the same reward as those who have worked all day. If this parable were all that the New Testament taught about reward we could reasonably conclude that all receive the same reward, but it is not. We must ask what is the point of the parable, since parables often teach one main point. The punch line of this parable is the generosity of God and the fact that Gentiles (late-comers) will be accepted alongside Jews: 'Am I not allowed to do what I choose with what belongs to me? Or do you begrudge my generosity?' (20:15). There is much else in the New Testament that implies that rewards will *not* be equal. The apostles are promised a special reward (Matt. 19:28). It is those whose work is of quality that receive a reward (1 Cor. 3:13–14). Martyrs will receive a special recognition (Rev. 6:11). If a reward is promised to a particular group or to people who do particular things, it implies that others do not receive it. To teach that all will receive the identical rewards would be highly demotivating, making a life of discipleship ultimately irrele-vant. If the laziest Christian received the same reward as the apostle Paul, who poured out his life for his ministry and died as a martyr, that would suggest God does not put a high value on our work.

Do our good works merit reward?

'Reward' is clearly a biblical word, but 'merit' is not. The terminology of 'merit' was introduced in the early church, but the Reformers were unhappy with it, though not unwilling to use it in certain contexts. Calvin regarded the word as a non-scriptural term, prone to abuse, used to describe 'the value of good works'.[26] He was emphatic in denying the merit of our good works. It is not legitimately inferred from Scripture, nor does it follow from the fact that God rewards our works. God in his generosity 'bestows unearned rewards upon works that merit no such thing'.[27]

There are three questions to ask concerning merit.

1 Can we boast as if we performed 'good works' all on our own? The answer is no. Our good works are the fruit of the Spirit, but although it is God who does

---

[26] *Inst.* 3:15:2.
[27] *Inst.* 3:15:3.

them in us they are still *our* good works, done by grace. The two sides of this come out well in Philippians 2, where Paul writes, 'Work out your own salvation with fear and trembling, for it is God who works in you, both to will and to work for his good pleasure' (Phil. 2:12–13). Augustine repeatedly affirmed that 'when God crowns our merits he crowns his own gifts'. They are our merits, but their source is God.

2 Do our 'good works' strictly *merit* reward? The answer is no. The doctrine of double justification explains that God values our works above their intrinsic worth.

3 Do our 'good works' have value before God? Calvin repeatedly denies that our works have any worth,[28] and states that our works have value *only* because of God's fatherly generosity in accepting and approving them after we have been justified by faith. He says this so many times and so emphatically that it is hard to explain it as merely rhetorical exaggeration. But it would seem to contradict the very structure of his doctrine of double justification – that they are accepted when their imperfections are covered. The implication of this would seem to be that what remains when the faults are pardoned is indeed of value. When God accepts them he is accepting imperfect virtue, not vice. To say that they are worthless is to belittle the work of the Holy Spirit, who inspires the works.[29]

---

[28] E.g., *Inst.* 3:18:6–7.
[29] For more on Calvin's teaching on this topic, see Raith, *After Merit.*

20
Assurance of salvation

Can we be sure of our salvation?

The sixteenth-century Reformers taught that it is possible to have assurance of salvation, to be certain that one's sins are forgiven and that one is right with God. That has also been the consistent position of the evangelical tradition. Such confidence before God is a great strength of that tradition, but it is always in danger of lapsing into self-confidence or arrogance. 'Let anyone who thinks that he stands take heed lest he fall' (1 Cor. 10:12). The final verse of Toplady's hymn 'A debtor to mercy alone' seems to have lost sight of this warning:

> Yes, I to the end shall endure,
> As sure as the earnest is given;
> More happy, but not more secure,
> The glorified spirits in heaven.

There is a consensus about the possibility of assurance, but much disagreement about the details of this. One can talk about the classic Protestant view of justification, but must talk of a *range* of views on assurance. This can be seen by asking three questions.

Is assurance *integral* to saving faith?

Is assurance of salvation integral to saving faith or is it merely a subsequent possibility? Is it part of the basic package, as it were, or an optional extra? The first view was the majority position at the Reformation, being held by Luther, Melanchthon and Calvin. Calvin's definition of saving faith is basically the conviction that God is favourable to me, as we saw in chapter 18. Trusting in the promises of God implies trusting that we have received what is promised, so assurance is implicitly part of saving faith. This position is well summarized by the answer in the 1563 *Heidelberg Catechism* to the question 'What is true faith?':

> True faith is not only a sure knowledge, whereby I hold for truth all that
> God has revealed to us in his word, but also a hearty trust, which the

Holy Ghost works in me by the gospel, that not only to others, but to me also, forgiveness of sin, everlasting righteousness, and salvation, are freely given by God, merely of grace, only for the sake of Christ's merits.[1]

There is a pastoral danger with this position. If assurance is integral to saving faith, does that mean that those who are unsure of their salvation are thereby proved not to be real Christians? That is not what Luther and others meant; rather the *nature* of saving faith is such that salvation is implicitly assured, whether or not people feel it. Genuine Christians may sometimes lack assurance, for a variety of reasons: because they have been taught to look for assurance in the wrong place, because their faith is weak or because in this life faith always struggles with doubt. The fact that saving faith implies assurance does not mean that believers always grasp that implication. It means that assurance is to be found through faith, through trusting in Christ; not that believers always grasp that clearly.

There was, however, an alternative Reformed tradition according to which assurance is something separate from saving faith, which may well come later, like two different courses of a meal. This position was taught by Bullinger, who greatly influenced the English Reformation, and is also found in the *Westminster Confession of Faith* (1647), which became the doctrinal basis for English-speaking Presbyterianism:

> Such as truly believe in the Lord Jesus, and love him in sincerity, en-deavouring to walk in all good conscience before him, may in this life be certainly assured that they are in a state of grace, and may rejoice in the hope of the glory of God: which hope shall never make them ashamed . . .
>
> This infallible assurance doth not so belong to the essence of faith but that a true believer may wait long and conflict with many difficulties before he be partaker of it: yet, being enabled by the Spirit to know the things which are freely given him of God, he may, without extraordinary revelation, in the right use of ordinary means, attain thereunto.[2]

There were some at that time who saw assurance of salvation as a 'second blessing', for more on which see the excursus to chapter 27.

In some groups, such as the Scottish Free Presbyterians (not to be confused with the Free Church of Scotland, the 'Wee Frees') this has led to assurance becoming a rare phenomenon. They point out that sheep (who outnumber

---

[1] *Heidelberg Catechism*, q. 21 (*RefConf* 2:774).
[2] *Westminster Confession of Faith* 18:1, 3 (*RefConf* 4:254).

people in the Scottish Highlands and Islands) bear a mark of ownership on their ears, which can be seen by all but the sheep themselves. The implication of this analogy is that it will be clear to others that someone is a true Christian, but they themselves may have great difficulty realizing it. In fact, doubting one's salvation has sometimes been seen as a mark of humility and as evidence that one *is* a Christian.

If assurance is not an aspect of saving faith, if it is something to be sought *after* coming to faith, then where is it to be sought? What are the grounds of assurance and, in particular, what is the *primary* ground for assurance?

What is the *primary* ground of assurance?

How can we come to an assurance of salvation? Various potential grounds for assurance have been suggested and most can claim some biblical support. But it is important to distinguish between the *primary* ground on which it is based and others that can give added support. We shall explore these in turn with reference especially to Calvin's doctrine of assurance.[3]

Election

Some have seen Calvin's doctrine of predestination as undermining assurance and it is certainly true that in the seventeenth century predestination caused many to doubt their salvation. Calvin was aware of this possibility and guarded against it in his *Institutes*. We can be tempted to doubt our election and to seek assurance in the wrong way. The wrong way is to ask the question 'Am I elect?' and to seek the answer by speculation about the divine will, about God's decrees. Whoever tries this 'tangles himself in innumerable and inextricable snares; then he buries himself in an abyss of sightless darkness'.

> Consequently, if we fear shipwreck, we must carefully avoid this rock, against which no one is ever dashed without destruction . . . those engulf themselves in a deadly abyss who, to make their election more certain, investigate God's eternal plan apart from his Word.[4]

To speculate directly about one's election is presumption and folly since God has never published a list of the elect. God's Book of Life has never been published. Faith and assurance must rest not on what God has chosen to hide

---

[3] For more on this, see Lane, 'Calvin's Doctrine of Assurance Revisited'. For a contrary view, see Beeke, *Assurance of Faith*, chs 1–4, 6.

[4] *Inst.* 3:24:4.

but on what he has revealed – Christ and the Gospel.[5] It is only in Christ that we are elect and pleasing to God and so it is to him that we must turn. 'We have a sufficiently clear and firm testimony that we have been inscribed in the book of life if we are in communion with Christ.' In other words, assurance of salvation teaches us that we are elect, not vice versa. Here, as elsewhere, the order of being and the order of knowing are reversed. Our election precedes and is the cause of our experiencing salvation; but it is through knowing ourselves as God's children that we come to realize he has chosen us. 'It is [God's] will that we be content with his promises, and not inquire elsewhere whether he will be disposed to hear us.'[6]

Predestination is not simply a potential cause of shipwreck. It is also an aid to assurance and Calvin can even claim that we have no other sure ground of confidence and that predestination is the best confirmation of our faith, from which we reap rich fruits of consolation. This is because election teaches us that salvation is all of grace, that it depends not on our merit but on God's will. To believers who are *already* persuaded of their election and salvation, this is a great comfort. Because their salvation is totally the work of God they can rest assured that God will complete that which he has begun.[7] Election reminds believers that their salvation is ultimately dependent not on their own will and efforts but on God's purposes and that it is therefore as immovable as God's eternal election (Rom. 8:33; Phil. 1:6).

Good works / fruit of the Spirit

Some Christians seek assurance from their good works, from the fruit of the Holy Spirit in their lives. Calvin firmly opposed any such attempt to base our assurance on something within ourselves. He observed that our works and the state of our hearts always fall short of perfection. 'For there is nowhere that fear [of God] which is able to establish full assurance. And the saints are conscious of possessing only such an integrity as intermingled with many vestiges of the flesh.'[8] Any attempt to base assurance on our imperfect works is doomed to failure since the tender conscience will soon see the inadequacy of the foundation. The result of relying upon our works is that our 'conscience feels more fear and consternation than assurance'.[9] Claiming assurance on such a basis shows that we do not recognize our own imperfection and opens the door to self-trust.

---

[5] *Inst.* 3:24:4–5.
[6] *Inst.* 3:24:5.
[7] *Inst.* 3:21:1.
[8] *Inst.* 3:14:19.
[9] *Inst.* 3:14:20.

But the New Testament clearly teaches that holiness is a test of the genuineness of our faith and Calvin openly acknowledged this. Our lives can be a proof to us that we are elect. 'One argument whereby we may prove that we are truly elected by God and not called in vain is that our profession of faith should find its response in a good conscience and an upright life.' But if the faithful may use this argument it is only 'in such a way that they place their sure foundations elsewhere'.[10] The argument from works may never be the *primary* ground of our confidence:

> We only know that we are God's children by His sealing His free adoption on our hearts by His Spirit and by our receiving by faith the sure pledge of it offered in Christ. Therefore, love is an accessory or inferior aid, a prop to our faith, not the foundation on which it rests.[11]

Calvin recognized that our works can strengthen or confirm our confidence, as evidences of God's work in us, and that they are a test of the genuineness of faith. But once they become the primary ground of assurance a *de facto* justification by works has been introduced which will lead either to despair or to a false self-confidence. Calvin acknowledges that 'newness of life, as the effect of divine adoption, serves to confirm confidence; but as a secondary support, whereas we must be founded on grace alone'.[12] It is important to understand what is meant by secondary support. It is not that Christ shows us the basis for salvation and that works then demonstrate to us that we have attained that salvation, with works functioning as the second stage of a process. Rather Christ and the gospel show us that we in particular are accepted by God, and this assurance or conviction is then strengthened when it is confirmed by further evidence.

Among the seventeenth-century English Puritans many sought to derive assurance from their works. People were encouraged to look within, to examine themselves and their works, and to seek assurance that way. This process was sometimes expressed in the form of a syllogism, a type of logical argument described by Aristotle. For example:

Whoever loves has been born of God; [1 John 4:7]
I love;
therefore I have been born of God.

---

[10] Comm. 2 Peter 1:10–11 (*Calvin's Commentaries: Epistles of Peter*, 333–334).
[11] Comm. 1 John 3:19 (*Calvin's Commentaries: First Epistle of John*, 278).
[12] Comm. 1 John 4:17 (*Calvin's Commentaries: First Epistle of John*, 295).

There are problems with this; it can lead to unhealthy introspection. If it involved only observable outward acts, then it would be easy; but how can we be sure our love is *real*? And how much love is required? And have we *really* forgiven someone? Introspection can lead to more and more self-examination and can easily cause those with a tender conscience to lose their assurance. If our assurance is based on our works, then we can easily end up either *trusting* or *doubting* ourselves. The more we become aware of our shortcomings, the less assurance we have.

However, works certainly do have an important role to play, not as the primary ground of assurance but as a reality check (for which see chapters 17 and 18). Our works must not contradict our claim to assurance of salvation.

Holy Spirit or experience

The Wesleys and the evangelical tradition in general introduced an emphasis on experience. John Wesley's conversion was about coming to assurance and experience played a crucial role in this:

> I felt my heart strangely warmed. I felt I did trust in Christ, Christ alone, for salvation: And an assurance was given me, that he had taken away *my* sins, even *mine*, and saved *me* from the law of sin and death.[13]

A few years later he wrote, 'I will still believe none is a true Christian till he experiences it,' though he later revised that view.[14] But experience fluctuates and Wesley lost his assurance for a time not long after his conversion. Experience can play a role in assurance, but it is unreliable as the primary ground, for various reasons. We need assurance not just when everything is going well but in the dark times, when God seems absent and we feel we are praying to a brick wall. Mystical writers refer to 'the dark night of the soul'. An assurance based on experience will not help at this point. Also, experience is not always evidence that we are genuine Christians. Matthew 7:21–23 describes people with a very dramatic charismatic experience (prophecy, casting out demons) to whom he declares at the end, 'I *never* knew you; depart from me, you workers of lawlessness.' Church history also provides many examples of the dangers of a false experience. These were chronicled by Ronald Knox in a classic work entitled *Enthusiasm*.[15]

---

[13] *Journal of John Wesley*, 35 (24 May 1738) (his italics).

[14] Cited by Wood, *Burning Heart*, 251. For his doctrine of assurance, see 250–259; Williams, *John Wesley's Theology Today*, 102–114.

[15] Knox, *Enthusiasm*. 'Enthusiasm' today is mostly a positive word, but in the eighteenth century it was very negative, more akin to 'fanaticism' today. Wesley famously stated, 'Above all else, flee enthusiasm!'

What about the role of the Holy Spirit? Paul twice refers to the Spirit's bearing witness to our adoption as God's children (Rom. 8:16; Gal. 4:6). John also states that we know God lives in us by the Spirit he has given us (1 John 3:24). Calvin recognizes the major role that the Holy Spirit plays in assurance. The outworking of the Spirit in our lives and in our good works is a secondary aid to assurance. The Spirit is the seal and pledge of our adoption and assures us that we are God's children. The Spirit is also given as the earnest of eternal life and assures us of our election.[16] Without the Holy Spirit as a witness in our hearts we falsely assume the name of Christians.[17]

The Holy Spirit is a witness to us of our election. But it is important to be clear how this happens. The Holy Spirit seals our adoption by confirming to us the promises of the Word.[18] It is not that the Holy Spirit gives us a private revelation that we are God's children. This would be to fall into the error of seeking assurance by asking if we are elect, of prying into God's secret will. It is not that the Gospel makes general promises and that the Holy Spirit informs us that these relate to us. This would be to divide the Spirit from the Word, which Calvin strongly condemns.[19] The Holy Spirit confirms our adoption by testifying to us concerning the truth of God's promises, by assuring us of the truth of the Gospel.[20] The testimony of the Spirit is not to be separated from the testimony of the Word. The Spirit brings assurance to us through the gospel, not by giving us personal messages separate from the gospel.

Faith

How do Christians know that God is their gracious Father? By believing the gospel. The evidence of our election is God's effectual calling of us, issuing in our faith.[21] It may therefore appear that for Calvin the ground of assurance is our faith. This could also be expressed in the form of a syllogism:

Whoever believes in him has eternal life; [John 3:16]
I believe in him;
therefore I have eternal life.

But there are problems with making our faith the primary ground of assurance. First, our faith is often weak and plagued with doubts. As Calvin

---

[16] *Inst.* 3:24:1–2.
[17] *Inst.* 3:2:39.
[18] *Inst.* 3:2:36.
[19] *Inst.* 1:9.
[20] See *Inst.* 1:7 on the inner witness of the Holy Spirit.
[21] *Inst.* 3:21:7; 3:24:2.

put it, our faith is always such that we need to pray, 'Lord, help our unbelief' (Mark 9:24).[22] 'Unbelief is, in all men, always mixed with faith.'[23] Also, such an approach easily leads to introspection and questioning the genuineness of our faith, especially because of the phenomenon of 'temporary faith' (see chapter 18), which threatens an assurance based primarily on our own faith. Similarly James warns against the danger of a dead faith (2:17). Clearly the awareness that one believes is a great encouragement to assurance, but to make it the primary ground is to load on to it more than it can bear.

Calvin acknowledges that those with temporary faith can feel some sort of assurance of salvation, though not the same as that experienced by genuine Christians.[24] But if such people can feel confidence, does that not undermine the confidence of true believers? Not necessarily. The fact that some people may be falsely assured does not mean that no one else can have assurance – just as the fact that some people may be convinced that two plus two equals five does not shake my belief that two plus two equals four. The many examples of false faith are not to undermine the Christian's confidence in the promises of God, especially those relating to final perseverance. We are not to abandon all confidence but only a 'crass and sheer confidence of the flesh, which bears in its train haughtiness, arrogance, and contempt of others, snuffs out humility and reverence for God, and makes one forget grace received'. We are to have such a fear that teaches us to receive the grace of God in humility, *without* lessening our confidence.[25]

Christ and the promises of the gospel

For Calvin the ground of assurance does not lie within ourselves. It is not our faith or our works or our experience of the Holy Spirit. These can play a secondary role as a confirmation of or an aid to our assurance. But the primary ground of assurance lies outside us. It is the Gospel, the mercy of God, the free promise of justification in Christ. I know that God is my gracious Father because of his love for me, shown in Christ and declared in his Word. The ground of assurance lies not within ourselves but rather in the promises of God, in Christ. 'Confidence of salvation is founded upon Christ and rests on the promises of the gospel.'[26]

If we have been chosen in [Christ], we shall not find assurance of our election in ourselves; and not even in God the Father, if we conceive him

---

[22] Short Treatise on the Lord's Supper 26 (*SWJC* 2:177–178).
[23] *Inst.* 3:2:24.
[24] *Inst.* 3:2:10–12.
[25] *Inst.* 3:24:7.
[26] Calvin, *Eternal Predestination of God* 2 (p. 56).

as severed from his Son. Christ, then, is the mirror wherein we must, and without self-deception may, contemplate our own election.[27]

The ground of assurance cannot be distinguished from the ground of faith itself – Christ and the promises of God. This follows since, for Calvin, assurance is not a second stage subsequent to faith but is simply faith itself writ large, an implication of faith. Since saving faith is not simply faith in the promises of God *in general* but faith that they apply *to me* (see chapter 18), faith in itself includes assurance. To put your trust in Christ and then to say that you are not sure is contradictory.

It may appear that Calvin has performed a sleight of hand. Since there is no salvation for those who do not believe, as Calvin clearly held, our salvation must depend upon our having believed, which makes faith the ground of our assurance. But this does not follow, for two reasons. First, assurance does not follow from faith as a second stage, as a logical deduction from the fact of my faith. If, as some later Calvinists have held, assurance of salvation is a logical consequence of the fact of my having believed, then it would follow that faith is the ground of assurance. But for Calvin faith and assurance are not separated in this way. Secondly, it is true that there is no salvation without faith but it is not faith that saves but Christ, so assurance, like faith, looks away from ourselves to Christ alone. When we have doubts, the remedy is not to engage in introspection but to turn to Christ and the gospel. Tight-rope walkers should always look ahead because if they look down at their feet they will almost certainly fall off the rope. So also, we should look ahead to Christ for assurance, not look within.

Paul tells us to examine ourselves, to see whether we are in the faith (2 Cor. 13:5). Calvin held to the need for self-examination, but this is not an introspective examination of my faith to see if it is genuine. That Calvin never recommends. It is not the testing of my faith by the fruit of the Spirit in my life. That is *a* test but Calvin is emphatic that the basis of assurance must lie elsewhere. Self-examination does not mean testing my works and deducing my election from them. It is not my faith that is examined but the *object* of my faith. Believers are to examine themselves to ensure that their trust is placed not in themselves but in Christ. They are to 'examine themselves carefully and humbly, lest the confidence of the flesh creep in and replace assurance of faith'.[28] Self-examination does not turn believers to themselves or to their faith

---

[27] *Inst.* 3:24:5.
[28] *Inst.* 3:2:11.

but back to Christ and the Gospel. Believers are not to compare their faith with that of the reprobate but to look to Christ and to place their trust in him.[29] It is not 'Am I *trusting* in Christ?' but 'Am I trusting in *Christ*?'

Can we be sure of *final* salvation?

Can we have assurance of *final* salvation or only of our present condition? In other words, does salvation come with a lifetime guarantee? The answer to this question hangs on whether genuine Christians can lose their salvation, an issue that will be discussed in chapter 28.

---

[29] *Inst.* 3:24:7.

21
Regensburg Colloquy[1]

The Protestant doctrine of justification raised new issues on which the Roman Catholic Church did not have a clearly defined position. As a result there were a variety of responses to the doctrine on the Catholic side, ranging from total rejection to considerable sympathy, and in some instances all but complete acceptance. In particular, there were Catholic humanists, disciples of Erasmus, who wanted to introduce reform within a Roman Catholic framework. They accepted the role of the pope and previously defined Roman Catholic doctrines, and wanted to introduce the doctrine of justification by faith into this framework.

Two main groups adopted this approach. There were reforming, humanist Catholics in Germany, such as Johann Gropper, who sought to introduce reform at Cologne and who wrote an influential *Handbook of Christian Instruction* (1538).[2] There was also a significant group of leading cardinals in Italy, called the *spirituali*, who had similar aims. These included Gasparo Contarini from Venice (1483–1542), who in 1511 had a conversion experience similar to Luther's. (Contarini wrote an account of this in a private letter that has only recently come to light,[3] so would not have been known in his lifetime.) In particular, Gropper and Contarini held that as Christians we remain dependent upon God's mercy, even at the last judgement. This belief, shared with Protestants, was the basis for a common understanding.[4]

---

[1] For a much fuller account, see Lane, *Regensburg Article 5*.
[2] Gropper, *Enchiridion Christianae Institutionis*.
[3] Gleason (ed.), *Reform Thought in Sixteenth-Century Italy*, 24–28.
[4] See Yarnold, '*Duplex Iustitia*'.

Colloquies

In the early years of the Reformation there were many colloquies, ecumenical dialogues, involving Catholic and Protestant theologians, aimed at resolving the differences between the two sides. These took place especially in the Holy Roman Empire, which included Germany and other neighbouring territories, such as northern Italy. This was not a unified state but was composed of a multitude of different states, under the largely nominal control of the Holy Roman Emperor. From 1519 to 1556 Charles V, king of Spain, held this role.

Today, with the benefit of hindsight, it is easy to say that these colloquies were a waste of time, that there was no way the two sides could be joined. That was not so obvious at the time, when Europe had not yet divided into rival rigidly demarcated confessions: Lutheran, Reformed and Roman Catholic. Also, there were compelling reasons for making the effort. First, the participants all believed that the New Testament pattern is for only one church, not a plethora of competing denominations. Secondly, they sought to resolve the religious issue in Germany in order to be able to release troops to respond to the Turkish threat. Having taken Hungary, the Turks besieged Vienna in 1529. Finally, the aim was to avoid civil war. This was no merely theoretical danger and in the seventeenth century Germany was devasted by the Thirty Years War between Catholics and Protestants (1618–48).

Regensburg Colloquy (1541)

The greatest chance of success came in three gatherings held in 1540 and 1541. These began with a colloquy at Hagenau in June and July 1540, which was adjourned to Worms. There it met in November and after long delays Philipp Melanchthon and the Catholic controversialist Johann Eck began to debate original sin in January, reaching agreement in a few days. At this point Nicholas Perrenot de Granvelle, the imperial chancellor, adjourned the debate to the coming Diet at Regensburg.[5] Meanwhile at Worms secret discussions had been taking place (chiefly between Gropper and Martin Bucer) to draw up the Regensburg Book, a collection of twenty-three articles, which was to be used as a basis for further discussion.

The anticipated colloquy took place at the Regensburg Diet, which opened on 5 April.[6] Contarini was present as the papal legate. The emperor selected

---

[5] The Diets were the deliberative assemblies of the Electors of the Holy Roman Emperor.
[6] On this colloquy, see Matheson, *Cardinal Contarini at Regensburg*.

the debaters/negotiators: Bucer, Melanchthon and Johann Pistorius on the Protestant side; Gropper, Eck and Julius Pflug on the Catholic side. Others, like Calvin, were present but not selected as debaters.

Bucer and Gropper were appointed as conciliators with the potential for reaching agreement. Melanchthon and Eck were appointed as hard-liners, whose presence was necessary for the credibility of the proceedings. Melanchthon came with strict instructions not to deviate from the *Augsburg Confession*. Pistorius and Pflug were both chosen as moderates with the aim of keeping Melanchthon and Eck in the minority.

At the emperor's insistence, the Regensburg Book became the basis for discussion. On 27 April the first four articles, on human innocence before the fall, free choice, the cause of sin and original sin were quickly agreed, building on the Worms agreement.

Article 5[7]

The fifth article, on justification, was discussed from 28 April to 2 May. Eck and Melanchthon both found the article in the Regensburg Book unsatisfactory and it was eventually agreed it should be set aside and that there be free discussion to draw up a new article. During the discussions Melanchthon, Eck and Gropper each produced drafts. Eventually, on 2 May, a version was produced (drawing heavily on Gropper's draft) to which all the parties gave their consent. (The text of the article is found at the end of this chapter.) Granvelle and Contarini were jubilant and the latter expressed his joy to Cardinal Alessandro Farnese (the pope's grandson) in Rome: 'God be praised, these Catholic and Protestant theologians resolved to agree on the article of justification, faith and works.' Eck needed some persuasion to sign. The initial response was predominantly positive.

So what did the article teach? The key idea was double righteousness, though that term is not used. Conversion brings about *both* inherent and imputed righteousness. We receive an inherent (infused or imparted) righteousness, which is an inner renewal by the Holy Spirit leading to love and good works. We also receive imputed righteousness, Christ's righteousness reckoned to our account. There is no question of having one without the other. The terminology of double righteousness is different to a greater or lesser extent from that used by all of the participants prior to the colloquy, but the substance of the two righteousnesses is what Protestants call 'justification' and 'sanctification'.

---

[7] On Article 5, see Lane, *Regensburg Article 5*.

Importantly, we are accepted by God on account of Christ and his merit, on account of imputed righteousness, *not* on the basis of inherent righteousness or the righteousness of works. Our inherent righteousness is real but imperfect, and is insufficient for our standing before God. Conversion leads to a real but imperfect inner transformation, which in turn gives birth to good works. Because of the imperfection of our inherent righteousness and of our works, we approach God not on that basis but only through Christ's gift of righteousness imputed to us, his role as mediator and his promises. Protestant concerns are effectively met by the clear and unambiguous insistence that acceptance is on the basis of imputed, not inherent, righteousness.

While God accepts us on the basis of imputed righteousness, he also at the same time gives us his Holy Spirit, through whom we become partakers of the divine nature, are renewed, have inherent righteousness, receive the infusion of love and begin to do good works and fulfil the law. We should grow in holiness and good works. The Catholic concern for love and good works is clearly and unambiguously met by the insistence on the simultaneous gift of the Holy Spirit and love leading to good works. Sanctification is presented not merely as a consequence (whether desirable or inevitable) of justification, but as a parallel and inseparable gift.

Coming to faith involves hating sin in mind and will and repenting, which occur through the prevenient movement of the Spirit. Our free choice has a role to play concurring in good works. Justification is by a living faith, that is a faith which works through love (Gal. 5:6), although the function of faith is to appropriate God's gifts. This proved to be the most controversial point in the article. The problem is not with what the article states, all of which can be substantiated from previous Protestant writings. Eck at the colloquy claimed that because we are justified by a faith that works through love, it is love rather than faith that justifies. This interpretation is manifestly contrary to what the article states, but Eck's claim caused Protestants to be suspicious of the article. Whatever Eck might have said at the colloquy (to justify the fact that he had signed the article) when he came to write about the article he expounded it as a blatantly Protestant document he regarded as heretical.

God has promised to reward our good works, in this life and the next. Eternal life is an inheritance based on promise, but works are rewarded to the extent that they are done in faith and from the Spirit. There is repeated reference to rewards, but no talk of merit.

It is all right to preach justification by faith alone, as long as repentance and good works are also preached. This is an important point, as we saw in considering the New Testament tension in chapter 17. Luther and Melanchthon had already warned against the dangers of a cheap grace without repentance, as we saw in chapter 18.

How was agreement reached? At the colloquy Gropper and Contarini both accepted Protestant ideas which had not previously appeared in their writings. This was not compromise for the sake of reaching an agreement, as both continued to hold and proclaim these ideas *after* the colloquy, even when it was dangerous to do so. Contarini died in 1542, with the Inquisition at his door. Gropper went quiet on these ideas from 1545, making clear in a letter to Pflug that it was better to keep silent about them, but at the end of his life again defended and reaffirmed them.[8]

Reaction to Article 5

The joy and hope engendered were to be short-lived. The colloquy soon began to founder, but that was because of differences on *other* doctrines, such as the infallibility of councils and transubstantiation,[9] not because of shortcomings in the statement on justification. Ironically it was the same Contarini who was willing to be flexible over justification who torpedoed the colloquy by his in-transigence over the word 'transubstantiation'. He insisted on its insertion, since it had been defined by a council, and would not countenance any compromise or delay. While the doctrine of justification had not been defined by the church, transubstantiation had been proclaimed by the Fourth Lateran Council. As with *all* of the colloquies, this one foundered eventually over the issue of authority. For the Reformers all had to be tested by Scripture; for the Catholics by the infallible pronouncements of the church. On 22 May the colloquy came to a close, the article on justification being its only significant achievement. On the 31st the revised version of the Regensburg Book was delivered to the emperor, together with nine new articles the Protestants had composed in opposition to some of the articles in the Book that had not been agreed.

Protestant reactions to Article 5 were mixed. Luther (who was not present) branded it patched and all-embracing. He claimed that the two ideas of justifi-cation by faith alone without works and faith working through love had been thrown and glued together. This is like sewing a new patch on to an old garment. Calvin (who was present) was much more positive:

You will be astonished, I am sure, that our opponents have yielded so much . . . Our friends have thus retained also the substance of the true

---

[8] The claims of this paragraph are defended in Lane, *Regensburg Article 5*.
[9] For details, see Matheson, *Cardinal Contarini at Regensburg*, 114–135.

doctrine, so that nothing can be comprehended within it which is not to be found in our writings; you will desire, I know, a more distinct explication and statement of the doctrine, and, in that respect, you shall find me in complete agreement with yourself. However, if you consider with what kind of men we have to agree upon this doctrine, you will acknowledge that much has been accomplished.[10]

It was widely acknowledged that the article was consistent with both the *Augsburg Confession* and Melanchthon's *Apology of the Augsburg Confession*.

On the Catholic side Contarini continued to commend and defend the article, as did Gropper and Pflug. Eck sought to distance himself from it. In Rome the pope did not want it to be widely seen so it was not read in consistory. Those who did see it said that though the sense might be Catholic, the wording was too ambiguous. The pope neither approved nor disapproved of the article. It is noteworthy that in these early stages the charge against Article 5 was ambiguity, not unorthodoxy, and even the hardline Cardinal Carafa (later Pope Paul IV) thought it could be given a Catholic interpretation.

Essentially both the Protestant and Catholic responses were twofold. Some maintained that the Regensburg article was compatible with their own teaching. Others regarded it as a compromising patchwork that was dangerously ambiguous rather than actually false. Both sides agreed that further explanation was necessary. They were concerned not so much with the content of Article 5 as fear of how the other side would exploit it.

The goal of the colloquy was agreement across the board, not on one article only. The enthusiasm that greeted Article 5 was enthusiasm for the prospect of agreement across the board, not enthusiasm for the idea of agreeing on one point only. As with negotiations within the European Union today, 'nothing is agreed until everything is agreed'. Any concessions made in negotiations do not come into force until the entire deal is agreed. Events were soon to prove how unrealistic this was. It should be noted that while failure to agree on other articles dramatically undermined the value of Article 5 in the context of the colloquy, it does not of itself indicate that the agreement on justification was not genuine.

After the breakdown of the colloquy those who had been willing to make concessions were criticized by their own sides. On all sides conciliation gave way to recrimination as the participants published works focusing not on the limited agreement reached but on the reasons for the failure of the colloquy.[11]

---

[10] Calvin to Farel (11 May 1541) (*SWJC* 4:260).

[11] Martin Bucer was an honourable exception, defending Article 5 at great length in his 1542 work *De vera . . . reconciliatione et compositione*.

The breakdown of the Regensburg Colloquy revealed the irreconcilable nature of the split between the two sides. One response was the reorganization of the Inquisition in 1542. Conciliation and negotiation had failed. The need now was for clear lines of demarcation. It was with that in mind that the Council of Trent (1545–63) was called. This set out to define Roman Catholic dogma in a firmly anti-Protestant manner, as in the *Decree on Justification* (1547), as we shall see in the next chapter.[12]

Appendix: the text of Article 5[13]

The justification of man

1 (1) No Christian should doubt that after the fall of our first parent all men are, as the apostle says, born children of wrath [Eph. 2:3] and enemies of God [Rom. 5:10] and thereby are in death [Rom. 5:21; Eph. 2:1] and slavery to sin [Rom. 6:16–20].

2 (1) Likewise, no Christian should question that nobody can be reconciled with God, nor set free from slavery to sin, except by Christ the one mediator between God and men [1 Tim. 2:5], by whose grace, as the apostle said to the Romans, we are not only reconciled to God [5:10] and set free from slavery to sin [6:18, 22], but also made sharers in the divine nature [2 Peter 1:4] and children of God [Rom. 8:14–16].

3 (1) Likewise, it is quite clear that adults do not obtain these blessings of Christ, except by the prevenient movement of the Holy Spirit, by which their mind and will are moved to hate sin. (2) For, as St. Augustine says, it is impossible to begin a new life if we do not repent of the former one. (3) Likewise, in the last chapter of Luke, Christ commands that repentance and forgiveness of sin should be preached in his name [24:47]. (4) Also, John the Baptist, sent to prepare the way of the Lord, preached repentance, saying: 'Repent, for the kingdom of heaven is drawing near' [Matt. 3:2]. (5) Next, man's mind is moved toward God by the Holy Spirit through Christ and this movement is through faith. Through this [faith] man's mind believes with certainty all that God has transmitted, and also with full certainty and without doubt assents to the promises made to us by God who, as stated in the Psalm, is faithful in all his words [145:13]. From there he acquires confidence on account of God's promise, by which he has

---

[12] For the contrast between Regensburg and Trent, see Lane, 'Tale of Two Imperial Cities: Justification at Regensburg and Trent'.

[13] Lane, *Regensburg Article 5 on Justification*, 329–333.

pledged that he will remit sins freely and that he will adopt as children those who believe in Christ, those I say who repent of their former life. (6) By this faith, he is lifted up to God by the Holy Spirit and so he receives the Holy Spirit, remission of sins, imputation of righteousness and countless other gifts.

4 (1) So it is a reliable and sound doctrine that the sinner is justified by living and effectual faith, for through it we are pleasing and acceptable to God on account of Christ. (2) And living faith is what we call the movement of the Holy Spirit, by which those who truly repent of their old life are lifted up to God and truly appropriate the mercy promised in Christ, so that they now truly recognize that they have received the remission of sins and reconciliation on account of the merits of Christ, through the free goodness of God, and cry out to God: 'Abba Father' [Rom. 8:15; Gal. 4:6]. (3) But this happens to no one unless also at the same time love is infused which heals the will so that the healed will may begin to fulfil the law, just as Saint Augustine said. (4) So living faith is that which both appropriates mercy in Christ, believing that the righteousness which is in Christ is freely imputed to it, and at the same time receives the promise of the Holy Spirit and love. (5) Therefore the faith that truly justifies is that faith which is effectual through love [Gal. 5:6]. (6) Nevertheless it remains true, that it is by this faith that we are justified (i.e. accepted and reconciled to God) inasmuch as it appropriates the mercy and righteousness which is imputed to us on account of Christ and his merit, not on account of the worthiness or perfection of the righteousness communicated to us in Christ.

5 (1) Although the one who is justified receives righteousness and through Christ also has inherent [righteousness], as the apostle says: 'you are washed, you are sanctified, you are justified, etc.' [1 Cor. 6:11] (which is why the holy fathers made use of [the term] 'to be justified' even to mean 'to receive inherent righteousness'), nevertheless, the faithful soul depends not on this, but only on the righteousness of Christ given to us as a gift, without which there is and can be no righteousness at all. (2) And thus by faith in Christ we are justified or reckoned to be righteous, that is we are accepted through his merits and not on account of our own worthiness or works. (3) And on account of the righteousness inherent in us we are said to be righteous, because the works which we perform are righteous, according to the saying of John: 'whoever does what is right is righteous' [1 John 3:7].

6 (1) Although fear of God, patience, humility and other virtues ought always to grow in the regenerate, because this renewal is imperfect and enormous

weakness remains in them, it should nevertheless be taught that those who truly repent may always hold with most certain faith that they are pleasing to God on account of Christ the mediator. For it is Christ who is the propitiator, the High Priest and the one who prays for us, the one the Father gave to us and with him all good things [Rom. 8:32].

7 (1) Seeing that in our weakness there is no perfect certainty and that there are many weak and fearful consciences, which often struggle against great doubt, nobody should be excluded from the grace of Christ on account of such weakness. Such people should be earnestly encouraged boldly to set the promises of Christ against these doubts and by diligent intercession to pray that their faith may be increased, according to the saying: 'Lord increase our faith' [Luke 17:5].

8 (1) Likewise, every Christian should learn that this grace and this regeneration have not been given to us so that we might remain idle in that stage of our renewal which we at first obtained, but so that we may grow in everything into him who is the head [Eph. 4:15]. (2) Therefore, the people must be taught to devote effort to this growth which indeed happens through good works, both internal and external, which are commanded and commended by God. To these works God has, in many passages from the Gospels, clearly and manifestly promised on account of Christ a reward – good things in this life, as much for the body as for the soul (as much as seems right to divine providence) and after this life in heaven. (3) Therefore, although the inheritance of eternal life is due to the regenerate on account of the promise, as soon as they are reborn in Christ, nevertheless God also renders a reward to good works, not according to the substance of the works, nor because they come from us, but to the extent that they are performed in faith and proceed from the Holy Spirit, who dwells in us, free choice concurring as a partial agent.

9 (1) The joy of those who have performed more and better works will be greater and more abundant, on account of the increase of faith and love, in which they have grown through exercises of that kind.

10 (1) Now those who say that we are justified by faith alone should at the same time teach the doctrine of repentance, of the fear of God, of the judgement of God and of good works, so that all the chief points of the preaching may remain firm, as Christ said: 'preaching repentance and the remission of sins in my name' [Luke 24:47]. (2) And that is to prevent this way of speaking from being understood other than has been previously mentioned.

22
Council of Trent

The breakdown of the Regensburg Colloquy revealed the irreconcilable nature of the split between the two sides. Conciliation and negotiation had failed. The need now was for clear lines of demarcation. In 1542 Pope Paul III called the Council of Trent. The council met in three phases: 1545–7, 1551–2 and 1562–3. It set out to define Catholic doctrine in opposition to Protestantism and to introduce disciplinary reform within the Roman Catholic Church. One of the most significant documents produced by the council was the *Decree on Justification*.[1]

The origins of the *Decree on Justification* (1547)

Debate opened on 21 June 1546 and the final version of the decree was promulgated on 13 January the following year.

There were five different drafts of the decree, drawn up by Cardinal Girolamo Seripando, who shared with Catholics like Contarini and Gropper a belief in the Christian's continuing need for mercy. He repeatedly sought to introduce this idea into his drafts, together with the idea of a double righteousness, but each time it was rejected by the Council.

Two issues proved to be especially contentious. The first was the doctrine of double righteousness.[2] This doctrine was put forward by Seripando, who held that the 'imperfect justice which the just man is able to attain deserves to be rewarded with eternal life only when it is complemented by Christ's justice'.[3] Therefore the Christian at the last judgement should 'appeal to God's mercy and put his trust in the merits of Christ'.[4] His was a doctrine of double righteousness according to which inherent righteousness is insufficient

---

[1] For a fuller account, see Lane, *Justification by Faith*, 60–85; McGrath, *Iustitia Dei*, 308–357. On the decree, see Jedin, *History of Council of Trent*, 2:166–196, 234–235, 239–261, 283–316.

[2] For discussions of this at Trent, see especially Jedin, *History of Council of Trent*, 2:241–249, 253–258, 284–288, 308. Also, Jedin, *Papal Legate at Council of Trent*, 348–392; Yarnold, '*Duplex Iustitia*', 213–222.

[3] Jedin, *Papal Legate*, 335.

[4] Jedin, *History of Council of Trent*, 2:284.

(because of our concupiscence) and needs to be complemented by imputed righteousness.[5]

In drawing up the second draft of the decree, submitted in August 1546, Seripando included a chapter 'On double righteousness'.[6] This was rejected by a committee, which changed the text to state, 'There are not two righteousnesses, which are given us, God's and Christ's, but one righteousness of God through Jesus Christ, that is love or grace, by which the justified are not merely reputed, but truly called and are righteous.'

Seripando raised the issue again in October, questioning the rejection of the doctrine of double righteousness, which was held by Catholic theologians in Italy and Germany, such as Contarini and Gropper.[7] There was some sympathy for Seripando at the level of practical piety, but his view was felt to be defective theologically. Some spoke of demanding eternal life as of right at the last judgement, while others thought that to boast there of good works was to be a Pharisee. Diego Lainez branded double righteousness a Lutheran novelty and warned against turning the throne of justice into a throne of mercy.[8]

Seripando was faced with the thankless task of producing the next draft and concluded it with a further reference to the continuing need for mercy:

> Because no one should judge himself, lest he fall into the devil's snare, the righteous should not cease to call on God's mercy for their sins, offences and negligencies and to trust in the merits of our Lord Jesus Christ.

This is because we shall be judged by the secret judgement of God at the end and ought not to judge ourselves before then.[9] In the revised version of the draft the inscrutability of God's judgement remains, but the opposite conclusion is drawn. Instead of the exhortation to call on mercy or trust Christ's merits there is the statement that

> nothing more is needed for the justified to be said (provided they have worked with that affection of love which is required in this mortal life) to have fully satisfied God's law and, as it were sprinkled everywhere with divine grace, to have truly merited eternal life.[10]

---

[5] Jedin, *Papal Legate*, 315–325.
[6] Jedin, *History of Council of Trent*, 2:241, 243.
[7] Jedin, *History of Council of Trent*, 2:247–248.
[8] Jedin, *History of Council of Trent*, 2:253–258.
[9] Jedin, *Papal Legate*, 377.
[10] Jedin, *Papal Legate*, 378.

This statement of the adequacy of works is repeated, with minor changes, in the final decree (ch. 16). Seripando felt betrayed and wrote in the margin that the whole passage was the work of someone who did not know what he was talking about or who was afraid of falling into Lutheran error.[11]

In November, feeling hard done by, Seripando gave an impassioned speech, defending his orthodoxy. Here he proposed two further additions in an attempt to retain the idea of the need for continuing mercy. The first was a statement that those who know that their love is inadequate should 'call upon God's mercy for the sake of the merits of Christ's Passion'.[12] The second was that where it was stated that the Christian should 'keep before his eyes the strict judgment of God' there should be added that this should lead to 'fleeing to the mercy of God through the merits of Christ with the sorrow of penitence'.[13] Both proposals were rejected.[14]

Seripando was thwarted at every point. His doctrine of double righteousness was rejected, though not formally condemned. His belief in the need for continuing mercy was rejected. Instead the sufficiency of inherent righteousness was affirmed.

The other disputed issue concerned the certitude of being in a state of grace, the Catholic way of describing assurance of salvation.[15] Here there were significant differences between those who held to an element of certitude and those who rejected it. Those who argued for some degree of certitude did so on the basis of 'the objective efficacy of the sacraments'.[16] To a large extent the differences lay in terminology and there was widespread acceptance of the idea of 'a moral certitude, which does not preclude self-deception'.[17] For a time it looked as if the council would not be able to make any positive statement on the topic, but at the last hour a compromise formula was agreed and included in the decree. Whereas double righteousness was clearly rejected by the council, with the question of certitude it was a matter of finding a form of words acceptable to both sides.

If these were the questions to be answered, of greater influence upon the form of the decree was the tripartite structure proposed at the beginning of the debates. There were three stages in the process of justification. First, the

---

[11] Jedin, *Papal Legate*, 378.
[12] Jedin, *History of Council of Trent*, 287–288.
[13] Jedin, *History of Council of Trent*, 2:288.
[14] Jedin, *History of Council of Trent*, 2:292.
[15] For discussions of this at Trent, see Jedin, *History of Council of Trent*, 2:249–253, 285–286, 288–290, 297–298.
[16] Jedin, *History of Council of Trent*, 2:251–252, 289.
[17] Jedin, *History of Council of Trent*, 2:252.

conversion of an adult unbeliever to the faith, a rare event in sixteenth-century Europe. Secondly, the means by which justified and baptized Christians preserve their justification, progress in it and attain to eternal glory. Thirdly, the way in which those who fall from grace can recover their forfeited justification.[18] The final decree broadly, but not totally, follows this structure. In expounding the decree we shall follow these three headings and add a fourth: certitude of being in a state of grace.

The decree begins with a positive exposition of the doctrine in sixteen chapters and concludes with thirty-three canons, each anathematizing a heretical statement. In what follows we shall expound the positive doctrine of the sixteen chapters.[19]

Stage I: initial justification of adults (chs 1–8)

The decree begins by describing how the adult convert becomes a Christian and is justified. All people have lost their innocence in Adam's sin and are children of wrath (Eph. 2:3). Neither Gentiles nor Jews could by their own efforts escape from their bondage to sin, but God sent his Son as a propitiator for our sins and those of the whole world (chs 1–2). Just as their unrighteousness stems from our birth in Adam, in order to be justified they need to be born again in Christ; that is, move from their fallen state in Adam to a state of grace and adoption. This move cannot take place without baptism or the desire for it (chs 3–4). With adults the first move is taken by God's predisposing grace, a call that comes from him without any merits on their part. They then have the free choice as to whether to assent to this grace and cooperate with it or to reject it. It is wrong to suppose either that we do nothing or that we can turn to God of our own free will without grace (ch. 5).

Cooperating with grace leads to a series of events that prepare us for justification. By hearing we come to believe that God is one who justifies the ungodly by his grace (Rom. 4:5). Recognizing that we ourselves are sinners and considering God's mercy, we turn from fear of divine justice to hope in God's mercy, trusting that God will be favourable to us for Christ's sake. We then begin to love God, the source of righteousness, and are thus moved to hate sin and repent of it. We then resolve to receive baptism, begin a new life and keep the commandments (ch. 6).

---

[18] Jedin, *History of Council of Trent*, 2:181–182.

[19] Quotations from the decree are my own translation, made with reference to previous translations, as in Leith (ed.), *Creeds of the Churches*, 408–424; Tanner (ed.), *Decrees of the Ecumenical Councils*, 2:671–681.

This process of preparation comes before justification itself, 'which is not only the remission of sins but also the sanctification and renewal of the inner person' whereby we change from being unrighteous to righteous, an enemy of God to his friend. Five different causes of justification are given. The *final* cause (the end or purpose for which a change is produced) is 'the glory of God and of Jesus Christ, and eternal life'. The *efficient* cause (the agent producing the change) is the merciful God, who freely washes and sanctifies us, sealing and anointing us with the Spirit. The *meritorious* cause (an intermediate cause that contributes to a change by making it worthy of taking place) is the Lord Jesus Christ, who merited our justification by his passion, making satisfaction for us to the Father. The *instrumental* cause (the means used to bring about a change) is 'the sacrament of baptism (the sacrament of faith) without which [faith] no one was ever justified'. Lastly, the sole *formal* cause (that which makes something to be what it is) is 'the righteousness of God – not that by which he himself is righteous, but that by which he makes us righteous' (ch. 7). It is noteworthy that of these five causes, four refer to God's action and only one to human activity. Since at the time of Trent the overwhelming majority of Catholics were baptized as infants, although the instrumental cause refers to human activity it involved mere passivity on the part of the one justified.

Having received the righteousness of God, 'we are renewed in the spirit of our mind. Thus we are not merely considered to be righteous [imputed righteousness] but are truly called righteous and are righteous [imparted righteousness]. We receive righteousness within us.' To be justified we need to receive the merits of Christ's passion but this involves the love of God being poured out in our hearts by the Holy Spirit and abiding in us. In justification we receive not just the forgiveness of sins but also the infusion of faith, hope and love. Faith without the addition of hope and love does not unite us with Christ and faith without works is dead. Newly baptized believers are summoned to keep the commandments in order to preserve their new righteousness spotless for the final judgement (ch. 7).

How are we to understand Paul's teaching that we are justified by faith and freely? This means that faith is 'the beginning of human salvation, the foundation and root of all justification'. Justification is a free gift because it is not merited by anything that precedes it, whether faith or works (ch. 8).

What are we to make of this? First, the waters are muddied by the fact that words have different meanings from those found in Protestant theology. Trent follows Catholic usage of viewing faith as intellectual head knowledge. The Reformers never thought that such a faith could save. Hope is described as a personal trust (trusting that God will be favourable to us for Christ's sake), in words remarkably similar to Calvin's definition of saving faith, on which see chapter 18. The definition of justification includes both forgiveness and renewal, which Protestants see as sanctification. Trent refuses the Protestant distinction between justification and sanctification. But it would be wrong to see this as merely a difference in definition, because the Protestant distinction and the Catholic refusal to make the distinction are both intimately linked to their respective views of justification.

Beyond these linguistic differences lies a serious doctrinal issue. Trent affirms that at conversion two things happen: we are inwardly renewed and are accounted righteous by God. The Reformers also agreed that the same two things happened. But on what *grounds* are we accounted righteous? For the Reformers this is clear – we are accounted righteous because of the righteousness of Christ that is reckoned to our account, imputed to us. At conversion we are indeed changed and renewed, but the ground for our acceptance by God is not this inward renewal but the 'alien' righteousness of Christ reckoned to us. What is the Tridentine position? Trent teaches that we are accepted by God on the basis of the righteousness he has implanted in us – this being the implication of the fact that the sole formal cause of justification is 'the righteousness of God – not that by which he himself is righteous, but that by which he makes us righteous' (ch. 7). The difference over the formal cause of justification has traditionally been identified as the fundamental difference between the two sides.[20]

The key issue is, on what basis does God accept us? For the Reformers, the converted Christian is renewed and begins to do good works, but both the renewal and the works remain imperfect. For acceptance by God we rely not on these imperfect works, but on God's mercy in Christ. (Regensburg Article 5 teaches the same.) For Trent we are accepted by God because we 'are truly called righteous and are righteous'. For the Reformers and for Article 5, we are accepted because of Christ's righteousness *imputed* to us; for Trent, we are accepted because the Holy Spirit has implanted righteousness within us, because of Christ's righteousness *imparted* to us.

Stage II: progression in justification (chs 7, 10–11, 16)

According to the Protestant definition, justification, like pregnancy, is binary – either you are or you are not. But since the Catholic definition includes sanctification (renewal by the Holy Spirit and becoming righteous) growth in

---

[20] E.g. by McGrath, *Iustitia Dei*, 417.

justification is both possible and necessary. The decree does not stop with the acquisition of justification. At conversion we receive a true and Christian righteousness and need to keep the commandments and preserve our righteousness spotless for the day of judgement and thus gain eternal life (ch. 7). The converted and justified Christian needs to grow in righteousness/justification, which we have received through Christ's grace, by daily discipleship and keeping the commandments of God and of the church. So, quoting a variant reading from the Latin Vulgate translation, 'He that is righteous, let him be further justified' (Rev. 22:11) (ch. 10).

Justification does not exempt us from keeping the commandments and we should not say they are impossible to observe, with God's help. We do not cease to be righteous by committing everyday venial sins. We should not be misled into thinking that 'faith alone' is enough, without discipleship, that we shall gain our inheritance and glory without first suffering with Christ. We are to seek God's glory and also to look for a reward (ch. 11).

God will reward the works of the faithful Christian. Eternal life at the end is held out 'both as a grace mercifully promised to the sons of God through Jesus Christ and as a reward to be faithfully rendered to their good works and merits, according to the promise of God himself'. It is indeed a gift of grace in that it is only by God's help that we can achieve it. It is only because, as head to the body and the vine to its branches, he strengthens us that we are able to perform meritorious works that please God. But at the same time

> nothing further is wanting to the justified, to prevent their being accounted to have, by those works which have been done in God, fully satisfied the divine law according to the state of this life, and to have truly merited eternal life.

This happens only because of God's grace at work within us. Our righteousness is our own, but it does not originate from us. 'Our' righteousness is the same righteousness imparted to us by God through Christ's merit. God has promised a reward for our works, but we must remember that our merits are his gifts and trust and glory in him, not in ourselves. Because of our proneness to offend, we should keep in mind God's severity and judgement as much as his mercy and goodness and not presume to judge ourselves (ch. 16).

From a Protestant point of view, the claim that we truly merit eternal life is arguably the most objectionable feature of the decree. It stands in sharp contrast both to Regensburg, Article 5, and to Seripando, both of which teach the imperfection of our works. Seripando attempted to include in the decree the statement that at the last judgement we need God's mercy as we fall short of fully satisfying God's standards, but the Council refused to include it.

Stage III: loss and recovery of justification (chs 13–15)

Since justified Christians 'are not merely considered to be righteous but are truly called righteous and are righteous' (ch. 7), what happens when they sin? Roman Catholic theology distinguishes between mortal sin, which severs our relationship with God and cuts us off from his grace, and less serious venial sins, which do not. When we commit a mortal sin we need to repent, to change heart, and then to go to confession, to the sacrament of penance. At baptism/initial justification, all sins are washed away. When we sin as Christians it is not so simple. Through penance the eternal punishment due to our sin is waived; that is, we are no longer headed for hell. But there is also a temporal punishment due to sin – to venial as well as mortal sins. (This is an idea that goes back to the third century and had developed considerably in the intervening years.) By sinning as Christians we dishonour God and need to offer him some compensation or satisfaction for this dishonour. How do we do that? By doing more than is strictly required; for example, by giving alms to the poor, by going on pilgrimage, by hearing mass, and so on. These 'extra' works are called works of supererogation. By doing them we offer satisfaction to God, thus paying off the debt we owe. Any debt remaining at the end of our life is paid by spending time in *purgatory*. This was seen as a place for those who are destined for heaven, but who need to settle their debts before they can enter. The pains of *purgatory* were seen as the same as those of *hell*, but with the important difference that *purgatory*, unlike hell, is only temporary. Another way of settling the debt is by earning or purchasing indulgences, either for oneself while alive or for one's departed relatives. And, of course, it was the sale of indulgences that sparked off the Reformation. In particular, it was the sale of indulgences to fund the building of the new St Peter's basilica in Rome, so that church can in a sense be seen as a monument to Luther and the Reformation!

It is those who persevere to the end who will be saved and we need to be vigilant lest we fall (ch. 13). If by sin we do fall away from the grace of justification, it is possible to regain it, through the sacrament of penance. This repentance of a Christian after falling is very different from that at baptism. It requires not only a change of heart but also the sacramental confession of one's sins (at least the desire to confess), priestly absolution and making satisfaction. God remits the eternal punishment due to our sin, but there remains a temporal punishment which is due and it is for this that we must offer satisfaction through fasting, almsgiving, prayers and the like (ch. 14). It is not only by falling from faith that the grace of justification is lost. Committing any other mortal sin causes it to be lost, even if faith remains (ch. 15).

The first eight chapters of the decree are about initial justification, which is basically by grace through faith. For the sixteenth-century Catholic this refers to their infant baptism, before they can remember. The Christian life as they actually experienced it was about salvation by merit. It was about struggling to pay off the temporal punishment for their sins by accruing merit, through fasting, visiting relics and other works of supererogation. People lived in fear of dying in debt and spending time in purgatory. A plenary indulgence, one that wipes the slate clean of all debt, was hugely attractive. This could be purchased or acquired by deeds like visiting Rome in a Holy Year.

Certitude of being in a state of grace (chs 9, 12–13)

Many of the Reformers saw assurance that our sins have been forgiven as a part of saving faith, as described in chapter 20. Trent disagrees strongly. One should believe firmly that forgiveness is only possible 'freely by the mercy of God for Christ's sake', but it is not part of saving faith to be confident that one's own sins are forgiven. We should not doubt God's mercy, Christ's merit or the efficacy of the sacraments; but at the same time we can be apprehensive about our own spiritual state since 'no one can know with a certainty of faith, which cannot be subject to error, that he has obtained the grace of God' (ch. 9). The decree does not deny that one may be fairly sure that one is right with God, but there is always the possibility of self-deception.

Even if we could be sure that we are right now in a state of grace, this would be no guarantee of final salvation, because of the possibility of sin and the uncertainty whether one will then repent. It is those who persevere to the end who will be saved and we cannot know that we shall not fall away and lose our salvation. One cannot know for certain whether one is elect: 'except by special revelation it cannot be known whom God has chosen for himself' (ch. 12). This statement was not meant to encourage people to look for such a special revelation, but was intended as an answer to the objection that the apostle Paul did seem to have an assurance of final salvation. We should hope firmly in God's help, but we cannot be sure of the final outcome with absolute certainty, although unless we neglect God's grace he will bring to completion the work that he has begun (ch. 13). God does not abandon those who are justified unless he is first abandoned by them (ch. 11).

It has been said that in the debates which gave birth to the decree four essential concerns recur. These are 'the defense of the necessity and worth of "cooperation" and works', 'the rejection of the idea that justification is given to the sinner *sola fide*', the rejection of any doctrine of justification that excludes grace and love, and 'the rejection of the certainty of salvation (certainty of forgiveness, certainty of faith)'.[21] These will be considered in chapter 24.

After Trent

The Tridentine *Decree on Justification* is one of the most impressive achievements of the council. The leaders of the council had reported to Rome that 'the significance of this Council in the theological sphere lies chiefly in the article on justification, in fact this is the most important item the Council has to deal with'.[22] But reading it can give one a false impression of the importance of the doctrine within Roman Catholicism. The decree was needed and the doctrine received the attention that it did because of the Protestant challenge. But for the inner life of the Catholic Church the doctrine was not very important. In 1566 Pope Pius V promulgated the first ever catechism for the whole Catholic Church, the so-called *Roman Catechism*, which draws on the documents from the council.[23] This is a substantial work and the English translation is nearly 500 pages long. It scarcely mentions justification, with a mere twelve to twenty passing references, mostly in the context of teaching on the sacraments. By contrast, the whole catechism is built around the sacramental system, which is central in a way that justification is not. For instance, there are about twenty pages on the sacrament of penance and the need to offer satisfaction for our sin. The sacramental system is as central to the catechism as the doctrine of justification is peripheral and the need to offer satisfaction for our sins receives the sustained exposition[24] denied to justification. Justification needed to be treated in response to the Protestant threat, but the heart of the Christian life in Catholicism is not justification but the sacramental system.

---

21 Pesch, 'Canons of Tridentine Decree on Justification', 181, 184, 186.
22 Cited in Jedin, *History of Council of Trent*, 2:171.
23 Donovan, *Catechism of the Council of Trent*.
24 Donovan, *Catechism of the Council of Trent*, 285–294.

23
Modern ecumenical dialogues

The second half of the twentieth century saw a series of ecumenical dialogues on the doctrine of justification, mostly but by no means exclusively between Lutherans and Catholics. We shall consider six key documents, culminating in the *Joint Declaration on the Doctrine of Justification* (1999), also touching on several others.[1]

Hans Küng, *Justification* (1957)[2]

Hans Küng's *Justification* was one of the two epoch-making theology doctoral theses of the twentieth century. In it he made the remarkable claim that Karl Barth's theology of justification is compatible with Catholic teaching. This was a bold claim as Barth's theology was not noted for its sympathy with Roman Catholicism. It was also bold because this was before the election of Pope John XXIII and the ensuing changes in attitude towards Protestantism.

> Protestants speak of a declaration of justice and Catholics of a making just. But Protestants speak of a declaring just which includes a making just; and Catholics of a making just which supposes a declaring just. Is it not time to stop arguing about imaginary differences?[3]

Barth responded with 'A Letter to the Author' in which he states that *if* Catholic teaching is as Küng expounds it then 'I must certainly admit that my view of justification agrees with the Roman Catholic view; if only for the reason that the Roman Catholic teaching would then be most strikingly in accord with mine!'[4] He goes on to question the accuracy of Küng's representation of Catholic teaching and says that it is for Catholic scholars to pronounce on that. In fact Küng's thesis was warmly received by Catholic scholars, with

---

[1] For a fuller account, see Lane, *Justification by Faith*, 87–126; Lane, 'Justification'.
[2] The date of the German original is 1957. I quote from the 1964 English translation.
[3] Küng, *Justification*, 211.
[4] Küng, *Justification*, xvii–xviii.

favourable reviews from, among others, Karl Rahner and Joseph Ratzinger (later Pope Benedict XVI).

The accuracy of Küng's analysis has been questioned, especially on the grounds that he focuses on initial justification and devotes little attention to issues like post-baptismal sin, satisfaction and penance. But the important point is that Roman Catholic theologians have largely accepted his thesis, resulting in a much greater openness towards the Protestant doctrine. This theological outcome remains a fact, regardless of the accuracy or otherwise of Küng's historical analysis.

Küng's attitude to Luther is an indicator of the change that took place in the twentieth century. At the beginning of the century, in his *Luther and Lutherdom* (1904), Heinrich Denifle portrayed Luther as a wicked heretic who debauched a nun by marrying her, and claimed that the root of Luther's doctrine of justification was his immorality. In the 1940s Joseph Lortz revised this traditional view, portraying Luther as a sincere theologian, who was led astray by the heretical late-medieval Nominalist theology he had been taught. Had he been taught the pure milk of Thomism the Reformation would never have happened. For Küng, however, Luther was not just sincerely misguided, but a prophetic figure who rediscovered elements of Pauline teaching, which the Catholic Church needed to learn – though Küng remained critical of Luther and by no means accepted all that he taught. This huge change over the course of the century came home to me once when I was in a Catholic Truth Society bookshop and found a book on Luther – in the section on saints!

Justification by Faith (Common Statement) (1985)

If the dialogue began with the Reformed theologian Barth it soon shifted to Lutherans. In 1972, the Joint Lutheran–Roman Catholic Study Commission's 'Malta Report' noted that 'today . . . a far-reaching consensus is developing in the interpretation of justification' and 'a far-reaching agreement in the understanding of the doctrine of justification appears possible' (§26).[5] This led to a number of Lutheran–Catholic dialogues. The first took place in the USA, being the seventh in a series of dialogues on different topics. There was a published volume,[6] and this contains the background papers as well as three chapters of Common Statement.

---

[5] Meyer and Vischer (eds), *Growth in Agreement*, 174.
[6] Anderson et al. (eds), *Justification by Faith: Lutherans and Catholics in Dialogue*.

The first chapter of Common Statement is a thorough survey of 'The History of the Question' from Augustine to today (§§5–93).

The second chapter (§§94–121) focuses on six key issues: forensic (i.e. imputed) justification; the sinfulness of the justified; the sufficiency of faith; merit; satisfaction; the criteria for what is 'authentically Christian'. Many of the difficulties with justification arise from 'the contrasting concerns and patterns of thought' of the two traditions. These used to be seen as contradictory, but historical research and ecumenical dialogue open up the possibility that they may rather be seen as complementary patterns and, 'even if at times in unavoidable tension, not necessarily divisive' (§94). This second chapter begins, therefore, by describing Catholic and Lutheran 'concerns and thought patterns', with their different emphases and ways of speaking (§97). The conclusion of the chapter is that

> Lutherans and Catholics can share in each other's concerns in regard to justification and can to some degree acknowledge the legitimacy of the contrasting theological perspectives and structures of thought. Yet, on the other hand, some of the consequences of the different outlooks seem irreconcilable. (§121)

The third chapter, 'Perspectives for Reconstruction' (§§122–160), surveys the biblical data, shrewdly noting that the biblical witness 'is richer and more varied than has been encompassed in either traditional Catholic or Lutheran approaches to justification'. This means that 'both sides need to treat each other's concerns and ways of interpreting Scripture with greater respect and willingness to learn than has been done in the past' (§149). The chapter notes growing convergences (relating especially to the six key issues) (§156). This chapter ends by repeating a joint affirmation with which the document had begun:

> Our entire hope of justification and salvation rests on Christ Jesus and on the gospel whereby the good news of God's merciful action in Christ is made known; we do not place our ultimate trust in anything other than God's promise and saving work in Christ. (§§4, 157)

This affirmation does not imply that no differences remain, but the authors ask whether these need to be 'church-dividing' (§4).

The Common Statement concludes with a Declaration (§§161–164). There is no pretence that differences do not remain. Some of the historic differences are seen as misunderstandings, some are seen as complementary understandings, but some are acknowledged to be irreconcilable differences.

This document has, rightly, been regarded as the most satisfactory ecumenical document on justification. It looks behind the different doctrines to discern the underlying concerns. It does not seek to explain all differences as misunderstandings or complementary understandings, but is prepared to acknowledge that there may be irreconcilable differences. This is a refreshing honesty not found in all ecumenical dialogues.

The condemnations of the Reformation era. Do they still divide? (1986)

In the early 1980s, while the American discussions were under way, there met in Germany a Joint Ecumenical Commission on the Examination of the Sixteenth-Century Condemnations, composed of Catholic and Lutheran theologians (with a few Reformed). Their task was to look specifically at the condemnations issued in the sixteenth century by each side against the teachings of the other on three topics: justification, the sacraments and the ministry. A final report was published in 1986,[7] and led to a lively controversy, especially among German Protestants. The Catholic response was more positive.

The report on justification looks at the anathemas contained in the thirty-three Canons of the Tridentine *Decree on Justification*, and asks of each whether they still apply to Protestants today. It focuses on seven areas: the depravity of human nature; concupiscence; the complete passivity of human beings toward God; the nature of justifying grace; justification through faith alone; the assurance of salvation; merit.[8] The conclusion reached is that the sixteenth-century condemnations do not apply *today*, though the introduction refers to failure to reach consensus over some condemnations.[9] They argue that some of the anathemas were attacking a caricature of Protestant teaching; some referred to extreme statements of Luther; and others referred to views that used to be held in the sixteenth century but are no longer held. (There is no mention of areas where Protestants converged with Catholics in the sixteenth century, but no longer today.) In most instances the case is argued persuasively, but not always. One gets the impression that every trick in the book will be used to prove that the anathemas do not apply today. Since there

---

[7] The date of the German original is 1986. ET Lehmann and Pannenberg (eds), *Condemnations of the Reformation Era*.

[8] Lehmann and Pannenberg (eds), *Condemnations of the Reformation Era*, 30–36.

[9] Lehmann and Pannenberg (eds), *Condemnations of the Reformation Era*, 68–69, 27.

is no claim that convergence has been reached in every area even today, the verdict on the condemnations reduces ultimately to a statement about the *good will* that exists between the parties today.

More helpfully, the report notes that the two traditions have differing concerns, with their accompanying strengths and weaknesses. Each side can acknowledge the validity of the other's concerns. Protestants focus attention on 'the misery of their sins, their resistance against God, and their lack of love for God and their neighbour' and therefore 'in faith put their whole trust in the saving God, are sure of his mercy, and try in their lives to match up to this faith'. The danger is that they 'think too little of God's regenerative power'. Catholics

> deeply penetrated by the limitless power of God, stress above all, in the event of justification also, God's glory and the victory of his gracious acts on behalf of men and women, holding human failure and half-heartedness toward these gracious acts to be, in the strict sense, of secondary importance.

The danger is that they do not take the misery of sin sufficiently seriously.[10]

ARCIC II, salvation and the church (1987)

In 1986, the Second Anglican–Roman Catholic International Commission (ARCIC II) produced an agreed statement on 'Salvation and the Church', which was published the following year,[11] and which acknowledged its indebtedness to *Justification by Faith*, the second document above. Its original contribution was to broaden the scope of the discussion to embrace both the doctrine of salvation as a whole and the corporate dimension of the church and sacraments. The introduction (§§1–8) briefly mentions sixteenth-century disputes and highlights four difficulties, which are the subject of the four major sections: 'Salvation and Faith' discusses the meaning of faith and its relation to assurance of salvation (§§9–11); 'Salvation and Justification' looks at the definition of justification and its relation to sanctification (§§12–18); 'Salvation and Good Works' tackles the necessity of works and their merit (§§19–24); 'The Church and Salvation' explores the role of the church in salvation (§§25–31). The conclusion includes the claim that 'our two Communions are agreed on the essential aspects of the doctrine of salvation and on the Church's role within it' (§32).

---

[10] Lehmann and Pannenberg (eds), *Condemnations of the Reformation Era*, 40.
[11] *Salvation and the Church*; also in Gros et al. (eds), *Growth in Agreement II*, 315–325.

This was a useful addition to the debate. Broadening the scope of the discussion to embrace both salvation as a whole and the corporate dimension was certainly helpful, but as the document is only a quarter of the length of the Common Statement in *Justification by Faith* the resulting statement is superficial by comparison. *Salvation and the Church* is a valuable document that furthered the move towards convergence, but its success was considerably more modest than its premature claim to have completed the task. The official Vatican response comments that it does not always avoid 'the doubts which surface in dialogue if one does not always seek a rigorous comparison between the respective positions, or if one is sometimes satisfied with a consensus which is almost entirely verbal, the fruit of reciprocal compromises'.[12]

'The Gift of Salvation' (1997)

In the United States, informal discussions took place between evangelicals and Catholics. As the discussions were between individuals, not institutions, the ensuing open statements have no official status. The first statement, 'Evangelicals and Catholics Together', was released on 29 March 1994,[13] with only a very brief statement about justification, for which it was criticized by some evangelical leaders. As an attempt to rectify this deficiency, another group met to draw up a second document, 'The Gift of Salvation', which was adopted on 7 October 1997.[14] This contains a much fuller common statement on justification, together with a list of questions requiring further exploration, which include

> the meaning of baptismal regeneration, the Eucharist, and sacramental grace; the historic uses of the language of justification as it relates to imputed and transformative righteousness; the normative status of justification in relation to all Christian doctrine; the assertion that while justification is by faith alone, the faith that receives salvation is never alone; diverse understandings of merit, reward, purgatory, and indulgences (§17).

There is an element of asymmetry about 'The Gift of Salvation' in that it was drawn up primarily to meet the needs of one party; that is, to meet the criticisms of 'Evangelicals and Catholics Together' and its signatories by other

---

[12] Congregation for the Doctrine of the Faith, 'Salvation and the Church', 387. For two other, less important, dialogues, see Lane, *Justification by Faith*, 111–113.

[13] 'Evangelicals and Catholics Together: Christian Mission'.

[14] George, 'Evangelicals and Catholics Together: New Initiative'.

evangelicals. As a result, 'The Gift of Salvation' looks evangelical, but is capable of being taken in a Catholic way. Its evangelical critics object not to what it says but to its silences and ambiguities.

Since these events there has been further such dialogue in the USA, again involving individuals rather than official representatives. In 2017 a volume was published, *Justified in Jesus Christ: Evangelicals and Catholics in Dialogue*,[15] containing the fruit of four years of dialogue on aspects of justification.

Joint Declaration on the Doctrine of Justification (1999)

The climax of our documents comes with the *Joint Declaration on the Doctrine of Justification*, the preparation of which took most of the 1990s. It was first published in 1997, but the initial reception was not very encouraging. In January 1998, a group of over 150 German theologians, led by Gerhard Ebeling and Eberhard Jüngel, signed a statement opposing it. In June 1998, however, the Lutheran World Federation published its official response to the declaration, based on the overwhelmingly positive responses received from member churches round the world. The same month the Vatican also published its official response to the declaration, calling for further clarification on a number of issues. Eventually a jointly agreed 'Annex' was composed and both sides agreed to sign an 'Official Common Statement' confirming the *Joint Declaration* in its entirety, to which was attached an 'Annex to the Official Common Statement'. This annex adds significant clarification and the final product is a considerable improvement on the original *Joint Declaration*. The *Joint Declaration*, together with the Official Common Statement and Annex, was signed by official representatives of the Lutheran World Federation and the Catholic Church at Augsburg on Reformation Day, 31 October 1999.[16] There is potential confusion in that the term *Joint Declaration on the Doctrine of Justification* applies strictly to the 1997 statement, but is commonly often used more broadly to include the Official Common Statement and Annex. However the term is used, the fact is that what was agreed is all three documents together.

The *Joint Declaration* begins with a preamble (§§1–7) setting the declaration in the context of earlier dialogues. The first section outlines the 'Biblical Message of Justification' (§§8–12) and is followed by a very brief section on

---

[15] Hoskins and Fleischacker (eds), *Justified in Jesus Christ*.
[16] Available from many sources, including Gros et al. (eds), *Growth in Agreement II*, 566–582. For assessment of it, see Blocher, 'Lutheran–Catholic Declaration on Justification'; Rusch (ed.), *Justification and Future of Ecumenical Movement*.

'The Doctrine of Justification as Ecumenical Problem', where it is affirmed that 'the corresponding doctrinal condemnations of the sixteenth century do not apply to today's partner' (§13). The third section, 'The Common Understanding of Justification' (§§14–18), sets out shared convictions:

> Together we confess: By grace alone, in faith in Christ's saving work and not because of any merit on our part, we are accepted by God and receive the Holy Spirit, who renews our hearts while equipping and calling us to good works. (§15)

The bulk of the declaration is found in the fourth section, 'Explicating the Common Understanding of Justification' (§§19–39), which focuses on seven issues: human powerlessness and sin in relation to justification; justification as forgiveness of sins and making righteous; justification by faith and through grace; the justified as sinner; law and gospel; assurance of salvation; the good works of the justified. For each of these issues there is a 'joint confession' agreed by both sides, followed by separate statements of the Lutheran and Catholic understandings. There is a brief final section entitled 'The Significance and Scope of the Consensus Reached' (§§40–44).

> The understanding of the doctrine of justification set forth in this *Declaration* shows that a consensus in basic truths of the doctrine of justification exists between Lutherans and Catholics. In light of this consensus the remaining differences of language, theological elaboration, and emphasis in the understanding of justification described in [§4] are acceptable. Therefore the Lutheran and the Catholic explications of justification are in their difference open to one another and do not destroy the consensus regarding the basic truths. (§40)

This has been described as a 'differentiated consensus'. To borrow a term from Lutheran-Reformed dialogue, the *Joint Declaration* adopts the approach of 'mutual affirmation and admonition'. If each side remains within the limits set by the commonly agreed statement, the remaining differences are not great enough to warrant mutual anathema (§§40–41).

Almost as long as the declaration itself is the appended 'Resources for the *Joint Declaration on the Doctrine of Justification*', a collection of material from the earlier dialogues offered in support of the claims of the declaration. The 'Annex to the Official Common Statement' sets out to elucidate the points raised by each side in their official responses to the declaration.

Some have argued that the commonly agreed statements of belief offer no more than a minimal core of basic Christian belief. This is not fair, but there is no pretence that significant differences do not remain between Catholic and Lutheran doctrines of justification, and these are enumerated, focusing especially on ecclesiological issues: 'ecclesiology, ecclesial authority, church unity, ministry, the sacraments' (§43).

This document is uniquely significant in that unlike all the other documents it has been solemnly ratified by the Catholic Church and the Lutheran World Federation at the highest level. On the other hand, it is not the most satisfactory document from the point of view of teasing out the real points of difference, for which the American *Justification by Faith* remains unsurpassed.

The impact of the *Joint Declaration on the Doctrine of Justification*

The *Joint Declaration on the Doctrine of Justification* claims 'a consensus in basic truths of the doctrine of justification' (§40). The crucial test of this will be its reception. How has it been received so far and has it actually made any difference?

The World Methodist Council took immediate steps to join in the achievement of the *Joint Declaration* and after due process in 2006 approved a brief 'Methodist Statement of Association with the *Joint Declaration on the Doctrine of Justification*', leading to an 'Official Common Affirmation' together with the signatories of the *Joint Declaration* in Seoul. In April 2016, the Anglican Consultative Council meeting in Lusaka welcomed and affirmed the substance of the *Joint Declaration*. In July 2017, during its General Council, the general secretary of the World Communion of Reformed Churches signed a declaration accepting formal association to the Joint Declaration. This took place in the Town Church at Wittenberg, where Luther regularly preached.

As with all such ecumenical documents, the big question is whether the *Joint Declaration* will make any difference to the way in which Lutherans and Catholics on the ground teach the doctrine of justification, and for that the training of the next generation of clergy is crucial. The *Joint Declaration* has achieved a considerable degree of acceptance on both sides and is widely taught in courses on grace and justification in Lutheran and Catholic seminaries and universities. On the other hand by no means all Lutheran institutions teach it positively and there remains a significant level of opposition on both sides. Christopher Malloy has written a penetrating critique from a Catholic perspective.[17]

---

[17] Malloy, *Engrafted into Christ*.

The Hope of Eternal Life (2011)

The American series 'Lutherans and Catholics in Dialogue' has yielded an eleventh volume entitled *The Hope of Eternal Life*, approved in 2010 after five years of meetings and preparation.[18] This builds on the foundation of the *Joint Declaration* in two ways, following the same basic method and tackling issues remaining from the *Joint Declaration*, such as satisfaction, purgatory, prayer for the dead, masses for the dead and indulgences (§§1–8, 156–271).

---

[18] Almen and Sklba (eds), *Hope of Eternal Life: Lutherans and Catholics in Dialogue.*

24

Key issues at stake

The popular caricature of the difference between Protestant and Catholic views of justification is justification by faith versus justification by works. There *are* real differences but they are much more subtle than that.[1]

Magisterium

The 'Magisterium' is the teaching authority of the Roman Catholic Church, found in the teaching of popes and councils. The Tridentine *Decree on Justification* was the response of the Magisterium to the Protestant doctrine of justification and the complaint of many Protestants is that this has not been disowned. That is true, but historically the Roman Catholic Church has changed not by repudiating its past doctrines but by reinterpreting them. So, for example, the traditional teaching has been that there is no salvation outside the (Catholic) Church. But since the nineteenth century the exception has been made of those who are outside of the Church because of 'invincible ignorance' and the Second Vatican Council teaches that sincere Buddhists and even atheists can be saved.[2] Before the council, in 1949 Father Leonard Feeney, an American priest, insisted on the traditional interpretation that only Roman Catholics are saved and he was eventually excommunicated for his stance. Rome stated that 'no salvation outside the Church' remains part of unchanging Catholic doctrine, but that it is not open to private interpretation.[3] Thus the church excommunicated a priest for holding to a traditional doctrine while all along insisting that Catholic doctrine is unchanging. The teaching of the Roman Catholic Church is what it teaches today, not what it taught at Trent or at any other time in the past.

So what does the Roman Catholic Church teach today? There are three authoritative sources to consider:

---

[1] For a fuller account, see Lane, *Justification by Faith*, 127–221; Lane, 'Justification'.
[2] E.g. *Lumen Gentium* 2:16 (Tanner (ed.), *Decrees of the Ecumenical Councils*, 2:861).
[3] Berkouwer, *Church*, 144–148, discusses Feeney and the earlier teaching of Pius IX.

1 The Second Vatican Council (1962–5) did not consider the doctrine of justification, but it did move towards viewing faith as placing one's trust in Christ and the gospel, as opposed to merely giving assent to doctrines.

2 The *Catechism of the Catholic Church* (1994) is a significant document being the first catechism for the whole Catholic Church since the 1566 *Roman Catechism*. Grace and Justification are covered in §§1987–2029, under the four headings of Justification, Grace, Merit and Christian Holiness. This summarizes key elements of the Tridentine *Decree on Justification*, with one significant addition, to be covered under 9. Merit and Reward, below.

3 The *Joint Declaration on the Doctrine of Justification* (1999) can be seen as an undertaking by the Roman Catholic Church to understand the earlier tradition (especially Trent) in line with the teaching of the *Joint Declaration*.

One might imagine that because the *Joint Declaration* was signed on behalf of the pope all Roman Catholics would accept it. That is not so. Some are very critical of it and there are those who maintain that the Tridentine *Decree on Justification* remains the authoritative Catholic statement and that the Second Vatican Council, the *Catechism of the Catholic Church* and the *Joint Declaration* have no dogmatic authority in this area.

Status of theological language

Doctrine is not like arithmetic, where there is only one correct answer. Doctrines are better understood as descriptive models. They are not purely subjective (like abstract art), but nor are they like the laws of gravity, for example. A better analogy would be different portraits of the same person. These will all be different and in principle may each be true, although it is possible to produce a portrait that is untrue. All representations are limited, while some can actually misrepresent. The four Gospels are four different portraits of Jesus, but complementary to each other. Different doctrines can also be compared to different world maps, different attempts to represent a three-dimensional reality in two-dimensional form. While maps can simply be erroneous, different maps can also be complementary rather than contradictory. Again, light can be described both as particles and as waves, and physicists regard these two models as complementary, not contradictory.

So where there are two different doctrines of justification it does not necessarily follow that only one of them can be true. Paul and James have different, but complementary, doctrines of justification.

Concerns

One of the most helpful features of the recent debates has been the focus on the fears and concerns of each side. It is much easier for each party to accept the validity of the concerns of its partner than to accept its formulation of the doctrine. So what are the respective concerns?

Protestants have been concerned to safeguard three points in particular:

- The seriousness of sin and our inability to save ourselves.
- The gratuity of salvation, which is a free gift from God.
- Our continuing dependence upon God's grace and mercy, rather than the merit of our own works.

Catholics have been concerned to safeguard three points in particular:

- The reality of the transformation brought by the Holy Spirit and God's grace.
- The need for human cooperation with God's grace.
- The need for, and value of, good works.

Both sets of concerns are valid and can claim support from the New Testament. Each side fears that its own concerns are being undermined by the other side. At the same time, each set of concerns is in danger of being unhelpfully one-sided. Put together they can be compared to the tension described in chapter 17. Through my own studies of this subject I have been made more aware of the valid concerns underlying Catholic theology. This has not led me to abandon a Protestant doctrine of justification, but it has made me more sensitive to ways in which that doctrine can be abused. For example, some Protestant formulations so emphasize human sin and our dependence upon mercy that they can be accused of belittling the regenerating work of the Holy Spirit.

Definition of justification

Reformation discussions of justification were bedevilled by the fact that the two sides were operating with different definitions of the word. Protestants carefully distinguished (without separating) justification and sanctification and defined the former in legal, forensic terms – basing this on Paul's use of the term. Catholics used the word 'justification' to cover both the regeneration and renewal brought by the Holy Spirit and the acceptance by God that followed from it –

following a long tradition going back to Augustine. Trent views God's saving work as a whole and refuses to make any clear and consistent distinction between justification and sanctification. To some extent, therefore, the two parties were talking past one another.

If the Reformers and Trent are talking about different things when they refer to 'justification' need these be incompatible? Was the dispute based entirely on a misunderstanding? The fact that the word is used differently, far from making them incompatible, opens up the *possibility* that apparently contradictory statements may in fact be compatible – as with those of Paul and James. If the Reformers and Trent use the term 'justification' with different meanings the issue is less 'Whose meaning is right?' than 'Are their different sounding pronouncements compatible?' Until the mid-twentieth century most theologians sought to accentuate the differences between the two sides, often by caricaturing their opponents. Since then, however, there has been a focus on understanding the other side and searching for common ground.

The difference in terminology reflects the different concerns of each side. Underlying the forensic definition of justification and the consequent distinction between justification and sanctification is the Protestant concern that salvation be based on nothing in us. Underlying the 'undifferentiated' Catholic definition is the concern to stress the unity of God's saving work and to avoid the danger of a purely notional righteousness which leaves the sinner unchanged. These two sets of concerns are not necessarily opposed to one another.

Basis for acceptance by God

What are the grounds on which we are reckoned or counted righteous? Trent and the Reformers agreed that this ground is Christ's righteousness given to us and that in conversion we are both inwardly changed by the Holy Spirit and counted righteous by God. So where does the difference lie? For the Reformers we are accounted righteous because Christ's righteousness is reckoned to our account – imputed righteousness. Trent is usually understood to teach that we are accounted righteous because Christ's righteousness is poured or infused into us by the Holy Spirit – imparted righteousness. This is a subtle, but real and fundamental, difference and lies at the root of many other differences.

Behind this difference lie different concerns. Catholics fear that the idea of imputed righteousness will lead to neglect of the transforming work of the Spirit and give rise to people with unchanged lives who have an assurance of salvation. Protestants fear that reliance upon imparted righteousness leads to a dependence upon one's own righteousness and a corresponding loss of assurance as well as a weak view of sin. Neither fear is unfounded.

Roman Catholics now are more open towards the Protestant view. Küng, in his *Justification*, suggests a way to resolve the conflict. He accepts that justification in the New Testament normally means a legal declaration of righteousness and argues that Catholics can accept this without the fear of lapsing into a purely verbal concept of justification that leaves us unchanged. How? He does this by seeing God's forensic declaration of righteousness as *effective*, as 'a declaring of justice which makes just'. God says that we are righteous and, as when he said 'Let there be light', his word does what it signifies. God does not merely *say* that we are righteous, he also *makes* us righteous.[4] That God does this is true, but do we become righteous instantly or is it a lifelong process?

Küng's proposal was adopted in subsequent dialogues. *Justification by Faith* affirms that 'By justification we are both declared and made righteous. Justification, therefore, is not a legal fiction. God, in justifying, effects what he promises; he forgives sin and makes us truly righteous' (§156.5). *Salvation and the Church* affirms that 'By pronouncing us righteous, God also makes us righteous' (§15). 'The Gift of Salvation' states that 'In justification, God, on the basis of Christ's righteousness alone, declares us to be no longer his rebellious enemies but his forgiven friends, and by virtue of his declaration it is so' (§7).

But there remains a serious problem. On what basis are we accounted righteous *after* conversion? The weakness of Küng's book is that he focuses mainly on initial justification and does not pay sufficient attention to our continuing acceptance by God. He could easily be taken to imply that *initially* God declares us righteous, through faith, that God then makes us righteous and that thereafter it is on *that* basis that we are accepted as righteous. Catholic theology has never had a problem with the idea that God justifies the ungodly (Rom. 4:5), but understands that only of *initial* justification. Thereafter we are justified because we are no longer ungodly but righteous. But Protestants hold that we are reckoned righteous through faith alone not just at the moment of conversion but throughout the Christian life. Küng in places seems to imply that justification and sanctification are two successive stages, with the latter following the former. The Tridentine decree is amenable to the idea of an effective declaration where God's initial acceptance of us is concerned, but not where subsequent acceptance is concerned. Protestants agree that justification goes hand in hand with renewal, but deny that the ensuing inherent righteousness is sufficient to make us acceptable to God without a continuing imputed righteousness.

---

[4] Küng, *Justification*, 199–211.

On what basis is the converted Christian accepted by God? This question is not directly answered in *Joint Declaration*, but there are two relevant statements. In its section on the common understanding of justification we read, 'By grace alone, in faith in Christ's saving work and not because of any merit on our part, we are accepted by God and receive the Holy Spirit, who renews our hearts' (§15). While this statement clearly holds together acceptance and renewal it seems to teach that acceptance is on the basis of faith in Christ's saving work, not on the basis of renewal – although the statement could be understood of initial justification rather than our continuing status. Later we have the Lutheran understanding that righteousness comes through the declaration of forgiveness and that justification is 'not dependent upon the life-renewing effects of grace in human hearts' (§23). The ensuing Catholic understanding does not contradict this, insisting only on the inseparability of 'God's forgiving grace' and the 'gift of new life' (§24). The *Joint Declaration* is not very explicit, but appears to be less amenable to the idea that we are accepted on the basis of imparted righteousness. Imputed righteousness is not mentioned explicitly, but we do read that God's righteousness is reckoned to all who trust in his promise (Gen. 15:6; Rom. 4:5) (§10).

Remaining sin

This is closely related to the previous issue. Those who argue that they are accepted on the basis of the transformation Christ has achieved in their lives and the imparted righteousness within them will be less eager to acknowledge sin in their lives than those who approach God on the basis that Christ has died for them. Both sides agreed that justified Christians are still plagued with concupiscence or lustful desires. But Trent, while conceding that the apostle Paul calls it 'sin', states that it is to be seen as result of sin and as an inclination towards sin, but not itself as sin. It is not properly sin unless we give in to it.[5] This means that Christians are acceptable to God despite suffering from concupiscence and that even light and daily (venial) sins do not impair their righteousness. It makes sense, therefore, to talk about meriting eternal life. The Reformers, by contrast, saw concupiscence as sin. In the words of Article 9 of the Thirty-nine Articles, 'concupiscence and lust hath of itself the nature of sin'. This is why, for example, Luther could say that the Christian is *simul iustus et peccator* (at the same time righteous and a sinner). For Protestants we always remain in need of God's mercy and cannot merit eternal life.

---

[5] *Decree on Original Sin* §5 (Tanner (ed.), *Decrees of the Ecumenical Councils*, 2:667).

Calvin in opposing the Tridentine *Decree on Justification* caricatures its authors in a way that brings out the contrasting attitudes to continuing sinfulness: 'To them scarcely anything short of murder is a sin; whoredom is a trivial mistake – the foulest lusts praiseworthy trials of virtue, a hidden wound of the conscience, a mere bagatelle.'[6]

This was one of the last issues to be resolved in the agreement of the *Joint Declaration*, and it was done by recognizing the tension in the New Testament set out in chapter 17. In the declaration itself the Lutheran position is stated to be that Christians are 'at the same time righteous and a sinner'. Looking at ourselves through the law we see that we remain 'totally sinners', but the sin that remains in the Christian is 'ruled' by Christ rather than ruling the Christian, so in this life 'Christians can in part lead a just life' (§29). The Vatican Response regarded this as unacceptable and the issue needed to be resolved in the Annex to the Official Common Statement. This affirms the reality of our inward renewal (2 Cor. 5:17) and that 'in this sense' the justified do not remain sinners. On the other hand, as Christians we still need to pray, 'God, be merciful to me, a sinner!' (Luke 18:13). 'To this extent, Lutherans and Catholics can together understand the Christian as *simul iustus et peccator*.' Although the two sides differ in their understanding of concupiscence, both can agree on holding together 'the reality of salvation in baptism and the peril from the power of sin' (Annex §§2A–B). Here we have both a recognition of the different concerns of each side and also an acknowledgement of the New Testament tension between the universality of sin and the call to lead righteous lives.

Sola fide

Justification by faith alone was from the beginning a key Reformation slogan, but despite this it is an easier issue to resolve than some of the others. Even in the sixteenth century many Roman Catholics admitted that it had a perfectly acceptable meaning. What concerned them was that teaching it might encourage people to have assurance without discipleship. This concern was also shared by most of the Reformers.

The Tridentine *Decree on Justification* condemns seven specific statements that contain the words 'faith alone', but does that not necessarily mean that there can never be a legitimate use of those words? The waters were muddied by the fact that each side understood the word 'faith' differently. For Trent faith is understood to refer to giving mental assent to doctrine. This was called

---

[6] *Acts of the Council of Trent: with the Antidote, 6th Session*, can. 30 (*SWJC* 3:161).

'unformed faith' and is insufficient for justification. Justification is not by naked faith but by a faith that is 'formed by love'. This caused many to claim that it is love rather than faith that justifies us.

The Reformers saw faith as more than mere mental assent, which on its own does not justify. Saving faith is a personal trust in Christ, involving the heart as well as the head. They denied that it was possible to be justified without also having hope and love, but insisted that it was only by faith (not by hope or love) that one becomes justified. For more on this see Chapter 18, above.

As *The Condemnations of the Reformation Era* recognizes, the different approaches reflect different concerns. The Reformers were concerned to safeguard the gratuity of God's free gift of justification; their opponents were concerned to safeguard the reality of the renewal that grace effects in our lives. Neither side overlooks what is important to the other and neither maintains what the other fears.[7] In the original *Joint Declaration* the Lutheran statement (§26) affirms justification by faith alone, but the joint confession (§25) does not mention it. Some Lutherans were not satisfied with this and in response the Annex makes a very significant statement: 'Justification takes place "by grace alone" . . . , by faith alone, the person is justified "apart from works"' (§2c). This formal affirmation of *sola fide* by the Catholic Church is a truly historic step.

Lapse and restoration

The greatest weakness of Küng's work is that he focuses on the *beginning* of justification, which for most Catholics occurs at infant baptism, but largely ignores the question of subsequent lapse and restoration, which is where the greatest divergence between the two sides is to be found. Trent teaches that those guilty of mortal sin need to repent and also to resort to the sacrament of penance, through which justification is restored. Through this sacrament the eternal punishment due to mortal sin is waived, but there remains a *temporal* punishment to be paid as a satisfaction to God.[8] This is the basis for purgatory (for those who die without having paid their debt) and indulgences (remitting some of the debt with approved activities). The issue of indulgences was, of course, the spark that ignited the Reformation.

Protestants have traditionally been concerned that this apparatus of satisfaction detracts from the free mercy of God in Christ. Catholics, on the other hand, have feared that the Protestant approach peddles a cheap grace that

---

[7] Lehmann and Pannenberg (eds), *Condemnations of the Reformation Era*, 52–53.
[8] *Decree on Justification*, ch.14.

underestimates the seriousness of sin in the life of the Christian. Once again, history suggests that neither fear is ungrounded.

Justification by Faith notes how both Lutherans and reforming Catholics in the sixteenth century protested against abuses arising from the idea of satisfaction. 'Many of these abuses were corrected by the reforms of the Council of Trent; others have gradually died out, but some, no doubt, still remain' (§115). Some areas need further study, such as 'Masses for special intentions, indulgences, and purgatory' (§116). The Lutherans concede the possibility that doctrines like purgatory might be preached and practised 'in ways consistent with justification by faith', in which case they need no longer be church-dividing (§153).

The *Joint Declaration* has nothing to say on this matter, except a brief mention in the section on 'The Justified as Sinner'. The joint confession there says that the justified 'are ever again called to conversion and penance' (§28). The accompanying Catholic statement affirms that those who 'voluntarily separate themselves from God' 'must receive pardon and peace in the sacrament of reconciliation' (§30). Failure to tackle this important topic is a serious weakness of the *Joint Declaration*. It is not even mentioned in the list of questions needing further clarification, except in as much as it is included in 'the sacraments' (§43). Ironically the signing of the *Joint Declaration* was followed weeks later by the beginning of the year 2000 with a Jubilee Indulgence in the Catholic Church.

Since then, however, satisfaction, purgatory and indulgences have received full attention in *Hope of Eternal Life*, with a significant degree of convergence. Key to this is the recognition that Catholic teaching now interprets purgatory primarily in terms of purification rather than punishment (§193). On the other hand, the issue of satisfaction is recognized as a topic still requiring further ecumenical discussion (§§252–258). From the third century occasional hints are found both for a time of purification after death and for a time to pay off the debt accrued by failure to offer satisfaction for our sins. In the Middle Ages and later the latter idea predominated. More recent Catholic theology plays down the idea of punishment (though without losing it completely) and instead emphasizes the idea of purification, as in the *Catechism of the Catholic Church* (§§1030–1032), though a different emphasis is found in §§1471–1479 on Indulgences.

Merit and reward

At the Reformation the Reformers were happy to talk about reward, but not about merit. Trent teaches that eternal life is both a grace promised in mercy and a reward for good works and merits. Indeed probably the most contentious statement of the decree is as follows:

> nothing further is wanting to the justified, to prevent their being accounted to have, by those works which have been done in God, fully satisfied the divine law according to the state of this life, and to have truly merited eternal life.[9]

The Reformers were not keen to call good works meritorious, but did not deny their merit as unequivocally as is sometimes supposed. Calvin and Melanchthon were prepared to describe eternal life as a reward of works, given because of God's promise. For more on this, see chapter 19.

Justification by Faith sets out the concerns of each party. 'Lutherans are inclined to hold that Catholic ways of thinking and speaking about merit can lead to a legalism that derogates from the unconditional character of God's justifying word' (§110). Catholics respond by acknowledging that 'merit has often been preached in a self-righteous way bordering on legalism, but they deny that the abuse of the doctrine invalidates the doctrine itself'. Minimizing God's gifts does not magnify the giver. Significantly they note that 'for any assurance of final perseverance and salvation . . . one must not trust in one's own merits but rather hope in God's continued mercy' (§111).

Various dialogue documents interpret merit in terms of the reward promised to good works, with which the Reformers were comfortable. So, *Justification by Faith* states that 'the good works of the justified, performed in grace, will be recompensed by God, the righteous judge, who, true to his promises, "will render to everyone according to his works"' (§156.11). Talk of reward can safeguard the concerns of both sides. It safeguards the reality of our inner transformation and the need for incentives to active obedience, without undermining the truths of our total dependence upon God's grace and continuing need for mercy. When they say that the reward is unmerited most Protestants wish to affirm that the reward given is out of all proportion to the works rewarded, not that the works rewarded are totally without value and indistinguishable from heinous crimes.

The *Joint Declaration* affirms that initial justification is unmerited, both in one of the joint confessions and in the accompanying Catholic statement (§§25, 27). Once justified, Christians are to bring forth good fruit and 'the works of love' (§37). According to the Catholic statement at that point, when

---

[9] *Decree on Justification*, ch. 16.

Catholics affirm the merit of works they mean that in Scripture a reward is promised to works and their intention is to emphasize our responsibility for our actions, not to deny that these works are gifts nor that justification itself is an unmerited gift of grace (§38). The Lutheran response is that our works are fruits and signs of justification and not our own merits and that eternal life is an 'unmerited "reward" in the sense of the fulfilment of God's promise to the believer' (§39). This is reaffirmed in *The Hope of Eternal Life* (§108).

There appears to be broad agreement except over the question of whether eternal life is a 'merited' reward, which need be no more than a linguistic difference. Is eternal life merited in the sense that it has been strictly earned? In the *Joint Declaration* the Catholic statement says that our works are 'gifts' and that justification is always 'the unmerited gift of grace' (§38). These statements simply reaffirm the Augustinian belief that our merits are God's gifts and do not address the present issue. More pertinent is the statement in the Annex that 'any reward is a reward of grace, on which we have no claim' (§2e). This could (but need not) be taken to exclude the idea of strictly earning the reward.

But what of the claim of the Tridentine *Decree on Justification* that we truly merit eternal life? Against this, there is a Catholic tradition of casting oneself on God's mercy at the end. The *Catechism of the Catholic Church*, in its section on Merit (§§2006–2011) states traditional Tridentine teaching but then significantly qualifies it by quoting this passage written by Thérèse of Lisieux (1873–97) at the close of her life in her book *Story of a Soul* (1897):

> After earth's exile, I hope to go and enjoy you in the fatherland, but I do not want to lay up merits for heaven. I want to work for your love alone . . . In the evening of this life, I shall appear before you with empty hands, for I do not ask you, Lord, to count my works. All our justice is blemished in your eyes. I wish, then, to be clothed in your own justice and to receive from your love the eternal possession of yourself. (§2011)

This looks like an affirmation that even justified Christians need God's mercy – the point that was accepted at Regensburg and which Seripando tried unsuccessfully to have inserted in the *Decree on Justification*. A communion prayer in the Church of England's Book of Common Prayer asks God to accept our dutiful service, 'not weighing our merits but pardoning our offences'. I had always assumed that this was a good example of Cranmer's introduction of justification by faith into the liturgy, and was surprised to discover that he had actually taken these words from the Latin mass.

Assurance of salvation

The Reformers were agreed about the possibility of assurance, though with significant differences concerning the relation between saving faith and assurance, as described in chapter 20. Trent rejected the Reformation claims, and allowed no more than a fallible assurance regarding our *present* status. The joint confession in the *Joint Declaration* is fairly bland, talking of 'rely[ing] on the mercy and promises of God' and being sure of 'the promise of God's grace in word and sacrament' (§34). The Lutheran statement distinguishes between being assured of salvation by looking to Christ and trusting only in him and a false security that comes from looking within (§35). The Catholic statement confirms the need to look away from our own experience to Christ's promise and not to consider that promise untrustworthy. But it also adds that 'Every person, however, may be concerned about his salvation when he looks upon his own weaknesses and shortcomings. Recognizing his own failures, however, the believer may yet be certain that God intends his salvation' (§36). A difference is still clearly discernible, even though the gulf may be less than in the sixteenth century.

The way forward

Considerable progress has been made on the issue of justification by the *Joint Declaration* and subsequently by *The Hope of Eternal Life*, building on the foundation of various dialogues. Misunderstandings have been cleared up and the two sides have drawn together, each listening to the concerns of the other. How solid the achievement will be depends on two factors: on the ability to persuade the doubters in each camp and on the willingness of each church not just to approve of the agreement but to embrace it in its own teaching of justification.

25
Forgiveness and fear

The psalmist links the two topics of this chapter by telling God that 'with you there is forgiveness, that you may be feared' (130:4), a combination that appears counterintuitive to us today.

Forgiveness

Forgiveness is in many ways a Christian distinctive. The Christian faith involves forgiveness to an extent that Judaism and Islam do not.[1] When the victims of high-profile crime or their relatives declare their forgiveness for the criminals who are responsible it is common for the media to comment on this. In a high proportion of cases, those forgiving are Christians. This can be a powerful witness to the gospel. The parable of the unforgiving servant (Matt. 18:21–35) explains why Christians in particular should be forgiving. Since God in Christ has forgiven us so much, it is grotesque for us to refuse to forgive others. The parable ends by stating that God will not forgive us if we do not forgive our brothers and sisters from the heart and the same idea comes in the Lord's Prayer (Matt. 6:12, 14–15).

This looks very straightforward. I used to think that I knew exactly what forgiveness meant until I received a letter with a number of questions on the issue. For example, should we forgive those who are not sorry for what they have done and do not repent of it? What exactly do we mean when we speak of 'forgiveness'? We shall consider these and other questions in dialogue with Miroslav Volf's popular and influential book *Free of Charge*.

---

[1] In *The Sunflower* Simon Wiesenthal tells of how a dying SS officer asked him as a Jew to forgive him for his crimes against the Jews. Wiesenthal does not do so and asks the reader to think what they would have done in his place (98). Fifty-three people respond to his question. Movingly, Desmond Tutu speaks for forgiveness, citing the inspirational example of Nelson Mandela (266–268).

Implications of forgiveness

Forgiving is sometimes confused with condoning. To condone an act is to say that it was not wrong; to forgive it implies that it was wrong. Again, to accept forgiveness is to acknowledge that the act was wrong. If someone offered to forgive me for eating an apple last thing at night I would decline, since there is nothing wrong in the act – assuming I had not stolen their apple, that is! This is true both of our relationship to one another and of our relationship to God. Miroslav Volf argues that God offers forgiveness to all and to accept it implies acknowledging and confessing that we have done wrong. Conversely, to refuse to acknowledge our faults is to refuse forgiveness.[2] While there is some truth in this, to acknowledge one's fault is not necessarily to repent of it, as we saw in chapter 10. Repentance involves more than just acknowledging that one is a sinner, more than just being sorry or regretful. The Greek word *metanoia* means a change of mind and heart, a change of behaviour, a turning from sin to God. Repentance includes the hatred of sin and turning one's back on it.

Three examples illustrate this point. Philip Yancey tells of his encounter with a man who was intending to leave his wife and children and wished Yancey to tell him in advance that God would forgive him.[3] The man acknowledged that his planned action was sinful and desired forgiveness for it, but clearly was not repentant, as the sequel demonstrated. Graham Greene tells the story in his novel *The Power and the Glory* of a man who betrays a priest to the authorities in anti-clerical Mexico, which will cost the priest his life, while at the same time asking the priest to give him absolution and to give him his blessing. There is a similar character in Shusaku Endo's historical novel *Silence*, about the time in the seventeenth century when the Japanese attempted to eradicate Christianity. Kichijiro betrays a priest for money and then seeks absolution from the same priest. These extreme examples serve to make the point that repentance involves more than just acknowledgement that one is a sinner and seeking forgiveness.

Forgiveness and repentance

Miroslav Volf argues that God forgives all people unconditionally, and that our repentance follows as a response to this – but not as a condition for forgiveness.[4] There is some truth in it. Paul tells us that 'while we were still sinners, Christ died for us' (Rom. 5:8). God's forgiveness is freely offered to everybody. But the

---

[2] Volf, *Free of Charge*, 153–154.
[3] Yancey, *What's So Amazing About Grace?* 179–180.
[4] Volf, *Free of Charge*, 177–183.

preaching in Acts makes it clear that this offer is not unconditional. In his Pentecost sermon Peter tells his hearers to 'repent . . . for the forgiveness of your sins' (2:38). Shortly after he tells another audience to 'repent therefore, and turn again, that your sins may be blotted out' (3:19). In order actually to *receive* forgiveness we need to repent. Jesus taught that 'repentance and forgiveness of sins should be proclaimed in his name to all nations' (Luke 24:47).

Forgiveness and punishment

In 1986 a horrific event took place where a gang of burglars broke into a vicarage in Ealing, seriously injured two men and raped the vicar's daughter. After the event the family extended their forgiveness to their assailants. In 1987 the judge at the trial sentenced them to less time for the rape than the burglary, on the controversial ground that 'the trauma suffered by the victim was not so great'. This led to an outcry and to a change in the law allowing appeals against unduly lenient sentences. In particular, the victims also protested against the leniency.[5] This raises an important question. Is it inconsistent to forgive someone and then later to protest against the leniency of their sentence?

Miroslav Volf argues that since God has forgiven us there is no room for retributive justice. In support he cites Romans: 'Repay no one evil for evil . . . Do not be overcome by evil, but overcome evil with good' (12:17, 21).[6] But this is to ignore the wider context of the passage. Individuals are indeed taught not to seek revenge, but on what grounds? 'Never avenge yourselves, but leave it to the wrath of God, for it is written, "Vengeance is mine, I will repay, says the Lord"' (12:19). We are not to seek revenge not because there is no retribution to come but because that is God's role, not ours. And how does God exercise that role? In part by delegating it to the state, as Paul goes on to explain (13:1–5). '[The ruler] is God's servant for your good. But if you do wrong, be afraid, for he does not bear the sword in vain. For he is the servant of God, an avenger who carries out God's wrath on the wrongdoer' (13:4). The fact that we are not to seek revenge far from implying that the state should not do so either, is based precisely on the fact that this role is given to the state.

But suppose the criminal has truly repented and been forgiven by God. Does that mean that the state should also forgive? No. Such an approach would simply lead to spurious professions of conversion by career criminals. After the Second World War a number of leading Nazi war criminals were brought

---

[5] See <https://en.wikipedia.org/wiki/Jill_Saward>, accessed 5 June 2020.
[6] Volf, *Free of Charge*, 160–171.

to repentance and faith through the ministry of an American army chaplain. They were forgiven by God but still had to face execution for their crimes.

So it is not inconsistent to forgive someone for a crime, and still want to see judicial punishment administered by society. Forgiving someone does not mean there should be no consequences. That is not to deny that there are occasions where a more lenient sentence is warranted because of the particular circumstances of the case. But always to waive punishment would simply encourage a crime wave.

After the end of apartheid, in the 1990s, there was in South Africa a 'Truth and Reconciliation Commission', chaired by Archbishop Desmond Tutu. This gave those who had committed human rights abuses under the apartheid regime the opportunity to confess to this and to receive amnesty. In Northern Ireland likewise, the Good Friday Agreement included an amnesty for large numbers of members of paramilitary groups, both Republican and Loyalist, who were serving sentences for violent crimes. There is a common motivation behind both. In both countries there had been a long conflict between rival communities and crimes had been committed on both sides, though not necessarily in equal proportions. The aim in each case was to end a long-running conflict and to bring about reconciliation between two communities. This is a valid motivation, though both processes have had their critics. The important point, though, is that the circumstances were exceptional and this is not a precedent for offering an amnesty to armed robbers, say.

Similar issues apply in the disciplining of children. It is right to forgive them when they do wrong, but it is also necessary that at least sometimes there should be consequences of wrongdoing. The book of Proverbs especially has much to say about the importance of disciplining children and how failure to do so harms them in the long run.

Types of forgiveness

William Perkins (1558–1602) was a prominent Elizabethan clergyman and theologian who was a leading figure in the Puritan movement. He wrote a work of casuistry, which has been defined as 'seeking to resolve moral problems by extracting or extending theoretical rules from a particular case, and reapplying those rules to new instances'.[7] His *The Cases of Conscience* was published in 1606, after his death. There he asks how one should forgive an injury and very helpfully distinguishes between four different types of forgiveness.[8]

---

[7] The word also has very negative overtones today, following from the dubious methods used by some casuists in the past.
[8] Book 3, ch. 3, q. 1 in Merrill (ed.), *William Perkins*, 174–175.

The first is 'forgiveness of revenge'. We are not to requite evil for evil by thought, word or deed. Vengeance is the Lord's and there is no room for revenge or hatred. Feelings of revenge and hatred are always wrong. It was very sad to see on television relatives of victims of Myra Hindley, for example, who were so consumed by their hatred of her that they had themselves become victims. When you forgive, says Lewis Smedes, 'you set a prisoner free, but you discover that the real prisoner was yourself'.[9] By contrast, 'not forgiving [is] like scratching at a sore to keep the healing scab from forming'.[10] Eva Kor, a Jewish twin who was a victim of Josef Mengele's experiments, came to forgive her tormentors and described how it healed her soul and set her free.[11]

The second is 'forgiveness of private punishment'. We are not to seek to get our own back on people as this is equally precluded by the fact that vengeance is the Lord's. As we have already argued, this is in part delegated to the state.

The third is 'forgiveness of judgement'. We are not required to overlook the fact that a sinful act is sinful. (As we have seen, forgiving someone implies that they have done wrong.) But if someone has made satisfaction for their offence we should no longer hold it against them.

The fourth is 'forgiveness of satisfaction'. This we are not required to give. If someone drives into your car, you should forgive them but you are still entitled to claim the cost of repairing the car. To forgive someone who has committed a crime against you does not mean that you do not want the law to take its course. Punishment can be waived, but need not be and cannot always be. If children are always spared punishment for their misdemeanours they will never learn to change.

One is not required to offer the 'forgiveness of satisfaction' but one may do so. As a teenager I was cycling with a friend in the Netherlands and we accidentally collided with one another and went into a parked car, scratching the side. The driver was standing nearby and I can still remember my relief when he waved us on, waiving his right to satisfaction. That was an act of grace for which I am still grateful.

Forgiving is often linked with forgetting. Under the New Covenant God forgives our iniquity and remembers our sin no more (Jer. 31:34). What does that mean? This is not forgetting in the sense that God becomes ignorant of it, but forgetting in that he no longer holds it against us. It is in this way that we forgive one another, no longer harping back to the offence.[12]

---

[9] Smedes, *Forgive and Forget*, 133.
[10] Smith, *House of Unexpected Sisters*, 88.
[11] From her obituary in *The Times*, 16 July 2019, 53.
[12] Augustine, *City of God* 22:30 (NPNF 2:510–511), makes a similar distinction regarding our forgetting evil in the Age to Come.

Forgiveness without repentance?

In the light of this discussion we can return to the question posed at the beginning. Should we forgive those who are not sorry for what they have done and do not repent of it? There are two different views on this, which were seen in Neville and Doreen Lawrence, the parents of Stephen Lawrence. Neville stated in 2018, on the twenty-fifth anniversary of the murder, that he had managed to forgive Stephen's killers, one of the hardest things to say, through embracing his Christian faith. He said that this forgiveness had made his life a lot better. By contrast, Doreen had earlier stated that she could not forgive them because to forgive someone requires that they show remorse, which they had not done.[13]

Without suggesting that there are no differences, these two positions are to some extent complementary. We have seen that God gave Christ for us while we were still his enemies (Rom. 5:6–10) and that we are offered forgiveness in the gospel, but that we need to repent and accept this forgiveness. Similarly we are called to forgive people in the sense of putting aside our anger, bitterness, resentment, hatred and desire for revenge, of having a heart of forgiveness – and to do this whether or not they repent or show remorse. But forgiveness in the full sense of the restoration or creation of a relationship requires a response on the part of the perpetrator. It is not enough to wait for them to repent or apologize and then offer forgiveness; as with the gospel the forgiveness needs to be offered first and may indeed be the catalyst that starts the process of repentance. Jesus did not wait for the soldiers to repent before praying, 'Father, forgive them, for they know not what they do' (Luke 23:34). The early Christian apocryphal writing *The Testaments of the Twelve Patriarchs* contains the advice that if someone who sins against us repents and confesses, we should forgive them 'But if he be shameless and persisteth in his wrongdoing, even so forgive him from the heart, and leave to God the avenging.'[14]

Fear of God

Psalm 130:4 appears counterintuitive today:

> But with you there is forgiveness,
> that you may be feared.

---

[13] See <https://www.bbc.co.uk/news/uk-43775801 and https://www.theguardian.com/uk-news/2018/apr/15/stephen-lawrences-father-says-he-forgives-his-sons-killers>, accessed 20 November 2019.
[14] *Gad* 6:3, 7 (Charles (ed.), *Testaments of the Twelve Patriarchs*, 85–86). Volf, *Free of Charge*, 179–181, argues that we should forgive those who refuse to repent.

Many Christians see no room for fear in the Christian life, but that is mistaken. Not all think that way. There was a church noticeboard that carried the message 'Read the Bible – it'll scare the hell out of you!' Psalm 25:14 states that 'the friendship of the LORD is for those who fear him, and he makes known to them his covenant'.

Tension

Those who say that there is no place for fear in the Christian life often cite 1 John 4:18: 'perfect love casts out fear'. When it comes to punishment, Romans 8:1 tells us 'there is now no condemnation for those who are in Christ Jesus'. Yet on the other hand Proverbs 9:10 states, 'The fear of the LORD is the beginning of wisdom', a sentiment also expressed elsewhere (Job 28:28; Ps. 111:10; Prov. 1:7). Jesus told his disciples not to fear persecutors who might kill them. 'But I will warn you whom to fear: fear him who, after he has killed, has authority to cast into hell. Yes, I tell you, fear him!' (Luke 12:4–5).

How are these different passages to be reconciled? Christians have wrestled with this question from early times and there is a remarkable consistency in the solution offered. We should distinguish between a servile fear of punishment and the filial respect due to God as our Father. Maximus the Confessor in the seventh century put it like this:

> The fear of the Lord is twofold. The first type is produced in us from threats of punishment, and from it arise in proper order self-control, patience, hope in God, and detachment, from which comes love. The second is coupled with love itself and constantly produces reverence in the soul, lest through the familiarity of love it becomes presumptuous of God.[15]

The 'Second Use of the Law'

The servile fear of punishment relates to what the Reformers called the 'Second Use of the Law', its role in restraining the ungodly. (We met the three uses of the law in chapter 7.) People are kept from gross sin or crime by fear of the law, because they fear God's punishment. This may be a fear that God will judge us directly, either here and now or at the end. More likely it is a fear of God's punishment through the state, as described in Romans 13:1–5. Or it may be fear of natural consequences, such as sexually transmitted diseases. Basically people are restrained by fear of the consequences. The second use of the law is vital for

---

[15] Maximus the Confessor, *Four Hundred Chapters on Love* 1:81 (Maximus the Confessor, *Selected Writings*, 44).

law and order – anarchy is a great evil. But it does not produce heart obedience; sin is restrained, not cured. Just as the brake lights all come on just before the speed camera, so also there is a cloud of exhaust fumes just after the camera as people accelerate away. The law restrains people from sin, but does not generally lead to a change of heart. People facing the prospect of a terminal disease may reform their lives to some extent, but should the danger pass they are liable to revert to their former ways.

Fear and conversion

Does fear have any role in conversion? Is it a legitimate tool for the evangelist to use? The first point to note is that fear alone is not a sufficient motive for conversion. True conversion involves hatred of sin, not just fear of the consequences. Proverbs 8:13 states that 'the fear of the LORD is hatred of evil' – not 'the fear of the LORD is fear of the consequences!' Hatred of sin has over the ages been recognized as the mark of a genuine repentance. As Augustine put it, 'the man who only fears the flames of hell is afraid not of sinning, but of being burned; but the man who hates sin as much as he hates hell is afraid to sin.'[16] John Cassian noted the contrast between fear of the consequences and hatred of sin:

> There is a great difference between those who extinguish the inner fire of sin by means of fear of hell or hope of future reward and those who have a horror of sin itself and of uncleanness, moved by love for God. These keep themselves pure simply because they love purity and long for it, . . . motivated not by fear of punishment but by delight in virtue. Such people do not take the opportunity to sin when no one is looking, nor are they corrupted by the secret allurements of thoughts. They keep the love of virtue in their hearts, and anything opposed to it they not only do not admit into their heart but actually hate with the utmost horror . . . He who abstains from the delights of sin because of fear will, as soon as the obstacle of fear is removed, return once more to what he loves and thus will not acquire any stability in good, nor will he ever be free of temptation.[17]

True obedience is a glad and willing obedience from the heart that arises from the love of God and the hatred of sin. Conversion requires not just fear of punishment but hatred of sin and love of righteousness. But that does not mean

---

[16] Augustine, *Letter* 145:4 (NPNF 1:496). Again, it is sinful to desire what is forbidden and to abstain merely from fear of punishment (*City of God* 14:10 (NPNF 2:271)).

[17] Cassian, *Conferences* 11:8 (NPNF² 11:418, changed).

that fear has no role to play. It is not a *sufficient* motive, but it can be a step on the way to a purer motive. The psalmist states:

> Before I was afflicted I went astray,
> but now I keep your word.
> (119:67)

Children need an element of coercion to make them do the right thing, but the outcome of a successful upbringing will be that they now do such things of their own accord. But the coercion succeeds only if they do then move to this next stage.

Fear in the Christian life

Does fear have a role to play in the Christian life? It is true that 'perfect love casts out fear', but that refers to *perfect* love. It does not say that a wilfully disobedient Christian need not be afraid. And even where there is perfect love there remains the 'fear' of reverence and respect. An electrician may well love electricity, as it is his livelihood, but he should retain a fear of it in the sense that electricity could kill him. When the Forth bridge was built, one of the builders was as agile as a monkey and had no fear at all of heights. This led him to dispense with a safety harness – until the day he fell to his death. Cristian Seera, a professional bull jumper, commented that 'The fear is always there . . . The fear is what keeps you safe. You have to have a bit of fear.'

This relates to the 'Third Use of the Law', to guide and exhort the believer, to show us how to live. Psalm 119 expresses a delight in this role of the law. The Reformers were not agreed about this Third Use.[18] For Calvin this was the 'principal use' of the law because it corresponds to its proper purpose, which is to bring about obedience. Luther, however, disagreed, arguing that law has no place in living the Christian life – except inasmuch as it points us back to Christ whenever we sin.[19] (That is the 'First Use of the Law', described in chapter 7.) The Lutheran *Formula of Concord* (1577), however, affirms the validity of the Third Use of the Law.[20]

In fact Luther and Calvin are not as opposed as they may appear. Luther's objection was not aimed at the idea of the law showing us how to live. He was thinking of law as threat – 'do this, or else'; he was thinking of law as expressing

---

[18] For different views on the relation between law and gospel, see Bahnsen et al., *Five Views on Law and Gospel*.

[19] Althaus, *Theology of Martin Luther*, 270–273.

[20] *BkConc* 502–503, 587–591.

God's wrath against sin. This was the way in which he thought of law before his conversion experience, which involved seeing Christ as the one who liberates us from this wrath. With this sense of law in mind he said that the Law has nothing to do with the Christian as a *believer*, only as a *sinner*. The prime motivation for Christian obedience is not to escape God's wrath, but when Christians sin, the law points them back to Christ again (first use of the law). Imagine a flock of sheep in a field that has an electric fence. While the sheep graze in the centre of the field they need not worry about the electric fence, but if they seek to stray outside the field the electric fence is there to send them back where they belong. So, for example, the warnings in Hebrews 10:26–31 are there for those tempted to abandon their allegiance to Christ. This is how Luther saw the law relating to Christians.

There is an important truth in what Luther said, and one all the Reformers held. The Christian life is not primarily about obeying laws or keeping rules. God is looking not for reluctant outward conformity to a code but a willing obedience born of love, a free joyful obedience from the heart. The primary source of law for the Christian is God's law written on our hearts. The promise of the New Covenant is that 'I will put my law within them, and I will write it on their hearts' (Jer. 31:33). This is the work of the Holy Spirit: 'I will put my Spirit within you, and cause you to walk in my statutes and be careful to obey my rules' (Ezek. 36:27). The Holy Spirit gives us love for God and neighbour.

Love is the *motivation* for all true obedience (1 Cor. 13:1–3). Indeed love is also the *content* of all true obedience. God asks nothing of us except what love dictates. Jesus and Paul both propound love as a summary of the law (Matt. 22:37–40; Rom. 13:8–10). God does not call us to do anything more than to love him and our neighbour, but the law is there to explain to us the *meaning* of love.

So is love all that we need for moral guidance? Can we say with Augustine, 'Love, and do what you will'?[21] This is often quoted today; what is less often mentioned is that he used this principle in order to justify the coercion of heretics! That illustrates perfectly the reason why love is not enough, why we need the law to interpret to us what love actually means. Jesus said, 'If you love me, you will keep my commandments' (John 14:15). Consider the case of a little child crossing the road with his mother. Because he does not understand the dangers he needs to obey her commands and do what she says.

According to the Babylonian Talmud, a Gentile approached the rabbi Hillel and offered to convert if he could teach him the whole Torah while he stood on one foot. Hillel's answer was, 'That which is despicable to you, do not do to

---

[21] *Homilies on 1 John* 7:8 (LCC 8:316).

others. This is the whole Torah and the rest is commentary. Go and learn it.'[22] The point of the story is not that we can dispense with the commentary. How often have we heard those who have abandoned their families justify it by saying, 'We did it for love' – meaning they were driven by their hormones? All sorts of crimes have been committed in the name of 'love'. Those who wish to liberalize laws often do so by citing specific examples and appealing to love. Thus divorce laws should become lax, because this is loving for those who are unhappily married – but there is a price to be paid by abandoned spouses and children and by those whose marriages will fail in the future because of easy access to divorce. Euthanasia should be made available out of love for those who are suffering – but there will be a price to be paid by elderly folk pressurized by greedy relatives to embrace it. (As the quip goes, 'Where there is a will, there is a relative!')

This point is made by the heroine in Charlotte Brontë's *Jane Eyre*, who discovers at the altar that her husband to be is already married. 'Love' would have told her to go ahead with the wedding, but

> Laws and principles are not for the times when there is no temptation: they are for such moments as this, when body and soul rise in mutiny against their rigour; stringent are they; inviolate they shall be. If at my individual convenience I might break them, what would be their worth? They have a worth – so I have always believed; and if I cannot believe it now, it is because I am insane – quite insane: with my veins running fire, and my heart beating faster than I can count the throbs. Preconceived opinions, foregone determinations, are all I have at this hour to stand by: there I plant my foot.[23]

The relation between love and law can be compared to that between water and pipes. Without the pipes to channel and direct it, water can do more harm than good. On the other hand, the most perfect piping system in the world is of no use whatsoever unless there is water to flow through it. Likewise the piping system of the law is useless without the water of love, while the latter can be dangerous when not directed by the former.

---

[22] *Šabbat* 31a.
[23] Brontë, *Jane Eyre*, 317.

26
Self-love and self-esteem

Self-love

Jesus taught that the two great commandments are to love God with all our heart, soul, mind and strength and to love our neighbour as ourselves (Mark 12:28–31). Despite the fact that Jesus explicitly refers to two commandments, some today maintain that there are in fact *three* commandments, the third being to love ourselves. Augustine recognizes that there are two (not three) commands, but he also refers to three proper objects of our love – God, self and neighbour.[1] It should be noted, though, that the self-love advocated by Augustine and others is very different from the psychological self-esteem advocated by many today.[2]

There is little support for the idea that we are commanded to love ourselves either from commentaries on this passage (and parallels) or from Christian tradition. The command *assumes* the fact of self-love, as does Paul in Ephesians: 'Husbands should love their wives as their own bodies. He who loves his wife loves himself. For no one ever hated his own flesh, but nourishes and cherishes it, just as Christ does the church' (5:28–29).

Karl Barth refers to the claim that there is a third commandment in Mark 12:28–31, and rejects it. The second commandment presupposes, but does not command us to love ourselves. 'Self-love means, and must mean, to be alone with ourselves, to seek ourselves, to serve ourselves, to think of ourselves.' This is what we do and the commandment recognizes this. The commandment to love our neighbour as ourselves is not a legitimation of this self-love but a limitation of it. It is 'the judgement on my self-love and not its indirect justification'.[3] Earlier he states of our self-love, 'God will never think of blowing on this fire, which is bright enough already.'[4]

---

[1] *City of God* 19:14 (NPNF 2:410).
[2] For Augustine's views on this, see O'Donovan, *Problem of Self-Love in Saint Augustine.* Barth gives an account of the idea that we are commanded to love one another in Christian tradition in *Church Dogmatics* I/2, 387–388.
[3] *Church Dogmatics* I/2, 450–451.
[4] *Church Dogmatics* I/2, 387–388.

We must not confuse 'love' with 'like'. Many people with negative self-esteem[5] do not *like* themselves. That is not the issue here. The radical nature of Jesus' command to love our enemies (Matt. 5:44) includes the command to love those we do not like. We are not commanded to like our neighbours as we like ourselves.

There is also a sense in which self-love can be bad, as described in 2 Timothy 3:2: 'For people will be lovers of self, lovers of money, proud, arrogant, abusive, disobedient to their parents, ungrateful . . .'. Such people do *not* love their neighbours as themselves, but insist on putting their own interests first.[6] When I was first preparing this material and receiving advice from a colleague he rightly pointed out that what he was doing was loving me as himself by putting himself out for me.

The issue here is whose interests we are looking out for. Whose face did you wash this morning? Presumably your own. The command to love our neighbours means looking out for their interests. Paul calls upon each of his readers to 'look not only to his own interests, but also to the interests of others' (Phil. 2:4). Why should we do this? He immediately tells us to 'have this mind among yourselves, which is yours in Christ Jesus' and follows that with an account of how Jesus emptied himself to take the form of a servant and was obedient to the point of death on a cross (2:5–8). The second commandment is all about putting ourselves out for others, just as we do for our own self-interest.

The emphasis today on loving ourselves fits well with the narcissistic trends of modern Western culture:[7]

There once was a nymph named Narcissus,
Who thought himself very delicious;
So he stared like a fool
At his face in a pool,
And his folly today is still with us.[8]

A blatant example of this trend is the recent rise of the practice of 'sologamy' or marrying oneself.

---

[5] I have followed McGrath and McGrath, *Self-Esteem*, 15, in referring to negative rather than low self-esteem. Dryden, *How to Accept Yourself*, 1, prefers 'self-depreciation'.

[6] Calvin refers to self-love as a 'noxious pest' or a 'deadly pestilence' (*Inst.* 3:7:4).

[7] See Vitz, *Psychology as Religion*.

[8] Cited by Stott, *Cross of Christ*, 275.

Self-esteem

Secular views

Given the great emphasis on self today, many people argue that our prime need is for self-esteem.[9] The popular view in modern psychology, deriving from Carl Rogers, is that our fundamental problem is negative self-esteem, and it is the role of therapy to rectify that. But self-esteem is not an unmitigated good and can be a bad thing if it is unwarranted. It can easily lead to a lack of realism and a false pride. In America, which has been heavily influenced by the emphasis on self-esteem, students' perception of their competence in maths has steadily risen, while their actual achievement has declined. In a 1989 study of eight nations, the American students had the highest estimate of their mathematical competence, the Korean students the lowest. In terms of actual competence, the Koreans scored the highest and the Americans the lowest.[10]

Modern Western culture sees the fundamental problem as negative self-esteem, while Christian tradition has always identified pride as the fundamental problem. Which is right? The psychologist Terry Cooper, building on the work of Karen Horney, argues that they may both be right, that pride and self-contempt often go together, that they are not so much alternatives as two sides of the same coin, being different manifestations of the same problem. He illustrates this with a table that contrasts healthy self-esteem and a neurotic pride that leads to self-contempt (see Table 3).[11]

A number of factors can lead to negative self-esteem. There is a gender issue in that males are more prone to pride and self-assertiveness and females are more likely to lack self-esteem or even suffer from self-contempt. There can also be a genetic factor in that negative self-esteem can run in families. Upbringing undoubtedly plays a role in that being consistently belittled in home or at school has its effect. Sexual abuse can also lead to self-contempt.

It is also important to distinguish between different types of pride. Cooper expounds four types described by Reinhold Niebuhr: pride of power; intellectual pride; pride of virtue, morality and self-righteousness; spiritual pride.[12] Again, egotism (an inflated sense of one's own importance, feelings of superiority) is not the same as egoism (a preoccupation with oneself, whether or not

---

[9] For a sharp critique of modern trends, see Harrison, *Big Ego Trip*.
[10] See e.g. <http://www.latimes.com/news/opinion/la-op-selfhelp1jan01,1,4617597.story>, accessed 5 June 2020.
[11] Cooper, *Sin, Pride and Self-Acceptance*, 142.
[12] Cooper, *Sin, Pride and Self-Acceptance*, 49–55.

Table 3 Contrast between healthy self-esteem and neurotic pride

Healthy self-esteem	Neurotic pride
Healthy self-esteem is based on a realistic assessment of oneself.	Neurotic pride is based on the creation of an imaginary self with glorified characteristics that one 'ought' to have.
Healthy self-esteem pursues goals in harmony with one's true being and potential.	Neurotic pride creates a false self that searches relentlessly for glory and triumph.
Healthy self-esteem rests primarily on qualities of character.	Neurotic pride rests primarily on accomplishments, attainments or relationships that have prestige value.
Healthy self-esteem acknowledges and accepts personal faults and liabilities without losing self-respect and self-love.	Neurotic pride claims unbounded virtues but needs constant affirmation, is easily hurt and is self-depreciating.
Healthy self-esteem accepts reality as it is.	Neurotic pride feels entitled to special favour, privilege and immunity.
Healthy self-esteem recognizes and accepts moral limitations and fallibility.	Neurotic pride minimizes actual moral flaws and magnifies the value of mere intellectual assent to high ideals.
Healthy self-esteem recognizes the activities of one's personal 'dark side'.	Neurotic pride denies, suppresses or ignores these issues, projects them onto others, or justifies them, as necessary for survival.
Healthy self-esteem may suffer a temporary sense of guilt and regret when one does not live up to his or her ideals.	Neurotic pride wallows in shame, humiliation and self-contempt when one falls short.
Healthy self-esteem is concerned more about reality than image.	Neurotic pride is concerned more about image than reality.
Healthy self-esteem can embrace personal failure without feeling panic or rage.	Neurotic pride cannot endure anything less than perfection without extreme self-recrimination.
Healthy self-esteem accepts vulnerability.	Neurotic pride despises vulnerability and lashes back vindictively when pride is wounded.
Healthy self-esteem accepts responsibility for oneself.	Neurotic pride forgets, justifies, explains away or blames others for personal failure.

one feels superior). There are correspondingly two sides of humility. In opposition to egotism, humility gives us a realistic perception of ourselves. Paul told the Romans not to think of themselves more highly than is justified, but with a sound judgement (12:3). Humility is recognizing the truth about ourselves when it comes to sin. It is based on a realistic self-appraisal. Bernard of Clairvaux described it as a virtue through which we have a low opinion of ourselves, because we know ourselves well.[13] In opposition to egoism, humility is self-forgetfulness, not being self-absorbed, as C. S. Lewis pointed out.[14] We are not encouraged to self-love, or self-loath, but self-forget. Or as Rick Warren aptly put it, 'Humility is not thinking less of yourself; it is thinking of yourself less.'[15] It is esteeming and valuing others above ourselves and looking after their interests (Phil. 2:3–4). There is also a difference between pride and vanity or vainglory. The vain person seeks the praise and approval of others; the proud person despises the views of others.[16]

It is important to distinguish between humility and negative self-esteem. Humility is not to be confused with a grovelling attitude or with a false modesty. It is not pretending to be what we know we are not. Nor is it to be confused with a polite self-deprecation or with other social conventions, which have a proper place. It is reported that the Duke of Wellington once closed a letter to a junior officer with the conventional 'I remain, Sir, your most humble and obedient servant,' and then added, 'you know damn well I'm not!'

Christian critique of secular views[17]

Three Christian doctrines especially challenge secular views on self-esteem.

The doctrine of sin. Some secular therapists encourage people to accept themselves as they are, because they are fine. One even finds Christians coming up with comments like 'God loves us just as we are, because that's how he made us.' If this is referred to our physical characteristics (height, hair colour, etc.) this is all right, but if it is applied to our moral character it is far from true. It completely ignores the fact that sin has turned us into something very different from what God intended. It would not be legitimate to argue that 'God loves me just as I am, because that's how he made me – a serial killer.' (For the record, I am not a serial killer!) That approach ignores the basic structure of creation – sin – redemption – glory, set out in chapter 1.

We cannot completely disclaim responsibility for our outward appearance. It is often said that when advised to invite someone to join his cabinet, Abraham Lincoln declined on the grounds that he did not like his face. On being told that the man was not responsible for his face, Lincoln replied that

---

13 Bernard of Clairvaux, *Steps of Humility and Pride* 1:2 (*Treatises II*, 30).

14 Lewis, *Mere Christianity*, 111–112.

15 Warren, *Purpose Driven Life*, 148.

16 For more on this, see Lewis, *Mere Christianity*, 109–111; DeYoung, *Vainglory: Forgotten Vice*.

17 For this and the next section, see McGrath and McGrath, *Self-Esteem*.

everyone over forty is.[18] Lincoln's point was not that we are responsible for being ugly, for example, but that by the age of 40 a person's character is often manifested in their face.

Absolute moral standards. Some secular theories speak of accepting ourselves as we are, with all our flaws, without any moral judgement. Acceptance is achieved by bypassing moral accountability. What the Christian faith offers us is the opportunity to accept ourselves while fully recognizing our faults, without glossing over our moral failings.

Losing one's life. The distinctively Christian approach is that the way to find ourselves is to say 'no' to ourselves. The way to find salvation is to lose our lives and ourselves for the sake of Christ and the gospel. 'If anyone would come after me, let him deny himself and take up his cross and follow me. For whoever would save his life will lose it, but whoever loses his life for my sake and the gospel's will save it' (Mark 8:34–35).

Christian basis for self-esteem

While the Christian faith undercuts the secular basis for self-esteem, it does have a basis of its own. It is not opposed to self-esteem as such but to the wrong sort of self-esteem. True self-esteem is primarily based not on our own self-image, but on God's image of us (1 Cor. 4:4–5), on who we are in Christ. There are a number of points to consider, viewing ourselves as created, as fallen, as being redeemed and as destined for glory. We need to see ourselves in the light of that. Also, it is important that this perspective does not stop at the head but goes on to penetrate the heart.

Created in the image of God. Christian doctrine teaches that we are not simply the accidental products of a blind and meaningless process of evolution, but beings made in the image of God (Gen. 1:26–27). This gives us a huge dignity and significance beyond what any secular ideology can give. We are not worthless.

Christ died for us. Not only are we made in God's image, but God also 'shows his love for us in that while we were still sinners, Christ died for us' (Rom. 5:8). 'God so loved the world, that he gave his only Son . . .' (John 3:16). It is hard to see what greater affirmation God could give. Unworthy we may be, but certainly not worthless.[19] God treats us as of immense value and this is a tremendous basis for self-esteem.

---

[18] For the story, see <https://www.reddit.com/r/answers/comments/147wvx/why_did_lincoln_say_every_man_over_forty_is>, accessed 21 November 2019. For whether Lincoln actually said this, see Brewster, *Lincoln's Gamble*, 283.

[19] A point made by Stott, *Cross of Christ*, 283–284, citing Anthony Hoekema.

There is an issue here. I am created in God's image and God loved me so much that he gave Christ for me. True, but the same is also true of everyone else. What many people are looking for is not so much a basis for self-esteem, but a basis for esteeming themselves higher than others. Little girls who are taught to regard themselves as princesses are being told that they are superior to other little girls. The Christian faith does indeed provide a basis for a healthy self-esteem, but at the same time we are told, 'in humility count others more significant than yourselves' (Phil. 2:3). The quest for self-esteem must not be a cover for pride.

Justified by faith. As Christians we are justified by faith, we are put right with God and accepted as righteous in his sight. This is clearly a basis for self-esteem. It also enables us to square the circle that secular theories cannot, by holding two things together in tension. God judges sin – and also accepts us. We are beloved of God, despite being miserable sinners and moral failures. We do not have to pretend that God loves us because we are great people inside; in fact he knows everything about us yet still loves us. God makes uncompromising moral demands on us, but at the same time we are unconditionally accepted by him in Christ – the tension described in chapter 17. It follows that we can have self-esteem without lowering our standards of what is right and wrong or deluding ourselves that we are marvellous people with nothing deeply wrong with us. The Christian faith enables us to accept that we have been accepted, despite being unacceptable.[20]

Adopted as God's children. God does not 'merely' forgive us and declare us not guilty, massive though that is. He also adopts us as his children. This is an amazing affirmation of God's love and of our worth in his eyes.

A new creation. As Christians we are put right with God and adopted into his family. But that is only half of the picture. We are not only justified but also sanctified. 'If anyone is in Christ, he is a new creation' (2 Cor. 5:17). And being a new creation means nothing less than being conformed to the image of Christ (Rom. 8:29). As fallen we are unworthy, but through sanctification we become progressively more worthy.

Gifted and talented. God has given each one of us, in different ways, talents and gifts. The gifts of the Spirit are described in a number of New Testament passages, especially Romans 12:6–8, 1 Corinthians 12:8–10, 28–30, Ephesians 4:11–13. God apportions them to each one individually as he wills, for the common good (1 Cor. 12:6–7, 11). We are called to discern and exercise the gift(s) we have been given. This is also a basis for self-esteem.

---

[20] Tillich, *Courage to Be*, 165. Dryden, *How to Accept Yourself*, 16–29, argues that the cure for self-depreciation is not self-esteem, but 'unconditional self-acceptance'.

Promised reward. God is pleased with our good works, and rewards them. Though not perfect they are not worthless. For more on this see chapter 19.

Destined for glory. John promises us that when Jesus appears 'we shall be like him' (1 John 3:2) and Peter tells us that we shall become 'partakers of the divine nature' (2 Peter 1:4). How then can we have negative self-esteem?

Dealing with negative self-esteem

Despite the truths that we have just considered, it remains true that many Christians suffer from a harmfully negative self-esteem. As mentioned above, many factors can cause this, including gender, genes, upbringing and experience of abuse.

The cure for negative self-esteem lies in the truths just considered. So why does it persist? It is often stated that the longest journey in the world is the few inches from the head to the heart. Giving assent to something in the head is different from wholeheartedly believing it in one's heart. It takes time for the truths listed above to make that journey. It is a gradual process. It is not like the demolition of a dam, with the sudden release of vast quantities of water, but more akin to a slow coffee percolator. For some people therapy can be useful in unearthing hidden factors from earlier life that bind them to negative self-esteem or to addictive sins. (The same considerations apply to those who find it hard to accept that God has forgiven them.)

How should pastors and preachers handle this? The important point is that we need both affirmation *and* constructive criticism; it is not one or the other. Criticism alone discourages; affirmation alone leads to complacency. This is the tension described in chapter 17. As we saw in chapter 19, God is easy to please (which avoids discouragement) but hard to satisfy (which avoids complacency). But there is a difficulty here that has been recognized since the time of Gregory the Great.[21] There is always the danger that the wrong people hear the wrong message. Those who are lacking in self-esteem will hear only the criticism and become even more aware of their shortcomings, whereas those who are lazy or over self-confident will hear only the affirmation and become more complacent. The advantage of one-to-one pastoring is that there is no ambiguity about who is meant when one says, 'You are the man!' (2 Sam. 12:7).

There is a modern trend towards worship as therapy, the worship of God becoming a way of massaging our ego. On YouTube there is a hilarious spoof

---

[21] Gregory the Great, *Pastoral Rule* Part 3. Chapter 17 (NPNF² 12 Part 2, 41–42) is especially relevant to our theme.

worship song, entitled 'It's all about me'.[22] Some worship songs inappropriately put 'me' and 'my feelings' at the centre. There is a beautiful song entitled 'Above all powers' that very movingly describes Christ's sacrificial love for us, until it ends with the grotesquely narcissistic claim that he 'thought of me above all'. As Rick Warren aptly observed, there is only one person who thinks of me above all – and that is me! Of course, the gospel *does* apply to us individually. Paul could say:

> I have been crucified with Christ. It is no longer I who live, but Christ who lives in me. And the life I now live in the flesh I live by faith in the Son of God, who loved me and gave himself for me.
> (Gal. 2:20)

But when our worship is expressed in an individualistic or self-centred way that is wrong.

Since the 1960s there has been a widespread revision of liturgies. The Anglican Church produced various revisions of the Book of Common Prayer, culminating in 2000 with *Common Worship*. The Roman Catholic Church after Vatican II translated its liturgy from Latin into the vernacular languages. At the same time the content was modified with the deliberate aim of removing 'negative themes', playing down references to sin and repentance, for example.[23] A quick comparison of a traditional hymn book with a book of modern worship songs shows a similar trend. The majority of modern choruses and worship songs emphasize themes like glory and power, with relatively little mention of sin and its cure. Even worse, in many of them we sing about ourselves and our feelings, rather than who God is and what he has done. A proper balance is required between all these aspects, or we risk betraying the gospel. As Luther pointed out, without sin, there is no need for salvation, and therefore no gospel at all.[24] The good news presupposes the bad news!

In the Book of Common Prayer there are prayers of confession in which we acknowledge that we are 'miserable offenders' or 'miserable sinners'.[25] Today some object that this is bad for our self-image, to which the response is that we *are* miserable offenders. Jesus tells the Laodiceans that 'you say, I am rich, I have prospered, and I need nothing, not realizing that you are wretched, pitiable, poor, blind, and naked' (Rev. 3:17) and the word 'pitiable' is 'miserable'

---

[22] See <https://www.youtube.com/watch?v=t9dvVp0Nxjo>, accessed 21 November 2019.
[23] Cf. Richgens, 'Close of the Gregorian Era', 58–61, 64–65.
[24] Althaus, *Theology of Martin Luther*, 257–258.
[25] General Confession and Morning and Evening Prayer; Litany.

in some other translations. As I have argued, our self-image should not be based on a denial of our sinfulness.[26] Augustine states that God's grace heals those who do not proudly boast of an imaginary blessedness but instead humbly confess their actual misery.[27]

---

[26] See Davies, *Down Peacock's Feathers*, based on the General Confession from the Book of Common Prayer, in which 'we acknowledge and bewail our manifold sins and wickedness, which we, from time to time, most grievously have committed, by thought, word and deed, against thy divine Majesty, provoking most justly thy wrath and indignation against us'.

[27] *City of God* 10:28 (NPNF 2:199).

Part 4

LIVING THE CHRISTIAN LIFE: SANCTIFICATION

27

Sanctification

What is sanctification?[1]

As we saw in chapter 16, the Reformers made a clear distinction between justification and sanctification. Justification refers to our standing before God, our acceptance by God; sanctification refers to our moral state, to our renewal by God's grace. While justification is binary (you either are or you are not), sanctification is progressive and we should become increasingly sanctified. These are the ways in which theology usually defines the terms and for theology it is helpful to keep to clear definitions. The Bible, however, is a collection of 'occasional' writings by different authors and we cannot assume they all shared the same definitions or even that they were each consistent in their own writings. For more on this see chapter 24.

In English we have two different families of words, relating to holiness and sanctification. Words like 'saint' and 'sanctify' derive from Latin and French, while words like 'holy' and 'holiness' derive from German. In the original Greek, and also in Latin, there is only one family of words, not two. So to be sanctified is to be holy, which means to be set apart for God (e.g. 2 Tim. 2:21). The process of sanctification follows from this. Paul regularly addresses the recipients of his letter as 'saints' or 'holy' – even the Corinthians who had much to learn about sanctification! So while sanctification is normally regarded as progressive, there is also a sense of 'definitive' or 'positional' sanctification.[2] As we shall see, there is a sense in which sanctification involves 'becoming what we are'.

Sanctification can be viewed either negatively (the elimination of sin) or positively (transformation into the image of Christ). These are sometimes called 'mortification' (putting to death) and 'vivification' (making alive). The *Westminster Confession of Faith* (1647) gives a comprehensive definition:

---

[1] For discussion of a number of different views, see Dieter et al., *Five Views on Sanctification*; Alexander (ed.), *Christian Spirituality: Five Views of Sanctification*.

[2] Peterson, *Possessed by God*.

They, who are once effectually called, and regenerated, having a new heart, and a new spirit created in them, are further sanctified, really and personally, through the virtue of Christ's death and resurrection, by His Word and Spirit dwelling in them: the dominion of the whole body of sin is destroyed, and the several lusts thereof are more and more weakened and mortified; and they more and more quickened and strengthened in all saving graces, to the practice of true holiness, without which no man shall see the Lord.[3]

Elimination of sin

In chapter 2 we saw that sin can be viewed from a range of perspectives: as pride, as unbelief, as selfishness, as self-centredness (being curved in on ourselves), and so on. Sanctification involves the reversal of these. Pride is replaced by humility; unbelief is banished by faith; selfishness gives way to love of God and neighbour; the self-centred life becomes God-centred.

Paul gives a list of the works of the flesh: 'sexual immorality, impurity, sensuality, idolatry, sorcery, enmity, strife, jealousy, fits of anger, rivalries, dissensions, divisions, envy, drunkenness, orgies, and things like these' (Gal. 5:19–21). Sanctification involves the replacement of these by the fruit of the Spirit: 'love, joy, peace, patience, kindness, goodness, faithfulness, gentleness, self-control' (Gal. 5:22–23). There are similar lists in 2 Peter 1:5–7 and 1 Corinthians 13:4–7 and each is a representative list, not an exhaustive one. In all of these lists love is pre-eminent, since God is love. Another way of viewing them is as descriptions of a Christlike character.

Sinning leads to bondage to sin and sanctification involves liberation from sin. Paul describes the way in which this happens through life in the Spirit (Rom. 8:1–17). But shortly before he describes the situation of those desiring to do good (Rom. 7:15–25). Controversy has raged as to whether this describes pre-Christian experience, suboptimal Christian experience or one side of normal Christian experience to be held in tension with that described in Romans 8.[4]

Transformation into the image of Christ

The heart of sanctification is being transformed into the likeness of Christ, becoming more like him (2 Cor. 3:18). This is a thoroughly positive goal and is

---

[3] Ch. 13:1 (*RefConf* 4:249).
[4] For various views on this see Wilder (ed.), *Perspectives on Our Struggle with Sin*.

vastly more than a list of 'dos and don'ts'. Yet it is also a hugely ambitious goal and the more comfortable target of becoming more respectable fades into insignificance by comparison. Being transformed into Christ's likeness will involve us in pain and hardship and at times we may well wish that God would settle for second best.

> It is a serious thing to live in a society of possible gods and goddesses, to remember that the dullest and most uninteresting person you can talk to may one day be a creature which, if you saw it now, you would be strongly tempted to worship, or else a horror and a corruption such as you now meet, if at all, only in a nightmare.[5]

The extent of transformation is shown by Paul in his command to 'present your bodies as a living sacrifice . . . Do not be conformed to this world, but be transformed by the renewal of your mind' (Rom. 12:1–2). J. B. Phillips famously translated this as 'Do not let the world squeeze you into its mould.' This points to conformity to God's will in mind and action. The extent of transformation is also shown by the two great commandments, to love God and neighbour (Matt. 22:37–40).

In chapter 3 it was suggested that Adam and Eve ceased to live in dependence upon the Spirit of God but set themselves up as their own moral arbiters. If the essence of the fall is to live as autonomous moral agents rather than in dependence upon the Spirit of God, then *by definition* its consequence must be the loss of the moral integration that results from turning away from God. The situation is so serious that it calls for no less than a heart transplant: 'I will give you a new heart, and a new spirit I will put within you. And I will remove the heart of stone from your flesh and give you a heart of flesh' (Ezek. 36:26).

If we have been given a new heart and if we now seek to live in dependence upon the Holy Spirit, why do we still sin? The effects of sin are so dire that they cannot be reversed overnight. An analogy may help to explain this. After the war part of Germany came under Russian control and in 1949 became the German Democratic Republic (East Germany). This Communist state was cut off by the Iron Curtain from the Federal Republic of Germany, until the fall of the Berlin Wall in 1989. In 1990 East Germany was integrated into the Federal Republic and since then has been part of that country. Yet even now there are profound social and cultural differences between the East and the

---

[5] Lewis, 'The Weight of Glory', in *Screwtape Proposes a Toast*, 109.

rest. Reunification and what has followed (which can be compared to justification and sanctification) have not yet undone the effects of forty years of alienation between East and West Germany.

Discipleship

To be transformed into the likeness of Christ involves discipleship. Three important aspects of discipleship are seen in Luke 9:23: 'If anyone would come after me, let him deny himself and take up his cross daily and follow me.' So discipleship is as follows.

Following Christ. To follow Christ means being his disciple, learning from him.

Denying oneself. What does this mean? Giving up chocolates for Lent? It is much more than that. It means saying 'No' to ourselves, to our own desires, and saying 'Yes' to God's will. This applies in two ways: Negatively it means not doing that which is wrong, such as lying or stealing, yet it also means more than this. Positively it means seeking God's will for our lives and being willing to follow wherever he leads. This may, for example, involve a call to remain single – not because celibacy is superior in its own right but in order to devote oneself to God's service. It involves responding to the promptings of the Holy Spirit and being malleable; it involves saying 'No' to self-will.

Taking up one's cross daily. Luke's Gospel is the only one to include the word 'daily'. This is not a once-for-all call but one for each and every day. Taking up or bearing one's cross does not mean putting up patiently with the hardships of life, be this a pain in the back (sports injury) or a pain in the backside (awkward relatives). It means voluntary acceptance of and submission to the will of God.

The process of sanctification can be compared to the two different strategies for dealing with excess weight. Corsets do not cure it but they hold it in and conceal it. Their effect is immediate. By contrast, taking exercise and eating a sensible diet take time to work, but deal with the problem and cure it. When it comes to sanctification we are faced with two similar strategies. We can restrain our sinful nature so that its worst effects are avoided – we can hold back our anger and not come to blows with others, and we can contain our lust and not go to the point of committing adultery. Restraining sin in this way is important, but it is not enough. We need also to seek a cure. We need to work on our anger and lust, not just contain them. While those battling excess weight may opt to go for one strategy without the other, with sanctification both are important.

Why is it that some non-Christians appear to be better people than many Christians, as we considered in chapter 19? This is a serious question. The key issue is not whether a particular Christian is better or worse than a particular non-Christian (something hard to measure anyway) but whether a particular person becomes better when they become a Christian. If they do not, we have grounds for questioning (not denying) whether they are indeed true Christians. But here and now we are all a 'work in progress'. The person with a foul temper who is converted may still have a volatile temper and compare badly with others who are not Christians, but the more significant question is whether they are becoming *less* foul tempered as they grow in grace.[6]

Becoming what we are

Another major aspect of sanctification is that we should 'become what we are'. Christians are united with Christ and share in his history. We are crucified with Christ and 'united with him in a death like his' (Rom. 6:5–8). We are also raised with him, and seated with him in the heavenlies (Eph. 2:6; Col. 3:1).

When did this happen? We were crucified with Christ in AD 33 or thereabouts and enter into this at our baptism/conversion. When we are baptized into Christ we are baptized into his death (Rom. 6:3–4). There is the story of the Frenchman who took British nationality. After the naturalization ceremony he was asked what difference it made. 'Put it like this,' he answered, 'This morning the Battle of Waterloo was a defeat; now it is a victory.' The outcome of the battle had not changed, but his relationship to it had. Likewise at conversion we move from being in Adam to being in Christ. We need by faith to reckon this to be true (Rom. 6:11). We also need to work it out in our lives. We have already died with Christ (Col. 3:3), but we must go on to 'put to death therefore what is earthly' and 'put on then, as God's chosen ones, holy and beloved, compassion, kindness, humility, meekness, and patience . . .' (3:5–14). We *have died* with Christ, but we also need to *put to death* all that is sinful. We enjoy the new life in Christ 'already, but not yet'.

We are living in the period between the first and second comings of Christ, when we enjoy the benefits of salvation already in part, but not yet fully – 'already, but not yet'. The recipients of the letter to the Hebrews were told that they were in the last days (1:1–2). This did not mean that the end was necessarily about to happen. The last days were introduced by the first coming of Christ, but they will not come to fruition until the second coming. This

---

[6] For more helpful comments on this question, see Lewis, *Mere Christianity*, 172–180.

situation can be compared to that of engagement, where two people are already committed to one another but have not yet reached the commitment of marriage. In Ephesians 1:14 the Holy Spirit is called 'the guarantee of our inheritance until we acquire possession of it', and the word for 'guarantee' or 'down payment' (*arrabōn*) is the word used in modern Greek for an engagement ring. Our present experience of salvation is also described as the first fruits of a harvest. We enjoy 'the firstfruits of the Spirit' (Rom. 8:23).

Is sanctification God's work or ours?

Is sanctification something we receive passively by faith, or something we acquire by our own effort, working for it? This is a silly polarization as both are true.

The New Testament describes sanctification as the work of God and calls upon us to rest passively in it. Jesus told his disciples that they could bear fruit only by abiding in him (John 15:4). Paul told the Galatians that it was no longer he who lived but Christ who lived in him. 'The life I now live in the flesh I live by faith in the Son of God, who loved me and gave himself for me' (Gal. 2:20). He prayed that God would sanctify the Thessalonians completely and that their whole spirit and soul and body 'be kept blameless at the coming of our Lord Jesus Christ' (1 Thess. 5:23).

These passages portray sanctification as God's work and it would be possible, but mistaken, to read them as encouraging us to be merely passive. Other passages tell us to strive for sanctification. As we have just seen, the statement that we have died, and our life is hidden with Christ in God (Col. 3:3) is immediately followed by the command to put to death what is earthly in us and to put on a number of virtues (3:5–14). Those who live according to the flesh will die, but those who by the Spirit put to death the deeds of the body will live (Rom. 8:12–13).

Both sides are held together in Philippians 2:12–13: 'Work out your own salvation with fear and trembling, for it is God who works in you, both to will and to work for his good pleasure.' God does it but we have to work it out in our lives by our own efforts. In 2 Peter 1:3–7 Peter begins with the statement that God's 'divine power *has granted to us* all things that pertain to life and godliness'. He continues by urging his readers to '*make every effort* to supplement your faith with virtue . . .'

There is a slogan that used to be used by those advocating the one side only: 'Don't wrestle, nestle.' In fact we are called to do both: wrestle *and* nestle! Another such slogan is 'Let go and let God.' This similarly presents one side only of the picture. Some preachers have pointed to Exodus 14:13–14, where

Moses tells the people of Israel, facing the threat of an Egyptian army, to 'Fear not, stand firm, and see the salvation of the LORD, which he will work for you today . . . The LORD will fight for you, and you have only to be silent.' In the very next verse, however, the Lord tells Moses to get on and do something: 'Why do you cry to me? Tell the people of Israel to go forward.'

Paul refers to love, joy, peace, and so on, as 'fruit', but that does not mean they come automatically. It is not like growing hair while one sleeps; it requires our choices and our effort. We need to walk by the Spirit (Gal. 5:16–25). It is the Holy Spirit who bears the fruit but we cannot just lie back and leave it to the Spirit – just as farmers and gardeners cannot leave all the work to the rain and sun.

Corporate sanctification

Just as sin is not purely individual but has a corporate dimension (see chapter 2), so also there is a corporate dimension to sanctification. As we engage in the task of sanctification we are greatly influenced both by society at large and by the church as a community when it comes to what is and is not acceptable. A few examples will illustrate this.

Divorce was rare in Western societies until the 1950s but with the progressive liberalization of divorce laws since the 1960s it has now reached epidemic proportions. What was once stigmatized by society is now completely acceptable and very easily obtained. Marriage has changed from a lifelong commitment to a rolling contract. The church has not remained immune from this and the majority of Western churches now accept divorce.[7] The result is that a Christian couple going through difficult times in their marriage are now far more likely to resort to divorce than to persevere with the marriage. They make their individual decisions, but these are hugely influenced by social pressures.[8]

Many Christians today, including pastors, struggle with pornography. The ready acceptance of this in society at large – its legalization and availability on the internet – makes it much more likely that a Western Christian today will have this problem, compared with one living in the 1950s.

Lest it be thought I am a grumpy old man looking back at a past golden age let me point to two areas where the movement has been in the other direction.

---

[7] For different views on this, see House (ed.), *Divorce and Remarriage*; Strauss (ed.), *Remarriage After Divorce*.

[8] For a study that supports the peer effects of divorce, see <http://douthat.blogs.nytimes.com/2010/06/24/how-divorce-spreads>, accessed 5 June 2020.

In the 1950s casual racism was endemic and socially acceptable. In the 1970s I heard Christian students make racial comments that would be totally unacceptable today, when the social pressure is strongly against racism. A hundred years ago anti-Semitism was normal, but attitudes have changed significantly (but not completely) since the Holocaust. Hitler gave anti-Semitism a bad name.

In the eighteenth century it was acceptable to own and trade in slaves. It is well known that the hymn writer John Newton, of 'Amazing grace' fame, was a former slave trader. What is less well known is that he continued in this occupation for a time *after* his conversion. Indeed he stated that 'During the time I was engaged in the slave-trade, I never had the least scruple as to its lawfulness. I was upon the whole satisfied with it, as the appointment Providence had marked out for me.'[9] When he later campaigned for its abolition he brought to the campaign his valuable first-hand knowledge of the slave-trade.[10] The achievement of reformers like William Wilberforce was not just to change the law but eventually to change social attitudes. I have not heard of any Christians today tempted to engage in people trafficking.

Christians do not engage in sanctification as hermetically sealed individuals. We are all greatly influenced by what is deemed by the church to be acceptable or unacceptable. This is why church discipline is very important, whether exercised informally (peer pressure) or formally. In turn, the church is not hermetically sealed from society at large. Changes in social attitudes often lead to changed attitudes within the church community. This can be a good thing as, for example, the church no longer accepts racism or the marginalization of the disabled. It can also be a bad thing as the church is influenced by social attitudes towards, for example, cohabitation or materialism. As Western society increasingly rejects the Christian values it has inherited from the past this is likely to become a growing problem, as it was for the church living in a pagan society in the early centuries.

To what extent should the government legislate for morality? How much this is desirable or possible will vary from context to context. The idea that the government should not legislate on moral issues is ridiculous. Should murder be legal? Or enslaving people? Those who argue against moral legislation usually mean that they want the greatest possible *sexual* freedom, though usually they will draw the line at paedophilia. Legislating contrary to public opinion can be counter-productive. The Prohibition of alcohol in the USA between 1918 and 1933 did an immense amount of harm, facilitating

---

[9] Newton, *Life of Rev. John Newton*, 95.
[10] Pollock, *Amazing Grace: John Newton's Story*, 111.

the rise of gangsterism. On the other hand, legislation can help to change social attitudes, as has happened with racism and smoking.

Excursus: second blessing?

John the Baptist promised that, unlike him, Jesus would baptize with the Holy Spirit (Matt. 3:11; Mark 1:8; Luke 3:16; John 1:33). To what does this refer? In chapter 10 we argued that receiving the Spirit is one of the features of Christian initiation (becoming a Christian) and it is to this that baptism in the Spirit refers. Paul tells the Corinthians that *all* believers (not just some) have been baptized in one Spirit into one body and made to drink of one Spirit (1 Cor. 12:13).

Over the centuries various minority groups have taught that there is a 'second blessing' subsequent to conversion – something that not all Christians have but which all Christians should seek to attain. This is often called a baptism in, with or of the Holy Spirit.[11] We shall review four different ways in which this approach was applied in four different centuries.

Puritans and assurance

In chapter 20 we saw that the 'alternative' Reformation view saw assurance as something subsequent to conversion, to be sought at a later date. How then should assurance be sought? Some at the time proposed looking within to see the evidence of faith or of sanctification. We should examine ourselves and then deduce that we are Christians on the basis of the evidence. Others commended another, simpler approach – the direct witness of the Holy Spirit, seen as an intuitive rather than rational process. The Holy Spirit witnesses to us directly by his presence. This idea was developed by the seventeenth-century Puritans Richard Sibbes and Thomas Goodwin.[12] They referred to it as the anointing or sealing of the Holy Spirit, appealing to Ephesians 1:13–14. They were misled by the bad translation of the King James Version, which reads '*after* that ye believed, ye were sealed with that holy Spirit of promise'. (Most modern translations render this as '*when* . . . you believed', removing the suggestion that this sealing takes place at a later date, as a subsequent experience.) They also appealed to Paul's teaching on the witness of the Spirit.

In chapter 11 we saw that John Wesley's 'conversion' involved coming to a full assurance of faith, similar to the experience described by Sibbes and

---

[11] On this issue, see Brand, *Perspectives on Spirit Baptism*. Confirmation is seen as a second stage following baptism (see chapter 10), but is not seen as a baptism of the Spirit. The *Catechism of the Catholic Church* relates baptism in the Spirit to new birth, not to confirmation (§720).

[12] See Eaton, *Baptism with the Spirit*, 60–92.

Goodwin. In the last century this teaching was revived by Martyn Lloyd-Jones, who referred explicitly to Sibbes and Goodwin.[13]

Wesleys and entire sanctification

In the eighteenth century John and Charles Wesley taught that there is a second blessing for *holiness*, bringing the gift of entire sanctification or Christian perfection, which we shall consider further in chapter 30. Others have not taught perfection but have held that there is a crisis experience that lifts people from carnal to spiritual Christians and brings about a life of victory over sin.[14]

Torrey and power in service

In the nineteenth century the American evangelist and Bible teacher R. A. Torrey taught that the baptism with the Holy Spirit is a distinct post-conversion experience. He was clear that this was *not* for assurance of salvation, not for holiness and not for gifts like speaking in tongues. The Holy Spirit came upon Jesus shortly before the beginning of his ministry and Torrey correspondingly saw this baptism as empowerment for an effective and powerful ministry. Torrey received this doctrine from his fellow evangelist D. L. Moody and he himself had the experience in 1871.

Torrey wrote a very influential work entitled *What the Bible Teaches* (1898). This contains a chapter on 'Baptism with the Holy Spirit'.[15] This he sees as a definite experience and one that is 'distinct from, additional to, and subsequent to' regeneration. So while every believer has the Holy Spirit and ideally all should receive baptism with the Holy Spirit immediately after their conversion, neglect of the topic means that in fact not all Christians have received it. It is possible to be regenerated by the Spirit without receiving baptism with the Spirit. The purpose of the baptism, he continues, is not to make us 'happy or holy' but to impart to us 'supernatural power or gifts in service'. 'It has to do with gifts for service rather than with graces of character.'[16] Citing 1 Corinthians 12 especially, he observes that this gifting varies from person to person, according to God's will. He mentions that 'many in the early church' spoke in tongues, while today the Spirit gives gifts for evangelism, teaching and such like. But baptism with the Spirit 'always imparts power in service' and 'boldness

---

[13] Lloyd-Jones, *Joy Unspeakable*. On this, see Eaton, *Baptism with the Spirit*, 125–253.

[14] For one such view, see the exposition of the Keswick view by J. Robertson McQuilkin in Dieter et al., *Five Views on Sanctification*, 151–183.

[15] Torrey, *What the Bible Teaches*, 269–280 (book 3, ch. 7). Three years earlier he had published a book entitled *Baptism of the Holy Spirit: How to Receive This Promised Gift*, which contains the same teaching and calls the baptism of the Spirit a 'second blessing'.

[16] Torrey, *What the Bible Teaches*, 271–273.

in testimony and service'.[17] He summarizes his argument as follows: 'Baptism with the Holy Spirit is *the* Spirit of *God* coming upon the believer, filling his mind with a real apprehension of truth, and taking possession of his faculties, imparting to him gifts not otherwise his that qualify him for the service to which God has called him.'[18]

Torrey argued that this baptism is necessary for Christian ministry and that we should follow the example of Jesus himself, who did not begin his ministry until he had received this anointing with the Holy Spirit. So *all* Christians should seek this blessing for whatever service they are called to. Interestingly, Torrey recognizes that Peter was filled with the Spirit more than once, recognizes the need for 'a new filling of the Holy Spirit for each new emergency of Christian service'.[19]

Pentecostalism and speaking in tongues

Pentecostalism started at the beginning of the twentieth century in the United States. Its original setting was within the holiness movement and so baptism in the Spirit was seen as the *third* blessing. The first is conversion; the second is entire sanctification; the third is baptism in the Holy Spirit. The vessel needs to be cleansed (by entire sanctification) before it can be filled (by the Spirit). Other early Pentecostals came from a Baptist or Reformed background and did not hold to the Wesleyan doctrine of entire sanctification. For them (as for most Pentecostals subsequently) baptism in the Spirit is the *second* blessing.

Whatever position is taken on entire sanctification, Pentecostals traditionally believe that all Christians are born again of the Spirit and that there is a subsequent experience of baptism in the Holy Spirit. Speaking in tongues is usually seen as the outward evidence that one has received this baptism. Indeed until 2007 the Assemblies of God churches held that speaking in tongues was *the* criterion of having received the baptism in the Holy Spirit.

Conclusion

I do not question that many of those who claim to have received one or more of these different 'baptisms' have in fact had a genuine experience of the Holy Spirit, and these can be immensely significant in the path of discipleship – though not all alleged experiences of the Spirit are positive or helpful. That is not the point at issue – which is whether there is one particular 'baptism in the

---

[17] Torrey, *What the Bible Teaches*, 274, 275.
[18] Torrey, *What the Bible Teaches*, 276.
[19] Torrey, *What the Bible Teaches*, 279.

Holy Spirit' to which all Christians should aspire and without which, by implication, a Christian is falling short.

Some may wish to suggest that the four doctrines expounded above are differing descriptions of the same event and that they can be seen as evidence for a continuity of teaching, albeit with variations. That is not so. They are very different experiences. Having assurance of salvation is not the same as being entirely sanctified. Empowerment for ministry is something quite different again and one can easily imagine someone who has a rock solid assurance and is leading a holy life, but is not empowered for ministry. That these are not simply four descriptions of the same event can be seen from the way in which Torrey differentiated the baptism in the Holy Spirit from holiness and from the way in which the first Pentecostals held that the baptism in the Holy Spirit came after entire sanctification, as something quite distinct. The four groups were not describing the same gift in different ways but were teaching about four *different* 'second blessings'.

The error lies in setting up one particular experience as intended for all Christians – and also in calling this 'the baptism of the Spirit'. There is no *one* experience that is intended for all Christians. Nor are such experiences what is meant in the New Testament by the baptism of the Spirit. That refers to the *initial* receiving of the Spirit at conversion, as we saw in chapter 10.

Finally, it should be noted that if any one of the above versions of second blessing is in fact intended for all Christians, then this is one of the best kept secrets in church history. The number holding to any of the first three versions are quite small. Today there are significant numbers of Christians holding to the Pentecostal version, but there were hardly any prior to the twentieth century. If any of these versions is in fact intended for all Christians it is remarkable that so few have been aware of that fact over the twenty centuries of Christian history.

28
Perseverance and apostasy

Can truly converted Christians lose their salvation?

This is a controversial topic. What makes it such is the untidiness of real life. It would be much simpler if all converted Christians simply persevered to the end without falling away. But that is not what we see. Shockingly, even one of the twelve apostles, chosen by Jesus, fell away and was lost. Apostasy, rejection of the faith one once had, is a sad fact of life. So how do we make sense of this theologically? A number of views have been held over the years and we shall look at four of these. First, we must review the teaching of the New Testament, asking three different questions.

New Testament teaching

Is perseverance to the end necessary for salvation?

In other words, is it necessary for salvation not just to start the Christian life, not just to become a Christian, but also to continue in it to the end, to remain a Christian? The consensus of the New Testament is that such perseverance is necessary. Final salvation is not unconditional, contrary to the claims of many today.

To give a few examples, we read in Mark 13:13 that it is those who endure to the end who will be saved. Paul assures the Colossians that Christ will present them 'holy and blameless and above reproach' – but this is on condition that they 'continue in the faith, stable and steadfast, not shifting from the hope of the gospel' (1:21–23). Hebrews refers to 'the holiness without which no one will see the Lord' (12:14). Hebrews also contrasts 'those who shrink back and are destroyed' with 'those who have faith and preserve their souls' (10:39).

There is nothing in the New Testament that suggests that salvation is possible without persevering to the end. That does not mean we need to live a sinless life – for more on which see chapter 30. It does not mean that Christians will not fall for a time or lapse into grave sin and then be restored, as happened with Peter when he denied Christ three times. We remain forgiven sinners – but sinners who are in the process of sanctification. As we saw in chapter 17, judgement is according to works, which means that sanctification is not an optional extra.

Is it possible to lose salvation?

Here again the New Testament answer is 'Yes'. This is stated in many different places. Jesus warns that 'every branch of mine that does not bear fruit [the Father] takes away' and that anyone who does not abide in him 'is thrown away like a branch and withers; and the branches are gathered, thrown into the fire, and burned' (John 15:2, 6). Hebrews contains two passages which warn in forthright terms of the danger of apostasy.[1]

> It is impossible [to restore again to repentance] those who have once been enlightened, who have tasted the heavenly gift, and have shared in the Holy Spirit, and have tasted the goodness of the word of God and the powers of the age to come, if they then fall away, since they are crucifying once again the Son of God to their own harm and holding him up to contempt.
> (6:4–6)

> If we go on sinning deliberately after receiving the knowledge of the truth, there no longer remains a sacrifice for sins, but a fearful expect-ation of judgement, and a fury of fire that will consume the adversaries.
> (10:26–27)

Those who turn away and are lost are also described in 2 Peter 2:20–22.

Is this just a theoretical possibility, something that will not in fact happen? The parable of the sower indicates that it is not just a possibility, but something that happens and is indeed to be expected. In his explanation of the parable Jesus explains that the ones sown on rocky ground are those who 'when they hear the word, immediately receive it with joy'. And they 'have no root in themselves, but endure for a while; then, when tribulation or persecution arises on account of the word, immediately they fall away' (Mark 4:16–17). Again, if one of the twelve apostles, chosen by Jesus, could fall away and be lost, who is exempt? Even Paul did not see himself as exempt, but disciplined his body, fearing disqualification (1 Cor. 9:27).

---

[1] For different views on these passages, see Bateman (ed.), *Four Views on Warning Passages in Hebrews*.

Will God keep Christians from completely falling away?

Here also the New Testament seems to say 'Yes'. While Jesus in John 15 refers to those who do not persevere, in chapter 10 he promises that his sheep will never perish and that no one will snatch them from his or his Father's hand (27–29). Paul, who disciplined himself to avoid disqualification, promised the Philippians that 'he who began a good work in you will bring it to completion at the day of Jesus Christ' (1:6). He also assured the Romans that

> neither death nor life, nor angels nor rulers, nor things present nor things to come, nor powers, nor height nor depth, nor anything else in all creation, will be able to separate us from the love of God in Christ Jesus our Lord.
> (8:38–39)

The same point is also taught elsewhere, but less clearly.

So the New Testament teaches three different things: *perseverance* is necessary for salvation; there is a real (not just theoretical) danger of *falling away* and losing our salvation; and yet God will *keep* those who are his. How can we hold these three points together? It is easy to hold to two of them and the danger is that people highlight two of the points, claim that as the teaching of Scripture and then deal with the third point on the basis that 'since we know what Scripture teaches . . .' In particular, doing justice to both the second and third points is tricky. We shall examine different attempts to do this, looking at three historic views that have been widely held and then at a more recent proposed solution.[2]

Four views

Augustine and the Catholic tradition

Augustine distinguished between three different stages of God's grace, of the Holy Spirit's working within us. The first is prevenient grace, where God takes the initiative and works within us to draw us to himself. This is something God does without us, and so is called *operating grace*. Once we are born again and converted we are now working together with the Holy Spirit and so this

---

[2] For another discussion of different views, see Pinson (ed.), *Four Views on Eternal Security*.

stage is called *cooperating grace*. While operating grace refers to the beginning of the Christian life, cooperating grace refers to the working of the Spirit in the life of the converted Christian in the process of sanctification. In the process of the Christian life, as we have seen, there remains the possibility of falling away and losing salvation. Augustine held that the power of sin is so great and we are so weak that we shall fall away unless God grants us the third stage of grace, the *gift of perseverance*. Without this gift we shall not manage to continue to the end and attain final salvation. He expounds this in one of his last books, entitled *The Gift of Perseverance*.[3]

Augustine held that because perseverance is a gift of God it is something for which we should pray. In support of this he quoted from the Lord's Prayer: 'lead us not into temptation, but deliver us from evil' (Matt. 6:13). There are two different ways in which God can answer this prayer. One way is obviously by giving us the grace to carry on and not fall away. Another, less obvious, way is by taking us from this life if he foresees that we shall otherwise fall away.

Crucially Augustine held that not all Christians receive the gift of perseverance. While it is given in answer to prayer, this is not something we can earn or merit by our piety or virtue. It is given only to the elect, to those whom God has chosen – on which see chapter 9. Augustine held that not all genuinely converted Christians, not all who have received prevenient and efficacious grace and have been born again, are elect. It is possible to be genuinely converted by God's grace and to lead a Christian life for a time, and then to fall away (of one's own choice) and be lost. The moral of this is that no one can be certain of final salvation and the death bed becomes crucial. Augustine told the story of an 84-year-old man who had lived a celibate life with his wife for 25 years – and then took a concubine.[4] The message is clear: no one can think they are out of danger.

How does Augustine hold together the three points from the New Testament? He clearly held to the need to persevere to the end. He reconciled the second and third points from the New Testament by referring the possibility of losing salvation to Christians as a whole and the promise of perseverance to the smaller (and unknown) number of the elect.

Catholic theology has not always followed Augustine's views on grace and election, but it has consistently held to the possibility of losing one's salvation. This was the position set forth in the Council of Trent's *Decree on Justification*, on which see chapter 22. Our state at the time of *death* is crucial; someone who

---

[3] NPNF 5:523–552; Augustine, *Four Anti-Pelagian Writings*, 271–337.
[4] Augustine, *Against Julian* 3:11:22.

has lived a bad life but repented at the end will be saved, but someone who has lived a Christian life but then fallen away at the end will be lost.

It should be noted, though, that some Catholic theologians today hold out the *hope* that at the end all will be saved, without stating this dogmatically. Significantly this number includes Pope John Paul II, writing in a private capacity.[5]

Calvin and the Reformed tradition

Calvin held to the perseverance of all true believers. Salvation requires persever-ance to the end, but God keeps true Christians from finally falling away. All who have true saving faith *will* persevere to the end and be saved, because Christ keeps them to the end as he has promised. Some may fall away for a time, but God will restore them (*Inst.* 3:24:6–9). So Christians can be assured of final salvation.

That position was reaffirmed in response to Arminianism at the Synod of Dort in 1618–19, on which see chapters 8 and 9. This acknowledges that we are weak and sinful and prone to fall, but also affirms that through God's preser-vation we shall persevere and attain to salvation. That does not mean it will be easy: the Christian life is a struggle. We should have assurance, but without any complacency.[6]

The Reformed position holds firmly to the need to persevere and to the promise of perseverance.[7] But what about the warning passages? These are there to keep us from falling away, by showing us the consequence of apostasy. And what about those who *do* fall away? There are two possible explanations. They may be true believers who have fallen away for a time, but in due course will repent and return. Alternatively it may be that they were never true believers and that they will not repent or return. John refers to those who appeared for a time to be 'of us' but who left so that it might be plain that they were not 'of us' (1 John 2:19). In Acts, Simon Magus 'believed' and was baptized, but soon proved himself not to be genuine (8:13, 18–23). Paul tells us 'The Lord knows those who are his' (2 Tim. 2:19). The parable of the wheat and the tares indicates that we cannot in this world discern infallibly who are the righteous (Matt. 13:24–30, 36–43).

How does Calvin hold together the three points from the New Testament? He clearly held to the need to persevere to the end and to God's promise to keep us from falling. What about the other point, the possibility of losing

---

[5] John Paul II, *Crossing the Threshold of Hope*, 185–187.

[6] Canons of Dort, Fifth Head (*RefConf* 4:144–151). Collier, *Debating Perseverance*, 59–92, shows that some at Dort, especially among the British delegation, argued for Augustine's position on this issue.

[7] For a recent exposition, see Schreiner and Caneday, *Race Set Before Us*.

salvation? Calvin seeks to do justice to this by referring it to those with temporary faith rather than genuine Christians, but this rather mutes the warnings of the New Testament where the latter are concerned.

Arminius and Arminianism

Arminius was ambivalent about whether true believers can fall away and lose their salvation.[8] In the year after Arminius's death his followers met and produced what was known as the *Remonstrance*, on which see chapters 8 and 9, containing five points of doctrine. The fifth point concerned the possibility of losing salvation, in which they affirmed that God gives sufficient grace to enable Christians to persevere to the end, but that they were not yet sure whether it is possible for true Christians to lose their salvation:

> Whether [true Christians] are not able through carelessness ... to abandon the beginning of their subjection to Christ, and embracing again this present world, to forsake the holy doctrine once delivered to them, to let a good conscience slip away, and to despise grace, must be more accurately sought from the sacred Scripture before we are able to teach others with full persuasion of our minds. (Article 5)[9]

By contrast, John Wesley, the father of evangelical Arminianism, was clear that it *is* possible to fall away and lose salvation, and argued that position in his *Serious Thoughts upon the Perseverance of the Saints*.[10] The majority of Arminians have followed Wesley on this.[11] It would appear to be a more logical position, given that the importance of human free will is one of the concerns underlying Arminianism. It is odd to state that we have free will as to whether or not to begin the Christian life, but do not have free will concerning continuing to the end. So most Arminians hold that Christ and the Holy Spirit assist us in our struggle against the world, the flesh and the devil (as stated in Article 5 of the *Remonstrance*) but that we retain the option of rejecting him.

This can be compared to the situation of a shipwrecked sailor who has been rescued by a lifeboat. The sailor is now out of danger from the elements, but retains the freedom to jump back into the water should he so wish. Put like

---

[8] Arminius, 'Declaration of Sentiments' (*Works of James Arminius*, 1:664–667); 'Apology or Defence Against Thirty-one Defamatory Articles', art. 1–2 (1:738–742). Cf. Bangs, *Arminius*, 216–219, 348–349.

[9] *RefConf* 4:44, with some Greek words omitted.

[10] McGonigle, *Sufficient Grace*, 179–183.

[11] For a defence of this from a New Testament scholar, see Marshall, *Kept by the Power of God*.

that the analogy is reassuring, but the reality is less so. No rescued sailor in their right mind would jump back into the water, but the incentives to abandon the Christian walk are far more persuasive. There is the lure of sin, there is the pressure to conform to society around, and there can be intellectual doubts and questioning. A better analogy would be someone who is very sick and has been accepted onto a gruelling and painful course of medical treatment. They will not be expelled from the programme, but there is no guarantee they will not themselves give up on it.

How do Arminians hold together the three points from the New Testament? They clearly hold to the need to persevere to the end and to the possibility of losing salvation. God's promises to keep us from falling are given as an encouragement that we are not on our own and that God protects us, but they are subordinated to the idea that the ultimate choice is ours and we can choose to turn our back on salvation.

'Once saved always saved'

The three historic views discussed so far agree on the need to persevere to the end, and that only those who persevere will be saved. Where they differ is about whether this perseverance is certain, whether the Christian faith comes with a 'lifetime guarantee'. More recently, however, a fourth view has emerged, according to which all who are converted will be saved regardless of how they then live. They will be saved even if they immediately renounce their faith and lead a life of debauched atheism.[12] The warning passages of the New Testament refer to loss of *reward* rather than loss of salvation. Many people today find this view attractive, but it is blatantly unbiblical. There is much in the New Testament that makes it clear that discipleship is not an optional extra and that remaining faithful is a condition of salvation. The whole letter to the Hebrews focuses on warning Jewish believers not to forsake Christ *and thus lose their salvation*. Also much of the teaching of Jesus warns against thinking that a profession of faith is of use if it is not backed up by our lives. Salvation requires perseverance.

Apart from being unbiblical, this approach is dangerous, for a number of reasons. It encourages a false complacency, the idea that there can be salvation without discipleship. Also it encourages a 'tip and run' approach to evangelism that is concerned only to lead people to make a 'decision', with scant concern about how these 'converts' will subsequently live. This is in marked contrast to the attitude of the apostle Paul, who was deeply concerned about his converts' lifestyle and discipleship. One needs only to read Galatians or 1 Corinthians

---

12 The authors of this view are here shamed, but not named.

to see that he did not hold to this recent view. The author of Hebrews was desperately concerned that his readers might lose their salvation by abandoning Christ and reverting to Judaism. These three letters make no sense if salvation is guaranteed by one single 'decision for Christ'. This view is pastorally disastrous.

Conclusion

The second and third points from the New Testament are in tension with each other. There is a real (not just theoretical) danger of *falling away* and losing our salvation; and yet God will *keep* those who are his. How can we hold these two points together? Augustine, Calvin and Arminius each have their ways of doing so. Their followers will not agree with each other, but there still remains a great deal of potential ground in common.

First, all should agree that the two points have different pastoral functions. The warnings against falling away and losing salvation are for those who are tempted to give up – like the Jewish Christians addressed by Hebrews. They are also for those who are becoming complacent, for those who are in danger of drifting away or of letting down their guard. The promises that God will keep us are for those who are striving to remain faithful and are fearful of their weakness. The two Hebrews passages (6:4–12; 10:26–39) both contain a blend of warning and encouragement. The danger, as always, is that each group hears the wrong message – that the complacent focus on God's promise and the diligent focus on the danger of apostasy. Practically Arminians and Calvinists can largely agree about the message each group needs; reconciling the points is in theory much harder.

A key to reconciling them can be to distinguish more clearly between outward appearance and inward reality. In chapter 12 we considered two stories, two different ways of talking about being a Christian, the one referring to inner reality, the other to outward appearance. When someone becomes a Christian this can be described at two different levels. Outwardly they profess to have faith, claim to have repented and there should be some change in their outward behaviour. They will be baptized and become members of the church, becoming *professing Christians*. Inwardly they believe and repent, are born again and love God from the heart, becoming *genuine Christians*. Ideally the outward and inward are in harmony, but not always in reality. Not all professing Christians are genuine Christians. Not all who think they have faith and repentance actually have true faith and repentance. We cannot see people's faith and repentance – not even in those whom we know the best. We can hear only what they say and observe what they do outwardly – and that only when we are watching them.

The same is true of our lives as Christians. There remains the contrast between outward appearance and inward reality. These are not unrelated or unconnected with each other, but nor are they identical with each other. The situation is not helped by the fact that we are all to a greater or lesser extent hypocrites – we display to others a condition that is better than the reality within.

It is important to remember that we cannot read other people's hearts – indeed, it is hard enough to read our own hearts much of the time. All that we see of others is their outward behaviour; it is only God who can read people's hearts. The Reformers argued that we should accept people on face value as professing Christians, making what they called a judgement of *charity*. We do not make a judgement of *faith*, we do not know for certain which professing Christians are or are not genuine.[13] In short, we give people the benefit of the doubt. When people turn away we must not presume to judge whether they are genuine Christians who are straying or pseudo-Christians declaring their true state. We must beware of passing judgement on specific individuals. We never know what happens in people's hearts, especially at the end. Katharine Tynan published a volume of 'poems in wartime', including one called 'The Great Mercy', about a cavalryman who is shot and killed. This contains the lines

Betwixt the saddle and the ground
Was mercy sought and mercy found.[14]

Distinguishing clearly between outward appearance and inward reality helps to resolve the New Testament tension. Those who *profess* to be Christians are liable to fall away and be lost. This is confirmed by biblical teaching, by biblical examples (like Judas) and by common experience. This is also the reality for pastors looking out over their flock – there is no guarantee that the people they see before them will not fall away and be lost. In fact one might say that statistically it is almost certain that some will do so. The Arminian would say such people had lost their salvation while the Calvinist would say they never really had it. This difference has been summed up in a popular ditty:

The Arminian knows he's got salvation, but is afraid he'll lose it;
The Calvinist knows he can't lose it, but is afraid he doesn't have it.

---

[13] E.g. Calvin, *Inst.* 4:1:8.
[14] Tynan, *Flower of Youth*, 51–52.

(While this applies to some Calvinists, others follow Calvin in holding that we can have assurance of final salvation.) The practical reality remains much (but not entirely) the same whatever one's theology. Also, on both views there will be genuine Christians who will stray for a time before returning to the path of discipleship.

Where the two positions clearly diverge is when we consider the question of our own salvation. Does assurance of present salvation guarantee final salvation? In the cold light of logic it would appear that we cannot believe both in the certainty of final salvation and in the real possibility of losing it. But the Christian life is a matter of practical living, not just theory. There is a tension here similar to that described in chapter 17. Pastorally the warnings are given to keep us from straying when we are tempted; the promises are given to encourage us when we doubt our strength to persevere. Arminians and Calvinists can agree on that much, even while differing on the theory.

29

Simple lifestyle

Simple lifestyle

An issue of great importance to Christians in the developed world is how to cope with affluence. With a few exceptions, people living in the developed world today enjoy an affluence unknown to all but a few, arguably unknown to all without exception, until very recently in human history. Consider for a start some of the things unavailable in 1900: air travel, space travel, radio, television, computers, Internet, mobile/cell phones, effective contraception and the year-round availability of food from around the world. If we go back to 1850 we have to add electrical power, cars, telephones. If we also consider what was available (or, more to the point, *not* available) back then by way of medicine, dentistry, plumbing, anaesthetics and painkillers, we realize just how privileged we are.

Given the extraordinary affluence we enjoy, it is not surprising that more and more people seek to derive their satisfaction from the things of this world alone. This is today both a moral and a spiritual issue. It is a moral issue in a world where hundreds of millions still face the threat of starvation – though we must not fall into the trap of treating economics as a 'zero sum game', whereby one person's wealth necessarily implies someone else's poverty. In the last generation affluence has increased in the West while levels of extreme poverty in the developing world have fallen at rates unparalleled in previous history.[1] It is a moral issue when our consumption is set against the finitude of the world's resources and the impact of our behaviour on the environment. It is also a spiritual issue. John Wesley wondered whether, ironically, true scriptural Christianity does not contain within itself the seeds of its own decline: 'For wherever true Christianity spreads it must cause diligence and frugality, which, in the natural course of things, must beget riches. And riches naturally beget pride, love of the world, and every temper that is destructive of Christianity.'[2]

---

[1] See e.g. Norberg, *Progress*, 63–82.
[2] Wesley, *Sermon* 122:17 ('The Causes of the Inefficacy of Christianity'), in Wesley, *Sermons*, 4:95–96.

A similar danger is noted in the book of Proverbs:

Give me neither poverty nor riches;
feed me with the food that is needful for me,
lest I be full and deny you
and say, 'Who is the LORD?'
(30:8–9)

Article 9 of the 1974 Lausanne Covenant referred to the need for Christians to develop a simple lifestyle.[3] Following from this the Lausanne committee organized an international Consultation on the topic that met at High Leigh, near London, in 1980. This led to the publication of an agreed statement entitled *An Evangelical Commitment to Simple Lifestyle* and to a volume including the papers presented at the Consultation.[4]

In handling this issue two dangers are to be avoided. The first is that of an affluent materialism that runs counter to the teaching of the Gospels, living as if a materially satisfying life on this earth is our ultimate goal. While as Christians we would never admit to holding such a world-view, too often our life choices make this denial sound hollow. The opposite danger is that of an ascetic legalism that seeks to tell Christians what they may or may not have. Such an approach can soon become dated – such as the teaching at one stage that it was all right for Christians to have a black and white television, but not a colour television. How can we combat materialism without lapsing into legalism? Calvin sets out five general principles that in my view translate well into other cultures and can be applied in the twenty-first-century West as well as in sixteenth-century Geneva, principles that can enable us to steer a path between these two extremes.[5] So, while he never possessed a car or a computer, while he never enjoyed an ice-cream or an iPad, his teaching can guide us as to how to handle these delights. This teaching is found especially, but not exclusively, in the five chapters of his *Institutes* devoted to the Christian life (Book 3, chapters 6–10), chapters he considered to be of such great importance that he had them printed as a booklet on their own, in 1550.

---

[3] See <http://www.lausanne.org/covenant>, accessed 5 June 2020.
[4] Nichols, *Evangelical Commitment*; Sider (ed.), *Lifestyle in the Eighties*.
[5] I am significantly indebted for this to Ronnie Wallace, both for a talk that I heard him give and for Wallace, *Calvin's Doctrine of Christian Life*, esp. II.4; III.3, 6.

Calvin on the Christian life

In the first chapter (6) Calvin sets out general principles about the Christian life and the things that should motivate us to pursue it. He then moves on to the specific command to deny ourselves, take up our cross and follow Jesus (Matt. 16:24). Chapter 7 focuses on the need for self-denial, the need to say 'No' to ourselves and to submit to God. This is the key to progress in the Christian life. Calvin continues his exposition of Matthew 16:24 with a chapter (8) on bearing the cross, which is an aspect of self-denial. He interprets bearing the cross especially as suffering patiently whatever tribulations God may send our way. Chapter 9 is devoted to the theme of meditation on the future life. It is only through doing this that we can have the right attitude towards this present life, as is described in the final chapter (10).

As a teenager Calvin studied in the Collège de Montaigu in Paris, which was profoundly influenced by the late medieval *Devotio Moderna* (Modern Devotion), exemplified especially by Thomas à Kempis's so-called *Imitation of Christ*.[6] In these chapters we see the clear imprint of the *Devotio Moderna*, but translated from a medieval monastic to a Protestant 'secular' setting. Calvin's target readership is not monks in a medieval monastery but Christians living in the world. Thomas's asceticism undergoes a radical transformation in the light of Reformation doctrine.

Calvin's five principles

Calvin sets out five principles in these chapters (and elsewhere) that point the way to avoiding affluent materialism without lapsing into legalism. As he notes, this is a slippery topic that 'slopes on both sides into error'. To disallow any use of material things that is not actually required by necessity is to go too far and to 'fetter consciences more tightly than does the Word of the Lord'. But there remains the opposite danger of excusing licentious indulgence on the grounds that the only constraint is the dictates of our consciences: 'Consciences neither ought to nor can be bound here to definite and precise legal formulas; but inasmuch as Scripture gives general rules for lawful use, we ought surely to limit our use in accordance with them.'[7]

---

[6] 'So-called' because this was originally the title of only the first chapter of the first book. Since it therefore appeared at the head, it inaccurately became the title for the whole work. Calvin never mentions either Thomas or *The Imitation of Christ*.

[7] *Inst.* 3:10:1.

The aim of the chapters on the Christian life is to point the godly to a rightly ordered life by briefly setting out a universal rule to determine their duties.[8] We turn now to the five principles.

Detachment from this world

We need to recognize that in this world we are pilgrims, not permanent residents: we are on a journey.[9] In the light of this we are to be detached from the things of this world, a detachment based on the perspective of eternity. Two things go hand in hand: hope for our future destiny and contempt for the present life. When we are tempted to seek fulfilment and happiness in the things of this life, God corrects us by sending tribulations, the discipline of the cross.[10] We are, says Calvin, faced with a straight choice: 'either the world must become worthless to us or hold us bound by intemperate love of it'. This is why God sends us trials and tribulations. Even with them, it is hard for us to look beyond this life; if here and now we enjoyed 'an enduring round of wealth and happiness' it would be well-nigh impossible. There is much around us to remind us of our transience and mortality, but despite this we very easily 'return to our thoughtless assurance of earthly immortality'.[11] This is a radical perspective that challenges rich and poor alike. Where people live by this principle it is a powerful witness, especially in our materialistic age.

There are two rival grounds for detachment from this world. For the Platonist it flows from the inferiority of the physical, material, temporal world in comparison with an unchanging, timeless eternity. For Calvin the primary grounds for this detachment are the fact that sin has spoiled God's good creation and the future hope of heavenly glory. It flows from biblical eschatology, not Greek dualism. (For more on this, see chapter 1.) Despite the 'infinite miseries' that may come our way, we are still to regard this life as a gift of God's generosity. Detachment from the world and contempt of the present life is based not upon a denial of the goodness of God's creation but upon a comparison of our present state with what is to come.[12]

This perspective leads Calvin to speak very negatively about the present life. He encourages believers to view heaven as their homeland and earth as a place of exile.[13] How well we have learned this lesson can be seen by a simple test – our attitude to death. Calvin regards it as monstrous that 'many who boast

---

8 *Inst.* 3:6:1.
9 *Inst.* 3:7:3.
10 *Inst.* 3:9:1.
11 *Inst.* 3:9:2.
12 *Inst.* 3:9:3.
13 *Inst.* 3:9:4.

themselves Christians are gripped by such a great fear of death, rather than a desire for it, that they tremble at the least mention of it'. He is fully aware that death holds a natural dread for us, but faith should enable us to overcome this. 'If we should think that through death we are recalled from exile to dwell in the fatherland, in the heavenly fatherland, would we get no comfort from this fact?' Indeed Calvin argues that Christians should 'joyfully await the day of death and final resurrection'.[14] Where Christians exemplify this victory over the fear of death it is a powerful witness in our society. I am reviewing these words in isolation at home during the COVID-19 pandemic, when the issue of facing death suddenly becomes much more relevant.

Use without enslavement

We are not to strive for worldly wealth or honours. This does not mean that we should renounce them in an ascetic manner. Rather 'if we must pass simply through this world, there is no doubt that we ought to use its good things in so far as they help rather than hinder our course'.[15] What is wrong is not possessing them but being enslaved to them, which happens very easily. George Verwer once announced in a talk that Operation Mobilisation had received a gift of a pair of silver candle sticks and then added, 'Let's praise the Lord for liberating our brother from these candlesticks.' The general response was laughter, but he protested that he meant what he had said. Experience convinces me more and more that he was right. Not only is it easy to become enslaved to one's possessions; it is very hard not to become enslaved. The things we own can easily end up owning us. If reluctance to part with them is the criterion, then I have to plead guilty. It is significant that Jesus said not 'Where your heart is, there your treasure will be also', but 'Where your treasure is, there your heart will be also' (Matt. 6:21). A simple test is how willing we are to do without them.

So Calvin's counsel is that we should make use of the things of this world, but with a right perspective. We should use them so far as they help us on our way. We should accept them as God's good gifts. Failure to do so means to be 'guilty of grave ingratitude toward God himself'.[16] This is far from a Platonic asceticism that pursues renunciation for its own sake. In themselves they are good gifts of God and are to be accepted as such, but *in comparison with* our future goal we should despise them as worthless. We should meditate on the eternal life to come, compared with which this life is to be 'despised and

---

[14] *Inst.* 3:9:5.
[15] *Inst.* 3:10:1.
[16] *Inst.* 3:9:3.

trampled under foot'.[17] Simplicity of lifestyle is not an end in itself, but the consequence of a set of priorities.

In Hans Christian Andersen's fairy tale 'The Tinderbox', a soldier entered a room full of bronze coins and filled his pockets with them. Then he moved to a room full of silver coins, which led him to empty his pockets and fill them with silver coins instead. Thereafter he moved to another room, full of gold coins, and the silver coins duly suffered the same fate as the bronze coins. It is not that the bronze and silver coins were not valuable – they were. But *in comparison with* the gold coins they were worthless and a distraction. It is all a matter of priorities.

This does not point to asceticism. These are God's gifts and there is no virtue in rejecting them. A simple lifestyle is not an end in itself and can indeed become self-indulgence. At one point I used to feel vaguely guilty about my possessions, until I spent some time in a Global South country, without a car or computer. The lack of a car meant that if we were unable to buy any bread on our weekly shop I would need to take out most of the following morning just to get bread. This was not an efficient use of time. If I were to give students handouts written in my handwriting on the grounds that my simple lifestyle precluded the use of a computer, that would be an act of self-indulgence that would most certainly not be appreciated by the students. The good things of this world are given for us to use. But at the same time this set of priorities relativizes them and warns us against becoming enslaved to them, against making idols of them.

Moderation, not legalistic asceticism

We are not to be enslaved to the things of this world, but are to use them with moderation. On the one hand we are to avoid a legalistic asceticism. An important principle is that the correct way to use God's gifts is to use them for the purpose for which they were created. There is much in this world that is given to us to enjoy, not just for necessary use, such as the beauty and smell of flowers. God created food 'not only to provide for necessity but also for delight and good cheer'. In short, many things are attractive and are given to us for enjoyment as well as practical use.[18] It is legitimate to use wine not just for necessity but also in order to be merry. But it will come as no surprise to hear that, for Calvin, 'this mirth must however be tempered with sobriety'.[19] In our enjoyment we should pursue a path of frugality, not extravagance. The need for this becomes the

---

[17] *Inst.* 3:9:4.
[18] *Inst.* 3:10:2.
[19] Comm. Ps. 104:15 (*Commentary on Book of Psalms* 4:157).

greater the wealthier we become. The rich are to avoid all excess, whether gluttony, drunkenness, the display of superfluous wealth, or whatever. All should be done with thankfulness to God but, 'where is your thanksgiving if you so gorge yourself with banqueting or wine that you either become stupid or are rendered useless for the duties of piety and of your calling?'[20] 'The more kindly [God] indulges us, the more solicitously ought we to restrict ourselves to a frugal use of his gifts. For we know how unbridled are the appetites of the flesh.'[21]

There is a middle path here between self-indulgence and legalism. On the one hand we are not to be bound by fixed formulas; on the other hand we should indulge ourselves as little as possible. We are to cut off 'all show of superfluous wealth, not to mention licentiousness, and diligently . . . guard against turning helps into hindrances'.[22] When it comes to wine, Calvin supported the temperance movement – that is, those who advocate a moderate enjoyment of wine, not those who hijacked the movement to teach abstinence rather than temperance.

Elsewhere Calvin warns against the dangers of legalistic asceticism, for 'when consciences once ensnare themselves, they enter a long and inextricable maze, not easy to get out of'.

> If any man should consider daintier food unlawful, in the end he will not be at peace before God, when he eats either black bread or common victuals, while it occurs to him that he could sustain his body on even coarser foods.[23]

Calvin taught that we should be content with what we have. The poor should accept their lot patiently and avoid an immoderate desire for what they do not have.[24] 'To covet wealth and honors, to strive for authority, to heap up riches, to gather together all those follies which seem to make for magnificence and pomp, our lust is mad, our desire boundless.'[25]

Paul also teaches that we should be content:

> But if we have food and clothing, with these we will be content. But those who desire to be rich fall into temptation, into a snare, into many senseless and harmful desires that plunge people into ruin and destruction. For the

---

[20] *Inst.* 3:10:3.
[21] Comm. Gen 43:33 (*Commentaries on Genesis* 2:363).
[22] *Inst.* 3:10:4.
[23] *Inst.* 3:19:7.
[24] *Inst.* 3:10:5.
[25] *Inst.* 3:7:8.

love of money is a root of all kinds of evils. It is through this craving that some have wandered away from the faith and pierced themselves with many pangs.
(1 Tim. 6:8–10)

Does this mean that it is wrong to seek to better one's lot? Does it mean that a young married couple who live in a rented one-bedroom apartment should be content to remain living there even when they have eleven children? The trouble with some teaching on this topic is that if one were to take it seriously that would be the outcome. That is not, however, what Calvin taught. It is not the desire for more that he criticizes, but an *immoderate* desire. Those who cannot bear poverty patiently will in turn abuse wealth when they acquire it.[26] In his commentary on Psalm 4:7 he explains:

Although the faithful desire and seek after their worldly comforts, yet they do not pursue them with immoderate and irregular ardour; but can patiently bear to be deprived of them, provided they know themselves to be objects of the divine care.[27]

The godly should 'neither desire nor hope for, nor contemplate, any other way of prospering than by the Lord's blessing'.[28] We should not *greedily* strive after riches and honours, but always 'look to the Lord so that by his guidance we may be led to whatever lot he has provided for us'. In particular, this means not seeking these things through underhand or illegitimate means. If we have our priorities right, 'then will a bridle be put on us that we may not burn with an immoderate desire to grow rich or ambitiously pant after honors'.[29]

What we have here is a counter-cultural challenge at the level of our priorities. This is a radical challenge especially to our modern affluent and materialist society. It is also a challenge to rich and poor alike, not just to the rich. Poor people as much as rich are liable to strive for wealth. Where this contentment is found it is a powerful witness to the Gospel. At London School of Theology, where I teach, we have some students who have sold their homes in order to be able to train for Christian ministry. Such sacrifice exemplifies the sort of detachment Calvin had in mind.

---

[26] *Inst.* 3:10:5.
[27] Calvin, *Commentary on Book of Psalms* 1:49. It is *lusting* after more that is sinful.
[28] *Inst.* 3:7:8.
[29] *Inst.* 3:7:9.

So the young couple will rightly aspire to own their own home of such a size as is appropriate for the eleven children. But they will not pursue that goal as a first priority, achieving it by bending the rules of honesty, by such hard work as deprives their children of love, by pursuing wealth at the cost of their commitment to the people of God and the work of God. It is all a question of priorities, of ultimate goals. The house will be seen as a good gift of God and will be enjoyed, but it will not be mistaken for the ultimate goal, which lies beyond this life, nor will it become the prime objective for this life.

Stewardship

Fundamental to a Christian attitude to possessions is to regard them as belonging to God. We should 'resign . . . all our possessions to the Lord's will'.[30] All of our money and possessions are entrusted to us by God and for the common good:

> Whatever benefits we obtain from the Lord have been entrusted to us on this condition: that they be applied to the common good of the church. And therefore the lawful use of all benefits consists in a liberal and kindly sharing of them with others . . . All the gifts we possess have been bestowed by God and entrusted to us on condition that they be distributed for our neighbor's benefit.[31]

As a US Internal Revenue Service auditor is alleged to have said, 'The trick is to stop thinking of it as "your" money.' Our money and possessions are meant to be shared. We are required to exercise stewardship over *all* that God has given us. It is not that 10% or some other proportion belongs to God and the rest is ours to dispose of as we will. When we have paid our taxes to the state, what remains is ours to dispose of as we will, within the law. Stewardship of possessions is not like that. It *is* about giving a certain amount, but it is also about how we use the rest. 'We are the stewards of everything God has conferred on us by which we are able to help our neighbor, and are required to render account of our stewardship.'[32] We need to handle all that we have as stewards who must give account. All that we have is from God and is given in trust for us to use for his glory.

> Let us remember by whom such reckoning is required: namely him who has greatly commended abstinence, sobriety, frugality and moderation, and has also abominated excess, pride, ostentation and vanity;

---

[30] *Inst.* 3:7:8.
[31] *Inst.* 3:7:5.
[32] *Inst.* 3:7:5.

who approves no other distribution of good things than one joined with love.[33]

Generosity

All that is ours is given to us for the common good. We are also called to be generous with those in need. But *how much* should we give? The legalistic answer is to give a fixed percentage. It can be helpful to have a percentage figure as a guide, if only to ensure that we do not become totally selfish, but we should never imagine that the extent of Christian giving can be limited to this. It is not about paying a certain percentage, as if we were paying taxes. The legalistic way can be challenging, especially if the percentage is high, but it falls short because it implies that what is left is totally ours.

The Christian standard Calvin applies is not a legalistic one but simply generosity. This has two implications. Generosity is not a legal category. Generous people give because they want to give (2 Cor. 9:7), not because a law requires it. When I complete my tax returns for the year I take care to ensure that I pay not a penny more than the law requires. That is completely legitimate where income tax is concerned, but is not the spirit we should bring to Christian giving. Christian giving asks not 'How little can I get away with?' but 'How much can I afford to give?' We should give generously, as we are able. Calvin expresses this in a way most will find extremely challenging: 'Each man will so consider with himself that in all his greatness he is a debtor to his neighbors, and that he ought in exercising kindness toward them to set no other limit than the end of his resources.'[34]

But while we should give generously, we should also give prudently rather than prodigally, ensuring that our resources are put to good use.

Interestingly, Calvin's advice here is very similar to John Wesley's own answer to the dilemma he had posed. Wesley saw only one way of escaping the corrupting influence of riches. Those who gain all they can (by working diligently) and save all they can (by which he meant not investing it in shares or a savings account but living as frugally as possibly, spending as little as possible) must also give all they can.[35] Wesley decided at an early age how much he needed to live and continued to live on that amount despite the fact that his income increased considerably. Calvin and Wesley both lived out consistently what they taught on this subject. There would be very few indeed in the

---

[33] *Inst.* 3:10:5.
[34] *Inst.* 3:7:7.
[35] Wesley, *Sermon* 122:18, in Wesley, *Sermons*, 4:96. Wesley spells this out more fully in his *Sermon 50* ('The Use of Money'), in Wesley, *Sermons*, 2:266–280.

developed world today who could make that claim, but following imperfectly from a distance is perhaps a second best. It is reassuring that Calvin introduces his teaching on the Christian life by stating that 'I do not so strictly demand evangelical perfection that I would not acknowledge as a Christian one who has not yet attained it.'[36] Calvin offers a target at which we should aim.

The other implication concerns the manner in which we give. Generosity implies giving with compassion, not the cold charity that treats its objects with contempt. Of course, those in need are often unworthy, so Calvin urges us to look beyond that to the image of God in them, 'which with its beauty and dignity allures us to love and embrace them'.[37] Our giving should flow from a heart concern for others.

> [Those who give] must put themselves in the place of him whom they see in need of their assistance, and pity his ill fortune as if they themselves experienced and bore it, so that they may be impelled by a feeling of mercy and humaneness to go to his aid just as to their own.[38]

Conclusion

I would like to suggest that these five principles are a useful guide as to how we should handle the things of this world:

- We should maintain a level of detachment from this world, recognizing that we are pilgrims, not permanent residents.
- We should use the things of this world so far as they help us on our way, without becoming enslaved to them.
- We should accept the good things of this life as gifts from God, but make use of them frugally, without extravagance.
- We should recognize that we are but stewards of all we have and that it is given to us for the common good.
- We should give generously, in terms of both the spirit in which we give and the quantity of giving.

---

[36] *Inst.* 3:6:5.
[37] *Inst.* 3:7:6.
[38] *Inst.* 3:7:7.

30
Perfection?

Is perfection attainable in this life?

Over the centuries various groups have claimed that the answer is 'Yes'. This chapter will focus mainly on one of the more moderate claims, which has been very influential.

John Wesley, *A Plain Account of Christian Perfection*

John Wesley taught a doctrine of Christian perfection, for which he received some criticism. In 1766 he published his *Plain Account of Christian Perfection*,[1] in which he set out both to explain his doctrine and to prove that he had held it consistently since 1725. He saw this doctrine as the distinctive doctrine of Methodism and its *raison d'être* – though he also said the same about his doctrine of assurance!

This doctrine is still held by some Methodist and Wesleyan groups, but the majority have either dropped or reinterpreted it. One exponent of Wesley's theology claimed that by Christian perfection Wesley meant no more than that Christians can avoid wilful habitual sin. If that were true he would not have faced the opposition he did, but in fact his doctrine goes far further than that. Wesley held that it was possible in this life to avoid *any* 'sins of the heart', a truly radical claim. It is misleading to describe avoiding wilful habitual sin as perfection. If all that is needed to be perfect is to avoid wilful sin, then I am perfect for about a third of the time – while I am asleep! There is a lot more to sin than wilful sin. Someone who is selfish and proud may manage to avoid wilful sin for a time, but remains selfish and proud.

---

[1] References will be to the section numbers in the original, followed by the page numbers in the 1925 Epworth edition/the page numbers in Wesley, *Doctrinal and Controversial Treatises II*. For Wesley's doctrine see Williams, *John Wesley's Theology Today*, 167–190; McGonigle, *Sufficient Grace: John Wesley's Evangelical Arminianism*, 241–264.

Sin

Different views on sanctification in general, and perfection in particular, often go back to different views of sin. For instance, the Council of Trent claimed that concupiscence or lustful desire is to be seen as a result of sin and as an inclination towards sin, but not itself as sin. It is not properly sin unless we give in to it,[2] while the Protestant view is that it is itself a sin. Different views of sin will produce different views on sanctification.

Wesley held firmly to an Augustinian doctrine of sin, and famously stated that anyone who denied the doctrine of original sin was 'but an heathen still'. The result of the fall is the 'entire depravation of the whole human nature' so that we are 'totally corrupted'.[3] Unbelievers have no righteousness before God and are unable to make the first move towards him. This is why Wesley held to his doctrine of prevenient grace, on which see chapter 8. Where Wesley differed from Augustine was in believing that *everybody* receives prevenient grace – although, of course, some choose to reject it. Unlike some who have held to a doctrine of perfection, Wesley cannot be accused of having a low view of sin.

Two types of sin

Fundamental to Wesley's idea of Christian Perfection is the distinction between two types of sin:[4]

- 'sin properly so-called', which is the '*voluntary* transgression of a known law';
- 'sin improperly so-called', which is the 'involuntary transgression of a divine law, known or unknown' – that is, any unintended deviation from the perfect will of God.

This distinction is fundamental to Wesley's doctrine of Christian perfection, as we shall see. Some have been very critical of it, claiming that 'a sin is a sin is a sin'. That is not an adequate answer, as we saw in chapter 2. The Bible differentiates between unintentional and defiant sin (Num. 15:27–31), between sins of ignorance and deliberate sins (Luke 12:47–48), between light and grave sins (John 19:11) and between mortal and non-mortal sins (1 John 5:16–17).

---

[2] *Decree on Original Sin* §5 (Tanner (ed.), *Decrees of the Ecumenical Councils* 2:667).
[3] *Sermon* 44:III:1–2 ('Original Sin') in Wesley, *Sermons*, 2:182–184.
[4] *Plain Account of Christian Perfection* §19 (45/169–170).

Entire sanctification

Wesley assumed that all Christians are entirely sanctified just before the moment of death. So if that is the case, why wait until then? It would be much better to receive entire sanctification now, so that we live more effectively as Christians. And it *is* possible, says Wesley, to receive it now. It simply requires faith – faith that God *can* do what he has promised and faith that he is able and willing to do it *now*. This is an instantaneous crisis experience like conversion, and like conversion it leads on to a moment-by-moment process.[5] Having received entire sanctification it is possible to lose it – and then later to regain it. Entire Sanctification consists of perfect love expelling all sin and controlling the heart, which leads to unbroken fellowship with Christ.[6] This is Christian perfection.

Wesley never claimed to have attained to Christian perfection himself, but given that he says it can be achieved by a simple step of faith it is inconceivable he would not have taken that step himself. The fact that he made no such claim presumably reflects his concern that the debate should be focused on the doctrine itself, and not on a scrutiny of his life.

Christian perfection

Wesley sought to tread a middle path between two opposite extremes. On the one side there is the error of 'angelism', the belief that we can on this earth achieve perfection. The opposite error is complacency, the belief that no perfection is attainable in this life, the willingness just to accept the fact that we are 'miserable sinners'. Some have suggested this middle path reflects an Anglican *via media*, but presenting one's position as the middle way between opposite extremes is a well-established form of argument. Others have commented that he is offering a middle way between half a dozen fanatics on the one side and 99.9% of all Christians on the other! Wesley might retort that the fact that so many Christians live in complacency is no excuse for following them.

In opposition to these two errors Wesley teaches a *relative* perfection. What does that mean? Entire sanctification means the avoidance of 'sin properly so-called', but not of 'sin improperly so-called'. It is not the avoidance of *all* sin. It does not bring exemption from ignorance, from errors of judgement, or from physical infirmities, such as lapses of memory. Entire sanctification does not free us from temptation.[7] But it does bring a real *moral* perfection – loving God with all our heart, soul, mind and strength and having the mind

---

[5] *Plain Account of Christian Perfection* §§14, 18, 25, 26 (27/154, 41/167, 81/106, 106–107/187–188).
[6] *Plain Account of Christian Perfection* §§15, 19 (29/155, 51–52/174).
[7] *Plain Account of Christian Perfection* §§12, 15, 19, 25 (16/146–147, 28/155, 42–43/168, 75–76/101–102).

of Christ. Christian perfection leaves no room for any sins of the heart. The perfect Christian will have no pride or selfishness, these having been expelled by love.[8] Christian perfection means 'love filling the heart, expelling pride, anger, desire, self-will; rejoicing evermore, praying without ceasing, and in everything giving thanks'.[9]

So consider the case of entirely sanctified students due to attend a lecture. They are still liable to miss the lecture because they were unaware of it, because they mistakenly did not allow sufficient time for the journey to the lecture, because they inadvertently overslept or because they simply forgot. They may also be tempted simply to skip it, but Christian perfection means that they will not fall for that temptation. Nor will they miss it because of negligence, such as failure to check the time of the lecture when they know they should do so.

Wesley has been heavily criticized for his talk of a 'relative perfection' and some have argued that this is a contradiction in terms. I do not agree. *If* it is true that we can attain to this degree of entire sanctification, with love expelling all sin from the heart, then that is certainly worthy of the name perfection. Wesley's claim is truly radical.

It may come as a surprise to learn that Wesley held that for the entirely sanctified Christian there is still room for growth. There is no such thing as perfection that is not capable of continual increase.[10] How can that be? Perfect love fills the heart – but the heart can grow in capacity. Also, Christians can get better at avoiding 'sins improperly so-called'. So, for example, inexperienced Christians might find themselves inadvertently offending people, but through experience learn how to avoid that.

Wesley would neither teach nor deny *sinless* perfection.[11] Why was that? It is because of the two different meanings of 'sin'. The entirely sanctified Christian is sinless where 'sin properly so-called' is concerned, but not where 'sin improperly so-called' is concerned.

Grounds for the doctrine

Wesley used a number of arguments to support his doctrine of Christian perfection.

Deathbed sanctification.[12] Wesley starts with the assumption that all Christians are entirely sanctified just before death. That Christians are made perfect

---

[8] *Plain Account of Christian Perfection* §§12, 13, 17 (19–21/148–150, 22–23/151, 33/159).

[9] *Plain Account of Christian Perfection* §25 (74/100).

[10] *Plain Account of Christian Perfection* §19, 25 (53/175, 85/110).

[11] *Plain Account of Christian Perfection* §19 (45/170).

[12] *Plain Account of Christian Perfection* §17 (34/160).

at the point of death is widely held. For example, the *Westminster Confession of Faith* states that at death the souls of the righteous are 'made perfect in holiness'.[13] But it is a different matter to claim that this happens before death, and Wesley's argument relies on that being true.

Perfection or maturity? The King James Version often translates the Greek word *teleios* as 'perfect', where modern translations translate it as 'mature' (e.g. in Phil. 3:15; Col. 1:28) or by some other word. Wesley relies on the KJV translation and so claims more from the passages than is warranted.

God's promises.[14] Wesley repeatedly argues from God's promises, in particular his promises to make us perfect. So, for example, Paul states:

> Christ loved the church and gave himself up for her, that he might sanctify her, having cleansed her by the washing of water with the word, so that he might present the church to himself in splendour, without spot or wrinkle or any such thing, that she might be holy and without blemish. (Eph. 5:25–27)

God *will* do this – but when? The context seems to imply that this will be at the end, when Christ returns. Wesley appears to be guilty of an 'over-realized eschatology' claiming for here and now what is reserved for the end. He does not give sufficient weight to the New Testament tension between 'already' and 'not yet'.

New Testament prayers.[15] Wesley also appeals to New Testament prayers, such as 1 Thessalonians 5:23–24:

> May the God of peace himself sanctify you completely, and may your whole spirit and soul and body be kept blameless at the coming of our Lord Jesus Christ. He who calls you is faithful; he will surely do it.

Here the same considerations apply. This is the goal at which we are aiming and to which God will bring us, but will this process be completed before the end of this life? Paul here refers to 'the coming of our Lord Jesus Christ'.

God has commanded perfection.[16] Wesley argues that because God commands us to be perfect, this must be possible. Jesus told his disciples to be 'perfect, as your heavenly Father is perfect' (Matt. 5:48) – though to be perfect as God is does sound like 'angelism'. He also commanded them to love God with all their heart

---

[13] Ch. 32:1 (*RefConf* 4:271).
[14] *Plain Account of Christian Perfection* §§17, 23 (35–36/161, 61/181).
[15] *Plain Account of Christian Perfection* §§17, 23 (36–37/161–162, 62/182).
[16] *Plain Account of Christian Perfection* §§17, 23 (37/162, 61/181).

soul, and mind and to love their neighbours as themselves (Matt. 22:37–39). But this argument falls into the error of supposing that 'ought' implies 'can', on which see chapter 7. Paul states that 'through the law comes' not knowledge of our ability but 'knowledge of sin' (Rom. 3:20). As Paul wrote to the Philippians, 'not that I have already obtained this or am already perfect, but I press on to make it my own, because Christ Jesus has made me his own' (3:12).

Positive features of the doctrine

I think that Wesley's doctrine of Christian Perfection is mistaken, but that we can also learn from it. First, Wesley's focus in entire sanctification is on *love*, on sin being expelled from the heart by perfect love. In striving for sanctification it is possible to be focused too much on specific sins. These matter, but are only the symptoms of the basic problem, which is lack of love. On the two commandments to love 'depend all the Law and the Prophets' (Matt. 22:40). Wesley puts his finger on the heart of the problem and points accurately to the cure – love expelling sin from the heart.

Secondly, while one might disagree about what is possible in this life, the call and challenge to press on towards perfection is good. This call comes clearly in a number of Charles Wesley's hymns, which can still be sung wholeheartedly by those who (unlike the Wesleys) do not expect their fulfilment in this life:

O for a heart to praise my God,
a heart from sin set free!
a heart that always feels thy blood
so freely spilt for me.

A heart in every thought renewed
and full of love divine,
perfect and right and pure and good,
a copy, Lord, of thine.

Thy nature, gracious Lord, impart;
come quickly from above;
write thy new name upon my heart,
thy new, best name of Love.

Love divine, all loves excelling,
Joy of heaven to earth come down;
fix in us thy humble dwelling;
all thy faithful mercies crown!

Jesus, thou art all compassion!
Pure unbounded love thou art;
visit us with thy salvation!
Enter every trembling heart.

Finish, then, thy new creation;
pure and spotless let us be.
Let us see thy great salvation
perfectly restored in thee.

Changed from glory into glory,
till in heaven we take our place,
till we cast our crowns before thee,
lost in wonder, love, and praise.

J. H. Noyes

Wesley's doctrine of entire sanctification has been held by a number of different groups since his time. A more extreme form of perfectionism was found in upstate New York, the base of John Humphrey Noyes, who was a big noise on the American revivalist scene. He pronounced himself sinless in 1834. He claimed that entire sanctification means not just that it is possible not to sin, but that one is no longer able to sin. This was a fatal move that led on to the idea that 'I cannot sin, *whatever I do*.' The outcome was sexual license. Noyes advocated 'spiritual marriage', to be sealed by a 'new physical sacrament'. As has been wryly observed, it may indeed have been physical, but there was nothing particularly new about it![17] Noyes was not alone in making this fatal step.[18]

Conclusion

As we saw in chapter 7, Pelagius held to the possibility of perfection (even without God's grace), while Augustine came to see that Christians are *not yet* cured of sin but *being* cured. He came to see the church more as a hospital for those being cured, than a club for those already fully cured. Accordingly, at the conclusion of his *Spirit and the Letter* he notes that 'In the righteousness that is to be made perfect, much progress in this life has been made by that man who knows by his progress how far he is from the perfection of

---

[17] For more, see Thomas, *Man Who Would Be Perfect*.
[18] As is documented by Knox, *Enthusiasm*, ch. 22.

righteousness.'[19] This approach is found in the last verse of William Cowper's hymn 'Hark, my soul, it is the Lord':

> Lord, it is my chief complaint
> That my love is weak and faint;
> Yet I love thee, and adore;
> O for grace to love thee more!

The Christian life involves struggle. Conversion brings a real change within us. We now love God and desire to serve him. Sin no longer *reigns* within us, but it still *remains* within us. We are plagued by sinful desires and lust that lead us to sin. So the Christian life is a daily struggle against sin. Conversion is the beginning, not the end, of the struggle against sin. John Wesley himself observed that many Christians imagine at conversion that the battle is over, only to discover that it has only just begun:

> How naturally do those who experience such a change [conversion] imagine that all sin is gone! That it is utterly rooted out of their heart, and has no more any place therein! How easily do they draw that inference, 'I *feel* no sin; therefore I *have* none.' It does not *stir;* therefore it does not *exist:* it has no *motion;* therefore it has no *being.* But it is seldom long before they are undeceived, finding sin was only suspended, not destroyed. Temptations return and sin revives, showing it was but stunned before, not dead. They now feel two principles in themselves, plainly contrary to each other: 'the flesh lusting against the Spirit' [Gal. 5:17], nature opposing the grace of God.[20]

We should look for a slow but steady progress towards the goal of perfection. Unfortunately there are no short cuts, no quick fixes. We should expect to sin less and less, but not expect to be sinless. Calvin expresses well the idea of slow steady progress:

> Let each one of us, then, proceed according to the measure of his puny capacity and set out upon the journey we have begun. No one shall set out so inauspiciously as not daily to make some headway, though it be slight. Therefore, let us not cease so to act that we may make some unceasing

---

[19] §64 (LCC 8:248).
[20] *Sermon* 43:5–6 ('The Scripture Way of Salvation'), in Wesley, *Sermons,* 2:158–159. (Also found in Leith (ed.), *Creeds of the Churches,* 362–363.)

progress in the way of the Lord. And let us not despair at the slightness of our success; for even though attainment may not correspond to desire, when today outstrips yesterday the effort is not lost. Only let us look toward our mark with sincere simplicity and aspire to our goal; not fondly flattering ourselves, nor excusing our own evil deeds, but with continuous effort striving toward this end: that we may surpass ourselves in goodness until we attain to goodness itself. It is this, indeed, which through the whole course of life we seek and follow. But we shall attain it only when we have cast off the weakness of the body, and are received into full fellowship with him.[21]

---

[21] *Inst.* 3:6:5.

Epilogue: future glory

In chapter 1 we saw that sin and grace need to be set in the wider context of creation – sin – grace – future glory. After a brief discussion of creation the bulk of the book has been devoted to the topics of sin and grace. Sin is universal (chapter 2) as a result of the original sin (chapter 3) consequent on the fall (chapter 4). Sin has many effects (chapter 2) and leads to guilt and judgement (chapter 5) and to the wrath of God (chapter 6).

Grace takes many forms, in line with the varieties of meanings of the term (introduction). Grace involves the inner workings of the Holy Spirit (chapters 7–8), distributed according to God's predestination, however that be understood (chapter 9). Through grace we are converted and become Christians (chapters 10–11). This involves baptism, and there are debates as to who should receive this and as to its efficacy (chapters 12–15). Becoming a Christian leads to our being justified or put right with God (chapters 16–18), which raises questions about the role of good works (chapter 19). We can be assured of our standing as children of God (chapter 20). Justification has been a topic of controversy between Protestants and Catholics since the time of the Reformation and there have been attempts both then and today to bring the two sides together (chapters 21–24). Justification is relevant to other topics such as the meaning of forgiveness and the role of fear (chapter 25) and the place of self-love and self-esteem (chapter 26). Conversion brings sanctification as well as justification (chapter 27). A related issue is whether it is possible for true Christians to fall away and lose their salvation (chapter 28). One challenge that faces Christians today is how to cope with the temptations of affluence (chapter 29). Finally, is it possible for Christians to attain perfection in this life (chapter 30)?

To see sin and grace in their wider context we need briefly to consider future glory.

Parousia

Future hope in the New Testament focuses on the parousia, when Christ will return and the dead will rise. At that point we all will attain salvation together – it is a corporate event, not private and individual. Peter refers to 'an inheritance that is imperishable, undefiled, and unfading, kept in heaven for you, who by God's power are being guarded through faith for a salvation ready to be revealed in the last time' (1 Peter 1:4–5). Peter does not say that we *go* to heaven to receive our inheritance. The idea that salvation is going to heaven is a Gnostic idea that has crept in through the back door. The Gnostics believed we are essentially souls, a divine spark destined to return to its heavenly home. The material and bodily realm is bad and salvation means escaping it. The early church rejected Gnosticism, but at this point was influenced by it. For Paul the survival of the soul without the resurrection of the body (salvation as 'going to heaven') was no gospel (1 Cor. 15:12–14). Imagine a future with no brain.

Tom Wright summarizes the New Testament hope not as 'life after death' (going to heaven when we die) but as 'life after life after death' – that is, resurrection after an intervening period. This is not some modern invention. The three ancient creeds all refer to the parousia and resurrection of the dead without any reference to the idea that we 'go to heaven when we die':

> [Christ] will come again with glory to judge the living and the dead . . .
> We look forward to the resurrection of the dead and the life of the age to come.
> (Nicene Creed)

> From [heaven] [Christ] will come to judge the living and the dead . . .
> I believe in . . . the resurrection of the flesh and eternal life.
> (Apostles Creed)

> [Christ] will come from [heaven] to judge the living and the dead. When he comes, all men will rise again with their bodies and will render account for their own deeds.
> (Athanasian Creed)

Life in the new age

What will our future destiny be like? The fullest account comes in Revelation 21 – 22. There we read that there will be no more pain, sorrow or death: 'He will wipe away every tear from their eyes, and death shall be no more, neither shall there be mourning, nor crying, nor pain any more, for the former things have passed away' (21:4). We shall be able to recognize each other – otherwise we would be less human than we are now. There will be no more sin; otherwise the final state would prove not to be final after all. We shall be unable to sin – not in the way an addict deprived of cigarettes is unable to smoke, but in the sense that those who are perfectly good have no desire to do evil. The time of trial and testing will be over. The coming kingdom will be God's reign of justice in which all evil is overcome. This refers not just to the evil we ourselves have done but also to the wrongs we might have suffered, such as bullying, sexual abuse or persecution. Positively, 'we know that when he appears we shall be like him, because we shall see him as he is' (1 John 3:2). This is the goal of sanctification – transformation into the image of Christ (chapter 27). We have the assurance that this goal will be attained, so 'everyone who thus hopes in him purifies himself as he is pure' (1 John 3:3). The implication of this future is not that we can sit back now because the end is assured, but that it is worth striving now because victory is assured.

There are many other questions we might like to ask. What will we be doing? Playing harps? Gardening? Will Calvin be there? (My daughter's pet budgie, not the Reformer!) We simply do not know. 'Beloved, we are God's children now, and what we will be has not yet appeared' (1 John 3:2). Or, as Luther graphically put it, 'We know no more about eternal life than children in the womb of their mother know about the world they are about to enter.'[1] This is a slight exaggeration, but his basic point is correct. Although what we know is very imprecise, it is enough to give us confidence and hope for the future. There is much else that we would like to know, but we know what we need to know for the purposes of our Christian walk now and the progress of sanctification.

---

[1] In his Table Talk, cited by Althaus, *Theology of Martin Luther*, 425.

Texts for further study

For those wanting to go deeper, or for those wishing to use this book as a textbook for a taught course, a selection of these classic texts can be read in conjunction with particular chapters:

Ch. 2 J. C. Ryle, *Holiness: Its Nature, Hindrances, Difficulties, and Roots*, Ch. 1.

Chs 3–4 Augustine, *City of God* Book 14 (NPNF 2:262–283).[1] Augustine, *The Merits and Remission of Sins and the Baptism of Infants*, Book 1 (NPNF 5:15–43).[2]

Ch. 6 Jonathan Edwards, *Sinners in the Hands of an Angry God*.[3]

Chs 7–8, 16 Augustine, *The Spirit and the Letter* (NPNF 5:80–114).[4]

Ch. 8 Canons of the Second Council of Orange.[5]

Chs 8, 9, 29 *Remonstrance*.[6]

Ch. 10 Heinrich Bullinger, *Decades*, Decade 4, Sermon 2.[7]

Ch. 11 Cyprian, *Letter 1 to Donatus* (ANF 5:275–280).

Ch. 12 Cyril of Jerusalem, *Catechetical Lectures* 3 and 20 (NPNF[2] 7:14–18, 147–148).

Ch. 13 Tertullian, *Baptism* (ANF 3:669–679).[8]

Ch. 14 World Council of Churches, *Baptism Eucharist and Ministry: Baptism*.[9]

Chs 18–19 Calvin, *Institutes* 3:11–17.[10]

Melanchthon, *Apology of the Augsburg Confession*, Article 4.[11]

---

[1] There are a number of more recent translations.

[2] For a more modern translation, see Rotelle (ed.), *Works of Saint Augustine* I/23:34–78.

[3] Sermon 7 in Edwards, *Select Works of Jonathan Edwards*, vol. 2, 183–199.

[4] For more modern translations, see Augustine, *Later Works*, 193–250; Rotelle (ed.), *Works of Saint Augustine* I/23:144–194.

[5] Leith (ed.), *Creeds of the Churches*, 37–45.

[6] *RefConf* 4:41–44.

[7] Bullinger, *Decades*, 3:55–114.

[8] For a more modern translation, see Evans, *Tertullian's Homily on Baptism*.

[9] In addition to the WCC edition, also found in Leith, *Creeds of the Churches*, 606–617.

[10] For notes to the text and guidance as to which parts to read, see Lane, *Reader's Guide to Calvin's Institutes*, 112–120.

[11] *BkConc* 120–173.

Chs 18, 20 Calvin, *Institutes* 3:2.[12]
Ch. 21 Regensburg Colloquy, Article 5.[13]
Ch. 22 Council of Trent, *Decree on Justification*.[14]
Chs 23–24 *Joint Declaration on the Doctrine of Justification*.[15]
Ch. 26 Bernard of Clairvaux, *The Steps of Humility and Pride*.[16]
Ch. 27 Thomas à Kempis, *The Imitation of Christ* Book 1.[17]
Ch. 28 Augustine, *The Gift of Perseverance* (NPNF 5:523–552).[18]
Ch. 29 Calvin, *Institutes* 3:6–10.[19]
Ch. 30 J. Wesley, *A Plain Account of Christian Perfection*.[20]

---

[12] For notes to the text and guidance as to which parts to read, see Lane, *Reader's Guide to Calvin's Institutes*, 97–100.

[13] Appendix to ch. 21.

[14] Leith, *Creeds of the Churches*, 408–424; Tanner (ed.), *Decrees of the Ecumenical Councils*, 2:671–681.

[15] Available from many sources, including Gros et al. (eds), *Growth in Agreement II*, 566–582.

[16] Bernard of Clairvaux: *Treatises II*, 25–82.

[17] There are many translations, one of which is listed in the bibliography. It is claimed to be the most widely read book in the world after the Bible.

[18] For a more modern translation, see Augustine, *Four Anti-Pelagian Writings*, 271–337.

[19] For notes to the text and guidance as to which parts to read, see Lane, *Reader's Guide to Calvin's Institutes*, 105–111.

[20] There is a 1952 Epworth edition and the text is also found in Wesley, *Doctrinal and Controversial Treatises II*.

Bibliography

Alexander, Donald L. (ed.), *Christian Spirituality: Five Views of Sanctification* (Downers Grove: InterVarsity Press, 1988).

Alexander, T. Desmond, Brian S. Rosner, D. A. Carson and Graeme Goldsworthy (eds), *New Dictionary of Biblical Theology* (Leicester: Inter-Varsity Press, 2000).

Almen, L. G., and R. J. Sklba (eds), *The Hope of Eternal Life: Lutherans and Catholics in Dialogue XI* (Minneapolis: Lutheran University Press, 2011).

Althaus, Paul, *The Theology of Martin Luther* (Philadelphia: Fortress, 1966).

Anderas, Phil, *Renovatio: Martin Luther's Augustinian Theology of Sin, Grace and Holiness* (Göttingen: Vandenhoeck & Ruprecht, 2019).

Anderson, H. George, T. Austin Murphy and Joseph A. Burgess (eds), *Justification by Faith: Lutherans and Catholics in Dialogue VII* (Minneapolis: Augsburg, 1985).

Arminius, James, *The Works of James Arminius: The London Edition*, 3 vols (Grand Rapids: Baker, 1986).

Armstrong, John H. (ed.), *Understanding Four Views on Baptism* (Grand Rapids: Zondervan, 2007).

Atkinson, James, *The Trial of Luther* (London: B. T. Batsford, 1971).

Attridge, Harold W. (ed.), *The Apostolic Tradition: A Commentary by Paul Bradshaw, Maxwell Johnson and Edward Phillips* (Minneapolis: Fortress, 2002).

Augustine, Saint, *Against Julian*, The Fathers of the Church, vol. 35 (Washington, D.C.: Catholic University of America Press, 1957).

——, *City of God* (London: Penguin, 1984).

——, *Four Anti-Pelagian Writings*, The Fathers of the Church, vol. 86 (Washington, D.C.: Catholic University of America Press, 1992).

——, *Later Works*, tr. John Burnaby, LCC 8 (London: SCM; Philadelphia: Westminster, 1955).

——, *Letters*, vol. 5, The Fathers of the Church, vol. 32 (Washington, D.C.: Catholic University of America Press, 1956).

Bahnsen, Greg L., Walter C. Kaiser, Douglas J. Moo, Wayne G. Strickland and Willem A. VanGemeren, *Five Views on Law and Gospel* (Grand Rapids: Zondervan, 1996).

Baillie, John, *Baptism and Conversion* (London: Oxford University Press, 1964).

Bangs, Carl, *Arminius: A Study in the Dutch Reformation* (Eugene: Wipf & Stock, 1998).

Barclay, John M. G., *Paul and the Gift* (Grand Rapids: Eerdmans, 2015).

____, *Paul and the Subversive Power of Grace*, Grove Biblical Series B80 (Cambridge: Grove, 2016).

Barr, James, *The Semantics of Biblical Language* (Oxford: Oxford University Press, 1961).

Barrett, C. K., *From First Adam to Last: A Study in Pauline Theology* (London: Adam & Charles Black, 1962).

Barrett, Matthew, and Ardel B. Caneday (eds), *Four Views on the Historical Adam* (Grand Rapids: Zondervan, 2013).

Barth, Karl, *Church Dogmatics*, 14 vols (Edinburgh: T&T Clark, 1956–77).

____, *Deliverance to the Captives* (London: SCM, 1961).

Basinger, David, and Randall Basinger (eds), *Predestination and Free Will: Four Views of Divine Sovereignty and Human Freedom* (Downers Grove: InterVarsity Press, 1986).

Bateman, Herbert W. (ed.), *Four Views on the Warning Passages in Hebrews* (Grand Rapids: Kregel, 2007).

Bauckham, Richard, *James* (London: Routledge, 1999).

Beasley-Murray, G. R., *Baptism in the New Testament* (London: Macmillan, 1962).

____, *Baptism Today and Tomorrow* (London: Macmillan, 1966).

Beeke, Joel R., *Assurance of Faith: Calvin, English Puritanism, and the Dutch Second Reformation* (New York: Peter Lang, 1991).

____, 'Reading the Best in Puritan Literature', *Reformation and Revival Journal* 5:2 (spring 1996), 117–158.

____, 'Theodore Beza's Supralapsarian Predestination', *Reformation and Revival Journal* 12:2 (spring 2003), 69–84.

Béguerie, Philippe and Claude Duchesneau, *How to Understand the Sacraments* (London: SCM, 1991).

Beilby, James K., and Paul Rhodes Eddy (eds), *Justification: Five Views* (Downers Grove: InterVarsity Press, 2011).

Berkouwer, Gerrit C., *The Church* (Grand Rapids: Eerdmans, 1976).

____, *Divine Election* (Grand Rapids: Eerdmans, 1960).

Bernard of Clairvaux, *Treatises II: The Steps of Humility and Pride; On Loving God*, Cistercian Fathers Series 13 (Kalamazoo: Cistercian, 1980).

Bettenson, Henry (ed.), *Early Christian Fathers* (Oxford: Oxford University Press, 1969).

Bettis, Joseph D., 'Is Karl Barth a Universalist?', *SJT* 20 (1967), 423–436.

Black, David Alan (ed.), *Perspectives on the Ending of Mark: Four Views* (Nashville: B&H Academic, 2008).

Blocher, Henri A. G., *In the Beginning: The Opening Chapters of Genesis* (Leicester: Inter-Varsity Press, 1984).

———, 'The Lutheran–Catholic Declaration on Justification', in Bruce L. McCormack (ed.), *Justification in Perspective: Historical Developments and Contemporary Challenges* (Grand Rapids: Baker, 2006), 197–217.

———, *Original Sin: Illuminating the Riddle* (Leicester: Inter-Varsity Press, 1997).

Bonhoeffer, Dietrich, *Christ the Center* (New York: Harper & Row, 1966).

———, *The Cost of Discipleship* (London: SCM, 1959).

Bornkamm, Heinrich, *Luther in Mid-Career 1521–30* (London: Darton, Longman & Todd, 1983).

Boston, Thomas, *Human Nature in Its Fourfold State* (London: Banner of Truth, 1964).

Bradshaw, Paul F., 'The Profession of Faith in Early Christian Baptism', *EvQ* 78 (2006), 101–115.

Brand, Chad Owen (ed.), *Perspectives on Election: Five Views* (Nashville: B&H, 2006).

———, *Perspectives on Spirit Baptism: Five Views* (Nashville: B&H, 2004).

Breward, Ian (ed.), *The Work of William Perkins*, Courtenay Library of Reformation Classics 3 (Appleford, Berkshire: Sutton Courtenay, 1970).

Brewster, Todd, *Lincoln's Gamble: The Tumultuous Six Months That Gave America the Emancipation Proclamation and Changed the Course of the Civil War* (New York: Scribner, 2015).

Brontë, Charlotte, *Jane Eyre* (London: J. M. Dent, 1950).

Brown, Peter, *Augustine of Hippo: A Biography* (London: Faber and Faber, 1967).

Bucer, Martin, *De vera ecclesiarum in doctrina, ceremoniis, et disciplina reconciliatione et compositione* (Strassburg: Wendel Rihel, 1542).

Bullinger, Henry, *The Decades*, vol. 3 (Cambridge: Cambridge University Press, 1851).

Butterfield, Herbert, *Christianity and History* (London: Collins, 1957).

Calvin, John, *The Bondage and Liberation of the Will: A Defence of the Orthodox Doctrine of Human Choice Against Pighius*, ed. Anthony N. S. Lane, tr. Graham I. Davies (Grand Rapids: Baker, 1996).

____, *Calvin's Commentaries: The Acts of the Apostles 14–28*, tr. John W. Fraser (Edinburgh: Saint Andrew, 1966).

____, *Calvin's Commentaries: The Epistle of Paul the Apostle to the Hebrews and the First and Second Epistles of St Peter*, tr. William B. Johnston (Edinburgh: Saint Andrew, 1963).

____, *Calvin's Commentaries: The Gospel According to St John 11–21 and the First Epistle of John*, tr. T. H. L. Parker (Edinburgh: Saint Andrew, 1961).

____, *Commentaries on the First Book of Moses Called Genesis*, tr. John King, 2 vols (Grand Rapids: Eerdmans, 1949 reprint).

____, *Commentary on the Book of Psalms*, tr. James Anderson, 5 vols (Grand Rapids: Eerdmans, 1949 reprint).

____, *Concerning the Eternal Predestination of God* (London: James Clarke, 1961).

____, *Institutes of the Christian Religion*, ed. John T. McNeill, tr. Ford Lewis Battles, LCC 20–21 (London: SCM; Philadelphia: Westminster, 1960).

____, *Selected Works of John Calvin*, ed. Henry Beveridge (Calvin Translation Society edn) (Grand Rapids: Baker, 1983 reprint of various nineteenth-century editions).

____, *Theological Treatises*, ed. John K. S. Reid, LCC 22 (London: SCM; Philadelphia: Westminster, 1954).

Carson, D. A., *Christ and Culture Revisited* (Nottingham: Apollos, 2008).

____, *The Intolerance of Tolerance* (Nottingham: Inter-Varsity Press, 2012).

Carson, D. A., Peter T. O'Brien and Mark A. Seifrid (eds), *Justification and Variegated Nomism*, 2 vols (Tübingen: Mohr Siebeck 2001; Grand Rapids: Baker, 2004).

Catechism of the Catholic Church (London: Geoffrey Chapman, 1994).

Chadwick, Henry, *Augustine*, Past Masters (Oxford: Oxford University Press, 1986).

Chadwick, Owen, *John Cassian*, 2nd edn (Cambridge: Cambridge University Press, 1968).

Charles, R. H. (ed.), *The Testaments of the Twelve Patriarchs* (London: SPCK, 1917).

Collier, Jay T., *Debating Perseverance: The Augustinian Heritage in Post-Reformation England* (New York: Oxford University Press, 2018).

Collins, Francis, *The Language of God: A Scientist Presents Evidence for Belief* (London: Simon & Schuster, 2007).

Colwell, John, 'The Contemporaneity of the Divine Decision: Reflections on Barth's Denial of "Universalism"', in Nigel M. de S. Cameron (ed.), *Universalism and the Doctrine of Hell* (Carlisle: Paternoster, 1993), 139–160.

Cone, Steven D., *Theology from the Great Tradition* (London: Bloomsbury T&T Clark, 2018).

Congregation for the Doctrine of the Faith, '"Salvation and the Church": Observations of the Congregation for the Doctrine of the Faith', *One in Christ* 24 (1988), 377–387.

Cooper, Terry D., *Sin, Pride and Self-Acceptance: The Problem of Identity in Theology and Psychology* (Downers Grove: InterVarsity Press, 2003).

Crabbe, Peter, *Concilia Omnia*, 2 vols (Cologne: Peter Quentel, 1538).

Cranfield, C. E. B., *A Critical and Exegetical Commentary on the Epistle to the Romans*, ICC, vol. 1 (Edinburgh: T & T Clark, 1975).

Crisp, Oliver, 'On Barth's Denial of Universalism', *Them* 29:1 (October 2003), 18–29.

Davies, D. R., *Down Peacock's Feathers* (London: Centenary, 1942).

——, *The Sin of Our Age* (London: Geoffrey Bles, 1947).

DeYoung, Rebecca Konyndyk, *Vainglory: The Forgotten Vice* (Grand Rapids: Eerdmans, 2014).

Dieter, Melvin E., Anthony A. Hoekema, Stanley M. Horton, J. Robertson McQuilkin and John F. Walvoord, *Five Views on Sanctification* (Grand Rapids: Zondervan, 1987).

Dodd, C. H., *The Epistle of Paul to the Romans*, 2nd edn (London: Collins, 1959).

Donovan, Jeremiah (tr.), *The Catechism of the Council of Trent* (Dublin: Richard Coyne; London: Keating and Browne, 1829).

Dryden, Windy, *How to Accept Yourself* (London: Sheldon, 1999).

Dunn, J. D. G., *Baptism in the Holy Spirit* (London: SCM, 1970).

Eaton, Michael A., *Baptism with the Spirit: The Teaching of Dr Martyn Lloyd-Jones* (Leicester: Inter-Varsity Press, 1989).

Edwards, Jonathan, *The Select Works of Jonathan Edwards*, vol. 2 (London: Banner of Truth, 1959).

Endo, Shusaku, *Silence* (London: Penguin, 1988).

'Evangelicals and Catholics Together: The Christian Mission in the Third Millennium', *First Things* 43 (May 1994), 15–22.

Evans, Ernest (ed.), *Tertullian Adversus Marcionem*, vol. 1 (Oxford: Clarendon, 1972).

_____, *Tertullian's Homily on Baptism* (London: SPCK, 1964).

Evans, Robert F., *Pelagius: Inquiries and Reappraisals* (London: A. & C. Black, 1968).

Farley, Benjamin Wirt, *The Providence of God* (Grand Rapids: Baker, 1988).

Ferguson, Everett, *Baptism in the Early Church: History, Theology, and Liturgy in the First Five Centuries* (Grand Rapids: Eerdmans, 2009).

_____, 'Inscriptions and the Origin of Infant Baptism', *JTS* 30 (1979), 37–46.

Finn, Richard, *Asceticism in the Graeco-Roman World* (Cambridge: Cambridge University Press, 2009).

Fischer, John Martin, Robert Kane, Derk Pereboom and Manuel Vargas, *Four Views on Free Will* (Oxford: Blackwell, 2007).

Foord, Martin, 'God Wills All People to Be Saved – Or Does He? Calvin's Reading of 1 Timothy 2:4', in Mark D. Thompson (ed.), *Engaging with Calvin* (Nottingham: Apollos, 2009), 179–203.

Forsyth, P. T., *The Cruciality of the Cross* (London: Hodder & Stoughton, 1909).

Fowler, Stanley K., *More Than a Symbol: The British Baptist Recovery of Baptismal Sacramentalism* (Carlisle: Paternoster, 2002).

George, Timothy, 'Evangelicals and Catholics Together: A New Initiative', *CT*, 8 December 1997, 34–38.

Gilson, Étienne, *The Spirit of Medieval Philosophy* (London: Sheed & Ward, 1936).

Gleason, Elisabeth G. (ed.), *Reform Thought in Sixteenth-Century Italy* (Chico: Scholars Press, 1981).

Greene, Graham, *The Power and the Glory* (Harmondsworth: Penguin, 1971).

Grenz, Stanley J., *Theology for the Community of God* (Carlisle: Paternoster, 1994).

Gropper, Johann, *Enchiridion Christianae Institutionis* (Cologne: Peter Quentel, 1538).

Gros, Jeffrey, Harding Meyer and William G. Rusch (eds), *Growth in Agreement II: Reports and Agreed Statements of Ecumenical Conversations on a World Level 1982–1998* (Grand Rapids: Eerdmans; Geneva: World Council of Churches, 2000).

Grudem, Wayne, *Systematic Theology* (Leicester: Inter-Varsity Press, 1994).

Haidt, Jonathan, *The Righteous Mind: Why Good People Are Divided by Politics and Religion* (London: Penguin, 2013).

Halton, Charles (ed.), *Genesis: History, Fiction, or Neither? Three Views on the Bible's Earliest Chapters* (Grand Rapids: Zondervan, 2015).

Hamilton, Victor P., *The Book of Genesis Chapters 1–17* (Grand Rapids: Eerdmans, 1990).

Harrison, A. W., *The Beginnings of Arminianism to the Synod of Dort* (London: University of London Press, 1926).

Harrison, Glynn, *The Big Ego Trip: Finding Significance in a Culture of Self-Esteem* (Nottingham: Inter-Varsity Press, 2013).

Hartog, Paul, *Calvin on Christ's Death: A Word for the World* (Eugene: Wipf & Stock, 2020).

Hoffmann, R. Joseph, *Marcion: On the Restitution of Christianity. An Essay on the Development of Radical Paulinist Theology in the Second Century* (Chico: Scholars Press, 1984).

Hooker, Richard, *The Works of That Learned and Judicious Divine Mr Richard Hooker*, 3rd edn, ed. John Keble, vol. 3 (Oxford: Oxford University Press, 1845).

Hoskins, Steven, and David Fleischacker (eds), *Justified in Jesus Christ: Evangelicals and Catholics in Dialogue* (Bismarck: University of Mary Press, 2017).

House, H. Wayne (ed.), *Divorce and Remarriage: Four Christian Views* (Downers Grove: InterVarsity Press, 1990).

Hunsinger, George, *How to Read Karl Barth: The Shape of His Theology* (New York: Oxford University Press, 1991).

Husbands, Mark, and Daniel J. Treier (eds), *Justification: What's at Stake in the Current Debates* (Downers Grove: InterVarsity Press, 2004).

Janiak, Andrew, 'The Book of Nature, the Book of Scripture', *New Atlantis* 44 (winter 2015), 95–103.

Jedin, Hubert, *A History of the Council of Trent*, 2 vols (London: Thomas Nelson, 1957, 1961).

——, *Papal Legate at the Council of Trent: Cardinal Seripando* (London: B. Herder, 1947).

Jenson, Matt, *The Gravity of Sin: Augustine, Luther and Barth on homo incurvatus in se* (London: T&T Clark, 2006).

Jeremias, Joachim, *Infant Baptism in the First Four Centuries* (London: SCM, 1960).

——, *The Origins of Infant Baptism* (London: SCM, 1963).

Jewett, Paul K., *Infant Baptism and the Covenant of Grace: An Appraisal of the Argument That as Infants Were Once Circumcised, So They Should Now Be Baptized* (Grand Rapids: Eerdmans, 1978).

John Paul II, *Crossing the Threshold of Hope* (London: Jonathan Cape, 1994).

Johnson, Luke Timothy, *The Gospel of Luke*, Sacra Pagina Series, vol. 3 (Collegeville: Liturgical Press, 1991).

Jüngel, Eberhard, *Karl Barth: A Theological Legacy* (Philadelphia: Westminster, 1986).

Kant, Immanuel, *The Critique of Practical Reason* (Indianapolis: Bobbs-Merrill Educational, 1956).

____, *Metaphysical Elements of Justice: The Complete Text of the Metaphysics of Morals, Part I*, tr. John Ladd, 2nd edn (Indianapolis: Hackett, 1999).

Kelly, J. N. D., *Early Christian Doctrines*, 5th edn (London: Bloomsbury Academic, 1977).

Kempis, Thomas à, *The Imitation of Christ* (London: Penguin, 2013).

Kenny, Anthony, *A Path from Rome* (Oxford: Oxford University Press, 1985).

Kerr, Hugh T., and John M. Mulder (eds), *Famous Conversions: The Christian Experience* (Grand Rapids: Eerdmans, 1983).

Kierkegaard, Søren, *Works of Love*, ed. Howard V. Hong and Edna H. Hong (Princeton: Princeton University Press, 1995).

Knell, Matthew, *Sin, Grace and Free Will: A Historical Survey of Christian Thought*, 2 vols (Cambridge: James Clarke, 2017, 2018).

Knox, R. A., *Enthusiasm: A Chapter in the History of Religion with Special Reference to the XVII and XVIII Centuries* (Oxford: Oxford University Press, 1950).

Kreider, Alan, *The Change of Conversion and the Origin of Christendom* (Harrisburg: Trinity Press International, 1999).

Küng, Hans, *Justification: The Doctrine of Karl Barth and a Catholic Reflection* (London: Burns & Oates, 1964).

Ladd, George Eldon, *The Gospel of the Kingdom: Scriptural Studies in the Kingdom of God* (Grand Rapids: Eerdmans, 1959).

Lane, Anthony N. S., 'Becoming a Christian: Initiation in the New Testament and in British Evangelicalism', in D. Ngien (ed.), *The Interface of Science, Theology, and Religion: Essays in Honor of Alister E. McGrath* (Eugene: Pickwick, 2019), 11–28.

____, 'Calvin's Doctrine of Assurance Revisited', in David W. Hall (ed.), *Tributes to John Calvin: A Celebration of His Quincentenary* (Phillipsburg: P&R, 2010), 270–313.

____, 'Did the Apostolic Church Baptize Babies? A Seismological Approach', *TBul* 55:1 (2004), 109–130.

____, 'Dual-Practice Baptism View', in D. F. Wright (ed.), *Baptism: Three Views* (Downers Grove: InterVarsity Press, 2009), 139–171.

_____, 'Irenaeus on the Fall and Original Sin', in R. J. Berry and T. A. Noble (eds), *Darwin, Creation and the Fall* (Nottingham: Apollos, 2009), 130–148.

_____, *Justification by Faith in Catholic–Protestant Dialogue: An Evangelical Assessment* (London: T&T Clark, 2002).

_____, 'Justification', in Geoffrey Wainwright & Paul McPartlan (eds), *The Oxford Handbook of Ecumenical Studies* (Oxford: Oxford University Press, 2017; online edn).

_____, 'Lust: The Human Person as Affected by Disordered Desires', *EvQ* 78 (2006), 21–35.

_____, 'Presenting the Challenge: Christ and Culture', in London Bible College authors, *Christian Life and Today's World: Not Conformed but Transformed* (Bletchley: Scripture Union, 2002), 29–46.

_____, *A Reader's Guide to Calvin's Institutes* (Grand Rapids: Baker, 2009).

_____, *Regensburg Article 5 on Justification: Inconsistent Patchwork or Substance of True Doctrine?* (Oxford: Oxford University Press, 2019).

_____, 'Sola Scriptura? Making Sense of a Post-Reformation Slogan', in Philip E. Satterthwaite and David F. Wright (eds), *A Pathway into the Holy Scripture* (Grand Rapids: Eerdmans, 1994), 297–327.

_____, 'A Tale of Two Imperial Cities: Justification at Regensburg (1541) and Trent (1546–1547)', in Bruce L. McCormack (ed.), *Justification in Perspective: Historical Developments and Contemporary Challenges* (Grand Rapids: Baker, 2006), 119–145.

_____, 'What's So Dangerous About Grace?', *Whitefield Briefing* 6:4 (July 2001).

_____, 'The Wrath of God as an Aspect of the Love of God', in K. Vanhoozer (ed.), *Nothing Greater, Nothing Better* (Grand Rapids: Eerdmans, 2001), 138–167.

Lehmann, Karl, and Wolfhart Pannenberg (eds), *The Condemnations of the Reformation Era: Do They Still Divide?* (Minneapolis: Fortress, 1990).

Lehmann, Paul, 'The Anti-Pelagian Writings', in Roy W. Battenhouse (ed.), *A Companion to the Study of St. Augustine* (New York: Oxford University Press, 1955), 203–234.

Leith, John H. (ed.), *Creeds of the Churches: A Reader in Christian Doctrine from the Bible to the Present*, 3rd edn (Atlanta: John Knox, 1982).

Letham, Robert, *Systematic Theology* (Wheaton: Crossway, 2019).

_____, *Union with Christ: In Scripture, History, and Theology* (Phillipsburg: Crossway, 2011).

Lewis, Clive Staples, *The Four Loves* (London: Fontana, 1963).

_____, *Mere Christianity* (London: Fontana, 1955).

_____, *Screwtape Proposes a Toast and Other Pieces* (London: Fontana, 1965).

_____, *Surprised by Joy* (London: Collins, 1959).

_____, *Undeceptions* (London: Geoffrey Bles, 1971).

Lewis, W. H. (ed.), *Letters of C. S. Lewis* (New York and London: Harcourt Brace Jovanovich, 1966).

Lloyd-Jones, David Martyn, *Joy Unspeakable: The Baptism with the Holy Spirit* (Eastbourne: Kingsway, 1984).

_____, *Romans: An Exposition of Chapter 6: The New Man* (London: Banner of Truth, 1972).

Lucas, Ernest, *Can We Believe Genesis Today? The Bible and the Questions of Science*, 2nd edn (Leicester: Inter-Varsity Press, 2001).

Luther, Martin, *Luther's Works* (Philadelphia: Fortress; St. Louis: Concordia, 1955–86, 2008ff.).

McCue, James F., 'Luther and the Problem of Popular Preaching', *Sixteenth Century Journal* 16 (1985), 33–43.

McGonigle, Herbert Boyd, *Sufficient Grace: John Wesley's Evangelical Arminianism*, Studies in Evangelical History and Thought (Carlisle: Paternoster, 2001).

McGrath, Alister, *C. S. Lewis: A Life* (London: Hodder & Stoughton, 2013).

_____, *Evangelicalism and the Future of Christianity* (Downers Grove: InterVarsity Press, 1994).

_____, *Iustitia Dei: A History of the Christian Doctrine of Justification*, 3rd edn (Cambridge: Cambridge University Press, 2005).

_____, *Luther's Theology of the Cross: Martin Luther's Theological Breakthrough*, 2nd edn (Chichester: Wiley-Blackwell, 2011).

McGrath, Joanna, and Alister E. McGrath, *Self-Esteem: The Cross and Christian Confidence* (Wheaton: Crossway, 1992).

MacGregor, G. H. C., 'The Concept of the Wrath of God in the New Testament', *NTS* 7 (1960–61), 101–109.

Madueme, Hans, and Michael Reeves (eds), *Adam, the Fall, and Original Sin: Theological, Biblical, and Scientific Perspectives* (Grand Rapids: Baker, 2014).

Malloy, Christopher J., *Engrafted into Christ: A Critique of the Joint Declaration* (New York: Peter Lang, 2005).

Marcel, Pierre C., *The Biblical Doctrine of Infant Baptism* (Cambridge: James Clarke, 1953).

Marshall, I. Howard, *Kept by the Power of God: A Study of Perseverance and Falling Away*, 3rd edn (Carlisle: Paternoster, 1995).

____ (ed.), *Christian Experience in Theology and Life* (Edinburgh: Rutherford House, 1988).

Matheson, Peter, *Cardinal Contarini at Regensburg* (Oxford: Oxford University Press, 1972).

Maximus the Confessor, *Selected Writings*, tr. George C. Berthold, Classics of Western Spirituality (New York: Paulist Press, 1985).

Menninger, Karl, *Whatever Became of Sin?* (New York: Hawthorn, 1973).

Merrill, Thomas F. (ed.), *William Perkins, 1558–1602, English Puritanist: His Pioneer Works on Casuistry* (Nieuwkoop: de Graaf, 1966).

Meyer, Harding, and Lukas Vischer (eds), *Growth in Agreement: Reports and Agreed Statements of Ecumenical Conversations on a World Level* (New York: Paulist Press; Geneva: World Council of Churches, 1984).

Moltmann, Jürgen, *God in Creation: An Ecological Doctrine of Creation* (London: SCM, 1985).

Morris, Leon: *The Apostolic Preaching of the Cross*, 3rd edn (London: Tyndale, 1965).

Moule, Handley, *Charles Simeon: Biography of a Sane Saint* (London: IVF, 1965).

Naselli, David, and Mark A. Snoeberger (eds), *Perspectives on the Extent of the Atonement: Three Views* (Nashville: B&H Academic, 2015).

Neuner, J., and J. Dupois (eds), *The Christian Faith in the Doctrinal Documents of the Catholic Church* (London: Collins, 1983).

Newman, John Henry, *Fifteen Sermons Preached Before the University of Oxford* (London: Longmans, Green, 1900).

Newton, John, *The Life of the Rev. John Newton* (London: Religious Tract Society, 1864).

Nichols, Alan, *An Evangelical Commitment to Simple Lifestyle. Exposition and Commentary*, Lausanne Occasional Paper 20 (Wheaton: LCWE, 1980).

Niebuhr, H. Richard, *Christ and Culture* (London: Faber and Faber, 1952).

Niebuhr, Reinhold, *Beyond Tragedy: Essays on the Christian Interpretation of History* (London: Nisbet, 1938).

____, *The Nature and Destiny of Man*, vol. 1 (London: Nisbet, 1941).

Norberg, Johan, *Progress: Ten Reasons to Look Forward to the Future* (London: Oneworld, 2016).

Oberman, Heiko Augustinus, *The Harvest of Medieval Theology: Gabriel Biel and Late-Medieval Nominalism* (Cambridge: Harvard University Press, 1963).

O'Donovan, Oliver, *The Problem of Self-Love in Saint Augustine* (New

Haven: Yale University Press, 1980).

Olson, Roger E., *Arminian Theology: Myths and Realities* (Downers Grove: InterVarsity Press, 2006).

Owen, David, *Time to Declare* (London: Penguin, 1992).

Packer, J. I., *Knowing God* (London: Hodder & Stoughton, 1973).

Pascal, Blaise, *Pensées* (Harmondsworth: Penguin, 1966).

Pawson, David, *The Normal Christian Birth* (London: Hodder & Stoughton, 1989).

Pearse, Meic, *The Great Restoration: The Religious Radicals of the 16th and 17th Centuries* (Carlisle: Paternoster, 1998).

Perkins, William, *A Reformed Catholike* (London: Legat, 1597).

Pesch, Otto Hermann, 'The Canons of the Tridentine Decree on Justification. To Whom Did They Apply? To Whom Do They Apply Today?', in Karl Lehmann (ed.), *Justification by Faith: Do the Sixteenth-Century Condemnations Still Apply* (New York: Continuum, 1997), 175–216.

Peter Lombard, *The Sentences, Book 3: On the Incarnation of the Word* (Toronto: Pontifical Institute of Mediaeval Studies, 2008).

Peterson, David, *Possessed by God: A New Testament Theology of Sanctification and Holiness* (Leicester: Inter-Varsity Press, 1995).

Peterson, Robert A., and Michael D. Williams, *Why I Am Not an Arminian* (Downers Grove: InterVarsity Press, 2004).

Pinker, Steven, *The Blank Slate: The Modern Denial of Human Nature* (London: Penguin, 2002).

Pinson, J. Matthew (ed.), *Four Views on Eternal Security* (Grand Rapids: Zondervan, 2002).

Plantinga, Cornelius, *Not the Way It's Supposed to Be: A Breviary of Sin* (Leicester: Inter-Varsity Press, 1995).

Pollock, John, *Amazing Grace: John Newton's Story* (London: Hodder & Stoughton, 1981).

_____, *Wilberforce* (London: Constable, 1977).

Rahner, Karl, *Theological Investigations*, vol. 5 (London: Darton, Longman & Todd, 1966).

Raith, Charles, *After Merit: John Calvin's Theology of Works and Rewards* (Göttingen: Vandenhoeck & Ruprecht, 2016).

Ramm, Bernard, *Offense to Reason: A Theology of Sin* (San Francisco: Harper & Row, 1985).

Richgens, R. H., 'The Close of the Gregorian Era', *Ampleforth Journal* 76:2 (summer 1971), 55–65.

Robinson, H. Wheeler, *Baptist Principles* (London: Kingsgate, 1945).

Rotelle, John E. (ed.), *The Works of Saint Augustine. A Translation for the 21st Century*, Part I, vol. 23: *Answer to the Pelagians* (Hyde Park: New City, 1997).

Rusch, William G. (ed.), *Justification and the Future of the Ecumenical Movement: The Joint Declaration on the Doctrine of Justification* (Collegeville: Liturgical Press, 2003).

Ryle, J. C., *Holiness: Its Nature, Hindrances, Difficulties, and Roots* (London: James Clarke, 1956 reprint).

Sacks, Jonathan, *Faith in the Future* (London: Darton, Longman & Todd, 1995).

Salvation and the Church. An Agreed Statement by the Second Anglican-Roman Catholic International Commission ARCIC II (London: Church House and Catholic Truth Society, 1987).

Sanders, E. P., *Paul and Palestinian Judaism* (London: SCM, 1977).

Schreiner, Thomas, *Faith Alone: The Doctrine of Justification: What the Reformers Taught . . . and Why It Still Matters* (Grand Rapids: Zondervan, 2015).

Schreiner, Thomas R., and Ardel B. Caneday, *The Race Set Before Us: A Biblical Theology of Perseverance and Assurance* (Downers Grove: InterVarsity Press, 2001).

Schrotenboer, Paul (ed.), *An Evangelical Response to* Baptism, Eucharist and Ministry (Carlisle: Paternoster, 1992; on behalf of the World Evangelical Fellowship).

Scriven, Charles, *The Transformation of Culture* (Scottdale: Herald, 1988).

Seifrid, Mark A., *Christ, Our Righteousness: Paul's Theology of Justification* (Leicester: Apollos, 2000).

Shaw, Bernard: *Complete Plays* (London: Constable, 1931).

Shuster, Marguerite, *The Fall and Sin: What We Have Become as Sinners* (Grand Rapids: Eerdmans, 2004).

Sider, Ronald J. (ed.), *Lifestyle in the Eighties: An Evangelical Commitment to Simple Lifestyle* (Exeter: Paternoster, 1982).

Simon, Robert I., *Bad Men Do What Good Men Dream: A Forensic Scientist Illuminates the Darker Side of Human Behavior* (Washington, D.C.: American Psychiatric Press, 1996).

Smedes, Lewis B., *Forgive and Forget: Healing the Hurts We Don't Deserve* (London: Triangle/SPCK, 1984).

Smith, Alexander McCall, *The House of Unexpected Sisters* (London: Abacus, 2017).

Smith, Gordon T., *Beginning Well: Christian Conversion and Authentic Transformation* (Downers Grove: InterVarsity Press, 2001).

Snoddy, Richard M., *Quicunque Vult: The Act and Object of Saving Faith in the Thought of James Ussher* (Oxford: Oxford University Press, 2010).

Stanley, Alan P. (ed.), *Four Views on the Role of Works at the Final Judgment* (Grand Rapids: Zondervan, 2013).

Stephens, W. P., *The Theology of Huldrych Zwingli* (Oxford: Clarendon, 1986).

Stewart, Kenneth J., 'The Points of Calvinism: Retrospect and Prospect', *SBET* 26 (2008), 187–203.

_____, *Ten Myths About Calvinism: Recovering the Breadth of the Reformed Tradition* (Downers Grove: Inter-Varsity Press; Nottingham: Inter-Varsity Press, 2011).

Stott, John R. W., *The Cross of Christ* (Leicester: Inter-Varsity Press, 1986).

Stott, John, and Nick Miller (eds), *Crime and the Responsible Community* (London: Hodder & Stoughton, 1980).

Strauss, Mark L. (ed.), *Remarriage After Divorce in Today's Church: Three Views* (Grand Rapids: Zondervan, 2006).

Strong, Augustus H., *Systematic Theology* (London: Pickering & Inglis, 1906 reprint).

Stump, J. B., and Chad Meister (eds), *Original Sin and the Fall: Five Views* (Downers Grove: InterVarsity Press, 2020).

Tanner, Norman P. (ed.), *Decrees of the Ecumenical Councils*, 2 vols (London: Sheed & Ward; Washington, D.C.: Georgetown University Press, 1990).

TeSelle, Eugene, *Augustine the Theologian* (London: Burns & Oates, 1970).

Thielman, Frank, *Romans*, ZECNT (Grand Rapids: Zondervan, 2018).

Thiselton, Anthony C., *Discovering Romans: Content, Interpretation, Reception* (London: SPCK, 2016).

Thomas, Robert David, *The Man Who Would Be Perfect: John Humphrey Noyes and the Utopian Impulse* (Philadelphia: University of Pennsylvania Press, 1977).

Thompson, Michael B., *The New Perspective on Paul* (Cambridge: Grove, 2002).

Thorsen, Don, *The Wesleyan Quadrilateral: Scripture, Tradition, Reason and Experience as a Model of Evangelical Theology*, 2nd edn (Lexington: Emeth, 2005).

Tillich, Paul, *The Courage to Be* (London: Fontana, 1962).

Torrey, R. A., *What the Bible Teaches: A Thorough and Comprehensive Study of What the Bible Has to Say Concerning the Great Doctrines of Which It Treats* (New York: Fleming H. Revell, 1898).

Turner, Max, *Baptism in the Holy Spirit*, Renewal Series 2 (Cambridge: Grove, 2000).

——, *The Holy Spirit and Spiritual Gifts Then and Now* (Carlisle: Paternoster, 1996).

Tynan, Katharine, *Flower of Youth: Poems in Wartime* (London: Sidgwick & Jackson, 1915).

Vitz, Paul C., *Psychology as Religion: The Cult of Self-Worship*, 2nd edn (Grand Rapids: Eerdmans, 1994).

Volf, Miroslav, *Free of Charge: Giving and Forgiving in a Culture Stripped of Grace* (Grand Rapids: Zondervan, 2005).

Walgrave, J. H., 'Incarnation and Atonement', in T. F. Torrance (ed.), *The Incarnation* (Edinburgh: Handsel, 1981), 148–176.

Wallace, Ronald S., *Calvin's Doctrine of the Christian Life* (Edinburgh: Oliver & Boyd, 1959).

Walls, Jerry L., and Joseph R. Dongell, *Why I Am Not a Calvinist* (Downers Grove: InterVarsity Press, 2004).

Warren, Rick, *The Purpose Driven Life: What on Earth Am I Here For?* (Grand Rapids: Zondervan, 2002).

Watson, D. C. K., *My God Is Real* (London: Falcon, 1970).

Wawrykow, Joseph P., *The SCM Press A–Z of Thomas Aquinas* (London: SCM, 2005).

Wengert, Timothy J., *Law and Gospel: Philip Melanchthon's Debate with John Agricola of Eisleben over* Poenitentia (Grand Rapids: Baker; Carlisle: Paternoster, 1997).

Wesley, John, *Doctrinal and Controversial Treatises II*, ed. Paul Wesley Chilcote and Kenneth J. Collins, *The Works of John Wesley*, vol. 13 (Nashville: Abingdon, 2013).

——, *The Journal of John Wesley: A Selection*, ed. Elisabeth Jay (Oxford: Oxford University Press, 1987).

——, *A Plain Account of Christian Perfection* (London: Epworth, 1952).

——, *Sermons*, in Albert C. Outler (ed.), *The Works of John Wesley*, vols 1–4 (Nashville: Abingdon, 1984–7).

Westermann, Claus, *Genesis 1–11: A Commentary* (London: SPCK, 1984).

Wiesenthal, Simon, *The Sunflower: On the Possibilities and Limits of Forgiveness* (New York: Schocken, 1997).

Wilder, Terry L. (ed.), *Perspectives on Our Struggle with Sin: 3 Views of Romans 7* (Nashville: B&H, 2011).

Williams, Colin W., *John Wesley's Theology Today* (London: Epworth, 1969).

Wilson, K., *Everybody's Heard of Blondin* (Sevenoaks: Hawthorns, 1990).

Wood, A. Skevington, *The Burning Heart: John Wesley, Evangelist* (Exeter: Paternoster, 1967).

World Council of Churches, *Baptism, Eucharist and Ministry*, Faith and Order Paper No. 111 (Geneva: World Council of Churches, 1982).

Wright, David F., *Infant Baptism in Historical Perspective: Collected Studies* (Milton Keynes: Paternoster, 2007).

Wright, David F. (ed.), *Baptism: Three Views* (Downers Grove: InterVarsity Press, 2009).

_____, *Common Places of Martin Bucer* (Appleford, Abingdon: Sutton Courtenay, 1972).

Wright, N. T., *Paul and His Recent Interpreters* (London: SPCK, 2015).

Yancey, Philip, *What's So Amazing About Grace?* (Grand Rapids: Zondervan, 1997).

Yarnold, Edward, '*Duplex Iustitia*: The Sixteenth Century and the Twentieth', in Gillian R. Evans (ed.), *Christian Authority* (Oxford: Oxford University Press, 1988), 204–223.

Index of names and documents

Index of biblical references

Lightning Source UK Ltd.
Milton Keynes UK
UKHW020352211120
373782UK00006B/1658